P9-BIM-180

GREGG SHORTHAND DICTIONARY

Diamond Jubilee Series

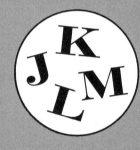

GREGG
SHORTHAND
DICTIONARY

John Robert Gregg
Louis A. Leslie
Charles E. Zoubek

Shorthand written by Charles Rader

GREGG   Diamond Jubilee Series

Gregg Division
McGraw-Hill Book Company
New York   Chicago   Dallas   San Francisco
Toronto   London   Sydney

GREGG SHORTHAND DICTIONARY, DIAMOND JUBILEE SERIES

Copyright © 1963 by McGraw-Hill, Inc. All Rights Reserved. Copyright 1949 by McGraw-Hill, Inc. All Rights Reserved. Printed in the United States of America. This book, or parts thereof, may not be reproduced in any form without permission of the publishers.

Library of Congress Catalog Card Number 61-17339

11 12 13 DODO-63 3

FOREWORD

Gregg Shorthand Dictionary, Diamond Jubilee Series, is divided into two parts:

Part One contains, in alphabetic order, the shorthand outlines for 34,055 words. These 34,055 words, however, represent a considerably larger vocabulary, as many simple derivatives of those words — those ending in *-ing* and *-s*, for example, which present no stenographic problem — have been omitted.

Part Two contains, in alphabetic order, the shorthand outlines for 1,314 entries for personal and geographical names.

It is easily possible to construct briefer outlines for many of the scientific and literary words for which full outlines are given in this dictionary. It is not advisable to do so, however, unless the writer is certain that he will use those briefer outlines with sufficient frequency to justify the effort of learning them. Otherwise, the brief, but half-remembered, outline will cause mental hesitation that will result in slower, rather than faster, writing.

Research techniques using high-speed motion pictures have proved that most shorthand writers actually write each outline at about the same speed, regardless of the speed of the dictation. That is why the writer who can take dictation at only 100 words a minute writes each outline as rapidly as it is written by another writer taking the same material at 200 words a minute. What, then, is the difference between the two writers?

The difference is that the writer who can write only 100 words a minute is wasting time thinking, pausing, hesitating. The writer who can write 200 words a minute does not need to stop to think. He writes the outlines little, if any, faster than the writer who can write only 100 words a minute; but the 200-word writer writes *continuously.*

The problem of increasing shorthand speed, therefore, is actually a problem of decreasing hesitations in writing. What causes hesitations in writing? They are caused by the struggle of the mind to remember and use the abbreviating material provided in the shorthand system.

The fewer shortcuts and exceptions the mind must remember and use, the easier it is for the writer to decrease or eliminate the hesitations that reduce speed. Therefore, any attempt by the writer to manufacture additional shortcuts is more likely to reduce his speed than to increase it, unless the new shortcuts are used in his daily work with such great frequency that they readily become automatized.

The experience of expert shorthand writers of every system is conclusive in establishing the inadvisability of attempting to gain speed by devising and learning lists of brief outlines. Longer outlines that are quickly constructed by the mind under pressure of dictation give the writer more speed; the attempt to remember and use large numbers of abbreviated outlines tends to reduce the writer's speed.

There is often room for some difference of opinion as to the most appropriate outline for a word. This dictionary offers outlines that have been discussed and considered by experts. Sometimes an apparently obvious improvement in an outline will actually create the danger of a conflict in reading. More often an outline different from that provided in this dictionary would be individually satisfactory but would not be consistent with the outlines for other members of the same word family.

Of one thing the reader may be sure — every outline in this dictionary is the result of serious thought and consideration. Where possible alternate outlines exist, each alternate has been discussed and considered. This dictionary as a whole represents the accumulated experience of all those who have worked with Gregg Shorthand since its first publication in 1888.

It is hoped that this volume will render a useful service to the shorthand writer by placing at his disposal a facile and fluent outline for any word in which he may be interested.

The Publishers

PART ONE

Part One of *Gregg Shorthand Dictionary, Diamond Jubilee Series,* contains 34,055 word entries, alphabetically arranged. This is a gross increase of 7,957 words over the previous edition. Actually, more than 8,000 new words were added, because it was found possible to drop some of the entries given in the previous edition. Many of the more than 8,000 new words were suggested by users of the *Gregg Shorthand Dictionary Simplified* or by the reading done by the authors.

Some words, like *sputnik, defector, plutonium, orbited, imperialistic, isotope,* and a number of others, were added because of their greatly expanded use in the field of "peaceful coexistence." Other words, like *stereophonic, transistor, tranquilizer, epoxy, fluoridate, video, togetherness, programed,* and *geriatrics,* were invented or came into general use in our speech since the publication of the *Gregg Shorthand Dictionary Simplified.* Some new words may be frowned upon, like *definitize, motivational, moonlighting;* but they have been included because the stenographer may have to write them from dictation.

Experience has proved that those using a shorthand dictionary often consult it for the simple words formerly omitted from shorthand dictionaries or for rare and unusual words likewise formerly omitted.

The present list, therefore, includes many of the apparently simple words formerly omitted. It includes many of the simple derivatives formerly omitted. Most readily apparent will be the addition of the many rare and unusual words that experience has proved are wanted by users of a list such as this.

Many words are included because the shorthand learner, while still in school, has occasion to use them in his schoolwork. For this reason many mathematical, mineralogical, chemical, physical, botanical, and physiological terms are included. For the same reason many literary words are included, words that are usually of no business value but that the high school or college learner uses in his schoolwork. The bulk of the vocabulary, however, consists of words generally used in business-office dictation.

It must be remembered, too, that in many types of office work the stenographer may have occasion to use these scientific or literary words. The editor's stenographer will need the literary words. The professor's secretary will need many of the mathematical or chemical or physiological words — according to the professor's field of interest.

Consistency, rather than brevity of outline, has been the guiding principle in the construction of the shorthand outlines in this *Gregg Shorthand Dictionary, Diamond Jubilee Series.* The fastest shorthand outline (within reasonable limits) is the outline that requires the least mental effort, the outline that is written consistently and analogically. The speed of a shorthand outline is not to be judged by its brevity to the eye, nor even by its facility for the hand; it is to be judged by the speed with which it may be constructed by the mind and supplied by the mind to the hand.

Many shorthand writers experience difficulty in understanding the principle that guides the shorthand author in devising shortcuts. If the preceding paragraph is true, why are there any shortcuts? Why not write out everything in full? The secret of the good shortcut is the frequency of use of the word or phrase. If a dictator says *as a matter of fact* fifty times a day, the shorthand writer should, of course, use a very brief shortcut for that phrase. Because of this extreme frequency of use, the shortcut will come as quickly to the mind as though the phrase had been written in full.

There is no value, however, in having every shorthand writer learn a shortcut for the phrase *as a matter of fact,* for some dictators may never use the phrase; and if it should occur infrequently in the dictation, the mental effort needed to recall the phrase would require far more time than would have been necessary to write it in full.

It is strongly urged, therefore, that the outline in this dictionary be accepted as the normal outline for any word unless that word occurs so frequently in the writer's dictation (at least several times a day) that learning a shortcut is thoroughly justified. A long list of seldom-used shortcuts can be a very heavy burden on the mind and will almost invariably result in decreasing one's writing speed rather than increasing it. As a famous shorthand reporter of an earlier generation once said: "The longer I write shorthand, the *longer* I write shorthand."

aaaaaaaaaaaaaaaaa
aaaaaaaaaaaaaaaaa
aaaaaaaaaaaaaaaaa
aaaaaaaaaaaaaaaaa
aaaaaaaaaaaaaaaaa
aaaaaaaaaaaaaaaaa
aaaaaaaaaaaaaaaaa
aaaaaaaaaaaaaaaaa
aaaaaaaaaaaaaaaaa
aaaaaaaaaaaaaaaaa

ab'a·cus
a·baft'
ab'a·lo'ne
a·ban'don
a·ban'doned
a·ban'don·ment
a·base'
a·based'
a·base'ment
a·bash'
a·bat'a·ble
a·bate'
a·bat'ed
a·bate'ment
ab'bess
ab'bey
ab'bot
ab·bre'vi·ate
ab·bre'vi·at'ed
ab·bre'vi·a'tion
ab'di·cate
ab'di·cat'ed

ab'di·ca'tion
ab·do'men
ab·dom'i·nal
ab·duct'
ab·duc'tion
a·bed'
ab'er·ra'tion
ab'er·ra'tion·al
a·bet'
a·bet'ted
a·bet'tor
a·bey'ance
ab·hor'
ab·horred'
ab·hor'rence
ab·hor'rent
a·bide'
a·bil'i·ty
ab'ject
ab'ju·ra'tion
ab·jure'
ab·jured'

ab·jure'ment
ab'la·tive
ab'laut
a·blaze'
a'ble
a'ble-bod'ied
ab·lu'tion
a'bly
ab'ne·ga'tion
ab·nor'mal
ab·nor·mal'i·ty
ab·nor'mi·ty
a·board'
a·bode'
a·bol'ish
a·bol'ished
ab'o·li'tion
ab'o·li'tion·ism
ab'o·li'tion·ist
a·bom'i·na·ble
a·bom'i·na·bly
a·bom'i·nate

a·bom'i·na'tion	ab'sence	ab·stract'ed
ab'o·rig'i·nal	ab'sent	ab·stract'ed·ly
ab'o·rig'i·ne	ab'sen·tee'	ab·strac'tion
a·bor'tive	ab'sen·tee'ism	ab·strac'tion·ist
a·bound'	ab'sent·ly	ab'stract·ly
a·bound'ing·ly	ab'sinthe	ab·struse'
a·bout'	ab'so·lute	ab·struse'ness
a·bove'	ab'so·lute·ly	ab·surd'
ab·rade'	ab'so·lute·ness	ab·surd'i·ty
ab·rad'ed	ab'so·lu'tion	ab·surd'ly
ab·ra'sion	ab'so·lut·ism	a·bun'dance
ab·ra'sive	ab'so·lut·ist	a·bun'dant
ab're·ac'tion	ab·solve'	a·bun'dant·ly
a·breast'	ab·solved'	a·buse'
a·bridge'	ab·sorb'	a·bused'
a·bridged'	ab·sorbed'	a·bu'sive
a·bridg'ment	ab·sorb'en·cy	a·bu'sive·ly
a·broad'	ab·sorb'ent	a·bu'sive·ness
ab'ro·gate	ab·sorb'ing·ly	a·but'
ab'ro·gat'ed	ab·sorp'tion	a·but'ment
ab'ro·ga'tion	ab·sorp'tive	a·but'tal
ab'ro·ga'tive	ab·stain'	a·but'ted
ab·rupt'	ab·stained'	a·but'ter
ab·rupt'ly	ab·stain'er	a·bysm'
ab·rupt'ness	ab·ste'mi·ous	a·bys'mal
ab'scess	ab·ste'mi·ous·ly	a·byss'
ab'scessed	ab·ste'mi·ous·ness	a·ca'cia
ab·scis'sa	ab·sten'tion	ac'a·dem'ic
ab·scis'sion	ab'sti·nence	a·cad'e·mi'cian
ab·scond'	ab'sti·nent	a·cad'e·mies
ab·scond'ed	ab'sti·nent·ly	a·cad'e·my
ab·scond'er	ab'stract	A·ca'di·an

a·can'thus

ac·cede'

ac·ced'ed

ac·cel'er·an'do

ac·cel'er·ant

ac·cel'er·ate

ac·cel'er·at'ed

ac·cel'er·a'tion

ac·cel'er·a'tive

ac·cel'er·a'tor

ac·cel'er·a·to'ry

ac'cent

ac·cent'ed

ac·cen'tu·ate

ac·cen'tu·at'ed

ac·cen'tu·a'tion

ac·cept'

ac·cept'a·bil'i·ty

ac·cept'a·ble

ac·cept'ance

ac'cep·ta'tion

ac·cept'ed

ac'cess

ac·ces'si·bil'i·ty

ac·ces'si·ble

ac·ces'sion

ac·ces'so·ry

ac'ci·dence

ac'ci·dent

ac'ci·den'tal

ac'ci·den'tal·ly

ac·cip'i·trine

ac·claim'

ac·claimed'

ac'cla·ma'tion

ac·clam'a·to'ry

ac·cli'mate

ac·cli'mat·ed

ac'cli·ma'tion

ac·cli'ma·ti·za'tion

ac·cli'ma·tize

ac·cli'ma·tized

ac·cliv'i·ty

ac'co·lade'

ac·com'mo·date

ac·com'mo·dat'ed

ac·com'mo·dat'ing·ly

ac·com'mo·da'tion

ac·com'mo·da'tive

ac·com'pa·nied

ac·com'pa·ni·ment

ac·com'pa·nist

ac·com'pa·ny

ac·com'plice

ac·com'plish

ac·com'plished

ac·com'plish·ment

ac·cord'

ac·cord'ance

ac·cord'ed

ac·cord'ing·ly

ac·cor'di·on

ac·cost'

ac·cost'ed

ac·count'

ac·count'a·bil'i·ty

ac·count'a·ble

ac·count'an·cy

ac·count'ant

ac·count'ed

ac·cou'tered

ac·cou'ter·ment

ac·cred'it

ac·cred'it·ed

ac·cre'tion

ac·cru'al

ac·crue'

ac·crued'

ac·cu'mu·late

ac·cu'mu·lat'ed

ac·cu'mu·lates

ac·cu'mu·la'tion

ac·cu'mu·la'tive

ac·cu'mu·la'tor

ac'cu·ra·cy

ac'cu·rate

ac'cu·rate·ly

ac·cu·sa'tion

ac·cu'sa·tive

ac·cu'sa·to'ry

ac·cuse'

ac·cused'

ac·cus'er

ac·cus'ing·ly

ac·cus'tom

ac·cus'tomed

ace 9	ac'o·lyte	ac'ri·mo'ni·ous·ness
a·cerb'	ac'o·nite	ac'ri·mo'ny
a·cer'bic	a'corn	ac'ro·bat
a·cer'bi·ty	a·cous'tic	ac'ro·bat'ic
ac'e·tate	a·cous'ti·cal	ac'ro·bat'i·cal·ly
a·ce'tic	a·cous'ti·cal·ly	ac'ro·bat'ics
ac'e·tone	a·cous'tics	a·crop'o·lis
a·cet'y·lene	ac·quaint'	a·cross'
ache	ac·quaint'ance	a·cros'tic
ached	ac·quaint'ance·ship	act
a·chiev'a·ble	ac·quaint'ed	act'ed
a·chieve'	ac'qui·esce'	ac·tin'ic
a·chieved'	ac'qui·esced'	ac·tin'i·um
a·chieve'ment	ac'qui·es'cence	ac'tion
ach'ro·mat'ic	ac'qui·es'cent	ac'tion·a·ble
ach'ro·mat'i·cal·ly	ac·quire'	ac'ti·vate
a·chro'ma·to'sis	ac·quired'	ac'ti·vat'ed
ac'id	ac·quire'ment	ac'ti·va'tion
a·cid'i·fi·ca'tion	ac·quires'	ac'ti·va'tor
a·cid'i·fi'er	ac'qui·si'tion	ac'tive
a·cid'i·fy	ac·quis'i·tive	ac'tive·ly
a·cid'i·ty	ac·quis'i·tive·ness	ac·tiv'i·ties
ac'i·do'sis	ac·quit'	ac·tiv'i·ty
ac'id·proof'	ac·quit'tal	ac'tiv·ize
a·cid'u·late	ac·quit'ted	ac'tor
a·cid'u·lat'ed	a'cre	ac'tress
a·cid'u·lous	a'cre·age	ac'tu·al
ac·knowl'edge	ac'rid	ac'tu·al'i·ties
ac·knowl'edged	a·crid'i·ty	ac'tu·al'i·ty
ac·knowl'edg·ment	ac'rid·ly	ac'tu·al·ly
ac'me	ac'ri·mo'ni·ous	ac'tu·ar'i·al
ac'ne	ac'ri·mo'ni·ous·ly	ac'tu·ar'y

ac'tu·ate

ac'tu·at'ed

a·cu'i·ty

a·cu'men

a·cute'

a·cute'ly

a·cute'ness

ad'age

a·da'gio

ad'a·mant

ad'a·man'tine

a·dapt'

a·dapt'a·bil'i·ty

a·dapt'a·ble

ad'ap·ta'tion

a·dapt'ed

a·dapt'er

a·dap'tive

add

add'ed

ad·den'da

ad·den'dum

ad'der

ad'dict

ad·dict'ed

ad·dic'tion

ad·di'tion

ad·di'tion·al

ad·di'tion·al·ly

ad'di·tive

ad'dle

ad'dled

ad·dress

ad·dressed'

ad'dress·ee'

Ad·dres'so·graph

ad·duce'

ad·duced'

ad·duct'

ad·duc'tion

ad·duc'tive

ad·duc'tor

ad'e·noid

ad'e·nol'o·gy

ad'e·no'ma

a·dept'

ad'e·qua·cy

ad'e·quate

ad'e·quate·ly

ad'e·quate·ness

ad·here'

ad·hered'

ad·her'ence

ad·her'ent

ad·he'sion

ad·he'sive

ad·he'sive·ness

a·dieu'

ad'i·pose

ad'i·pos'i·ty

ad·ja'cen·cy

ad·ja'cent

ad'jec·ti'val

ad'jec·tive

ad·join'

ad·joined'

ad·journ'

ad·journed'

ad·journ'ment

ad·judge'

ad·judged'

ad·ju'di·cate

ad·ju'di·cat'ed

ad·ju'di·ca'tion

ad·ju'di·ca'tive

ad·ju'di·ca'tor

ad'junct

ad'ju·ra'tion

ad·jur'a·to'ry

ad·jure'

ad·jured'

ad·just'

ad·just'a·ble

ad·just'ed

ad·just'er

ad·just'ment

ad'ju·tan·cy

ad'ju·tant

ad·min'is·ter

ad·min'is·tered

ad·min'is·tra'tion

ad·min'is·tra'tive

ad·min'is·tra'tive·ly

ad·min'is·tra'tor

ad·min'is·tra'trix

ad'mi·ra·ble

ad'mi·ra·bly	ad·re'nal	ad·ven'ture·some
ad'mi·ral	ad·ren'al·ine	ad·ven'tur·ess
ad'mi·ral·ty	a·drift'	ad·ven'tur·ous
ad'mi·ra'tion	a·droit'	ad'verb
ad·mire'	a·droit'ly	ad·ver'bi·al
ad·mired'	a·droit'ness	ad·ver'bi·al·ly
ad·mis'si·bil'i·ty	ad·sorb'	ad'ver·sar'y
ad·mis'si·ble	ad·sorp'tion	ad·ver'sa·tive
ad·mis'sion	ad'u·la'tion	ad·verse'
ad·mit'	ad'u·la·to'ry	ad·verse'ly
ad·mit'tance	a·dult'	ad·ver'si·ty
ad·mit'ted	a·dul'ter·ant	ad·vert'
ad·mit'ted·ly	a·dul'ter·ate	ad'ver·tise
ad·mix'ture	a·dul'ter·at'ed	ad·ver'tise·ment
ad·mon'ish	a·dul'ter·a'tion	ad'ver·tis'er
ad'mo·ni'tion	a·dul'ter·er	ad·vice'
ad·mon'i·to'ry	a·dul'ter·ous	ad·vis'a·bil'i·ty
a·do'be	a·dul'ter·y	ad·vis'a·ble
ad'o·les'cence	a·dult'hood	ad·vise'
ad'o·les'cent	ad·um'brate	ad·vised'
a·dopt'	ad·um'brat·ed	ad·vis'ed·ly
a·dopt'ed	ad'um·bra'tion	ad'vi·see'
a·dop'tion	ad·vance'	ad·vise'ment
a·dop'tive	ad·vanced'	ad·vi'so·ry
a·dor'a·ble	ad·vance'ment	ad'vo·ca·cy
ad'o·ra'tion	ad·van'tage	ad'vo·cate
a·dore'	ad'van·ta'geous	ad'vo·cat'ed
a·dored'	ad'vent	ad·vow'son
a·dor'ing·ly	Ad'vent·ist	adz
a·dorn'	ad'ven·ti'tious	ae'gis
a·dorned'	ad·ven'ture	ae·o'li·an
a·dorn'ment	ad·ven'tur·er	ae'on

a′er·ate

a′er·at′ed

a′er·a′tion

a′er·a′tor

a·e′ri·al

a′er·o·nau′ti·cal

aes·thet′ic

a·far′

af′fa·bil′i·ty

af′fa·ble

af′fa·bly

af·fair′

af·fect′

af′fec·ta′tion

af·fect′ed

af·fect′ed·ly

af·fect′ing·ly

af·fec′tion

af·fec′tion·ate

af·fec′tion·ate·ly

af′fec·tiv′i·ty

af·fi′ance

af·fi′anced

af·fi′ant

af′fi·da·vit

af·fil′i·ate

af·fil′i·at′ed

af·fil′i·a′tion

af·fin′i·ty

af·firm′

af·firm′a·ble

af′fir·ma′tion

af·firm′a·tive

af·firm′a·to′ry

af·firmed′

af·fix′

af·fixed′

af·fla′tus

af·flict′

af·flict′ed

af·flic′tion

af·flic′tive

af′flu·ence

af′flu·ent

af·ford′

af·ford′ed

af·for′est

af·for′est·a′tion

af·fray′

af·fright′

af·fright′ed

af·front′

af·front′ed

af′ghan

a·field′

a·fire′

a·flame′

a·float′

a·foot′

a·fore′said′

a·fore′thought′

a·fore′time′

a·foul′

a·fraid′

a·fresh′

aft′er

aft′er·beat′

aft′er·care′

aft′er·clap′

aft′er·deck′

aft′er·din′ner

aft′er·ef·fect′

aft′er·glow′

aft′er·growth′

aft′er·guard′

aft′er·hatch′

aft′er·hold′

aft′er·im′age

aft′er·life′

aft′er·math

aft′er·most

aft′er·noon′

aft′er·part′

aft′er·taste′

aft′er·thought′

aft′er·time′

aft′er·ward

a·gain′

a·gainst′

a·gape′

ag′ate

ag′ate·ware′

a·ga′ve

age

aged

age′less

a'gen·cy	ag'i·ta'tor	ai'ler·on
a·gen'da	a·gleam'	ail'ment
a·gen'dum	ag'nate	aim
a'gent	ag·nos'tic	aim'less
a·ger'a·tum	ag·nos'ti·cism	air
ag·glom'er·ate	a·gog'	air'brush'
ag·glom'er·at'ed	ag'o·nize	air'-dry'
ag·glom'er·a'tion	ag'o·nized	aired
ag·glom'er·a'tive	ag'o·niz'ing·ly	air'field'
ag·glu'ti·nate	ag'o·ny	air'foil'
ag·glu'ti·na'tion	a·grar'i·an	air'i·ly
ag·glu'ti·na'tive	a·gree'	air'lin'er
ag'gran·dize	a·gree'a·bil'i·ty	air'mail'
ag·gran'dize·ment	a·gree'a·ble	air'man
ag'gra·vate	a·gree'a·ble·ness	air'plane'
ag'gra·vat'ed	a·greed'	air'port'
ag'gra·vat'ing·ly	a·gree'ment	air'ship'
ag'gra·va'tion	ag'ri·cul'tur·al	air'sick'
ag'gre·gate	ag'ri·cul'ture	air'space'
ag'gre·ga'tion	a·gron'o·my	air'tight'
ag·gres'sion	a·ground'	air'way'
ag·gres'sive	a'gue	air'wor'thy
ag·gres'sor	a·head'	air'y
ag·grieve'	a·hoy'	aisle
ag·grieved'	a·hun'gered	a·jar'
a·ghast'	aid	a·kim'bo
ag'ile	aid'ed	a·kin'
a·gil'i·ty	ai·grette'	al'a·bas'ter
ag'i·o	ai'guil·lette'	a·lac'ri·ty
ag'i·tate	ail	al'a·mo
ag'i·tat'ed	ai·lan'thus	a·larm'
ag'i·ta'tion	ailed	a·larmed'

a·larm′ing·ly

a·larm′ist

a·las′

al′ba·core

al′ba·tross

al·bi′no

al′bum

al·bu′min

al·bu′mi·nous

al′che·mist

al′che·my

al′co·hol

al′co·hol′ic

al′co·hol·ism

al′co·hol·ize

al′cove

al′der

al′der·man

al′der·man′ic

Al′der·ney

a′le·a·to′ry

a·lem′bic

a·lem′bi·cate

Al′e·mite

a·lert′

a·lert′ly

a·lert′ness

ale′wife′

al′ex·an′drite

al·fal′fa

al′ge·bra

al′ge·bra′ic

Al·ge′ri·an

a′li·as

al′i·bi

al′i·dade

al′ien

al′ien·a·bil′i·ty

al′ien·a·ble

al′ien·ate

al′ien·at′ed

al′ien·a′tion

al′ien·ist

a·light′

a·lign′

a·lign′ment

a·like′

al′i·men′ta·ry

al′i·men·ta′tion

al′i·mo′ny

al′i·quant

al′i·quot

a·live′

a·live′ness

a·liz′a·rin

al′ka·li

al′ka·lin′i·ty

all

al·lay′

al·layed′

al′le·ga′tion

al·lege′

al·leged′

al·leg′ed·ly

al·le′giance

al′le·gor′i·cal

al′le·go·rize

al′le·go′ry

al′le·gret′to

al·le′gro

al′ler·gen

al·ler′gic

al′ler·gy

al·le′vi·ate

al·le′vi·at′ed

al·le′vi·a′tion

al′ley

al′ley·way′

al·li′ance

al·lied′

al′li·ga′tor

al·lit′er·ate

al·lit′er·a′tion

al·lit′er·a′tive

al·lit′er·a′tive·ly

al′lo·ca·ble

al′lo·cate

al′lo·cat′ed

al′lo·ca′tion

al′lo·cu′tion

al′lo·path

al′lo·path′ic

al·lop′a·thy

al·lot′

al·lot′ment

al·lot′ted

al·low'

al·low'a·ble

al·low'ance

al·lowed'

al·low'ed·ly

al·loy'

al·loy'age

al·loyed'

all'spice'

al·lude'

al·lud'ed

al·lure'

al·lured'

al·lure'ment

al·lur'ing·ly

al·lu'sion

al·lu'sive

al·lu'sive·ly

al·lu'sive·ness

al·lu'vi·al

al·lu'vi·um

al·ly'

al'ma·nac

al·might'y

al'mond

al'mon·er

al'most

alms

alms'house'

a·lo'di·um

al'oe

a·loft'

a·lo'ha

a·lone'

a·long'

a·long'side'

a·loof'

a·loof'ly

al·o·pe'ci·a

a·loud'

al·pac'a

al'pha·bet

al'pha·bet'ic

al'pha·bet'i·cal

al'pha·bet·ize

al·read'y

al'so

al'tar

al'tar·piece'

al'ter

al'ter·a·ble

al'ter·a'tion

al'ter·a'tive

al'ter·cate

al'ter·ca'tion

al'tered

al'ter·nate

al'ter·nat'ed

al'ter·na'tion

al·ter'na·tive

al'ter·na'tor

al·though'

al'ti·graph

al·tim'e·ter

al'ti·pla'no

al·tis'si·mo

al'ti·tude

al'to

al'to·geth'er

al'tru·ism

al'tru·ist

al'tru·is'tic

al'tru·is'ti·cal·ly

al'um

a·lu'mi·na

a·lu'mi·nate

a·lu'mi·nif'er·ous

a·lu'mi·no'sis

a·lu'mi·num

a·lum'na

a·lum'nae

a·lum'ni

a·lum'nus

al·ve'o·lar

al·ve'o·lus

al'ways

a·lys'sum

a·mal'gam

a·mal'gam·ate

a·mal'gam·at'ed

a·mal'gam·a'tion

a·man'u·en'sis

am'a·ranth

am'a·ran'thine

a·mass'

a·massed'

am'a·teur'
am'a·teur'ish
am'a·teur'ism
am'a·tive
am'a·tive·ness
am'a·to'ry
a·maze'
a·mazed'
a·maze'ment
a·maz'ing·ly
Am'a·zon
Am'a·zo'ni·an
am·bas'sa·dor
am·bas'sa·do'ri·al
am·bas'sa·do'ri·al·ly
am·bas'sa·dress
am'ber
am'ber·gris
am'bi·dex·ter'i·ty
am'bi·dex'trous
am'bi·dex'trous·ly
am'bi·dex'trous·ness
am'bi·ent
am'bi·gu'i·ty
am·big'u·ous
am·big'u·ous·ly
am·big'u·ous·ness
am·bi'tion
am·bi'tious
am·bi'tious·ly
am·biv'a·lence
am·biv'a·lent

am'ble
am·bro'si·a
am·bro'si·al
am·bro'si·al·ly
am'bro·type
am'bu·lance
am'bu·lant
am'bu·la·to'ry
am'bus·cade'
am'bush
a·mel'io·rate
a·mel'io·rat'ed
a·mel'io·ra'tion
a·mel'io·ra'tive
a'men'
a·me'na·bil'i·ty
a·me'na·ble
a·mend'
a·mend'ed
a·mend'ment
a·men'i·ty
A·mer'i·can
A·mer'i·can·i·za'tion
A·mer'i·can·ize
am'e·thyst
a'mi·a·bil'i·ty
a'mi·a·ble
am'i·ca·bil'i·ty
am'i·ca·ble
a·mid'ships
a·midst'
a·miss'

am'i·ty
am'me'ter
am·mo'ni·a
am·mo'ni·um
am'mu·ni'tion
am·ne'si·a
am'nes·ty
a·moe'ba
a·mong'
a·mongst'
a·mor'al
am'o·rous
am'o·rous·ly
am'o·rous·ness
a·mor'phous
a·mor'ti·za'tion
a·mor'tize
a·mor'tized
a·mount'
a·mount'ed
a·mour'
am·per'age
am'pere
am'per·sand
am·phib'i·an
am·phib'i·ous
am·phib'i·ous·ly
am'phi·the'a·ter
am'pho·ra
am'ple
am'pli·fi·ca'tion
am'pli·fied

am'pli·fi'er	a·nal'y·sis	an'cil·lar'y
am'pli·fy	an'a·lyst	and
am'pli·tude	an'a·lyt'ic	an·dan'te
am'ply	an'a·lyt'i·cal	and'i'ron
am·pul'la	an'a·lyt'i·cal·ly	an'ec·dot'age
am'pu·tate	an'a·lyze	an'ec·dote
am'pu·tat'ed	an'a·lyzed	a·ne'mi·a
am'pu·ta'tion	an'a·lyz'er	an'e·mom'e·ter
am'pu·ta'tive	an'am·ne'sis	an'e·mom'e·try
am'pu·tee'	an·ar'chic	a·nem'o·ne
a·muck'	an·ar'chi·cal	a·nent'
am'u·let	an'arch·ism	an'er·oid
a·muse'	an'arch·ist	an'es·the'si·a
a·mused'	an'arch·y	an'es·the'si·ol'o·gy
a·muse'ment	an·as'tig·mat'ic	an'es·the'sis
a·mus'ing·ly	a·nath'e·ma·tize	an'es·thet'ic
a·nab'o·lism	an'a·tom'ic	an'es·thet'i·za'tion
a·nach'ro·nism	an'a·tom'i·cal	an·es'the·tize
a·nach'ro·nis'tic	a·nat'o·mist	an·es'the·tized
a·nach'ro·nous	a·nat'o·mize	an'eu·rysm
an'a·con'da	a·nat'o·mized	a·new'
an'a·gram	a·nat'o·my	an'gel
an'a·lects	an'ces'tor	an·gel'ic
an'al·ge'si·a	an'ces'tors	An'ge·lus
an'al·ge'sic	an·ces'tral	an'ger
an'a·log'i·cal	an'ces'try	an'gered
a·nal'o·gies	an'chor	an'gle
a·nal'o·gous	an'chor·age	an'gled
a·nal'o·gous·ly	an'chored	an'gler
an'a·logue	an'cho·rite	An'gli·can
a·nal'o·gy	an·cho'vy	An'glo-Sax'on
a·nal'y·ses	an'cient	An·go'ra

an'gri·er

an'gri·est

an'gri·ly

an'gry

an'guish

an'guished

an'gu·lar

an'gu·lar'i·ty

an'gu·la'tion

an·hy'drous

an'i·line

an'i·mad·ver'sion

an'i·mal

an'i·mate

an'i·mat'ed

an'i·mat'ed·ly

an'i·ma'tion

an'i·ma'tor

an'i·mism

an'i·mist

an'i·mis'tic

an'i·mos'i·ty

an'i·mus

an'ise

an'ise·root'

an'kle

an'kle·bone'

an'klet

an'ky·lo'sis

an'nal·ist

an'nals

an·neal'

an·nealed'

an·nex'

an'nex·a'tion

an'nex·a'tion·ist

an·nexed'

an·ni'hi·late

an·ni'hi·lat'ed

an·ni'hi·la'tion

an'ni·ver'sa·ry

an'no·tate

an'no·tat'ed

an'no·ta'tion

an·nounce'

an·nounced'

an·nounce'ment

an·nounc'er

an·noy'

an·noy'ance

an·noyed'

an·noy'ing·ly

an'nu·al

an'nu·al·ly

an·nu'i·tant

an·nu'i·ty

an·nul'

an'nu·lar

an·nulled'

an·nul'ment

an·nun'ci·a'tion

an·nun'ci·a'tor

an'ode

an'o·dyne

a·noint'

a·noint'ed

a·nom'a·lies

a·nom'a·lous

a·nom'a·lous·ly

a·nom'a·ly

a·non'

an'o·nym'i·ty

a·non'y·mous

a·non'y·mous·ly

a·noph'e·les

an·oth'er

an'swer

an'swer·a·ble

an'swered

ant

ant·ac'id

an·tag'o·nism

an·tag'o·nist

an·tag'o·nis'tic

an·tag'o·nis'ti·cal·ly

an·tag'o·nize

an·tag'o·nized

ant·arc'tic

an'te

ant'eat'er

an'te·ced'ent

an'te·cham'ber

an'te·date'

an'te·dat'ed

an'te·lope

an'te·na'tal

an·ten'na

an·te'ri·or

an'te·room'

an'them

an·thol'o·gies

an·thol'o·gist

an·thol'o·gize

an·thol'o·gy

an'thra·cite

an'thrax

an'thro·poid

an·thro·po·log'i·cal

an·thro·pol'o·gy

an'ti·bod'y

an'tic

an'ti·christ'

an·tic'i·pate

an·tic'i·pat'ed

an·tic'i·pa'tion

an·tic'i·pa·to'ry

an'ti·cli'max

an'ti·cline

an'ti·dote

an'ti·gen

an'ti·knock'

an'ti·mo'ny

an·tin'o·my

an·tip'a·thies

an·tip'a·thy

an·tiph'o·nal

an·tip'o·des

an'ti·quar'i·an

an'ti·quar'y

an'ti·quat'ed

an·tique'

an·tiqued'

an·tiq'ui·ty

an'ti·sep'sis

an'ti·sep'tic

an'ti·sep'ti·cal·ly

an'ti·so'cial

an'ti·tank'

an·tith'e·ses

an·tith'e·sis

an'ti·thet'i·cal

an'ti·tox'in

an'ti·trust'

ant'ler

ant'lered

an'to·nym

an'trum

an'vil

anx·i'e·ty

anx'ious

anx'ious·ly

an'y

an'y·bod'y

an'y·one

an'y·thing

an'y·way

an'y·where

a·or'ta

a·or'tic

a·pace'

a·part'

a·part'ment

ap'a·thet'ic

ap'a·thet'i·cal·ly

ap'a·thy

a·pe'ri·ent

a·per'i·tive

ap'er·ture

a'pex

a'pex·es

a·pha'si·a

a'phid

aph'o·rism

aph'o·ris'tic

a'pi·a·rist

a'pi·ar'y

ap'i·cal

ap'i·ces

a·piece'

a·poc'a·lypse

a·poc'ry·phal

ap'o·gee

a·pol'o·get'ic

a·pol'o·get'i·cal

a·pol'o·gies

a·pol'o·gist

a·pol'o·gize

a·pol'o·gized

a·pol'o·gy

ap'o·plec'tic

ap'o·plex'y

a·pos'ta·sy

a·pos′tate

a·pos′tle

ap′os·tol′ic

ap′os·tol′i·cal

a·pos′tro·phe

a·pos′tro·phize

a·poth′e·car′y

ap′o·thegm

a·poth′e·o′sis

ap·pall′

ap·palled′

ap·pall′ing·ly

ap′pa·nage

ap′pa·ra′tus

ap′pa·ra′tus·es

ap·par′el

ap·par′eled

ap·par′ent

ap′pa·ri′tion

ap·peal′

ap·pealed′

ap·peal′ing·ly

ap·pear′

ap·pear′ance

ap·peared′

ap·peas′a·ble

ap·pease′

ap·peased′

ap·pease′ment

ap·peas′ing·ly

ap·pel′lant

ap·pel′late

ap′pel·la′tion

ap′pel·lee′

ap·pend′

ap·pend′age

ap′pen·dec′to·my

ap·pend′ed

ap·pen′di·ci′tis

ap·pen′dix

ap·pen′dix·es

ap′per·ceive′

ap′per·ceived′

ap′per·cep′tion

ap′per·cep′tive

ap′per·tain′

ap′per·tained′

ap′pe·tite

ap′pe·tiz′er

ap′pe·tiz′ing·ly

ap·plaud′

ap·plaud′ed

ap·plause′

ap′ple

ap′ple·jack′

ap′ple·nut′

ap′ple·sauce′

ap·pli′ance

ap′pli·ca·bil′i·ty

ap′pli·ca·ble

ap′pli·cant

ap′pli·ca′tion

ap′pli·ca′tor

ap·plied′

ap′pli·qué′

ap·ply′

ap·point′

ap·point′ed

ap·point′ee′

ap·poin′tive

ap·point′ment

ap·por′tion

ap·por′tioned

ap·por′tion·ment

ap′po·site

ap′po·si′tion

ap·prais′al

ap·praise′

ap·praised′

ap·prais′er

ap·prais′ing·ly

ap·pre′ci·a·ble

ap·pre′ci·a·bly

ap·pre′ci·ate

ap·pre′ci·at′ed

ap·pre′ci·a′tion

ap·pre′ci·a′tive

ap·pre′ci·a′tive·ly

ap′pre·hend′

ap′pre·hend′ed

ap′pre·hend′ing·ly

ap′pre·hen′sion

ap′pre·hen′sive

ap′pre·hen′sive·ly

ap′pre·hen′sive·ness

ap·pren′tice

ap·pren'ticed

ap·pren'tice·ship

ap·prise'

ap·prised'

ap·proach'

ap·proach'a·ble

ap·proached'

ap'pro·ba'tion

ap'pro·ba'tive

ap'pro·ba'tive·ness

ap·pro'pri·ate

ap·pro'pri·at'ed

ap·pro'pri·ate·ly

ap·pro'pri·ate·ness

ap·pro'pri·a'tion

ap·prov'al

ap·prove'

ap·proved'

ap·prov'ing·ly

ap·prox'i·mate

ap·prox'i·mat'ed

ap·prox'i·mate·ly

ap·prox'i·ma'tion

ap·pur'te·nance

ap·pur'te·nant

a'pri·cot

A'pril

a'pron

ap'ro·pos'

apse

ap'sis

apt

ap'ti·tude

apt'ly

apt'ness

aq'ua·ma·rine'

aq'ua·relle'

a·quar'i·um

aq'ua·scu'tum

a·quat'ic

aq'ua·tint'

aq'ue·duct

a'que·ous

aq'ui·line

Ar'ab

ar'a·besque'

A·ra'bi·an

Ar'a·bic

ar'a·bil'i·ty

Ar'ab·ist

ar'a·ble

a·rach'nid

a·rach'noid

a·rag'o·nite

Ar'a·ma'ic

ar'ba·lest

ar'bi·ter

ar'bi·tra·ble

ar'bi·trage

ar·bit'ra·ment

ar'bi·trar'i·ly

ar'bi·trar'i·ness

ar'bi·trar'y

ar'bi·trate

ar'bi·trat'ed

ar'bi·tra'tion

ar'bi·tra'tive

ar'bi·tra'tor

ar'bor

ar·bo're·al

ar·bo're·ous

ar'bo·re'tum

ar·bu'tus

arc

ar·cade'

ar·cad'ed

Ar·ca'di·a

ar·ca'num

arch

ar'chae·ol'o·gist

ar'chae·ol'o·gy

ar·cha'ic

arch'an'gel

arch'an·gel'ic

arch'bish'op

arch'dea'con

arch'di'o·cese

arch'du'cal

arch'duch'ess

arch'duch'y

arch'duke'

arch'er

arch'er·fish'

arch'er·y

ar'che·typ'al

ar'che·type

arch'fiend'

ar'chi·pel'a·go

ar'chi·tect

ar'chi·tec·ton'ic

ar'chi·tec'tur·al

ar'chi·tec'tur·al·ly

ar'chi·tec'ture

ar'chi·trave

ar'chives

ar'chi·vist

arch'ly

arch'ness

arch'way

arc'tic

ar'dent

ar'dent·ly

ar'dor

ar'du·ous

ar'du·ous·ly

are

a're·a

a·re'na

ar'gent

ar'gen·tif'er·ous

ar'gon

Ar'go·naut

ar'got

ar'gu·a·ble

ar'gue

ar'gued

ar'gu·ment

ar'gu·men·ta'tion

ar'gu·men'ta·tive

Ar'gy·rol

a'ri·a

ar'id

a·rid'i·ty

a·right'

a·rise'

a·ris'en

a·ris·toc'ra·cy

a·ris'to·crat

a·ris'to·crat'ic

a·rith'me·tic

a·rith·met'i·cal

ark

arm

ar·ma'da

ar'ma·dil'lo

ar'ma·ment

ar'ma·ture

arm'chair

armed

Ar·me'ni·an

arm'ful

arm'hole'

ar'mi·stice

arm'let

ar'mor

ar'mored

ar·mo'ri·al

ar'mor·y

arm'pit'

arm'rest'

arm'scye'

ar'my

ar'ni·ca

a·ro'ma

ar'o·mat'ic

a·round'

a·rouse'

ar·peg'gio

ar·raign'

ar·raigned'

ar·raign'ment

ar·range'

ar·ranged'

ar·range'ment

ar·rang'er

ar'ras

ar·ray'

ar·rayed'

ar·rear'age

ar·rears'

ar·rest'

ar·rest'er

ar·rhyth'mic

ar·riv'al

ar·rive'

ar·rived'

ar'ro·gance

ar'ro·gant

ar'ro·gant·ly

ar'ro·gate

ar'ro·gat'ed

ar'ro·ga'tion

ar′row	ar·tif′i·cer	a·sep′tic
ar′row·head′	ar′ti·fi′cial	ash
ar′row·head′ed	ar′ti·fi′ci·al′i·ty	a·shamed′
ar′row·wood′	ar′ti·fi′cial·ly	ash′en
ar′row·y	ar·til′ler·ist	ash′es
ar·roy′o	ar·til′ler·y	ash′lar
ar′se·nal	ar′ti·san	a·shore′
ar′se·nate	art′ist	ash′pit′
ar·sen′ic	ar·tis′tic	ash′wort′
ar·sen′i·cal	art′ist·ry	ash′y
ar′se·nide	art′less	A′sian
ar′se·nite	Ar′y·an	A′si·at′ic
ar′son	as	a·side′
ar′son·ist	as′a·fet′i·da	as′i·nine
art	as·bes′tos	as′i·nin′i·ty
ar·te′ri·al	as·cend′	ask
ar′ter·y	as·cend′an·cy	a·skance′
art′ful	as·cend′ant	a·skew′
art′ful·ly	as·cend′er	a·slant′
ar·thrit′ic	as·cen′sion	a·sleep′
ar·thrit′i·cal	as·cent′	asp
ar·thri′tis	as′cer·tain′	as·par′a·gus
ar′thro·plas′ty	as′cer·tain′ment	as′pect
ar′ti·choke	as·cet′ic	as′pen
ar′ti·cle	as·cet′i·cism	as·per′i·ty
ar′ti·cled	as·ci′tes	as·perse′
ar·tic′u·late	a·scor′bic	as·persed′
ar·tic′u·lat′ed	as′cot	as·per′sion
ar·tic′u·la′tion	as·cribe′	as′phalt
ar·tic′u·la′tive	as·cribed′	as·phal′tic
ar′ti·fact	as·crip′tion	as′pho·del
ar′ti·fice	a·sep′sis	as·phyx′i·a

as·phyx′i·ate

as·phyx′i·a′tion

as′pic

as·pir′ant

as′pi·rate

as′pi·rat′ed

as′pi·ra′tion

as′pi·ra′tor

as·pire′

as·pired′

as′pi·rin

as′sa·gai

as·sail′

as·sail′ant

as·sailed′

as·sas′sin

as·sas′si·nate

as·sas′si·nat′ed

as·sas′si·na′tion

as·sault′

as·sault′ed

as·say′

as·sayed′

as·say′er

as·sem′blage

as·sem′ble

as·sem′bled

as·sem′bler

as·sem′bly

as·sent′

as·sent′ed

as·sent′ing·ly

as·sert′

as·sert′ed

as·ser′tion

as·ser′tive

as·ser′tive·ly

as·sess′

as·sess′a·ble

as·sessed′

as·sess′ment

as·ses′sor

as·ses′sor·ship

as′set

as·sev′er·ate

as·sev′er·a′tion

as′si·du′i·ty

as·sid′u·ous

as·sid′u·ous·ly

as·sign′

as·sign′a·ble

as′sig·na′tion

as·signed′

as′sign·ee′

as·sign′ment

as′sign·or′

as·sim′i·la·ble

as·sim′i·late

as·sim′i·lat′ed

as·sim′i·la′tion

as·sim′i·la′tive

as·sim′i·la·to′ry

as·sist′

as·sist′ance

as·sist′ant

as·sist′ed

as·sists′

as·size′

as·so′ci·ate

as·so′ci·at′ed

as·so′ci·a′tion

as·so′ci·a′tive

as′so·nance

as′so·nant

as·sort′

as·sort′ed

as·sort′ment

as·suage′

as·suaged′

as·sum′a·ble

as·sum′a·bly

as·sume′

as·sumed′

as·sum′ed·ly

as·sump′sit

as·sump′tion

as·sur′ance

as·sure′

as·sured′

as·sur′ed·ly

as·sur′ed·ness

as·sur′er

As·syr′i·an

as′ter

as′ter·isk

a·stern′

as·ter·oid	as·tute'ly	a·tone'
as·the'ni·a	as·tute'ness	a·toned'
as·then'ic	a·sun'der	a·tone'ment
asth'ma	a·sy'lum	a'tri·um
asth·mat'ic	a'sym·met'ric	a·tro'cious
as'tig·mat'ic	a'sym·met'ri·cal	a·tro'cious·ly
a·stig'ma·tism	a·sym'me·try	a·troc'i·ty
as·ton'ish	at	at'ro·phied
as·ton'ish·ing·ly	at'a·rax'i·a	at'ro·phy
as·ton'ish·ment	at'a·vism	at'ro·pine
as·tound'	at'a·vis'tic	at·tach'
as·tound'ed	a'the·ism	at·tached'
as·tound'ing·ly	a'the·ist	at·tach'ment
a·strad'dle	a'the·is'tic	at·tack'
as·trag'a·lus	ath'e·nae'um	at·tack'er
as'tra·khan	A·the'ni·an	at·tain'
as'tral	ath'lete	at·tain'a·ble
a·stray'	ath·let'ic	at·tain'der
a·stride'	ath·let'ics	at·tained'
as·trin'gen·cy	a·thwart'	at·tain'ment
as·trin'gent	at'mos·phere	at'tar
as'tro·labe	at'mos·pher'ic	at·tempt'
as·trol'o·ger	at'oll	at·tempt'ed
as·trol'o·gy	at'om	at·tend'
as'tro·nau'tics	at'om·at'ic	at·tend'ance
as·tron'o·mer	a·tom'ic	at·tend'ant
as'tro·nom'i·cal	at'om·is'tic	at·ten'tion
as·tron'o·my	at'om·ize	at·ten'tive
as'tro·phys'i·cal	at'om·ized	at·ten'tive·ly
as'tro·phys'i·cist	at'om·iz'er	at·ten'tive·ness
as'tro·phys'ics	a·ton'al	at·ten'u·ate
as·tute'	a'to·nal'i·ty	at·ten'u·at'ed

at·ten'u·a'tion

at·test'

at'tes·ta'tion

at·tests'

at'tic

at·tire'

at·tired'

at'ti·tude

at'ti·tu'di·nize

at·tor'ney

at·tor'neys

at·tract'

at·tract'ed

at·trac'tion

at·trac'tive

at·trac'tive·ly

at·trib'ute

at·trib'ut·ed

at'tri·bu'tion

at·trib'u·tive

at·tri'tion

at·tune'

at·tuned'

a·twit'ter

a·typ'i·cal

au'burn

auc'tion

auc'tioned

auc'tion·eer'

au·da'cious

au·da'cious·ly

au·dac'i·ty

au'di·bil'i·ty

au'di·ble

au'di·bly

au'di·ence

au'di·o

au'di·om'e·ter

au'dit

au'dit·ed

au·di'tion

au'di·tor

au'di·to'ri·um

au'di·to'ry

au'ger

aught

aug·ment'

aug'men·ta'tion

aug·ment'a·tive

aug·ment'ed

au'gur

au'gured

au'gu·ry

au·gust'

Au'gust

aunt

au'ra

au'ral

au're·ole

au'ri·cle

au·ric'u·lar

au·rif'er·ous

au·ro'ra

au·ro'ral

aus'cul·tate

aus'cul·ta'tion

aus'pice

aus'pic·es

aus·pi'cious

aus·tere'

aus·tere'ly

aus·ter'i·ty

Aus·tral'ian

Aus'tri·an

au·then'tic

au·then'ti·cate

au·then'ti·cat'ed

au·then'ti·ca'tion

au'then·tic'i·ty

au'thor

au·thor'i·tar'i·an

au·thor'i·ta'tive

au·thor'i·ta'tive·ly

au·thor'i·ty

au'thor·i·za'tion

au'thor·ize

au'thor·ized

au'thor·ship

au'to·bi'o·graph'i·cal

au'to·bi·og'ra·phy

au·toch'tho·nous

au'to·clave

au·toc'ra·cy

au'to·crat

au'to·crat'ic

au'to·crat'i·cal·ly

au'to·graph

au'to·in·tox'i·ca'tion

au'to·mat'ic

au·tom'a·tism

au·tom'a·tize

au·tom'a·ton

au'to·mo·bile'

au·ton'o·mize

au·ton'o·mous

au·ton'o·my

au'top·sies

au'top·sy

au'to·sug·ges'tion

au'tumn

au·tum'nal

aux·il'ia·ry

a·vail'

a·vail'a·bil'i·ty

a·vail'a·ble

a·vailed'

av'a·lanche

av'a·rice

av'a·ri'cious

av'a·ri'cious·ly

av'a·tar'

a·venge'

a·venged'

av'e·nue

a·ver'

av'er·age

av'er·aged

a·ver'ment

a·verred'

a·verse'

a·ver'sion

a·vert'

a·vert'ed

a'vi·ar'y

a'vi·a'tion

a'vi·a'tor

av'id

a·vid'i·ty

av'id·ly

av'i·ga'tion

av'o·ca'do

av'o·ca'tion

a·void'

a·void'a·ble

a·void'ed

a·vow'al

a·vow'ed·ly

a·vun'cu·lar

a·wait'

a·wait'ed

a·wake'

a·wak'en

a·wak'ened

a·ward'

a·ward'ed

a·ware'

a·ware'ness

a·wash'

a·way'

awe

awe'some

aw'ful

aw'ful·ly

awk'ward

awk'ward·ly

awk'ward·ness

awl

awn'ing

a·woke'

a·wry'

ax

ax'i·om

ax'i·o·mat'ic

ax'is

ax'le

a·za'le·a

az'i·muth

Az'tec

az'ure

az'u·rite

B

bab'bitt
bab'ble
ba·boon'
ba'by
Bab'y·lo'ni·an
bac'ca·lau're·ate
bac'cha·nal
bac'cha·na'li·an
bach'e·lor
bach'e·lor·hood'
ba·cil'lus
back
back'ache'
back'board'
back'bone'
back'break'er
back'drop'
back'er
back'fire'
back'gam'mon
back'ground'
back'hand'

back'hand'ed
back'lash'
back'log'
back'saw'
back'slide'
back'slid'er
back'spin'
back'stage'
back'stamp'
back'stitch'
back'stop'
back'stroke'
back'track'
back'ward
back'ward·ness
back'wash'
back'wa'ter
back'woods'
ba'con
bac·te'ri·a
bac·te'ri·al
bac·te'ri·cid'al

bac·te'ri·cide
bac·te'ri·o·log'i·cal
bac·te'ri·ol'o·gy
bac·te'ri·um
bad
badge
badg'er
bad'i·nage'
bad'lands'
bad'ly
bad'min·ton
bad'ness
baf'fle
baf'fled
bag
ba·gasse'
bag'a·telle'
bag'gage
bagged
bag'pipe'
bail
bailed

bail'ee'

bail'iff

bail'i·wick

bail'ment

bait

baize

bake

Ba'ke·lite

bak'er

bak'er·y

bal'ance

bal'anced

bal·bo'a

bal·brig'gan

bal'co·ny

bald

bal'da·chin

bal'der·dash

bald'ness

bal'dric

bale

baled

bale'ful

balk

ball

bal'lad

bal'last

balled

bal'le·ri'na

bal'let

bal·let'o·mane

bal·lis'tics

bal·loon'

bal·loon'ist

bal'lot

ball'play'er

ball'room'

balm

bal'sa

bal'sam

bal'sam·if'er·ous

bal'us·ter

bal'us·trade'

bam·boo'

bam·boo'zle

bam·boo'zled

ban

ba'nal

ba·nal'i·ty

ba·nan'a

band

band'age

ban·dan'na

band'box'

ban·deau'

band'ed

ban'de·role

ban'di·coot

ban'dit

band'mas'ter

ban'do·leer'

band'stand'

ban'dy

bane'ful

bang

bang'board'

banged

bang'le

ban'ish

ban'ish·ment

ban'is·ter

ban'jo

bank

bank'book'

banked

bank'er

bank'rupt

bank'rupt cy

banned

ban'ner

banns

ban'quet

ban'quet·ed

ban'shee

ban'tam

ban'ter

ban'tered

ban'ter·ing·ly

ban'yan

ban'zai'

bap'tism

bap·tis'mal

Bap'tist

bap·tize'

bap·tized'

bap·tize'ment

bar

barb

bar·bar'i·an

bar·bar'ic

bar'ba·rism

bar·bar'i·ty

bar'ba·rous

bar'be·cue

barbed

bar'ber

bar'ber'ry

bar·bette'

bar'bi·can

bard

bare

bare'back'

bared

bare'faced'

bare'foot'

bare'head'ed

bare'ly

bare'ness

bar'gain

bar'gained

barge

barge'man

bar'i·tone

bar'i·um

bark

bar'ley

bar'maid'

barn

bar'na·cle

barn'yard'

bar'o·gram

bar'o·graph

ba·rom'e·ter

bar'o·met'ric

bar'on

bar'on·age

bar'on·ess

bar'on·et

bar'on·et·cy

ba·ro'ni·al

bar'o·ny

ba·roque'

bar'rack

bar'ra·cu'da

bar·rage'

bar'ra·try

bar'rel

bar'ren

bar'ren·ness

bar'ri·cade'

bar'ri·cad'ed

bar'ri·er

bar'ris·ter

bar'row

bar'ter

bar'tered

bas'al

ba·salt'

bas'cule

base

base'board'

based

base'less

base'ly

base'ment

base'ness

bas'er

bas'est

bash'ful

bas'ic

bas'i·cal·ly

ba·sil'i·ca

bas'i·lisk

ba'sin

ba'sis

bask

bas'ket

bas'ket·ball'

bas'ket·work'

bas'-re·lief'

bass

bas'si·net'

bas'so

bas·soon'

bass'wood'

bast'ed

bas'ti·na'do

bas'tion

bat

batch

bath

bathe

bathed
bath'er
bath'house'
ba'thos
bath'robe'
bath'room'
ba·tiste'
ba'ton'
bat·tal'ion
bat'ten
bat'tened
bat'ter
bat'tered
bat'ter·y
bat'tle
bat'tled
bat'tle·ment
bat'tle·ship'
bawl
bawled
bay'ber'ry
bay'o·net
bay'o·net'ed
bay'ou
ba·zaar'
be
beach
beached
beach'comb'er
bea'con
bead
bead'ed

bea'dle
bead'work'
bea'gle
beak
beak'er
beam
beamed
bean
bear
bear'a·ble
beard
beard'ed
bear'er
bear'ish
bear'skin'
beast
beast'li·ness
beast'ly
beat
beat'en
beat'er
be'a·tif'ic
be·at'i·fi·ca'tion
be·at'i·fy
beat'ings
be·at'i·tude
beau'te·ous
beau'ti·ful
beau'ti·ful·ly
beau'ti·fy
beau'ty
bea'ver

be·calm'
be·calmed'
be·came'
be·cause'
beck'on
beck'oned
be·cloud'
be·come'
be·com'ing·ly
be·com'ing·ness
bed
be·daub'
bed'bug'
bed'cham'ber
bed'clothes'
bed'ded
be·deck'
be·dev'il
be·dev'iled
bed'fel'low
be·diz'en
bed'lam
bed'post'
bed'rid'den
bed'rock'
bed'roll'
bed'room'
bed'side'
bed'spread'
bed'spring'
bed'stead
bed'time'

bee	be·hav'ior	bell'bird'
beech	be·hav'ior·al	bell'boy'
beef	be·hav'ior·ism	bel'li·cose
beef'steak'	be·head'	bel'li·cos'i·ty
bee'line'	be·head'ings	bel·lig'er·ence
beer	be·held'	bel·lig'er·en·cy
bees'wax'	be·he'moth	bel·lig'er·ent
bee'tle	be·hest'	bel·lig'er·ent·ly
be·fall'	be·hind'	bel'lowed
be·fell'	be·hold'	bel'lows
be·fit'	be·hold'en	be·long'
be·fog'	be·hold'er	be·longed'
be·fore'	be·hoove'	be·long'ings
be·fore'hand'	beige	be·lov'ed
be·friend'	be·jew'el	be·low'
be·fud'dle	be·jew'eled	belt
be·fud'dled	be·la'bor	belt'ed
beg	be·lat'ed	bel've·dere'
be·get'	be·lat'ed·ly	be·moan'
beg'gar	belch	be·moaned'
begged	be·lea'guer	be·mused'
be·gin'	be·lea'guered	bench
be·gone'	bel'fry	bend
be·go'ni·a	Bel'gi·an	bend'ed
be·got'	be·lie'	be·neath'
be·grime'	be·lief'	ben'e·dic'tion
be·guile'	be·liev'a·ble	ben'e·fac'tion
be·guiled'	be·lieve'	ben'e·fac'tor
be'gum	be·lit'tle	ben'e·fac'tress
be·gun'	be·lit'tled	ben'e·fice
be·half'	bell	be·nef'i·cent
be·have'	bel'la·don'na	ben'e·fi'ci·ar'y

ben'e·fit

ben'e·fit'ed

be·nev'o·lence

be·nev'o·lent

be·night'ed

be·nign'

be·nig'nan·cy

be·nig'nant

be·nig'ni·ty

bent

ben'zene

be·queath'

be·quest'

be·rate'

be·rat'ed

be·reave'

be·reaved'

be·reave'ment

ber'ry

berth

ber'yl

be·seech'

be·seeched'

be·seech'ing·ly

be·set'

be·side'

be·sides'

be·siege'

be·sieged'

be·smirch'

be·sot'ted

be·span'gle

be·speak'

Bes'se·mer

best

bes'tial

bes'ti·al'i·ty

be·stow'

be·stowed'

be·stride'

bet

be·take'

be·tide'

be·times'

be·to'ken

be·tray'

be·tray'al

be·tray'er

be·troth'

be·troth'al

bet'ter

bet'tered

bet'ter·ment

be·tween'

be·twixt'

bev'el

bev'eled

bev'er·age

bev'y

be·wail'

be·wailed'

be·ware'

be·wil'der

be·wil'dered

be·wil'der·ing·ly

be·wil'der·ment

be·witch'

be·witch'ing·ly

be·yond'

bez'el

bi·an'nu·al

bi·an'nu·al·ly

bi'as

bi'ased

bi'be·lot'

Bi'ble

Bib'li·cal

bib'li·o·graph'i·cal

bib'li·og'ra·phy

bib'u·lous

bi·cam'er·al

bi·car'bon·ate

bi·cen'te·nar'y

bi'ceps

bi·chlo'ride

bi·chro'mate

bi·cus'pid

bi'cy·cle

bid

bid'der

bide

bi·en'ni·al

bi·en'ni·um

bier

bi·fo'cal

big

big'a·mist

big'a·mous

big'a·my

big'ger

big'gest

big'horn'

bight

big'ot

big'ot·ed

big'ot·ry

bi'jou

bi·lat'er·al

bile

bilge

bil'i·ar'y

bi·lin'gual

bil'ious

bilk

bill

bill'board'

billed

bil'let

bil'let·ed

bill'fish'

bill'fold'

bill'head'

bil'liards

bil'lings

bil'lion

bil'lion·aire'

bil'low

bill'post'er

bill'stick'er

bi'me·tal'lic

bi·met'al·lism

bi·met'al·list

bi·month'ly

bin

bi'na·ry

bin·au'ral

bind

bind'er

bind'er·y

bind'ing·ly

bind'ings

bind'weed'

bin'go

bin'na·cle

bin·oc'u·lar

bi·no'mi·al

bi·og'ra·pher

bi'o·graph'ic

bi'o·graph'i·cal

bi'o·graph'i·cal·ly

bi·og'ra·phy

bi'o·log'i·cal

bi'o·log'i·cal·ly

bi·ol'o·gist

bi·ol'o·gy

bi'op·sy

bi·par'tite

bi'ped

bi'plane'

bi·po'lar

birch

bird

bird'lime'

bird'man'

birth

birth'day'

birth'mark'

birth'place'

birth'right'

bis'cuit

bi'sect

bish'op

bish'op·ric

bis'muth

bi'son

bisque

bit

bite

bit'er

bit'ing·ly

bit'ten

bit'ter

bit'ter·est

bit'ter·ly

bit'tern

bit'ter·ness

bit'ters

bit'ter·weed'

bi·tu'men

bi·tu'mi·nous

biv'ouac

bi·zarre'

black

black'ball'

black'ber'ry

black'bird'

black'board'

black'en

black'er

black'est

black'fish'

black'guard

black'head'

black'ish

black'jack'

black'leg'

black'mail'

black'mail'er

black'ness

black'smith'

black'strap'

black'thorn'

blad'der

blade

blame

blamed

blame'less

blame'less·ly

blame'less·ness

blame'wor'thy

blanch

blanc·mange'

bland

blan'dish

blan'dish·ing·ly

blan'dish·ment

bland'ly

bland·ness

blank

blanked

blank'er

blank'est

blan'ket

blank'ly

blare

blared

blar'ney

blas·pheme'

blas·phemed'

blas·phem'er

blas'phe·mous

blas'phe·my

blast

blast'ed

bla'tant

blaze

blazed

blaz'er

bla'zon

bla'zoned

bleach

bleached

bleach'er

bleak

bleat

bleed

bleed'er

blem'ish

blench

blend

blend'ed

blend'ings

bless

bless'ed·ness

bless'ings

blew

blight

blight'ed

blimp

blind

blind'ed

blind'er

blind'fold'

blind'ly

blind'ness

blink

blinked

blink'er

bliss

bliss'ful

bliss'ful·ly

blis'ter

blis'tered

blis'ter·ing·ly

blis'ter·y

blithe

blithe'ly

blithe'some

bliz'zard

bloat

bloat'ed

block

block·ade'

block·ad'ed

block·ad'er

block'head'

block'house'

blond

blood

blood'ed

blood'hound'

blood'i·est

blood'less

blood'let'ting

blood'line'

blood'root'

blood'shed'

blood'shot'

blood'stain'

blood'wood'

blood'y

bloom

bloomed

bloom'er

blos'som

blos'somed

blot

blotch

blot'ter

blouse

blow

blow'er

blow'fish'

blow'fly'

blow'gun'

blow'hard'

blow'hole'

blown

blow'off'

blow'out'

blow'pipe'

blow'torch'

blow'y

blub'ber

bludg'eon

bludg'eoned

blue

blue'fish'

blue'grass'

blue'nose'

blue'stock'ing

bluff

bluffed

bluff'er

blun'der

blun'dered

blun'der·buss

blun'der·er

blun'der·ing·ly

blunt

blunt'ed

blunt'ly

blunt'ness

blur

blurb

blurred

blurt

blush

blushed

blush'ing·ly

blus'ter

blus'tered

blus'ter·ing·ly

blus'ter·y

bo'a

board

board'ed

board'er

boast

boast'ed

boast'er

boast'ful

boast'ful·ly

boat

boat'load'

boat'man'

boat'swain'

bob'bin

bob'cat'

bob'o·link

bob'tail'

bode

bod'ice

bod'i·ly

bod′kin	bol′stered	bo·ni′to
bod′y	bolt	bon′net
bod′y·guard′	bolt′ed	bon′net·ed
bod′y·mak′er	bolt′head′	bo′nus
bog	bo′lus	bon′y
bo′gey	bomb	boo′by
bog′gle	bom·bard′	boo′dle
bog′gled	bom·bard′ed	book
bo′gus	bom′bard·ier′	book′bind′er
bog′wood′	bom·bard′ment	booked
Bo·he′mi·an	bom′bast	book′ings
boil	bom·bas′tic	book′ish
boiled	bombed	book′keep′er
boil′er	bomb′er	book′keep′ing
bois′ter·ous	bomb′proof′	book′let
bois′ter·ous·ly	bomb′shell′	book′lets
bo′la	bo·nan′za	book′mak′er
bold	bon′bon′	book′man
bold′er	bond	book′mark′
bold′est	bond′age	book′plate′
bold′face′	bond′ed	book′rack′
bold′ly	bond′hold′er	book′rest′
bold′ness	bond′man	book′sell′er
bo·le′ro	bond′slave′	book′shelf
bole′weed′	bonds′man	book′stall′
bo·liv′i·a	bone	book′stand′
bo·li′via′no	boned	book′worm′
boll	bone′fish′	boom
bo′lo	bone′less	boomed
bo·lom′e·ter	bone′set′	boom′er·ang
bol′she·vik	bon′fire′	boon
bol′ster	bon′go	boor

boor'ish

boost

boost'ed

boost'er

boot

boot'black'

boot'ed

boot'ee'

boot'er·y

booth

boot'jack'

boot'leg'

boot'leg'ger

boot'less

boot'strap'

boo'ty

booze

bo·rac'ic

bo'rate

bo'rax

Bor'deaux'

bor'der

bor'de·reau'

bor'dered

bore

bored

bo're·al

bo're·a'lis

bore'dom

bor'er

bore'some

bo'ric

bo'rine

bor'ings

born

bo'ron

bor'ough

bor'row

bor'rowed

bor'row·er

bor'row·ings

borsch

bosk'y

Bos'ni·an

bos'om

boss

bossed

boss'ism

boss'y

bo·tan'ic

bo·tan'i·cal

bot'a·nist

bot'a·nize

bot'a·nized

bot'a·ny

botch

botched

bot'fly'

both

both'er

both'ered

both'er·some

Both'ni·an

bot'tle

bot'tle·bird'

bot'tled

bot'tle·head'

bot'tle·hold'er

bot'tle·neck'

bot'tle·nose'

bot'tom

bot'tom·less

bot'tom·ry

bot'u·lism

bou'doir

bough

boughed

bought

bouil'la·baisse'

bouil'lon'

boul'der

bou'le·vard

bounce

bounced

bounc'er

bound

bound'a·ry

bound'ed

bound'en

bound'er

bound'less

boun'te·ous

boun'te·ous·ly

boun'ti·ful

boun'ty

bou·quet'

bour·geois'	boy'cott	brake'man
bour'geoi'sie'	boy'hood	bram'ble
bourse	boy'ish	bran
bout	boy'ish·ness	branch
bo'va·rysm	brace	branched
bo'vine	braced	branch'ling
bow	brace'let	brand
bow	brack'en	brand'ed
bowd'ler·ize	brack'et	bran'died
bowed	brack'et·ed	bran'dish
bowed	brack'ish	bran'dished
bow'el	brad'awl'	brand'-new'
bow'er	brag	bran'dy
bow'er·bird'	bragged	brash
bow'fin'	brag'ga·do'ci·o	brass
bow'ie	brag'gart	bras'sard
bow'knot'	Brah'man	brass'bound'
bowl	braid	brass'ie
bowled	braid'ed	brass'i·ness
bow'leg'ged	Braille	brass'y
bowl'er	brain	brat
bow'man	brained	brat'ling
bow'shot'	brain'fag'	bra·va'do
bow'sprit	brain'less	brave
bow'string'	brain'sick'	brave'ly
box	brain'work'	brav'er
box'board'	brain'y	brav'er·y
box'car'	braise	brav'est
boxed	braised	bra'vo
box'er	brake	bra·vu'ra
box'wood'	brake'age	brawl
boy	braked	brawled

brawl'er

brawn

brawn'y

bray

brayed

braze

brazed

bra'zen

bra'zened

bra'zier

bra·zil'ite

bra·zil'wood'

breach

breached

bread

bread'bas'ket

bread'board'

bread'ed

bread'fruit'

bread'root'

bread'stuff'

breadth

bread'win·ner'

break

break'a·ble

break'age

break'down'

break'er

break'fast

break'neck'

break'off'

break'out'

break'o·ver'

break'-through'

break'up'

break'wa'ter

breast

breast'band'

breast'bone'

breast'ed

breast'-fed'

breast'mark'

breast'pin'

breast'plate'

breast'weed'

breast'work'

breath

breathed

breath'less

bred

breech

breed

breed'er

breeze

breezed

breez'y

breth'ren

breve

bre·vet'

bre'vi·ar'y

bre·vier'

brev'i·ty

brew

brewed

brew'er

brew'er·y

brew'house'

bribe

bribed

brib'er·y

bric'-a-brac'

brick

brick'bat'

bricked

brick'lay'er

brick'ma'son

brick'yard'

brid'al

bride

bride'groom'

brides'maid'

bridge

bridged

bridge'head'

bridge'work'

bri'dle

bri'dled

brief

brief'er

brief'est

brief'ly

brief'ness

bri'er

brig

bri·gade'

brig'a·dier'

brig'and	bris'tle	broc'a·tel'
brig'and·age	bris'tled	broc'co·li
brig'an·tine	bris'tli·er	bro·chette'
bright	bris'tli·est	bro·chure'
bright'en	bris'tly	bro'gan
bright'er	Bri·tan'ni·a	brogue
bright'est	Bri·tan'nic	broil
bright'ly	Brit'i·cism	broiled
bright'ness	Brit'ish	broil'er
bright'work'	Brit'ish·er	broke
bril'liance	Brit'on	bro'ken
bril'lian·cy	brit'tle	brok'en·ly
bril'liant	brit'tle·ness	bro'ker
bril'lian·tine'	broach	bro'ker·age
bril'liant·ly	broached	bro'mate
bril'liant·ness	broad	bro'mide
brim	broad'ax'	bro·mid'ic
brim'ful'	broad'bill'	bro'mine
brimmed	broad'brim'	bron'chi·al
brim'stone'	broad'cast'	bron·chi'tis
brin'dled	broad'cast'er	bron'cho·scope
brine	broad'en	bron'chus
bring	broad'er	bron'co
brink	broad'est	bronze
brin'y	broad'leaf'	bronzed
bri·oche'	broad'loom'	brooch
bri·quette'	broad'ly	brood
brisk	broad'side'	brood'ed
brisk'en	broad'way'	brood'er
bris'ket	broad'wise'	brood'ling
brisk'ly	bro·cade'	brook
brisk'ness	bro·cad'ed	brook'let

broom

broom'weed'

broom'wood'

broth

broth'er

broth'er·hood

broth'er-in-law'

broth'er·li·ness

broth'er·ly

brougham

brought

brow

brown

brown'er

brown'est

brown'ie

browse

browsed

bru'in

bruise

bruised

bruit

brum'ma·gem

brunch

bru·net'

bru·nette'

brunt

brush

brushed

brush'ful

brush'less

brush'wood'

brush'work'

brusque

bru'tal

bru·tal'i·ty

bru·tal·i·za'tion

bru'tal·ize

bru'tal·ized

bru'tal·ly

brute

brut'ish

brut'ish·ly

brut'ish·ness

bub'ble

bub'bled

bub'bly

bu·bon'ic

buc'cal

buc'ca·neer'

buck

buck'board'

bucked

buck'et

buck'et·ed

buck'et·ful

buck'le

buck'led

buck'ler

buck'ram

buck'saw'

buck'shot'

buck'skin'

buck'wheat'

bu·col'ic

bud

bud'ded

bud'dy

budge

budged

budg'et

budg'et·ar'y

budg'et·ed

bud'wood'

bud'worm'

buff

buf'fa·lo

buff'er

buff'ered

buf'fet

buf·fet'

buf'fet·ed

buf·foon'

buf·foon'er·y

bug

bug'bear'

bugged

bug'gy

bu'gle

bu'gler

bu'gle·weed'

bug'proof'

bug'weed'

build

build'ed

build'er

build'ing

build'ings

built

bulb

bulb'ous

bulge

bulged

bulk

bulk'head'

bulk'i·er

bulk'i·est

bulk'y

bull

bull'doze'

bull'dozed'

bull'doz'er

bul'let

bul'le·tin

bull'fight'

bull'finch'

bull'frog'

bull'head'

bul'lion

bull'ish

bull'ock

bull'weed

bul'ly

bul'ly·rag'

bul'rush'

bul'wark

bum

bum'boat'

bump

bump'er

bump'i·er

bump'i·est

bump'kin

bump'y

bu'na

bunch

bunched

bun'dle

bun'dled

bung

bun'ga·low

bun'gle

bun'gled

bun'gler

bun'ion

bunk'er

bunk'house'

bunt

buoy

buoy'ant

buoy'ant·ly

bur'den

bur'dened

bur'den·some

bu'reau

bu·reauc'ra·cy

bu'reau·crat

bu·rette'

bur'gee

bur'geon

bur'geoned

bur'gess

bur'glar

bur'i·al

bu'rin

bur'lap

bur·lesque'

bur·lesqued'

bur'ly

burn

burned

burn'er

bur'nish

bur'nish·er

burn'out'

burnt

burr

bur'ro

bur'row

bur'rowed

bur'sar

bur·si'tis

burst

bur'y

bus

bus'es

bush

bushed

bush'el

bush'el·er

bush'ings

bus'i·ly

busi′ness	but′ter·ball′	bux′om
busi′ness·es	but′ter·cup′	buy
busi′ness·like′	but′tered	buy′er
bus′kin	but′ter·fat′	buzz
bust	but′ter·fish′	buz′zard
bus′tard	but′ter·fly′	buzzed
bus′tle	but′ter·nut′	buzz′er
bus′tled	but′ter·scotch′	by
bus′y	but′ter·y	by′gone′
bus′y·bod′y	but′ton	by′pass′
but	but′toned	by′path′
butch′er	but′ton·hole′	by′play′
butch′ered	but′ton·holed′	by′-prod′uct
butch′er·y	but′ton·weed′	By·ron′ic
but′ler	but′ton·wood′	by′stand′er
butt	but′tress	by′way′
but′ter	but′tressed	by′word′

C

cab	cac'tus·es	cai'tiff
ca·bal'	ca·dav'er	ca·jole'
cab'bage	ca·dav'er·ous	ca·joled'
cab'in	cad'die	ca·jol'er·y
cab'i·net	ca'dence	cake
ca'ble	ca·den'za	cake'walk'
ca'bled	ca·det'	cal'a·bash
ca'ble·gram	cad'mi·um	cal'a·mine
ca·boose'	Cad'mus	ca·lam'i·tous
cab'ri·o·let'	ca'dre	ca·lam'i·tous·ly
ca·ca'o	ca·du'ce·us	ca·lam'i·ty
cach'a·lot	cad'weed	cal·car'e·ous
cache	Cae·sar'e·an	cal'ci·fi·ca'tion
ca·chet'	cae·su'ra	cal'ci·fy
cach'in·na'tion	ca·fé'	cal'ci·mine
cack'le	caf'e·te'ri·a	cal'cine
cack'led	caf'fe·ine	cal·cined'
ca·coph'o·nous	cage	cal'ci·um
ca·coph'o·ny	caged	cal'cu·late
cac'ti	cairn	cal'cu·lat'ed
cac'toid	cais'son	cal'cu·la'tion
cac'tus	cais'soned	cal'cu·la'tor

cal'dron
cal'en·dar
cal'en·der
cal'en·dered
calf
calf'skin'
cal'i·ber
cal'i·brate
cal'i·brat'ed
cal'i·bra'tion
cal'i·co
cal'i·per
ca'liph
cal'is·then'ics
calk
calked
calk'er
call
cal'la
call'a·ble
called
cal'ler
cal·lig'ra·phy
cal·li'o·pe
cal·los'i·ty
cal'lous
cal'loused
cal'lous·ly
cal'low
cal'low·ly
cal'lus
calm

calmed
calm'er
calm'est
calm'ly
calm'ness
cal'o·mel
ca·lor'ic
cal'o·rie
cal'u·met
ca·lum'ni·ate
ca·lum'ni·at'ed
ca·lum'ni·a'tion
ca·lum'ni·a'tor
cal'um·ny
Cal'va·ry
calved
ca·lyp'so
ca'lyx
ca'ma·ra'de·rie
cam'ber
cam'bi·um
cam'bric
came
cam'el
cam'el·eer'
Cam'e·lot
Cam'em·bert'
cam'e·o
cam'er·a
cam'er·a·man'
cam'i·sole
cam'o·mile

cam'ou·flage
camp
cam·paign'
cam'pa·ni'le
camp'er
camp'fire'
cam'phor
cam'phor·ate
cam'phor·at'ed
cam'pus
can
ca·nal'
ca·nal'i·za'tion
ca·nar'y
can'can
can'cel
can'celed
can'cel·la'tion
can'cer
can'cer·ous
can'cer·weed'
can'de·la'brum
can'did
can'di·da·cy
can'di·date
can'did·ly
can'died
can'dle
can'dled
can'dle·fish'
can'dle·light'
can'dle·nut'

can'dle·stick'
can'dor
can'dy
can'dy·mak'er
cane
cane'brake'
ca'nine
can'is·ter
can'ker
can'kered
can'ker·ous
can'ker·weed'
can'ker·worm'
canned
can'ner
can'ner·y
can'ni·bal
can'ni·bal·ism
can'ni·ly
can'non
can'non·ade'
can'non·eer'
can'ny
ca·noe'
can'on
ca·non'i·cal
ca·non'i·cals
can'on·i·za'tion
can'on·ize
can'o·py
cant
can't

can'ta·loupe
can·tan'ker·ous
can·ta'ta
can·teen'
cant'er
can'tered
can'ti·cle
can'ti·cles
can'ti·le'ver
can'tle
can'to
can'ton
can·ton'ment
can'tor
can'vas
can'vased
can'vass
can'vassed
can'vass·er
can'yon
caou'tchouc
ca'pa·bil'i·ties
ca'pa·bil'i·ty
ca'pa·ble
ca'pa·bly
ca·pa'cious
ca·pac'i·tance
ca·pac'i·tate
ca·pac'i·tat'ed
ca·pac'i·tor
ca·pac'i·ty
cape

ca'per
ca'pered
ca'per·ings
cap'il·lar'i·ty
cap'il·lar'y
cap'i·tal
cap'i·tal·ism
cap'i·tal·ist
cap'i·tal·is'tic
cap'i·tal·ists
cap'i·tal·i·za'tion
cap'i·tal·ize
cap'i·tal·ized
cap'i·tol
ca·pit'u·late
ca·pit'u·lat'ed
ca·pit'u·lates
ca·pit'u·la'tion
ca'pon
capped
ca·price'
ca·pri'cious
cap·size'
cap·sized'
cap'stan
cap'sule
cap'tain
cap'tain·cy
cap'tion
cap'tious
cap'tious·ly
cap'tious·ness

cap'ti·vate

cap'ti·vat'ed

cap'ti·va'tion

cap'tive

cap·tiv'i·ty

cap'ture

cap'tured

car

ca'ra·ba'o

car'a·bi·neer'

car'a·cal

car'a·cole

ca·rafe'

car'a·mel

car'a·mel·ize

car'a·pace

car'at

car'a·van

car'a·van'sa·ry

car'a·vel

car'a·way

car'bide

car'bine

car'bo·hy'drate

car·bol'ic

car'bon

car'bon·ate

car'bon·at'ed

car·bon'ic

car'bon·if'er·ous

car'bon·ize

car'bon·ized

car'bo·run'dum

car'boy

car'bun·cle

car'bu·ret'or

car'cass

car'ci·no'ma

card

card'board'

card'ed

car'di·ac

car'di·gan

car'di·nal

car'di·nal·ate

car'di·o·gram'

car'di·o·graph'

car'di·ol'o·gy

care

cared

ca·reen'

ca·reened'

ca·reer'

care'free'

care'ful

care'ful·ly

care'less

care'less·ly

care'less·ness

ca·ress'

ca·ressed'

ca·ress'ing·ly

car'et

car'fare'

car'go

car'i·bou

car'i·ca·ture

car'i·es

car'il·lon

car'load·ings'

car·min'a·tive

car'mine

car'nage

car'nal

car'nal·ly

car·na'tion

car·nel'ian

car'ni·val

car·niv'o·rous

car'ol

car'oled

car'om

car'omed

ca·rot'id

ca·rous'al

ca·rouse'

ca·roused'

carp

car'pal

car'pen·ter

car'pet

car'pet·ed

car'riage

car'ried

car'ri·er

car'ri·on

car'rot·

car'rou·sel'

car'ry

cart

cart'age

cart'ed

car'tel

car'ti·lage

car'ti·lag'i·nous

car·tog'ra·phy

car'ton

car·toon'

car·touche'

car'tridge

carve

carved

carv'er

carv'ings

car'y·at'id

ca·sa'ba

cas·cade'

cas·cad'ed

cas·car'a

case

ca'se·in

case'ment

case'work'

cash

cash'book'

cash'box'

cashed

ca·shew'

cash·ier'

cash·iered'

cash'mere

ca·si'no

cask

cas'ket

cas·sa'tion

cas·sa'va

cas'se·role

cas'si·a

cas·si'no

cas'sock

cast

cas'ta·net'

caste

cast'er

cas'ti·gate

cas'ti·gat'ed

cas'ti·ga'tion

cas'tle

cast'off'

cas'tor

cas'tra·me·ta'tion

cas'u·al

cas'u·al·ly

cas'u·al·ty

cas'u·ist

cas'u·ist·ry

ca·tab'o·lism

cat'a·clysm

cat'a·comb

cat'a·falque

cat'a·lep'sy

cat'a·lep'tic

cat'a·logue

cat'a·logued

ca·tal'pa

ca·tal'y·sis

cat'a·lyst

cat'a·lyt'ic

cat'a·lyze

cat'a·mount

cat'a·pult

cat'a·ract

ca·tarrh'

ca·tarrh'al

ca·tas'tro·phe

cat'a·stroph'ic

cat'a·stroph'i·cal·ly

cat'a·ton'ic

Ca·taw'ba

cat'bird'

cat'boat'

cat'call'

catch

catch'er

catch'weed'

catch'word'

catch'y

cat'e·che'sis

cat'e·chet'i·cal

cat'e·chism

cat'e·chize

cat'e·gor'i·cal

cat′e·go·rize	cau·sal′i·ty	cease′less
cat′e·go′ry	cau·sa′tion	cease′less·ly
cat′e·nar′y	caus′a·tive	ce′cum
ca′ter	cause	ce′dar
ca′tered	caused	ce′dar·bird′
ca′ter·er	cause′less	cede
cat′er·pil′lar	cau′se·rie′	ced′ed
cat′fish′	cause′way′	ce·dil′la
cat′gut′	caus′tic	ced′ing
ca·thar′sis	cau′ter·i·za′tion	ceil′ings
ca·thar′tic	cau′ter·ize	cel′e·brant
cat′head′	cau′ter·ized	cel′e·brate
ca·the′dral	cau′ter·y	cel′e·brat′ed
cath′e·ter	cau′tion	cel′e·bra′tion
cath′e·ter·ize	cau′tion·ar′y	ce·leb′ri·ty
cath′ode	cau′tioned	ce·ler′i·ty
cath′o·lic	cau′tious	cel′er·y
ca·thol′i·cism	cav′al·cade′	ce·les′ta
cath′o·lic′i·ty	cav′a·lier′	ce·les′tial
ca·thol′i·cize	cav′al·ry	ce·les′tial·ly
cat′kin	ca′va·ti′na	cel′i·ba·cy
cat′like′	cave	cel′i·bate
cat′nip	ca′ve·at	cell
cat′tail′	cav′ern	cel′lar
cat′tle	cav′ern·ous	cel′lar·er
cat′walk′	cav′i·ar	cel′lar·et′
cau′cus	cav′il	cel′list
cau′cused	cav′i·ty	cel′lo
cau′dal	ca·vort′	cel′lo·phane
caught	cay·enne′	cel′lu·lar
cau′li·flow′er	cease	cel′lu·li′tis
caus′al	ceased	cel′lu·loid

cel'lu·lose	cen'tral·ize	cer'ti·o·ra'ri
Celt'ic	cen'tral·ized	cer'ti·tude
ce·ment'	cen·trif'u·gal	cer'vi·cal
ce'men·ta'tion	cen'tri·fuge	cer'vix
cem'e·ter'y	cen·trip'e·tal	ce'si·um
cen'a·cle	cen'trist	ces·sa'tion
cen'o·bite	cen·tu'ri·on	ces'sion
cen'o·taph	cen'tu·ry	cess'pool'
cen'ser	ce·phal'ic	ces'tus
cen'sor	ce·ram'ic	ce·ta'cean
cen'sored	ce're·al	chafe
cen·so'ri·al	cer'e·bel'lum	chaf'fer
cen·so'ri·ous	cer'e·bral	chaf'fered
cen'sor·ship	cer'e·bra'tion	chaf'finch
cen'sur·a·ble	cer'e·brum	chaff'weed'
cen'sure	cere'ment	cha·grin'
cen'sured	cer'e·mo'ni·al	cha·grined'
cen'sus	cer'e·mo'ni·al·ly	chain
cent	cer'e·mo'ni·ous	chained
cen'taur	cer'e·mo'ni·ous·ly	chain'work'
cen'te·nar'i·an	cer'e·mo'ni·ous·ness	chair
cen'te·nar'y	cer'e·mo'ny	chair'man
cen·ten'ni·al	ce·rise'	chaise
cen'ter	ce'ri·um	chal·ced'o·ny
cen'ter·board'	cer'tain	cha·let'
cen'tered	cer'tain·ly	chal'ice
cen'ter·piece'	cer'tain·ty	chalk
cen'ti·grade	cer·tif'i·cate	chalk'i·ness
cen'ti·me'ter	cer·tif'i·cat'ed	chal'lenge
cen'ti·pede	cer'ti·fi·ca'tion	chal'lenged
cen'tral	cer'ti·fied	cham'ber
cen'tral·i·za'tion	cer'ti·fy	cham'bered

cham′ber·lain	chap′lain	char′ter
cham′ber·maid′	chap′let	char′tered
cha·me′le·on	chap′ter	char·treuse′
cham′ois	char	char′y
cham·pagne′	char′ac·ter	chase
cham′per·ty	char′ac·ter·is′tic	chased
cham′pi·on	char′ac·ter·is′ti·cal·ly	chasm
cham′pi·on·ship′	char′ac·ter·i·za′tion	chas′sis
chance	char′ac·ter·ize	chaste
chanced	char′ac·ter·ized	chas′ten
chan′cel	cha·rade′	chas′tened
chan′cel·ler·y	char′coal′	chas′ten·ing·ly
chan′cel·lor	chard	chas·tise′
chan′cer·y	charge	chas·tised′
chan′de·lier′	charge′a·ble	chas′tise·ment
chan′dler	charged	chas′ti·ty
chan′dler·y	charg′er	chas′u·ble
change	char′i·ly	châ·teau′
change′a·ble	char′i·ness	chat′e·laine
changed	char′i·ot	chat′tel
change′less	char′i·ot·eer′	chat′ter
change′ling	char′i·ta·ble	chat′tered
chan′nel	char′i·ta·bly	chat′ter·er
chan′neled	char′i·ty	chat′ty
chant	char′la·tan	chauf·feur′
chant′ed	charm	chau′vin·ism
cha′os	charmed	cheap
cha·ot′ic	charm′ing·ly	cheap′en
cha·ot′i·cal·ly	char′nel	cheap′ened
chap′ar·ral′	charred	cheap′er
chap′el	chart	cheap′est
chap′er·on	chart′ed	cheap′ly

cheap'ness	chem'is·try	child
cheat	che·nille'	child'hood
cheat'ed	cher'ish	child'ish
cheat'er	che·root'	child'ish·ly
check	cher'ry	child'ish·ness
check'book'	cher'ub	child'less
checked	che·ru'bic	child'like'
check'er	cher'u·bim	chil'dren
check'er·board'	cher'vil	chil'i
check'ered	chess	chill
check'mate'	chess'board'	chilled
check'mat'ed	chess'man	chill'i·er
check'off'	chest	chill'i·est
check'rein'	ches'ter·field'	chill'ing·ly
cheek'y	chest'nut	chill'y
cheer	chev'ron	chime
cheered	chew	chimed
cheer'ful	chic	chi·me'ra
cheer'ful·ly	chi·can'er·y	chi·mer'i·cal
cheer'ful·ness	chick'a·dee	chim'ney
cheer'i·ly	chick'en	chim'pan·zee'
cheer'less	chick'weed'	chin
cheer'less·ly	chic'le	chi'na
cheer'y	chic'o·ry	chinch
cheese	chide	chin·chil'la
cheese'cake'	chief	chine
cheese'cloth'	chief'ly	Chi'nese'
chef	chief'tain	chink
chem'i·cal	chif'fon	chintz
chem'i·cal·ly	chif'fo·nier'	chip
che·mise'	chig'ger	chip'munk
chem'ist	chil'blain'	chipped

chip'per	chop	chron'i·cle
chi·rog'ra·phy	chop'house'	chron'i·cled
chi·rop'o·dist	chopped	chron'i·cler
chi'ro·prac'tor	chop'per	chron'i·cles
chirp	cho·ral'	chron'o·graph
chis'el	chord	chron'o·log'i·cal
chis'eled	cho·re'a	chron'o·log'i·cal·ly
chit'chat'	cho're·og'ra·phy	chro·nol'o·gy
chit'ter·ling	chor'is·ter	chro·nom'e·ter
chiv'al·ric	chor'tle	chron'o·met'ric
chiv'al·rous	cho'rus	chrys'a·lis
chiv'al·ry	chose	chrys·an'the·mum
chive	cho'sen	chrys'o·lite
chlo'ral	chow	chub'bi·ness
chlo'rate	chow'der	chub'by
chlo'ride	chrism	chuck
chlo'rin·ate	chris'ten	chuck'le
chlo'rine	Chris'ten·dom	chuck'led
chlo'rite	chris'tened	chuck'le·head'
chlo'ro·form	chris'ten·ings	chuck'ling·ly
chlo'ro·phyll	Chris'tian	chum
chlo·ro'sis	Chris'ti·an'i·ty	chum'my
choc'o·late	Christ'mas	chump
choice	chro'mate	chunk
choir	chro·mat'ics	chunk'i·ness
choir'boy'	chrome	chunk'y
choke	chro'mic	church
chok'er	chro'mite	church'man
chol'er	chro'mi·um	churl
chol'er·a	chro'mo·some	churl'ish
chol'er·ic	chron'ic	churl'ish·ly
choose	chron'i·cal·ly	churl'ish·ness

churn	cir'cu·lat'ed	cite
churned	cir'cu·la'tion	cit'ed
chute	cir'cu·la·to'ry	cit'i·zen
chut'ney	cir'cum·am'bi·ent	cit'i·zen·ry
chyle	cir·cum'fer·ence	cit'i·zen·ship'
ci·ca'da	cir·cum'fer·en'tial	cit'rate
cic'a·trix	cir'cum·flex	cit'ric
ci'der	cir'cum·lo·cu'tion	cit'ron
ci·gar'	cir'cum·loc'u·to'ry	cit'y
cig'a·rette'	cir'cum·nav'i·gate	civ'ic
cinch	cir'cum·scribe'	civ'il
cinc'ture	cir'cum·scribed'	ci·vil'ian
cinc'tured	cir'cum·spect	ci·vil'i·ty
cin'der	cir'cum·spec'tion	civ'i·li·za'tion
cin'e·ma	cir'cum·spect'ly	civ'i·lize
cin'e·mat'o·graph	cir'cum·spect'ness	civ'i·lized
cin'na·bar	cir'cum·stance	civ'il·ly
cin'na·mon	cir'cum·stanc·es	clack
cinque'foil'	cir'cum·stan'tial	claim
ci'on	cir'cum·stan'ti·al'i·ty	claim'ant
ci'pher	cir'cum·stan'ti·ate	claimed
ci'phered	cir'cum·stan'ti·at'ed	clair·voy'ance
cir'cle	cir'cum·vent'	clair·voy'ant
cir'cled	cir'cum·vent'ed	cla'mant
cir'cuit	cir'cum·ven'tion	clam'bake'
cir·cu'i·tous	cir'cus	clam'ber
cir·cu'i·tous·ly	cir·rho'sis	clam'bered
cir·cu'i·tous·ness	cir·rhot'ic	clam'my
cir'cu·lar	cir'rus	clam'or
cir'cu·lar·i·za'tion	cis'tern	clam'ored
cir'cu·lar·ize	cit'a·del	clam'or·ous
cir'cu·late	ci·ta'tion	clamp

clam'shell'

clan

clan·des'tine

clang

clanged

clang'or

clank

clanked

clan'nish

clan'ship

clans'man

clap

clapped

clap'per

clap'trap'

claque

clar'et

clar'i·fi·ca'tion

clar'i·fied

clar'i·fy

clar'i·net'

clar'i·on

clar'i·ty

clash

clasp

class

clas'sic

clas'si·cal

clas'si·cal·ism

clas'si·cal·ist

clas'si·cal·ly

clas'si·cist

clas'si·fi·ca'tion

clas'si·fied

clas'si·fi'er

clas'si·fy

class'mate'

class'room'

class'work'

clat'ter

clat'tered

clause

claus'tro·pho'bi·a

clav'i·chord

clav'i·cle

claw

clay

clean

cleaned

clean'er

clean'est

clean'li·ness

clean'ly

clean'ness

cleanse

cleans'er

clean'up'

clear

clear'ance

cleared

clear'er

clear'est

clear'head'ed

clear'ing·house'

clear'ly

clear'ness

cleat

cleat'ed

cleav'age

cleave

cleav'er

clef

cleft

clem'a·tis

clem'en·cy

clem'ent

clench

clere'sto'ry

cler'gy

cler'gy·man

cler'i·cal

cler'i·cal·ism

clerk

clev'er

clev'er·er

clev'er·est

clev'er·ness

clew

cli·ché'

click

cli'ent

cli'en·tele'

cliff

cli·mac'ter·ic

cli·mac'tic

cli'mate

cli·mat'ic	close'ness	club'man
cli'max	clos'er	cluck
climb	clos'est	clump
climbed	clos'et	clum'si·er
climb'er	clos'et·ed	clum'si·est
clinch	clo'sure	clum'si·ly
clinch'er	clot	clum'si·ness
cling	cloth	clum'sy
cling'ing·ly	clothed	clus'ter
clin'ic	clothes	clus'tered
clin'i·cal	clothes'pin'	clutch
cli·ni'cian	cloth'ier	clut'ter
clink	clot'ted	clut'tered
clinked	cloud	coach
clink'er	cloud'i·er	coach'man
clip	cloud'i·est	co·ad'ju·tor
clip'per	cloud'i·ness	co·ag'u·late
clip'pings	cloud'less	co·ag'u·lat'ed
clique	cloud'y	co·ag'u·lates
cloak	clout	co·ag'u·la'tion
clock	clout'ed	co·ag'u·la'tive
clock'wise'	clove	coal
clock'work'	clo'ven	co'a·lesce'
clod	clo'ver	co'a·lesced'
clog	clown	co'a·les'cence
cloi'son'né'	clowned	co'a·les'cent
clois'ter	clown'ish	co'a·li'tion
clois'tered	cloy	coal'sack'
clon'ic	cloyed	coarse
close	club	coars'en
closed	clubbed	coars'ened
close'ly	club'house'	coars'er

coars'est	co'co·nut'	cog'nate
coast	co·coon'	cog·ni'tion
coast'al	co'da	cog'ni·zance
coast'er	code	cog'ni·zant
coast'wise'	cod'ed	cog·no'men
coat	co'de·fend'ant	co·hab'it
coat'ed	co'de·ine	co·here'
coat'ings	co'dex	co·hered'
co·au'thor	cod'fish'	co·her'ence
coax	cod'i·cil	co·her'ent
coaxed	cod'i·fi·ca'tion	co·her'ent·ly
co·ax'i·al	cod'i·fy	co·her'er
coax'ing·ly	co'ed'	co·he'sion
co'balt	co'ed'u·ca'tion	co·he'sive
cob'ble	co'ef·fi'cient	co'hort
cob'bled	co·erce'	coif
co'bra	co·erced'	coif·fure'
cob'web'	co·er'cion	coign
co·caine'	co·er'cive	coil
coc'cyx	co·e'val	coiled
coch'i·neal'	co'ex·ec'u·tor	coin
cock·ade'	cof'fee	coin'age
cock'a·too'	cof'fer	co'in·cide'
cock'le	cof'fin	co'in·cid'ed
cock'le·shell'	cog	co·in'ci·dence
cock'ney	co'gen·cy	co·in'ci·den'tal
cock'pit'	co'gent	coined
cock'roach'	cog'i·tate	coin'er
cock'sure'	cog'i·tat'ed	co'in·sur'ance
cock'sure'ness	cog'i·ta'tion	co'in·sure'
cock'tail'	cog'i·ta'tive	co'in·sur'er
co'coa	co'gnac	coke

col'an·der

cold

cold'er

cold'est

cold'ly

cole'slaw'

col'ic

col'i·se'um

co·li'tis

col·lab'o·rate

col·lab'o·rat'ed

col·lab'o·ra'tion

col·lapse'

col·lapsed'

col·laps'i·ble

col'lar

col'lar·band'

col'lar·bone'

col·late'

col·lat'ed

col·lat'er·al

col·la'tion

col·la'tor

col·league'

col'lect

col·lect'ed

col·lect'i·ble

col·lec'tion

col·lec'tive

col·lec'tiv·ism

col·lec'tiv·ist

col·lec'tor

col·lec'tor·ship

col'lege

col·le'gi·ate

col·lide'

col·lid'ed

col'lie

col'lier

col·li'sion

col'lo·ca'tion

col·lo'di·on

col'loid

col·loi'dal

col·lo'qui·al

col'lo·quy

col'lo·type

col·lu'sion

col·lu'sive

co·logne'

co'lon

colo'nel

co·lo'ni·al

col'o·nist

col'o·ni·za'tion

col'o·nize

col'o·nized

col'on·nade'

col'o·ny

col'o·phon

col'or

col'or·a'tion

col'o·ra·tu'ra

col'ored

col'or·less

co·los'sal

Col'os·se'um

co·los'sus

col'por'teur

colt

col'um·bine

col'umn

co·lum'nar

co'ma

com'a·tose

comb

com'bat

com'bat·ant

com'ba·tive

com·bat'ive·ness

combed

com'bi·na'tion

com'bine

com·bined'

comb'ings

com·bust'

com·bus'ti·ble

com·bus'tion

come

co·me'di·an

com'e·dy

come'li·ness

come'ly

co·mes'ti·ble

com'et

com'fit

com'fort

com'fort·a·ble

com'fort·a·bly

com'fort·ed

com'fort·er

com'fort·less

com'ic

com'i·cal

com'ings

com'ma

com·mand'

com'man·dant'

com·mand'ed

com·man·deer'

com·mand'er

com·mand'er·y

com·mand'ing·ly

com·mand'ment

com·man'do

com·mem'o·rate

com·mem'o·rat'ed

com·mem'o·ra'tion

com·mem'o·ra'tive

com·mence'

com·menced'

com·mence'ment

com·mend'

com·mend'a·ble

com'men·da'tion

com·mend'a·to'ry

com·mend'ed

com·men'su·ra·ble

com·men'su·rate

com'ment

com'men·tar'y

com'men·ta'tor

com'ment·ed

com'merce

com·mer'cial

com·mer'cial·ism

com·mer'cial·i·za'tion

com·mer'cial·ize

com·min'a·to'ry

com·min'gle

com·min'gled

com'mi·nute

com'mi·nut'ed

com'mi·nu'tion

com·mis'er·ate

com·mis'er·a'tion

com'mis·sar'

com'mis·sar'i·at

com'mis·sar'y

com·mis'sion

com·mis'sioned

com·mis'sion·er

com·mit'

com·mit'ment

com·mit'ted

com·mit'tee

com·mo'di·ous

com·mod'i·ty

com'mo·dore'

com'mon

com'mon·al·ty

com'mon·er

com'mon·est

com'mon·ly

com'mon·place'

com'mon·wealth'

com·mo'tion

com'mu·nal

com·mune'

com·mu'ni·ca·ble

com·mu'ni·cant

com·mu'ni·cate

com·mu'ni·cat'ed

com·mu'ni·ca'tion

com·mu'ni·ca'tive

com·mun'ion

com·mu'ni·qué'

com'mu·nism

com'mu·nist

com·mu·nis'tic

com·mu'ni·ty

com'mu·ni·za'tion

com'mu·nize

com'mu·ta'tion

com'mu·ta'tor

com·mute'

com·mut'ed

com·mut'er

com·pact'

com·pan'ion

com·pan'ion·a·ble

com·pan'ion·ship

com·pan'ion·way'

com'pa·ny

com'pa·ra·bil'i·ty

com'pa·ra·ble

com·par'a·tive

com·pare'

com·pared'

com·par'i·son

com·part'ment

com'pass

com·pas'sion

com·pas'sion·ate

com·pas'sion·ate·ly

com·pat'i·bil'i·ty

com·pat'i·ble

com·pa'tri·ot

com·peer'

com·pel'

com·pelled'

com·pel'ling·ly

com'pend

com·pen'di·ous

com·pen'di·um

com'pen·sate

com'pen·sat'ed

com'pen·sa'tion

com'pen·sa'tor

com·pen'sa·to'ry

com·pete'

com·pet'ed

com'pe·tence

com'pe·tent

com'pe·tent·ly

com'pe·ti'tion

com·pet'i·tive

com·pet'i·tor

com'pi·la'tion

com·pile'

com·piled'

com·pil'er

com·pla'cence

com·pla'cen·cy

com·pla'cent

com·plain'

com·plain'ant

com·plained'

com·plain'ing·ly

com·plaint'

com·plai'sance

com·plai'sant

com'ple·ment

com'ple·men'tal

com'ple·men'ta·ry

com'ple·ment·ed

com·plete'

com·plet'ed

com·ple'tion

com·plex'

com·plex'ion

com·plex'i·ty

com·pli'ance

com·pli'ant

com'pli·cate

com'pli·cat'ed

com'pli·ca'tion

com·plic'i·ty

com·plied'

com'pli·ment

com'pli·men'ta·ry

com'plin

com·ply'

com·po'nent

com·port'

com·pose'

com·posed'

com·pos'er

com·pos'ite

com·po·si'tion

com·pos'i·tor

com'post

com·po'sure

com'pote

com'pound

com'pre·hend'

com'pre·hend'ed

com'pre·hen'si·bil'i·ty

com'pre·hen'si·ble

com'pre·hen'sion

com'pre·hen'sive

com·press'

com·press'i·bil'i·ty

com·press'ible

com·pres'sion

com·pres'sor

com·prise'

com'pro·mise

com'pro·mis'ing·ly

Comp·tom'e·ter

comp·trol'ler

com·pul'sion

com·pul'sive

com·pul'so·ry

com·punc'tion

com'pu·ta'tion

com·pute'

com·put'ed

com'rade

con·cat'e·na'tion

con'cave

con·cav'i·ty

con·ceal'

con·cealed'

con·ceal'ment

con·cede'

con·ced'ed

con·ceit'

con·ceit'ed

con·ceit'ed·ly

con·ceiv'a·ble

con·ceiv'a·bly

con·ceive'

con·ceived'

con'cen·trate

con'cen·trat'ed

con'cen·tra'tion

con·cen'tric

con'cept

con·cep'tion

con·cep'tu·al

con·cern'

con·cerned'

con'cert

con·cert'ed

con'cer·ti'na

con·ces'sion

con·ces'sion·aire'

conch

con·cil'i·ate

con·cil'i·at'ed

con·cil'i·a'tion

con·cil'i·a·to'ry

con·cise'

con·cise'ness

con'clave

con·clude'

con·clud'ed

con·clu'sion

con·clu'sive

con·clu'sive·ly

con·coct'

con·coct'ed

con·coc'tion

con·com'i·tant

con'cord

con·cord'ance

con'course

con·crete'

con·cur'

con·curred'

con·cur'rence

con·cur'rent

con·cus'sion

con·demn'

con·dem·na'tion

con·dem'na·to'ry

con·demned'

con'den·sa'tion

con·dense'

con·densed'

con·dens'er

con'de·scend'

con'de·scend'ing·ly

con'de·scen'sion

con·dign'

con'di·ment

con·di'tion

con·di'tion·al

con·di'tion·al·ly

con·di'tioned

con·dole'

con·do'lence

con'do·min'i·um

con'do·na'tion

con·done'

con·doned'

con'dor

con·du'cive

con·duct'

con·duct'ed

con·duc'tion

con·duc·tiv'i·ty

con·duc'tor

con'duit
con'dyle
cone
con·fec'tion
con·fec'tion·er
con·fec'tion·er'y
con·fed'er·a·cy
con·fed'er·ate
con·fed'er·a'tion
con·fer'
con'fer·ee'
con'fer·ence
con·ferred'
con·fess'
con·fess'ed·ly
con·fes'sion
con·fes'sion·al
con·fes'sor
con·fide'
con·fid'ed
con'fi·dence
con'fi·dent
con'fi·den'tial
con'fi·den'tial·ly
con'fi·dent·ly
con·fid'ing·ly
con·fig'u·ra'tion
con·fine'
con·fined'
con·fine'ment
con·firm'
con'fir·ma'tion

con·firmed'
con'fis·cate
con'fis·cat'ed
con'fis·ca'tion
con·fis'ca·to'ry
con'fla·gra'tion
con·flict'
con·flict'ed
con·flic'tion
con·flu·ence
con'flu·ent
con·form'
con·form'a·ble
con'for·ma'tion
con·formed'
con·form'er
con·form'i·ty
con·found'
con·found'ed
con'frere
con·front'
con'fron·ta'tion
con·front'ed
con·fuse'
con·fused'
con·fus'ed·ly
con·fus'ing·ly
con·fu'sion
con'fu·ta'tion
con·fute'
con·fut'ed
con·geal'

con·gealed'
con'ge·la'tion
con'ge·ner
con·gen'ial
con·ge·ni·al'i·ty
con·gen'i·tal
con·gest'
con·gest'ed
con·ges'tion
con·glom'er·ate
con·glom'er·a'tion
con·grat'u·late
con·grat'u·lat'ed
con·grat'u·lates
con·grat'u·la'tion
con·grat'u·la·to'ry
con'gre·gate
con'gre·gat'ed
con'gre·ga'tion
con'gre·ga'tion·al
con'gress
con·gres'sion·al
con'gru·ence
con'gru·ent
con·gru'i·ty
con'gru·ous
con'ic
con'i·cal
co'ni·fer
co·nif'er·ous
con·jec'tur·al
con·jec'ture

con·jec′tured

con′ju·gal

con′ju·gate

con′ju·gat′ed

con′ju·ga′tion

con·junc′tion

con·junc′tive

con·junc′ti·vi′tis

con′ju·ra′tion

con·jure′

con·jured′

con′jur·er

con·nect′

con·nect′ed·ly

con·nec′tion

con·nec′tive

con·nec′tor

con·niv′ance

con·nive′

con·nived′

con′nois·seur′

con′no·ta′tion

con·note′

con·not′ed

con·nu′bi·al

con′quer

con′quered

con′quer·or

con′quest

con′san·guin′i·ty

con′science

con′sci·en′tious

con′sci·en′tious·ly

con′scious

con′scious·ly

con′scious·ness

con′script

con·scrip′tion

con′se·crate

con′se·crat′ed

con′se·cra′tion

con′se·cra′tive

con·sec′u·tive

con·sen′sus

con·sent′

con·sent′ed

con′se·quence

con′se·quent

con′se·quen′tial

con′se·quent·ly

con′ser·va′tion

con·serv′a·tism

con·serv′a·tive

con·serv′a·to′ry

con·serve′

con·served′

con·sid′er

con·sid′er·a·ble

con·sid′er·ate

con·sid′er·a′tion

con·sid′ered

con·sign′

con·signed′

con′sign·ee′

con·sign′ment

con·sign′or

con·sist′

con·sist′en·cy

con·sist′ent

con·sis′to·ry

con·so·la′tion

con·sole′

con·soled′

con·sol′i·date

con·sol′i·dat′ed

con·sol′i·da′tion

con·sol′ing·ly

con′sols

con′som·mé′

con′so·nance

con′so·nant

con′so·nan′tal

con·sort′

con·sort′ed

con·spic′u·ous

con·spic′u·ous·ly

con·spir′a·cy

con·spir′a·tor

con·spir′a·to′ri·al

con·spire′

con·spired′

con′sta·ble

con·stab′u·lar′y

con′stan·cy

con′stant

con′stant·ly

con'stel·la'tion

con'ster·na'tion

con'sti·pa'tion

con·stit'u·en·cy

con·stit'u·ent

con'sti·tute

con'sti·tut'ed

con'sti·tu'tion

con'sti·tu'tion·al

con'sti·tu'tion·al'i·ty

con'sti·tu'tion·al·ly

con·strain'

con·strained'

con·straint'

con·strict'

con·strict'ed

con·stric'tion

con·struct'

con·struct'ed

con·struc'tive

con·strue'

con·strued'

con'sul

con'su·lar

con'su·late

con'su·lates

con·sult'

con·sult'ant

con'sul·ta'tion

con·sult'a·tive

con·sult'ed

con·sum'a·ble

con·sume'

con·sumed'

con·sum'er

con'sum·mate

con'sum·ma'tion

con·sump'tion

con·sump'tive

con'tact

con·ta'gion

con·ta'gious

con·tain'

con·tained'

con·tain'er

con·tam'i·nate

con·tam'i·nat'ed

con·tam'i·na'tion

con'tem·plate

con'tem·plat'ed

con'tem·pla'tion

con·tem·pla·tive

con·tem'po·ra'ne·ous

con·tem'po·rar'y

con·tempt'

con·tempt'i·ble

con·temp'tu·ous

con·tend'

con·tend'ed

con·tend'er

con·tent'

con·tent'ed

con·ten'tion

con·ten'tious

con·tent'ment

con'test

con'test·ant

con'tes·ta'tion

con'text

con·tex'tu·al

con·ti·gu'i·ty

con·tig'u·ous

con'ti·nence

con'ti·nent

con'ti·nen'tal

con·tin'gen·cy

con·tin'gent

con·tin'u·al

con·tin'u·al·ly

con·tin'u·ance

con·tin'u·ant

con·tin'u·a'tion

con·tin'ue

con·tin'ued

con'ti·nu'i·ty

con·tin'u·ous

con·tin'u·ous·ly

con·tin'u·um

con·tort'

con·tort'ed

con·tor'tion

con·tor'tion·ist

con'tour

con'tra·band

con'tra·bass'

con'tract

con·tract′ed

con·trac′tile

con·trac′tion

con·trac′tor

con·trac′tu·al

con′tra·dict′

con′tra·dic′tion

con′tra·dic′to·ry

con′tra·dis·tinc′tion

con′tra·in′di·cate

con′tra·in′di·ca′tion

con·tral′to

con·trap′tion

con′tra·ri·ly

con′tra·ri·ness

con′tra·ri·wise′

con′tra·ry

con′trast

con′tra·vene′

con′tra·ven′tion

con·trib′ute

con′tri·bu′tion

con·trib′u·tive

con·trib′u·tor

con·trib′u·to′ry

con′trite

con′trite·ly

con·tri′tion

con·triv′ance

con·trive′

con·trol′

con·trol′la·ble

con·trolled′

con·trol′ler

con′tro·ver′sial

con′tro·ver′sy

con′tro·vert

con′tu·ma′cious

con′tu·ma·cy

con′tu·me′li·ous

con′tu·me′ly

con·tuse′

con·tused′

con·tu′sion

co·nun′drum

con′va·lesce′

con′va·les′cence

con′va·les′cent

con·vec′tion

con·vene′

con·vened′

con·ven′ience

con·ven′ienc·es

con·ven′ient

con·ven′ient·ly

con·vent′

con·ven′tion

con·ven′tion·al

con·ven′tion·al′i·ty

con·ven′tion·al·ize

con·ven′tion·al·ly

con·ven′tu·al

con·ven′tu·al·ly

con·verge′

con·verged′

con·ver′gence

con·ver′gent

con·ver·sant

con′ver·sa′tion

con′ver·sa′tion·al

con′ver·sa′tion·al·ist

con·verse′

con·ver′sion

con·vert′

con·vert′ed

con·vert′i·bil′i·ty

con·vert′i·ble

con′vex

con·vex′i·ty

con·vey′

con·vey′ance

con·veyed′

con·vey′er

con·vict′

con·vict′ed

con·vic′tion

con·vince′

con·vinc′ing·ly

con·viv′i·al

con·viv′i·al′i·ty

con·viv′i·al·ly

con′vo·ca′tion

con·voke′

con·voked′

con′vo·lute

con′vo·lut′ed

con·vo·lu'tion

con·voy'

con·voyed'

con·vulse'

con·vul'sion

con·vul'sive

cook'book'

cook'er

cook'er·y

cook'house'

cool

cooled

cool'er

cool'est

cool'head'ed

cool'house'

coo'lie

cool'ly

cool'ness

coop

coop'er

coop'er·age

co-op'er·ate

co-op'er·at'ed

co-op'er·a'tion

co-op'er·a'tive

co-opt'

co-opt'ed

co-or'di·nate

co-or'di·nat'ed

co-or'di·na'tion

co-or'di·na'tor

coot

co'pal

co·part'ner

co·part'ner·ship

cope

coped

Co·per'ni·can

cop'ied

cop'i·er

cop'ing

co'pi·ous

co'pi·ous·ly

co'pi·ous·ness

cop'per

cop'per·head'

cop'per·plate'

cop'per·smith'

cop'pice

cop'ra

cop'y

cop'y·hold'er

cop'y·ist

cop'y·read'er

cop'y·right'

co'quet·ry

co·quette'

co·quet'tish

cor'a·cle

cor'a·coid

cor'al

cor'al·line

cord

cord'age

cord'ed

cor'dial

cor·dial'i·ty

cor'dial·ly

cord'ite

cor'don

Cor'do·van

cor'du·roy

cord'wood'

core

cored

co're·spond'ent

co·ri·an'der

Co·rin'thi·an

cork

cork'age

cork'screw'

cork'wood'

cor'mo·rant

corn

cor'ne·a

cor'ner

cor'nered

cor'ner·stone'

cor'net

corn'field'

corn'flow'er

cor'nice

corn'stalk'

cor'nu·co'pi·a

cor'ol·lar'y

co·ro'na

cor'o·nar'y

cor'o·na'tion

cor'o·ner

cor'o·net

cor'po·ral

cor'po·rate

cor'po·rate·ly

cor'po·ra'tion

cor'po·ra'tive

cor·po're·al

corps

corpse

cor'pu·lence

cor'pu·lent

cor'pus

cor'pus·cle

cor·pus'cu·lar

cor·ral'

cor·rect'

cor·rect'ed

cor·rec'tion

cor·rec'tion·al

cor·rec'tive

cor·rect'ly

cor·rect'ness

cor·rec'tor

cor're·late

cor're·lat'ed

cor're·la'tion

cor·rel'a·tive

cor're·spond'

cor're·spond'ed

cor're·spond'ence

cor're·spond'ent

cor·re·spond'ing·ly

cor're·sponds'

cor'ri·dor

cor·rob'o·rate

cor·rob'o·ra'tion

cor·rob'o·ra'tive

cor·rob'o·ra·to'ry

cor·rode'

cor·rod'ed

cor·ro'si·ble

cor·ro'sion

cor·ro'sive

cor'ru·gate

cor'ru·gat'ed

cor'ru·ga'tion

cor·rupt'

cor·rupt'ed

cor·rupt'i·bil'i·ty

cor·rupt'i·ble

cor·rup'tion

cor·rupt'ly

cor·sage'

cor'sair

corse'let

cor'set

cor·tege'

cor'tex

cor'ti·cal

co·run'dum

cor'us·cate

cor'us·cat'ed

cor'us·ca'tion

cor·vette'

co·ry'za

co·sig'na·to'ry

co·sign'er

cos'i·ly

co'sine

cos·met'ic

cos'me·ti'cian

cos'mic

cos·mog'o·ny

cos·mol'o·gy

cos·mop'o·lis

cos'mo·pol'i·tan

cos·mop'o·lite

cos'mos

Cos'sack

cost

cos'tal

cos'tive

cost'li·ness

cost'ly

cos'tume

cos·tum'er

co'sy

cot

co'te·rie

co·ter'mi·nous

co·til'lion

cot'tage

cot'ter

cot'ton

cot'ton·tail'

cot'ton·wood'

couch

cou'gar

cough

could

coun'cil

coun'ci·lor

coun'sel

coun'seled

count

count'ed

coun'te·nance

count'er

coun'ter·act'

coun'ter·at·tack'

coun'ter·bal'ance

coun'ter·blast'

coun'ter·change'

coun'ter·check'

coun'ter·claim'

coun'ter·clock'wise'

count'ered

coun'ter·feit

coun'ter·feit'er

coun'ter·foil'

coun'ter·ir'ri·tant

coun'ter·mand'

coun'ter·march'

coun'ter·mine'

coun'ter·of·fen'sive

coun'ter·pane'

coun'ter·part'

coun'ter·plot'

coun'ter·point'

coun'ter·shaft'

coun'ter·sign'

coun'ter·sink'

coun'ter·vail'

coun'ter·weight'

count'ess

count'less

coun'try

coun'try·man

coun'try·side'

coun'ty

coup

cou'pé'

cou'ple

cou'pler

cou'plet

cou'pling

cou'pon

cour'age

cou·ra'geous

cour'i·er

course

coursed

cours'er

court

court'ed

cour'te·ous

cour'te·sy

court'house'

cour'ti·er

court'li·ness

court'ly

court'-mar'tial

court'ship

court'yard'

cous'in

cove

cov'e·nant

cov'er

cov'er·age

cov'ered

cov'er·let

cov'ert

cov'et

cov'et·ed

cov'et·ous

cov'ey

cow'ard

cow'ard·ice

cow'ard·ly

cow'bell'

cow'boy'

cow'catch'er

cow'er

cowl

cow'lick'

co-work'er

cow'slip

cox'comb'

cox'swain		crane		craze	
coy		craned		cra'zi·er	
coy'ly		cra'ni·al		cra'zi·est	
coy'ness		cra'ni·om'e·try		cra'zi·ly	
coy'ote		cra'ni·ot'o·my		cra'zi·ness	
coz'en		cra'ni·um		cra'zy	
co'zi·er		crank		creak	
co'zi·est		crank'case'		creak'ing·ly	
co'zi·ly		cranked		cream	
co'zi·ness		crank'i·ly		creamed	
co'zy		crank'i·ness		cream'er·y	
crab		crank'y		cream'i·er	
crack		cran'ny		cream'i·est	
cracked		crape		cream'y	
crack'er		crash		crease	
crack'le		crass		cre·ate'	
crack'led		crass'ly		cre·at'ed	
cra'dle		crass'ness		cre·a'tion	
cra'dled		crate		cre·a'tive	
craft		crat'ed		cre·a'tive·ly	
craft'i·er		cra'ter		cre·a'tive·ness	
craft'i·est		cra·vat'		cre'a·tiv'i·ty	
craft'i·ly		crave		cre·a'tor	
craft'i·ness		craved		crea'ture	
crafts'man		cra'ven		crèche	
craft'y		cra'ven·ette'		cre'dence	
crag		crav'ings		cre·den'tial	
cram		craw'fish'		cre·den'za	
crammed		crawl		cred'i·bil'i·ty	
cramp		crawled		cred'i·ble	
cram'pon		cray'fish'		cred'it	
cran'ber'ry		cray'on		cred'it·a·bil'i·ty	

cred'it·a·ble

cred'it·ed

cred'i·tor

cre'do

cre·du'li·ty

cred'u·lous

cred'u·lous·ness

creed

creek

creel

creep

creep'er

creep'i·ness

cre'mate

cre'mat·ed

cre·ma'tion

cre'ma·to·ry

Cre·mo'na

cre'ole

cre'o·sote

crepe

crep'i·tant

crep'i·tate

crep'i·ta'tion

cre·scen'do

cres'cent

crest

crest'ed

crest'fall'en

cre'tin

cre'tin·ism

cre'tin·oid

cre'tin·ous

cre·tonne'

cre·vasse'

crev'ice

crew

crew'el

crib

crib'bage

crib'work'

crick'et

crime

crim'i·nal

crim'i·nal'i·ty

crim'i·nal·ly

crim'i·nol'o·gist

crim'i·nol'o·gy

crimp

crim'son

cringe

cringed

crin'kle

crin'kled

crin'o·line

crip'ple

crip'pled

cri'ses

cri'sis

crisp

crisp'er

crisp'est

crisp'ly

crisp'ness

criss'cross'

cri·te'ri·a

cri·te'ri·on

crit'ic

crit'i·cal

crit'i·cal·ly

crit'i·cism

crit'i·cize

crit'i·cized

cri·tique'

croak

croaked

croak'er

croak'ing·ly

croch'et

crock

crock'er·y

croc'o·dile

cro'cus

crook

crook'ed

crook'ed·ness

croon

crooned

croon'er

crop

cro·quet'

cro·quette'

cro'sier

cross

cross'bar'

cross'bow'

cross'bow'man

cross'bred'

cross'cut'

cross'hatch'

cross'ings

cross'o'ver

cross'road'

cross'walk'

cross'wise'

cross'word'

crotch'et

crouch

crouched

croup

crou'pi·er

crow

crow'bar'

crowd

crowd'ed

crown

crowned

crown'work'

cru'cial

cru'cial·ly

cru'ci·ble

cru'ci·fied

cru'ci·fix

cru'ci·fix'ion

cru'ci·form

cru'ci·fy

crude

crud'er

crud'est

cru'di·ty

cru'el

cru'el·ly

cru'el·ty

cru'et

cruise

cruis'er

crul'ler

crumb

crum'ble

crum'bled

crump

crum'pet

crum'ple

crum'pled

crunch

crup'per

cru·sade'

cru·sad'er

cruse

crush

crushed

crush'er

crush'ing·ly

crust

crust'ed

crust'i·er

crust'i·est

crust'y

crutch

crux

cry

cry'o·lite

crypt

cryp'tic

cryp'ti·cal

cryp'ti·cal·ly

cryp'to·gram

cryp'to·graph

cryp·tog'ra·phy

crys'tal

crys'tal·line

crys'tal·li·za'tion

crys'tal·lize

crys'tal·lized

crys'tal·loid

cub

cub'by·hole'

cube

cu'beb

cu'bic

cu'bi·cle

cub'ism

cu'bit

cuck'oo

cu'cum·ber

cud'dle

cud'dled

cudg'el

cudg'eled

cue

cuff

cuffed

cui·rass'

cui·sine'

cu'li·nar'y

cull

culled

cul'mi·nate

cul'mi·nat'ed

cul'mi·na'tion

cul'pa·bil'i·ty

cul'pa·ble

cul'prit

cult

cul'ti·vate

cul'ti·vat'ed

cul'ti·va'tion

cul'ti·va'tor

cul'tur·al

cul'tur·al·ly

cul'ture

cul'tured

cul'vert

cum'ber

cum'bered

cum'ber·some

cum'brous

cum'mer·bund'

cu'mu·la'tive

cu'mu·lus

cu·ne'i·form

cun'ning

cun'ning·ly

cup

cup'board

cup'cake'

cu'pel

cu'pel·la'tion

cup'ful

Cu'pid

cu·pid'i·ty

cu'po·la

cupped

cu'pric

cu'prous

cur

cur'a·ble

cu'ra·çao'

cu'ra·cy

cu·ra're

cu'rate

cur'a·tive

cu·ra'tor

curb

curbed

curd

cure

cured

cu·ret'tage

cu·rette'

cur'few

cu'rie

cu'ri·o

cu'ri·os'i·ties

cu'ri·os'i·ty

cu'ri·ous

cu'ri·ous·ly

curl

curled

curl'er

cur'lew

curl'i·cue

curl'y

cur·mudg'eon

cur'rant

cur'ren·cy

cur'rent

cur'rent·ly

cur·ric'u·la

cur·ric'u·lar

cur·ric'u·lum

cur'ry

curse

curs'ed

cur'sive

cur'so·ry

curt

cur·tail'

cur·tailed'

cur'tain

cur'te·sy

curt'ly

cur'va·ture

curve

curved

cur'vi·lin'e·ar

cush'ion

cush'ioned

cusp

cus'pi·dor

cuss'ed·ness

cus'tard

cus·to'di·al

cus·to'di·an

cus'to·dy

cus'tom

cus'tom·ar'i·ly

cus'tom·ar'y

cus'tom·er

cut

cu·ta'ne·ous

cut'a·way'

cut'back'

cute

cu'ti·cle

cut'lass

cut'ler·y

cut'let

cut'off'

cut'out'

cut'purse'

cut'ter

cut'tings

cut'tle·fish'

cut'weed'

cut'worm

cy'a·nate

cy·an'ic

cy'a·nide

cy'a·nite

cy·an'o·gen

cy'a·no'sis

cyc'la·men

cy'cle

cy'clic

cy'cloid

cy·clom'e·ter

cy'clone

cy·clon'ic

cy'clo·pe'di·a

cy'clo·pe'dic

Cy'clops

cy'clo·ra'ma

cyg'net

cyl'in·der

cy·lin'dric

cy·lin'dri·cal

cym'bal

cyn'ic

cyn'i·cal

cyn'i·cal·ly

cyn'i·cism

cy'no·sure

cy'press

Cy·ril'lic

cyst

cys·ti'tis

cyst'oid

cys'to·lith

czar

Czech

D

dab'ble
dachs'hund'
da·coit'
dae'dal
dae'mon
daf'fo·dil
daft
dag'ger
da·guerre'o·type
dahl'ia
dai'ly
dain'ti·er
dain'ti·est
dain'ti·ly
dain'ti·ness
dain'ty
dair'y
dair'y·maid'
dair'y·man
da'is
dai'sy
dal'li·ance

dal'ly
dal·ma'tian
dam
dam'age
dam'aged
dam'a·scene'
dam'a·scened'
da·mas'cus
dam'ask
dammed
dam'na·ble
dam·na'tion
damp
damp'en
damp'ened
damp'er
damp'est
damp'ness
dam'sel
dance
danc'er
dan'de·li'on

dan'dle
dan'dled
dan'druff
dan'dy
dan'ger
dan'ger·ous
dan'ger·ous·ly
dan'gle
dan'gled
Dan'ish
dank
dap'per
dap'ple
dap'pled
dare
dared
dar'ing·ly
dark
dark'en
dark'er
dark'est
dark'ly

dark'ness
dar'ling
darned
dart
dart'ed
dash
dash'board'
dashed
dash'ing·ly
das'tard·ly
da'ta
date
dat'ed
da'tive
da'tum
daub
daubed
daugh'ter
daugh'ter-in-law'
daunt
daunt'ed
daunt'less
dau'phin
dav'en·port
dav'it
daw'dle
daw'dled
dawn
dawned
day
day'book'
day'break'

day'dream'
day'light'
day'time'
daz'zle
daz'zled
dea'con
dead
dead'en
dead'ened
dead'fall'
dead'head'
dead'light'
dead'li·ness
dead'lock
dead'ly
deaf
deaf'en
deaf'ened
deaf'en·ing·ly
deaf'er
deaf'est
deal
deal'er
deal'ings
dean
dean'er·y
dear
dear'er
dear'est
dear'ly
dear'ness
dearth

death
death'bed'
death'blow'
death'less
death'like'
death'ly
de·ba'cle
de·bar'
de·bark'
de·barred'
de·base'
de·based'
de·base'ment
de·bat'a·ble
de·bate'
de·bat'ed
de·bat'er
de·bauch'
de·bauched'
de·bauch'er·y
de·ben'ture
de·bil'i·tate
de·bil'i·tat'ed
de·bil'i·ty
deb'it
deb'it·ed
de·bris'
debt
debt'or
de·bunk'
de'but
deb'u·tante'

dec'ade

de·ca'dence

de·ca'dent

de·cal'co·ma'ni·a

de·camp'

de·cant'

de·cant'er

de·cap'i·tate

de·cap'i·ta'tion

de-car'bon·ize

de·cath'lon

de·cay'

de·cayed'

de·cease'

de·ceased'

de·ce'dent

de·ceit'

de·ceit'ful

de·ceit'ful·ness

de·ceive'

de·ceived'

de·cel'er·a'tion

De·cem'ber

de'cen·cy

de·cen'ni·al

de'cent

de'cent·ly

de·cen'tral·i·za'tion

de·cen'tral·ize

de·cep'tion

de·cep'tive

de·cep'tive·ly

de·cep'tive·ness

de·cide'

de·cid'ed·ly

de·cid'u·ous

dec'i·mal

dec'i·mate

dec'i·mat'ed

dec'i·ma'tion

de·ci'pher

de·ci'pher·a·ble

de-ci'phered

de·ci'sion

de·ci'sive

de·ci'sive·ly

de·ci'sive·ness

deck

decked

deck'house'

deck'le

de·claim'

de·claimed'

dec'la·ma'tion

de·clam'a·to'ry

dec'la·ra'tion

de-clar'a·tive

de·clar'a·to'ry

de·clare'

de·clared'

de·clen'sion

dec'li·na'tion

de·cline'

de·clined'

de·cliv'i·ty

de·coc'tion

dé·col'le·tage

dé·col'le·té

de·com'pen·sate

de·com'pen·sa'tion

de'com·pose'

de·com·posed'

de'com·po·si'tion

dec'o·rate

dec'o·rat'ed

dec'o·ra'tion

dec'o·ra'tive

dec'o·ra'tor

dec'o·rous

dec'o·rous·ly

dec'o·rous·ness

de·co'rum

de·coy'

de·crease'

de·creased'

de·creas'ing·ly

de·cree'

de·creed'

de·crep'it

de·crep'i·tude

de·cre'tal

de·cried'

de·cry'

ded'i·cate

ded'i·cat'ed

ded'i·ca'tion

ded'i·ca·to'ry

de·duce'

de·duced'

de·duc'i·ble

de·duct'

de·duct'ed

de·duct'i·ble

de·duc'tion

de·duc'tive·ly

deed

deed'ed

deem

deemed

deep

deep'en

deep'ened

deep'er

deep'est

deep'ly

deep'ness

deer

deer'hound'

deer'skin'

deer'stalk'er

deer'weed'

de·face'

de·faced'

de·fal'cate

de·fal'cat·ed

de'fal·ca'tion

def'a·ma'tion

de·fam'a·to'ry

de·fame'

de·famed'

de·fault'

de·fault'ed

de·fault'er

de·fea'si·ble

de·feat'

de·feat'ed

de·feat'ism

de·fect'

de·fec'tion

de·fec'tive

de·fec'tor

de·fend'

de·fend'ant

de·fend'ed

de·fend'er

de·fense'

de·fen'si·ble

de·fen'sive

de·fen'sive·ly

de·fen'sive·ness

de·fer'

def'er·ence

def'er·en'tial

def'er·en'tial·ly

de·fer'ment

de·fer'ral

de·ferred'

de·fi'ance

de·fi'ant

de·fi'ant·ly

de·fi'cien·cy

de·fi'cient

def'i·cit

def'i·lade'

def'i·lad'ed

de·file'

de·filed'

de·file'ment

de·fin'a·ble

de·fine'

de·fined'

def'i·nite

def'i·nite·ly

def'i·nite·ness

def'i·ni'tion

de·fin'i·tive

de·fin'i·tive·ly

de·fin'i·tive·ness

de·fin'i·tize

de·flate'

de·flat'ed

de·fla'tion

de·fla'tion·ar'y

de·flect'

de·flect'ed

de·flec'tion

de·for'est·a'tion

de·form'

de'for·ma'tion

de·formed'

de·form'i·ty

de·fraud'

de·fraud'ed

de·fray'

de·frayed'

deft

deft'ly

deft'ness

de·funct'

de·fied'

de·fy'

de·gen'er·a·cy

de·gen'er·ate

de·gen'er·at'ed

de'gen·er·a'tion

deg'ra·da'tion

de·grade'

de·grad'ed

de·grad'ing·ly

de·gree'

de·hy'drate

de·hy'drat·ed

de'i·fi·ca'tion

de'i·fied

de'i·fy

deign

deigned

de'ism

de'ist

de'i·ty

de·ject'ed

de·ject'ed·ly

de·jec'tion

de·lay'

de·layed'

de·lec'ta·bil'i·ty

de·lec'ta·ble

de·lec·ta'tion

del'e·gate

del'e·gat'ed

del'e·ga'tion

de·lete'

de·let'ed

del'e·te'ri·ous

del'e·te'ri·ous·ly

de·le'tion

delft'ware'

de·lib'er·ate

de·lib'er·at'ed

de·lib'er·a'tion

de·lib'er·a'tive

del'i·ca·cy

del'i·cate

del'i·cate·ly

del'i·ca·tes'sen

de·li'cious

de·li'cious·ly

de·light'

de·light'ed

de·light'ful

de·light'ful·ly

de·lim'it

de·lim'i·ta'tion

de·lin'e·ate

de·lin'e·at'ed

de·lin'e·a'tion

de·lin'e·a'tive

de·lin'e·a'tor

de·lin'quen·cy

de·lin'quent

del'i·quesce'

del'i·ques'cence

del'i·ques'cent

de·lir'i·ous

de·lir'i·um

de·liv'er

de·liv'er·ance

de·liv'ered

de·liv'er·er

de·liv'er·y

del·phin'i·um

del'ta

del'toid

de·lude'

de·lud'ed

del'uge

del'uged

de·lu'sion

de·lu'sive

de luxe'

delve

de·mag'net·ize

dem'a·gog'ic

dem'a·gogue

de·mand'

de·mand'ed

de·mand'ing·ly

de'mar·ca'tion

de·mean'

de·meaned'

de·mean'or

de·ment'ed

de·men'ti·a

de·mer'it

dem'i·god'

de·mil'i·ta·rize

de·mise'

de·mo'bi·li·za'tion

de·mo'bi·lize

de·mo'bi·lized

de·moc'ra·cy

dem'o·crat

dem'o·crat'ic

dem'o·crat'i·cal·ly

de·moc'ra·ti·za'tion

de·moc'ra·tize

de·mol'ish

de·mol'ished

dem'o·li'tion

de'mon

de·mon'e·ti·za'tion

de·mon'e·tize

de'mo·ni'a·cal

de·mon'stra·ble

dem'on·strate

dem'on·strat'ed

dem'on·stra'tion

de·mon'stra·tive

dem'on·stra'tor

de·mor'al·i·za'tion

de·mor'al·ize

de·mor'al·ized

de·mot'ic

de·mount'able

de·mur'

de·mure'

de·mure'ly

de·mur'rage

de·murred'

de·mur'rer

den

de·na'ture

de·na'tured

den·drol'o·gy

de·ni'al

de·nied'

den'i·grate

den'i·zen

de·nom'i·nate

de·nom'i·nat'ed

de·nom'i·na'tion

de·nom'i·na'tion·al

de·nom'i·na'tor

de'no·ta'tion

de·note'

de·not'ed

de·noue'ment

de·nounce'

de·nounced'

dense

dens'er

dens'est

den'si·ty

dent

den'tal

den·tal'gi·a

dent'ed

den'ti·frice

den'tine

den'tist

den'tist·ry

den·ti'tion

den'u·da'tion

de·nude'

de·nun'ci·a'tion

de·nun'ci·a·to'ry

de·ny'

de·o'dor·ant

de·o'dor·ize

de·o'dor·ized

de·part'

de·part'ed

de·part'ment

de'part·men'tal

de'part·men'tal·ize

de·par'ture

de·pend'

de·pend'ed

de·pend'en·cy

de·pend'ent

de·per'son·al·ize

de·pict'

de·pict'ed

de·pic'tion

de·pil′a·to′ry

de·plete′

de·plet′ed

de·ple′tion

de·plor′a·ble

de·plore′

de·plored′

de·ploy′

de·ployed′

de·ploy′ment

de·po′lar·i·za′tion

de·po′lar·ize

de·po′nent

de·pop′u·late

de·pop′u·lat′ed

de·port′

de′por·ta′tion

de·port′ed

de·port′ment

de·pose′

de·posed′

de·pos′it

de·pos′i·tar′y

de·pos′it·ed

dep′o·si′tion

de·pos′i·tor

de·pos′i·to′ry

de′pot

dep′ra·va′tion

de·prave′

de·praved′

de·prav′i·ty

dep′re·cate

dep′re·cat′ed

dep′re·ca′tion

dep′re·ca·to′ry

de·pre′ci·ate

de·pre′ci·at′ed

de·pre′ci·a′tion

dep′re·da′tion

de·press′

de·pres′sant

de·pressed′

de·press′ing·ly

de·pres′sion

de·pres′sive

dep′ri·va′tion

de·prive′

de·prived′

depth

dep′u·ta′tion

de·pute′

de·put′ed

dep′u·tize

dep′u·tized

dep′u·ty

de·rail′

de·railed′

de·rail′ment

de·range′

de·ranged′

de·range′ment

der′by

der′e·lict

der′e·lic′tion

de·ride′

de·rid′ed

de·ri′sion

de·ri′sive

de·riv′a·ble

der′i·va′tion

de·riv′a·tive

de·rive′

de·rived′

der′mal

der′ma·ti′tis

der′ma·tol′o·gy

der′ma·to′sis

der′o·gate

der′o·gat′ed

der′o·ga′tion

de·rog′a·to′ry

der′rick

der′vish

des′cant

de·scend′

de·scend′ant

de·scent′

de·scribe′

de·scribed′

de·scrip′tion

de·scrip′tive

de·scry′

des′e·crate

des′e·crat′ed

des′e·cra′tion

de·sen'si·tize

de·sen'si·tiz'er

de·sert'

de·sert'ed

de·sert'er

de·ser'tion

de·serve'

de·served'

des'ic·cant

des'ic·cate

des'ic·cat'ed

des'ic·ca'tion

des'ic·ca'tive

de·sid'er·a'ta

de·sid'er·a'tum

de·sign'

des'ig·nate

des'ig·nat'ed

des'ig·na'tion

de·signed'

de·sign'ed·ly

de·sign'er

de·sir'a·bil'i·ty

de·sir'a·ble

de·sire'

de·sired'

de·sires'

de·sir'ous

de·sist'

de·sists'

desk

des'o·late

des'o·lat'ed

des'o·late·ly

des'o·la'tion

de·spair'

de·spaired'

de·spair'ing·ly

des'per·a'do

des'per·ate

des'per·ate·ly

des'per·a'tion

des'pi·ca·ble

de·spise'

de·spised'

de·spite'

de·spoil'

de·spoiled'

de·spond'en·cy

de·spond'ent

de·spond'ing·ly

des'pot

des·pot'ic

des'pot·ism

des'qua·ma'tion

des·sert'

des'ti·na'tion

des'tine

des'tined

des'ti·ny

des'ti·tute

des'ti·tu'tion

de·stroy'

de·stroyed'

de·stroy'er

de·struct'i·ble

de·struc'tion

de·struc'tive

des'ue·tude

des'ul·to'ri·ly

des'ul·to'ry

de·tach'

de·tach'a·ble

de·tached'

de·tach'ment

de·tail'

de·tailed'

de·tain'

de·tained'

de·tect'

de·tect'ed

de·tec'tion

de·tec'tive

de·tec'tor

de·ten'tion

de·ter'

de·ter'gent

de·te'ri·o·rate

de·te'ri·o·rat'ed

de·te'ri·o·ra'tion

de·ter'mi·na·ble

de·ter'mi·nant

de·ter'mi·na'tion

de·ter'mi·na'tive

de·ter'mine

de·ter'mined

de·ter'min·ism
de·terred'
de·ter'rent
de·test'
de·test'a·ble
de'tes·ta'tion
de·test'ed
de·throne'
de·throned'
det'o·nate
det'o·nat'ed
det'o·na'tion
det'o·na'tor
de·tour'
de·toured'
de·tract'
de·tract'ed
de·trac'tion
de·trac'tor
det'ri·ment
det'ri·men'tal
de·tri'tus
de·val'u·ate
de·val'u·at'ed
de·val'u·a'tion
dev'as·tate
dev'as·tat'ed
dev'as·tat'ing·ly
dev'as·ta'tion
de·vel'op
de·vel'oped
de·vel'op·ment

de·vel'op·men'tal
de'vi·ate
de'vi·at'ed
de'vi·a'tion
de·vice'
dev'il
dev'il·try
de'vi·ous
de'vi·ous·ness
de·vise'
de·vised'
de·vi'tal·ize
de·void'
de·volve'
de·volved'
de·vote'
de·vot'ed
de·vot'ed·ly
dev'o·tee'
de·vo'tion
de·vo'tion·al
de·vour'
de·voured'
de·vout'ly
dew
dew'y
dex'ter
dex·ter'i·ty
dex'ter·ous
dex'ter·ous·ly
dex'trose
di'a·be'tes

di'a·bet'ic
di'a·bol'ic
di'a·bol'i·cal
di·ac'o·nal
di'a·crit'i·cal
di'a·dem
di·aer'e·sis
di'ag·nose'
di'ag·nosed'
di'ag·no'ses
di'ag·no'sis
di'ag·nos'tic
di'ag·nos·ti'cian
di·ag'o·nal
di·ag'o·nal·ly
di'a·gram
di'al
di'a·lect
di'a·lec'tic
di'aled
di'a·logue
di·al'y·sis
di·am'e·ter
di'a·met'ric
di'a·met'ri·cal·ly
di'a·mond
di'a·pa'son
di'a·per
di·aph'a·nous
di'a·phragm
di'a·rist
di'a·ry

Di·as'po·ra	dif'fer·ence	di·lap'i·dat'ed
di·as'to·le	dif'fer·ent	di·lap'i·da'tion
di·as'tol'ic	dif'fer·en'tial	dil'a·ta'tion
di'a·ther'mic	dif'fer·en'ti·ate	di·late'
di'a·tom	dif'fer·en'ti·at'ed	di·lat'ed
di'a·tom'ic	dif'fer·en'ti·a'tion	di·la'tion
di'a·tribe	dif'fi·cult	dil'a·to'ry
dice	dif'fi·cul·ty	di·lem'ma
di·chot'o·mous	dif'fi·dence	dil'et·tan'te
di·chot'o·my	dif'fi·dent	dil'i·gence
Dic'ta·phone	dif·fract'	dil'i·gent
dic'tate	dif·frac'tion	dil'i·gent·ly
dic'tat·ed	dif·fuse'	di·lute'
dic·ta'tion	dif·fused'	di·lut'ed
dic·ta'tor	dif·fu'sion	di·lu'tion
dic'ta·to'ri·al	dig	dim
dic'ta·to'ri·al·ly	di·gest'	dime
dic·ta'tor·ship	di·gest'ed	di·men'sion
dic'tion	di·gest'i·ble	di·men'sion·al
dic'tion·ar'y	di·ges'tion	di·min'ish
Dic'to·graph	di·ges'tive	di·min'u·en'do
dic'tum	dig'gings	dim'i·nu'tion
did	dig'it	di·min'u·tive
di·dac'tic	dig'i·tal'is	dim'i·ty
die	dig'ni·fied	dim'ly
died	dig'ni·fy	dimmed
die'stock'	dig'ni·tar'y	dim'mer
di'et	dig'ni·ty	dim'mest
di'e·tar'y	di·gress'	dim'ness
di'e·tet'ics	di·gres'sion	dim'ple
dif'fer	dike	dine
dif'fered	di·lap'i·date	dined

din'er

din'gy

din'ner

di'no·saur

dint

di·oc'e·san

di'o·cese

di'o·ra'ma

diph·the'ri·a

diph'thong

di·plo'ma

di·plo'ma·cy

dip'lo·mat

dip'lo·mat'ic

dip'lo·mat'i·cal·ly

di·plo'ma·tist

di·plo'pi·a

dip'per

dip'so·ma'ni·a

dip'so·ma'ni·ac

di·rect'

di·rect'ed

di·rec'tion

di·rec'tion·al

di·rec'tive

di·rect'ly

di·rect'ness

di·rec'tor

di·rec'to·ry

dire'ful

dir'est

dirge

dir'i·gi·ble

dirt

dirt'i·ly

dirt'y

dis·a·bil'i·ty

dis·a'ble

dis·a'bled

dis'a·buse'

dis'ad·van'tage

dis·ad'van·ta'geous

dis'af·fect'ed

dis'af·fec'tion

dis'af·firm'

dis'af·firmed'

dis'a·gree'

dis'a·gree'a·ble

dis'a·gree'ment

dis'al·low'

dis'al·lowed'

dis'ap·pear'

dis'ap·pear'ance

dis'ap·peared'

dis'ap·point'

dis'ap·point'ment

dis'ap·pro·ba'tion

dis'ap·prov'al

dis'ap·prove'

dis·arm'

dis·ar'ma·ment

dis·armed'

dis·arm'ing·ly

dis'ar·range'

dis'ar·ranged'

dis'ar·ray'

dis'ar·tic'u·late

dis'as·so'ci·a'tion

dis·as'ter

dis·as'trous

dis'a·vow'

dis'a·vow'al

dis·band'

dis·band'ed

dis·bar'

dis·bar'ment

dis·barred'

dis'be·lieve'

dis'be·lieved'

dis'be·liev'er

dis'be·liev'ing·ly

dis·burse'

dis·burse'ment

disc

dis'card

dis·card'ed

dis·cern'

dis·cerned'

dis·cern'i·ble

dis·cern'ing·ly

dis·cern'ment

dis·charge'

dis·charged'

dis·ci'ple

dis·ci'ple·ship

dis'ci·pli·nar'y

dis'ci·pline

dis'ci·plined

dis·claim'

dis·claimed'

dis·close'

dis·clo'sure

dis·col'or

dis·col'or·a'tion

dis·col'ored

dis·com'fit

dis·com'fi·ture

dis·com'fort

dis'com·pose'

dis'com·posed'

dis'com·po'sure

dis'con·cert'

dis'con·nect'

dis'con·nect'ed

dis·con'so·late

dis'con·tent'

dis'con·tent'ed

dis'con·tin'u·ance

dis'con·tin'ue

dis'con·tin'ued

dis'cord

dis·cord'ance

dis·cord'ant

dis'count

dis'count·ed

dis·coun'te·nance

dis·cour'age

dis·cour'aged

dis·cour'age·ment

dis·cour'ag·ing·ly

dis·course'

dis·cour'te·ous

dis·cour'te·sy

dis·cov'er

dis·cov'ered

dis·cov'er·er

dis·cov'er·y

dis·cred'it

dis·cred'it·a·ble

dis·cred'it·ed

dis·creet'

dis·crep'an·cy

dis·crete'

dis·cre'tion

dis·cre'tion·ar'y

dis·crim'i·nate

dis·crim'i·nat'ed

dis·crim'i·na'tion

dis·crim'i·na·tive

dis·crim'i·na·to'ry

dis·cur'sive

dis'cus

dis·cuss'

dis·cuss'es

dis·dain'

dis·dained'

dis·dain'ful

dis·ease'

dis·eased'

dis·em'bar·ka'tion

dis'em·bar'rass

dis'em·bod'y

dis'en·chant'

dis'en·gage'

dis'es·tab'lish

dis'es·teem'

dis·fa'vor

dis·fea'ture

dis·fig'ure

dis·fig'ured

dis·fig'ure·ment

dis·fran'chise

dis·gorge'

dis·grace'

dis·grace'ful

dis·grun'tle

dis·guise'

dis·gust'

dis·gust'ed

dis·gust'ed·ly

dis·gust'ing·ly

dish

dis'ha·bille'

dis·har'mo·ny

dis·heart'en

di·shev'el

di·shev'eled

dis·hon'est

dis·hon'est·ly

dis·hon'or

dis·hon'or·a·ble

dis·hon'ored

dis·il·lu'sion

dis·in'cli·na'tion

dis·in·cline'

dis·in·clined'

dis·in·fect'

dis·in·fect'ant

dis·in·gen'u·ous

dis·in·her'it

dis·in·te·grate

dis·in·te·gra'tion

dis·in'ter·est·ed

dis·join'

dis·joined'

dis·join'ings

dis·joint'ed

dis·junc'tion

dis·junc'tive

disk

dis·like'

dis'lo·cate

dis'lo·cat'ed

dis'lo·ca'tion

dis·lodge'

dis·loy'al

dis·loy'al·ty

dis'mal

dis'mal·ly

dis·man'tle

dis·man'tled

dis·mast'

dis·mast'ed

dis·may'

dis·mayed'

dis·mem'ber

dis·mem'bered

dis·mem'ber·ment

dis·miss'

dis·miss'al

dis·mount'

dis·mount'ed

dis'o·be'di·ence

dis'o·be'di·ent

dis'o·bey'

dis'o·beyed'

dis'o·blige'

dis'o·blig'ing·ly

dis·or'der

dis·or'dered

dis·or'der·ly

dis·or'gan·ize

dis·or'gan·ized

dis·own'

dis·par'age

dis·par'age·ment

dis·par'ag·ing·ly

dis'pa·rate

dis·par'i·ty

dis·pas'sion·ate

dis·patch'

dis·patched'

dis·patch'er

dis·pel'

dis·pelled'

dis·pen'sa·ble

dis·pen'sa·ry

dis'pen·sa'tion

dis·pense'

dis·pensed'

dis·per'sal

dis·perse'

dis·persed'

dis·per'sion

dis·pir'it·ed

dis·place'

dis·place'ment

dis·play'

dis·please'

dis·pleas'ure

dis·port'

dis·pos'al

dis·pose'

dis·posed'

dis'po·si'tion

dis'pos·sess'

dis'pos·sessed'

dis·po'sure

dis·praise'

dis·proof'

dis'pro·por'tion

dis'pro·por'tion·ate

dis'pu·ta·ble

dis'pu·tant

dis'pu·ta'tion

dis'pu·ta'tious

dis·pute'

dis·put'ed

dis·qual'i·fi·ca'tion

dis·qual'i·fy

dis·qui'et·ed

dis·qui'e·tude

dis'qui·si'tion

dis·re·gard'

dis·re·pair'

dis·rep'u·ta·ble

dis·re·pute'

dis·re·spect'

dis·re·spect'ful

dis·robe'

dis·root'

dis·rupt'

dis·rup'tion

dis·rup'tive

dis'sat·is·fac'tion

dis·sat'is·fied

dis·sect'

dis·sect'ed

dis·sem'ble

dis·sem'i·nate

dis·sem'i·nat'ed

dis·sem'i·na'tion

dis·sen'sion

dis·sent'

dis·sent'er

dis·sen'tient

dis'ser·ta'tion

dis·serv'ice

dis'si·dence

dis'si·dent

dis·sim'i·lar

dis·sim'i·lar'i·ty

dis·sim'u·late

dis·sim'u·lat'ed

dis·sim'u·la'tion

dis'si·pate

dis'si·pat'ed

dis'si·pa'tion

dis·so'ci·ate

dis·so'ci·at'ed

dis·so'ci·a'tion

dis'so·lute

dis'so·lu'tion

dis·solv'a·ble·ness

dis·solve'

dis·solved'

dis'so·nance

dis'so·nant

dis·suade'

dis·sua'sion

dis'taff

dis'tal

dis'tance

dis'tant

dis·taste'

dis·taste'ful

dis·tem'per

dis·tend'

dis·ten'si·ble

dis·till'

dis'til·late

dis'til·la'tion

dis·tilled'

dis·till'er

dis·till'er·y

dis·tinct'

dis·tinc'tion

dis·tinc'tive

dis·tinct'ly

dis·tinct'ness

dis·tin'guish

dis·tin'guished

dis·tort'

dis·tort'ed

dis·tor'tion

dis·tract'

dis·tract'ing·ly

dis·trac'tion

dis·train'

dis·trained'

dis·traught'

dis·tress'

dis·trib'ute

dis'tri·bu'tion

dis·trib'u·tive

dis·trib'u·tor

dis'trict

dis·trust'

dis·trust'ful

dis·turb'

dis·turb'ance

dis·turbed'

dis·turb'er

dis·un'ion

dis'u·nite'

dis·use'

ditch

ditched

dith'y·ram'bic

dit'to

dit'ty

di·ur'nal

di'va·gate

di'van

dive

dived

div'er

di·verge'

di·verged'

di·ver'gence

di·ver'gent

di·verg'ing·ly

di·verse'

di·ver'si·fi·ca'tion

di·ver'si·fy

di·ver'sion

di·ver'sion·ar·y

di·ver'si·ty

di·vert'

di·vest'

di·vide'

di·vid'ed

div'i·dend

di·vid'er

di·vine'

di·vined'

di·vine'ly

di·vin'i·ty

di·vis'i·bil'i·ty

di·vis'i·ble

di·vi'sion

di·vi'sor

di·vorce'

di·vor'cee'

di·vorce'ment

di·vulge'

di·vulged'

diz'zi·er

diz'zi·est

diz'zi·ly

diz'zi·ness

diz'zy

do

doc'ile

do·cil'i·ty

dock

dock'et

dock'yard'

doc'tor

doc'tor·ate

doc'tri·naire'

doc'tri·nal

doc'trine

doc'u·ment

doc'u·men'ta·ry

doc'u·men·ta'tion

doc'u·ment'ed

dod'der

dodge

dodged

do'do

doe

doe'skin'

doff

dog

dog'cart'

doge

dog'ged

dog'ger·el

dog'ma

dog·mat'ic

dog'ma·tism

dog'ma·tize

dog'trot'

dog'wood'

doi'ly

do'ings

dol'drums

dole

doled

dole'ful

doll

dol'lar

dol'man

dol'phin

dolt

do·main'

dome

domed

do·mes'tic

do·mes′ti·cal·ly

do·mes′ti·cate

do·mes′ti·cat′ed

do′mes·tic′i·ty

dom′i·cile

dom′i·cil′i·ar′y

dom′i·nance

dom′i·nant

dom′i·nate

dom′i·nat′ed

dom′i·na′tion

dom′i·neer′

dom′i·neered′

dom′i·neer′ing·ly

dom′i·nie

do·min′ion

dom′i·no

do′nate

do′nat·ed

do·na′tion

don′a·tive

done

don′key

do′nor

doom

doomed

door

door′bell′

door′frame′

door′knob′

door′nail′

door′sill′

door′stop′

door′way′

door′yard′

dope

dor′mant

dor′mer

dor′mi·to′ry

dor′mouse′

dor′sal

do′ry

dos′age

dose

dos′si·er

dot

dot′age

do′tard

dote

dot′ing·ly

dot′ted

dou′ble

dou′bled

dou′bly

doubt

doubt′ed

doubt′ful

doubt′ful·ly

doubt′ing·ly

doubt′less

dough

dough′boy′

dough′nut′

dough′ty

dough′y

dour

dove

dove

dove′cot′

dove′tail′

dow′a·ger

dow′di·er

dow′di·est

dow′di·ly

dow′dy

dow′el

dow′eled

dow′er

down

down′cast′

down′fall′

down′heart′ed

down′hill′

down′pour′

down′right′

down′stairs′

down′town′

down′ward

down′y

dow′ry

dows′er

dox·ol′o·gy

doze

doz′en

drab

drach′ma

draft	dra'per·y	drear'i·er
draft'ed	dras'tic	drear'i·est
draft'ee'	draught	drear'i·ly
draft'i·er	draw	drear'i·ness
draft'i·est	draw'back'	drear'y
draft'i·ly	draw'bar'	dredge
draft'y	draw'bridge'	dredged
drag	draw'ee'	dreg
drag'gle	draw'er	drench
drag'gled	draw'ings	drenched
drag'net'	drawl	dress
drag'on	drawled	dressed
drag'on·fly'	drawn	dress'er
dra·goon'	draw'plate'	dress'ings
dra·gooned'	draw'string'	dress'mak'er
drain	dray	dress'y
drain'age	dray'age	drew
drained	dray'man	drib'ble
drain'er	dread	drib'bled
drake	dread'ed	dried
dra'ma	dread'ful	dri'er
dra·mat'ic	dream	dri'est
dra·mat'i·cal·ly	dreamed	drift
dra·mat'ics	dream'er	drift'wood'
dram'a·tist	dream'i·er	drill
dram'a·ti·za'tion	dream'i·est	drilled
dram'a·tize	dream'i·ly	drill'er
dram'a·tized	dream'i·ness	drink
dram'a·tur'gy	dream'land	drink'a·ble
drank	dream'less	drink'er
drape	dream'like	drip
drap'er	dream'y	drip'pings

drive	drudg'er·y	duc'tile
driv'el	drug	duc·til'i·ty
driv'en	drug'gist	dudg'eon
driv'er	drug'store'	due
drive'way'	dru'id	du'el
driz·zle	dru·id'i·cal	du'el·ist
driz'zled	drum	du·en'na
droll	drum'head'	du·et'
droll'er·y	drummed	duf'fel
drom'e·dar'y	drum'mer	duff'er
drone	drum'stick'	dug
dron'ing·ly	drunk	du'gong
drool	drunk'ard	dug'out'
drool'ings	drunk'en	duke
droop	dry	duke'dom
drop	dry'ly	dul'cet
drop'out'	dry'ness	dul'ci·mer
drop'per	du'al	dull
drop'pings	du'al·ism	dull'ard
drop'si·cal	du'al·is'tic	dull'er
drop'sy	du·al'i·ty	dull'est
dross	du·bi'e·ty	dull'ness
drought	du'bi·ous	du'ly
drove	du'cal	dumb
drown	duc'at	dumb'bell'
drowned	duch'ess	dum'my
drown'ings	duch'y	dump
drowse	duck	dump'ing
drow'si·ly	duck'ling	dump'ling
drow'si·ness	duck'pin'	dun
drow'sy	duck'weed'	dunce
drudge	duct	dune

dun'ga·ree'

dun'geon

dun'nage

dunned

dupe

du'plex

du'pli·cate

du'pli·cat'ed

du'pli·ca'tion

du'pli·ca'tor

du·plic'i·ty

du'ra·bil'i·ty

du'ra·ble

du·ral'u·min

dur'ance

du·ra'tion

du'ress

dur'ing

dusk'y

dust

dust'ed

dust'er

dust'i·er

dust'i·est

dust'y

du'te·ous

du'ties

du'ti·ful

du'ty

dwarf

dwarf'ish

dwell

dwel'lings

dwelt

dwin'dle

dwin'dled

dy·nam'ic

dy'na·mism

dy'na·mite

dy'na·mit'ed

dy'na·mo

dy'nas·ty

dys'en·ter'y

dys·func'tion

dys·pep'si·a

dys·pep'tic

dys'tro·phy

E

each	ear'shot'	East'er
ea'ger	earth	east'er·ly
ea'ger·ly	earth'en	east'ern
ea'ger·ness	earth'en·ware'	east'ern·er
ea'gle	earth'li·ness	east'ward
ea'glet	earth'ling	east'ward·ly
ear	earth'ly	eas'y
earl	earth'quake'	eas'y·go'ing
earl'dom	earth'ward	eat
ear'li·er	earth'work'	eat'a·ble
ear'li·est	earth'worm'	eat'en
ear'ly	ear'wax'	eat'er
ear'mark'	ear'wig'	eaves'drop'
earn	ease	ebb
earned	eased	ebbed
earn'er	ea'sel	eb'on·ize
ear'nest	ease'ment	eb'on·ized
ear'nest·ly	eas'i·er	eb'on·y
ear'nest·ness	eas'i·est	e·bul'li·ence
earn'ings	eas'i·ly	e·bul'li·ent
ear'ring'	eas'i·ness	eb'ul·li'tion
ear'rings'	east	ec·cen'tric

ec'cen·tric'i·ty

ec'chy·mo'sis

ec·cle'si·as'tic

ec·cle·se'si·as'ti·cal

ech'e·lon

ech'o

ech'oed

é·clair'

é·clat'

ec·lec'tic

ec·lec'ti·cism

e·clipse'

ec'logue

e'co·nom'ic

e'co·nom'i·cal

e'co·nom'i·cal·ly

e·con'o·mist

e·con'o·mize

econ'omized

econ'omy

ec'ru

ec'sta·sy

ec·stat'ic

ec·stat'i·cal·ly

ec'ze·ma

ed'dy

e'del·weiss

e·de'ma

edge

edged

edg'er

edge'ways'

edge'wise'

ed'i·bil'i·ty

ed'i·ble

e'dict

ed'i·fi·ca'tion

ed'i·fice

ed'i·fied

ed'i·fy

ed'it

ed'it·ed

e·di'tion

ed'i·tor

ed'i·to'ri·al

ed'i·to'ri·al·ize

ed'i·to'ri·al·ly

ed'u·ca·ble

ed'u·cate

ed'u·cat'ed

ed'u·ca'tion

ed'u·ca'tion·al

ed'u·ca'tion·al·ly

ed'u·ca'tor

e·duce'

eel

eel'pot'

eel'worm'

ee'rie

ef·face'

ef·face'ment

ef·fect'

ef·fect'ed

ef·fec'tive

ef·fec'tu·al

ef·fec'tu·al·ly

ef·fec'tu·ate

ef·fem'i·na·cy

ef·fem'i·nate

ef'fer·ent

ef'fer·vesce'

ef'fer·ves'cence

ef'fer·ves'cent

ef·fete'

ef'fi·ca'cious

ef'fi·ca·cy

ef·fi'cien·cy

ef·fi'cient

ef'fi·gies

ef'fi·gy

ef'flo·resce'

ef'flo·res'cence

ef'flo·res'cent

ef·flu'vi·a

ef·flu'vi·um

ef'flux

ef'fort

ef'fort·less

ef·fron'ter·y

ef·ful'gence

ef·ful'gent

ef·fu'sion

ef·fu'sive

ef·fu'sive·ly

ef·fu'sive·ness

e·gal'i·tar'i·an

egg'nog'

egg'plant'

egg'shell'

eg'lan·tine

e'go

e'go·cen'tric

e'go·cen·tric'i·ty

e'go·ism

e'go·is'tic

e'go·tism

e'go·tis'tic

e'go·tis'ti·cal

e·gre'gious

e'gress

e'gret

E·gyp'tian

ei'der

ei'ther

e·jac'u·late

e·jac'u·la'tion

e·ject'

e·jec'tion

e·ject'ment

e·jec'tor

e·lab'o·rate

e·lab'o·rate·ly

e·lab'o·ra'tion

e·lapse'

e·lapsed'

e·las'tic

e·las'tic'i·ty

e·lat'ed

e·la'tion

el'bow

el'bowed

el'bow·room'

eld'er

el'der·ber'ry

eld'er·ly

eld'est

e·lect'

e·lect'ed

e·lec'tion

e·lec'tion·eer'

e·lec'tive

e·lec'tor

e·lec'tor·al

e·lec'tor·ate

e·lec'tric

e·lec'tri·cal

e·lec'tri·cal·ly

e·lec'tri'cian

e·lec'tric'i·ty

e·lec'tri·fi·ca'tion

e·lec'tri·fy

e·lec'tro·cute

e·lec'tro·cu'tion

e·lec'trode

e·lec'tro·lier'

e·lec'trol'y·sis

e·lec'tro·lyt'ic

e·lec'tro·lyt'i·cal

e·lec'tro·lyze

e·lec'tro·mag'net

e·lec'trom'e·ter

e·lec'tro·mo'tive

e·lec'tron

e·lec'tron'ic

e·lec'tro·plate'

e·lec'tro·pos'i·tive

e·lec'tro·scope

e·lec'tro·type

e·lec'tro·typ'er

el'ee·mos'y·nar'y

el'e·gance

el'e·gant

el'e·gy

el'e·ment

el'e·men'tal

el'e·men'tal·ly

el'e·men'ta·ry

el'e·phant

el'e·phan·ti'a·sis

el'e·phan'tine

el'e·vate

el'e·vat'ed

el'e·va'tion

el'e·va'tor

elf'in

e·lic'it

e·lic'it·ed

e·lide'

el'i·gi·bil'i·ty

el'i·gi·ble

e·lim'i·nate

e·lim'i·nat'ed

e·lim′i·na′tion	e·lu′so·ry	em·bez′zle·ment
e·lim′i·na′tive	e·ma′ci·ate	em·bez′zler
e·li′sion	e·ma′ci·at′ed	em·bit′ter
e·lite′	e·ma′ci·a′tion	em·bit′tered
e·lix′ir	em′a·nate	em·bla′zon
E·liz′a·be′than	em′a·nat′ed	em′blem
elk	e·man′ci·pate	em·blem·at′ic
el·lip′sis	e·man′ci·pat′ed	em′blem·at′i·cal
el·lips′oid	e·man′ci·pa′tion	em·bod′ied
el·lip′tic	e·man′ci·pa′tor	em·bod′i·ment
el·lip′ti·cal	e·mas′cu·late	em·bod′y
elm	e·mas′cu·la′tion	em·bold′en
el′o·cu′tion	em·balm′	em·bold′ened
el′o·cu′tion·ist	em·balmed′	em′bo·lism
e·lon′gate	em·balm′er	em′bo·lus
e·lon′gat·ed	em·bank′ment	em·boss′
e·lon′ga′tion	em·bar′go	em·bossed′
e·lope′	em·bar′goed	em·brace′
e·lope′ment	em·bark′	em·braced′
el′o·quence	em′bar·ka′tion	em·bra′sure
el′o·quent	em·bar′rass	em′bro·cate
el′o·quent·ly	em·bar′rassed	em′bro·ca′tion
else	em·bar′rass·ment	em·broi′der
else′where	em′bas·sy	em·broi′dered
else′wise	em·bat′tle	em·broi′der·y
e·lu′ci·date	em·bat′tled	em·broil′
e·lu′ci·dat′ed	em·bel′lish	em·broiled′
e·lu′ci·da′tion	em·bel′lished	em′bry·o
e·lude′	em·bel′lish·ment	em′bry·ol′o·gy
e·lud′ed	em′ber	em′bry·on′ic
e·lu′sive	em·bez′zle	e·mend′
e·lu′sive·ness	em·bez′zled	e′men·da′tion

e·mend'ed

em·phat'i·cal·ly

en·a'ble

em'er·ald

em'pire

en·a'bled

e·merge'

em·pir'ic

en·act'

e·merged'

em·pir'i·cal

en·act'ed

e·mer'gence

em·pir'i·cism

en·act'ment

e·mer'gen·cy

em·place'ment

en·am'el

e·mer'gent

em·ploy'

en·am'eled

e·mer'i·tus

em·ployed'

en·am'ored

em'er·y

em·ploy'ee

en·camp'

e·met'ic

em·ploy'er

en·camp'ment

em'i·grant

em·ploy'ment

en·cap'su·late

em'i·grate

em·po'ri·um

en·caus'tic

em'i·grat'ed

em·pow'er

en'ce·phal'ic

em'i·gra'tion

em·pow'ered

en·ceph'a·li'tis

em'i·nence

em'press

en·chant'

em'i·nent

emp'tied

en·chant'ed

em'is·sar'y

emp'ti·ly

en·chant'ing·ly

e·mis'sion

emp'ti·ness

en·chant'ment

e·mit'

emp'ty

en·cir'cle

e·mit'ted

em'py·re'an

en·cir'cled

e·mol'li·ent

e'mu

en·cir'cle·ment

e·mol'u·ment

em'u·late

en'clave

e·mo'tion

em'u·lat'ed

en·close'

e·mo'tion·al

em'u·lates

en·closed'

e·mo'tion·al·ly

em'u·la'tion

en·clo'sure

em·pan'el

em'u·la'tive

en·co'mi·a

em'per·or

em'u·la·to'ry

en·co'mi·as'tic

em'pha·ses

em'u·lous

en·co'mi·um

em'pha·sis

e·mul'si·fi·ca'tion

en·com'pass

em'pha·size

e·mul'si·fi'er

en·core'

em'pha·sized

e·mul'si·fy

en·coun'ter

em·phat'ic

e·mul'sion

en·coun'tered

en·cour′age

en·cour′aged

en·cour′age·ment

en·cour′ag·ing·ly

en·croach′

en·croached′

en·croach′ment

en·cum′ber

en·cum′bered

en·cum′brance

en·cy′cli·cal

en·cy′clo·pe′di·a

en·cy′clo·pe′dic

en·cyst′

en·cyst′ed

end

en·dan′ger

en·dan′gered

en·dear′

en·deared′

en·deav′or

en·deav′ored

end′ed

en·dem′ic

end′ings

en′dive

end′less

end′less·ly

end′long′

en′do·crine

en′do·cri·nol′o·gy

en′do·derm

en·dog′e·nous

en·dorse′

en·dorse′ment

en·dow′

en·dowed′

en·dow′ment

en·due′

en·dued′

en·dur′a·ble

en·dur′ance

en·dure′

en·dured′

en·dur′ing·ly

end′ways

end′wise

en′e·my

en′er·get′ic

en′er·gize

en′er·gized

en′er·vate

en′er·va′tion

en·fee′ble

en·fee′bled

en′fi·lade′

en·fold′

en·force′

en·force′a·ble

en·forced′

en·force′ment

en·forc′er

en·fran′chise

en·fran′chised

en·gage′

en·gaged′

en·gage′ment

en·gag′ing·ly

en·gen′der

en·gen′dered

en′gine

en′gi·neer′

Eng′lish

Eng′lish·man

en·gorge′

en·gorge′ment

en·grain′

en·grained′

en·grave′

en·graved′

en·grav′er

en·gross′

en·grossed′

en·gross′er

en·gulf′

en·hance′

en·hanced′

en·hance′ment

en·har·mon′ic

e·nig′ma

e·nig·mat′ic

e·nig·mat′i·cal

en·join′

en·joined′

en·joy′

en·joy′a·ble

en·joyed'

en·joy'ment

en·large'

en·larged'

en·large'ment

en·larg'er

en·light'en

en·light'ened

en·light'en·ing·ly

en·light'en·ment

en·list'

en·list'ed

en·list'ment

en·liv'en

en·liv'ened

en·mesh'

en'mi·ty

en·no'ble

en·no'bled

e·nor'mi·ty

e·nor'mous

e·nough'

en·rage'

en·raged'

en·rap'ture

en·rap'tured

en·rich'

en·riched'

en·rich'ment

en·roll'

en·rolled'

en·roll'ment

en·shrine'

en·shrined'

en'sign

en'si·lage

en·slave'

en·slave'ment

en·sue'

en·sued'

en·sure'

en·sured'

en·tab'la·ture

en·tail'

en·tailed'

en·tan'gle

en·tan'gled

en·tan'gle·ment

en'ter

en'tered

en'ter·i'tis

en'ter·prise

en'ter·tain'

en'ter·tained'

en'ter·tain'er

en'ter·tain'ing·ly

en'ter·tain'ment

en·thrall'

en·thralled'

en·throne'

en·throned'

en·thu'si·asm

en·thu'si·ast

en·thu'si·as'tic

en·thu'si·as'ti·cal·ly

en·tice'

en·ticed'

en·tice'ment

en·tic'ing·ly

en·tire'

en·tire'ly

en·tire'ty

en·ti'tle

en·ti'tled

en'ti·ty

en·tomb'

en·tombed'

en·tomb'ment

en'to·mol'o·gist

en'to·mol'o·gy

en'trails

en'trance

en·tranc'ing·ly

en'trant

en·trap'

en·treat'

en·treat'ed

en·treat'y

en·trench'

en·trust'

en'try

en'try·way'

en·twine'

e·nu'cle·ate

e·nu'cle·a'tion

e·nu'mer·ate

e·nu′mer·at′ed

ep′i·gas′tric

eq′ua·bly

e·nu′mer·a′tion

ep′i·glot′tis

e′qual

e·nu′mer·a′tor

ep′i·gram

e′qualed

e·nun′ci·ate

ep′i·gram·mat′ic

e·qual′i·tar′i·an

e·nun′ci·at′ed

ep′i·graph

e·qual′i·ty

e·nun′ci·a′tion

ep′i·lep′sy

e′qual·i·za′tion

e·nun′ci·a′tor

ep′i·lep′tic

e′qual·ize

en·vel′op

ep′i·lep′toid

e′qual·ized

en′ve·lope

ep′i·logue

e′qual·iz′er

en·ven′om

e·piph′y·sis

e′qual·ly

en′vi·a·ble

e·pis′co·pa·cy

e′qua·nim′i·ty

en′vi·ous

e·pis′co·pal

e·quate′

en·vi′ron·ment

e·pis′co·pa′li·an

e·quat′ed

en·vi′ron·men′tal

e·pis′co·pate

e·qua′tion

en·vi′ron·men′tal·ly

ep′i·sode

e·qua′tor

en·vi′rons

ep′i·sod′ic

e′qua·to′ri·al

en·vis′age

e·pis′te·mol′o·gy

eq′uer·ry

en·vis′aged

e·pis′tle

e·ques′tri·an

en′voy

ep′is·to·lar′y

e·ques′tri·enne′

en′voys

e·pis′to·la·to′ry

e′qui·an′gu·lar

en′vy

ep′i·taph

e′qui·dis′tance

en′zyme

ep′i·tha·la′mi·um

e′qui·dis′tant

e′on

ep′i·the′li·um

e′qui·lat′er·al

e·phem′er·al

ep′i·thet

e′qui·lib′ri·um

ep′ic

e·pit′o·me

e′quine

ep′i·cure

e·pit′o·mize

e′qui·noc′tial

ep′i·cu·re′an

ep′i·zo·ot′ic

e′qui·nox

ep′i·dem′ic

ep′och

e·quip′

ep′i·der′mal

ep′och·al

eq′ui·page

ep′i·der′mic

ep′o·nym

e·quip′ment

ep′i·der′mis

ep·ox′y

e′qui·poise

ep′i·der′moid

eq′ua·ble

eq′ui·ta·ble

eq'ui·ta'tion

eq'ui·ty

e·quiv'a·lence

e·quiv'a·len·cy

e·quiv'a·lent

e·quiv'o·cal

e·quiv'o·cal·ly

e·quiv'o·cate

e·quiv'o·ca'tion

e'ra

e·rad'i·cate

e·rad'i·cat'ed

e·rad'i·ca'tion

e·rase'

e·rased'

e·ras'er

e·ra'sure

e·rect'

e·rect'ed

e·rec'tile

e·rec'tion

e·rect'ness

erg

er'go

er'got

er'mine

e·rode'

e·ro'sion

e·rot'ic

err

er'rand

er·ra'ta

er·rat'ic

er·rat'i·cal·ly

er·ra'tum

erred

er·ro'ne·ous

er'ror

erst'while'

er'u·dite

er'u·di'tion

e·rupt'

e·rup'tion

e·rup'tive

er'y·sip'e·las

es'ca·lade'

es'ca·la'tor

es'ca·pade'

es·cape'

es·cape'ment

es·cap'ist

es·carp'ment

es·cheat'

es·chew'

es'cort

es·cort'ed

es'cri·toire'

es'crow'

es·cutch'eon

Es'ki·mo

e·soph'a·gus

es'o·ter'ic

es·par'to

es·pe'cial

es·pe'cial·ly

Es'pe·ran'to

es'pi·o·nage

es'pla·nade'

es·pous'al

es·pouse'

es'prit'

es·py'

es·quire'

es·say'

es·sayed'

es'say·ist

es'sence

es·sen'tial

es·sen'tial·ly

es·tab'lish

es·tab'lished

es·tab'lish·ment

es·tate'

es·teem'

es·teemed'

es'ter

es·thet'ic

es'ti·ma·ble

es'ti·mate

es'ti·mat'ed

es'ti·ma'tion

es'ti·ma'tor

es'ti·vate

es·top'pel

es·trange'

es·tranged'

es·trange′ment	eu′phe·mis′tic	e′ven·ly
es′tu·ar′y	eu·pho′ni·ous	e′ven·ness
e·su′ri·ent	eu′pho·ny	e·vent′
etch	Eur·a′sian	e·vent′ful
etch′er	eu·re′ka	e·vent′ful·ly
etch′ings	Eu′ro·pe′an	e·ven′tu·al
e·ter′nal	Eu·sta′chi·an	e·ven′tu·al′i·ty
e·ter′nal·ly	eu·tec′tic	e·ven′tu·al·ly
e·ter′ni·ty	eu′tha·na′si·a	e·ven′tu·ate
eth′ane	e·vac′u·ate	ev′er
e′ther	e·vac′u·at′ed	ev′er·glade
e·the′re·al	e·vac′u·a′tion	ev′er·green′
e·the′re·al·ly	e·vade′	ev′er·last′ing
eth′i·cal	e·vad′ed	ev′er·last′ing·ly
eth′i·cal·ly	e·val′u·ate	ev′er·y
eth′ics	e·val′u·a′tion	ev′er·y·bod′y
eth·nol′o·gy	ev′a·nesce′	ev′er·y·day′
eth′yl	ev′a·nes′cence	ev′er·y·one′
e′ti·ol′o·gy	ev′a·nes′cent	ev′er·y·thing′
et′i·quette	e′van·gel′i·cal	ev′er·y·where′
e′tude	e·van′ge·list	e·vict′
et′y·mo·log′i·cal	e·vap′o·rate	e·vict′ed
et′y·mol′o·gy	e·vap′o·rat′ed	e·vic′tion
eu′ca·lyp′tus	e·vap′o·ra′tion	ev′i·dence
Eu′cha·rist	e·vap′o·ra′tor	ev′i·dent
eu′chre	e·va′sion	ev′i·den′tial
Eu·clid′e·an	e·va′sive	ev′i·den′tial·ly
eu·gen′ics	e·va′sive·ly	e′vil
eu′lo·gis′tic	e·va′sive·ness	e′vil·ly
eu′lo·gize	e′ven	e·vince′
eu′lo·gy	eve′ning	e·vinced′
eu′phe·mism	eve′nings	e·vis′cer·ate

ev'o·ca'tion

e·voc'a·tive

e·voke'

e·voked'

ev'o·lu'tion

ev'o·lu'tion·ar'y

ev'o·lu'tion·ist

e·volve'

ewe

ew'er

ex·ac'er·bate

ex·ac'er·ba'tion

ex·act'

ex·act'ed

ex·ac'tion

ex·act'i·tude

ex·act'ly

ex·act'ness

ex·ag'ger·ate

ex·ag'ger·at'ed

ex·ag'ger·a'tion

ex·alt'

ex'al·ta'tion

ex·alt'ed

ex·a'men

ex·am'i·na'tion

ex·am'ine

ex·am'ined

ex·am'in·er

ex·am'ple

ex·as'per·ate

ex·as'per·at'ed

ex·as'per·a'tion

ex'ca·vate

ex'ca·vat'ed

ex'ca·va'tion

ex'ca·va'tor

ex·ceed'

ex·ceed'ed

ex·ceed'ing·ly

ex·cel'

ex·celled'

ex'cel·lence

ex'cel·len·cy

ex'cel·lent

ex·cel'si·or

ex·cept'

ex·cept'ed

ex·cep'tion

ex·cep'tion·al

ex·cep'tion·al·ly

ex·cerpt'

ex·cess'

ex·cess'es

ex·ces'sive

ex·ces'sive·ly

ex·change'

ex·change'a·ble

ex·cheq'uer

ex·cip'i·ent

ex'cise

ex·ci'sion

ex·cit'a·bil'i·ty

ex·cit'a·ble

ex·cit'ant

ex'ci·ta'tion

ex·cite'

ex·cit'ed·ly

ex·cite'ment

ex·claim'

ex·claimed'

ex·cla·ma'tion

ex·clam'a·to'ry

ex·clude'

ex·clud'ed

ex·clu'sion

ex·clu'sive

ex'com·mu'ni·cate

ex'com·mu'ni·ca'tion

ex·co'ri·ate

ex·co'ri·at'ed

ex·co'ri·a'tion

ex·cres'cence

ex·cres'cent

ex·crete'

ex·cret'ed

ex·cre'tion

ex'cre·to'ry

ex·cru'ci·ate

ex·cru'ci·at'ing·ly

ex·cru'ci·a'tion

ex'cul·pate

ex'cul·pat'ed

ex'cul·pa'tion

ex·cur'sion

ex·cus'a·ble

ex·cuse'
ex·cused'
ex·cus'es
ex'e·cra·ble
ex'e·crate
ex'e·crat'ed
ex'e·cra'tion
ex·ec'u·tant
ex'e·cute
ex'e·cut'ed
ex'e·cu'tion
ex'e·cu'tion·er
ex·ec'u·tive
ex·ec'u·tor
ex·ec'u·trix
ex'e·ge'sis
ex·em'plar
ex·em'pla·ry
ex·em'pli·fi·ca'tion
ex·em'pli·fy
ex·empt'
ex·empt'ed
ex·emp'tion
ex'e·qua'tur
ex'er·cise
ex'er·cised
ex'er·cis'er
ex·ert'
ex·ert'ed
ex·er'tion
ex'ha·la'tion
ex·hale'

ex·haled'
ex·haust'
ex·haus'tion
ex·haus'tive
ex·haust'less
ex·hib'it
ex·hib'it·ed
ex'hi·bi'tion
ex·hib'i·tor
ex·hil'a·rate
ex·hil'a·rat'ed
ex·hil'a·ra'tion
ex·hort'
ex'hor·ta'tion
ex·hort'ed
ex·hu·ma'tion
ex·hume'
ex·humed'
ex'i·gen·cy
ex'i·gent
ex·ig'u·ous
ex'ile
ex'iled
ex·ist'
ex·ist'ed
ex·ist'ence
ex·ist'ent
ex'it
ex'o·dus
ex·on'er·ate
ex·on'er·at'ed
ex·on'er·a'tion

ex·or'bi·tant
ex·or'bi·tant·ly
ex'or·cise
ex'or·cised
ex'or·cism
ex·or'di·um
ex'o·ter'ic
ex·ot'ic
ex·ot'i·cism
ex·pand'
ex·pand'ed
ex·panse'
ex·pan'sion
ex·pan'sive
ex·pa'ti·ate
ex·pa'ti·at'ed
ex·pa'tri·ate
ex·pa'tri·a'tion
ex·pect'
ex·pect'an·cy
ex·pect'ant
ex'pec·ta'tion
ex·pect'ed
ex·pec'to·rant
ex·pec'to·rate
ex·pec'to·ra'tion
ex·pe'di·en·cy
ex·pe'di·ent
ex'pe·dite
ex'pe·dit'ed
ex'pe·di'tion
ex'pe·di'tion·ar'y

ex'pe·di'tious

ex'pe·di'tious·ly

ex·pel'

ex·pelled'

ex·pend'

ex·pend'ed

ex·pend'i·ture

ex·pense'

ex·pen'sive·ly

ex·pe'ri·ence

ex·pe'ri·enced

ex·pe'ri·enc·es

ex·per'i·ment

ex·per'i·men'tal

ex·per'i·men'tal·ly

ex·per'i·men·ta'tion

ex·per'i·ment·er

ex·pert'

ex·pert'ly

ex·pert'ness

ex'per'tise'

ex'pi·ate

ex'pi·a'tion

ex'pi·ra'tion

ex·pire'

ex·pired'

ex·plain'

ex·plained'

ex'pla·na'tion

ex·plan'a·to'ry

ex'ple·tive

ex'pli·ca·ble

ex'pli·cate

ex·plic'it

ex·plic'it·ly

ex·plode'

ex·plod'ed

ex'ploit

ex'ploi·ta'tion

ex·ploit'ed

ex'plo·ra'tion

ex·plor'a·to'ry

ex·plore'

ex·plored'

ex·plor'er

ex·plor'ing·ly

ex·plo'sion

ex·plo'sive

ex·po'nent

ex·po·nen'tial

ex·port'

ex'por·ta'tion

ex·pose'

ex·posed'

ex'po·si'tion

ex·pos'i·to'ry

ex·pos'tu·late

ex·pos'tu·lat'ed

ex·pos'tu·la'tion

ex·po'sure

ex·pound'

ex·press'

ex·pres'sion

ex·pres'sive

ex·pres'sive·ly

ex·press'ly

ex·press'man

ex·pro'pri·ate

ex·pro'pri·a'tion

ex·pul'sion

ex·punge'

ex·punged'

ex'pur·gate

ex'pur·gat'ed

ex'pur·ga'tion

ex'qui·site

ex'tant

ex·tem'po·ra'ne·ous

ex·tem'po·rar'y

ex·tem'po·re

ex·tem'po·ri·za'tion

ex·tem'po·rize

ex·tend'

ex·tend'ed

ex·ten'si·ble

ex·ten'sion

ex·ten'sive

ex·tent'

ex·ten'u·ate

ex·ten'u·at'ed

ex·ten'u·a'tion

ex·te'ri·or

ex·ter'mi·nate

ex·ter'mi·nat'ed

ex·ter'mi·na'tion

ex·ter'mi·na'tor

ex·ter′nal

ex·ter′nal·i·za′tion

ex·ter′nal·ly

ex·tinct′

ex·tinc′tion

ex·tin′guish

ex·tin′guished

ex·tin′guish·er

ex′tir·pate

ex′tir·pat′ed

ex′tir·pa′tion

ex·tol′

ex·tolled′

ex·tort′

ex·tort′ed

ex·tor′tion

ex·tor′tion·ate

ex′tra

ex·tract′

ex·tract′ed

ex·trac′tion

ex·trac′tive

ex′tra·cur-
ric′u·lar

ex′tra·dite

ex′tra·dit′ed

ex′tra·di′tion

ex·tra′ne·ous

ex·traor′di·nar′i·ly

ex·traor′di·nar′y

ex·trap′o·late

ex′tra·ter′ri·to′ri·al′i·ty

ex·trav′a·gance

ex·trav′a·gant

ex·trav′a·gan′za

ex·trav′a·sate

ex·trav′a·sa′tion

ex·treme′

ex·trem′ist

ex·trem′i·ty

ex′tri·cate

ex′tri·cat′ed

ex′tri·ca′tion

ex·trin′sic

ex′tro·ver′sion

ex′tro·vert′

ex·trude′

ex·trud′ed

ex·tru′sion

ex·u′ber·ance

ex·u′ber·ant

ex′u·date

ex·u′da′tion

ex·ude′

ex·ud′ed

ex·ult′

ex·ult′ant

ex′ul·ta′tion

ex·ult′ed

ex·ult′ing·ly

eye

eye′ball′

eye′brow′

eye′cup′

eyed

eye′lash′

eye′let

eye′lid′

eye′piece′

eyes

eye′shot′

eye′sight′

eye′strain′

eye′tooth′

eye′wash′

eye′wit′ness

F

Fa'bi·an

fa'ble

fa'bled

fab'ric

fab'ri·cate

fab'ri·cat'ed

fab'ri·ca'tion

fab'u·lous

fa·çade'

face

faced

fac'et

fa·ce'tious

fa'cial

fac'ile

fa·cil'i·tate

fa·cil'i·tat'ed

fa·cil'i·ty

fac'ings

fac·sim'i·le

fact

fac'tion

fac'tion·al

fac'tious

fac·ti'tious

fac'tor

fac'to·ry

fac·to'tum

fac'tu·al

fac'tu·al·ly

fac'ul·ta'tive

fac'ul·ty

fad'dist

fade

fad'ed

fad'ing·ly

Fahr'en·heit

fail

failed

fail'ing·ly

fail'ings

faille

fail'ure

faint

faint'ed

faint'heart'ed

faint'ly

faint'ness

fair

fair'er

fair'est

fair'ly

fair'ness

fair'way'

fair'y

fair'y·land'

faith

faith'ful

faith'less

faith'less·ly

fake

fak'er

fal'con

fall

fal·la'cious

fal'la·cy

fall'en

fal'li·bil'i·ty

fal'li·ble

fal'low

false

false'hood

false'ly

false'ness

fal·set'to

fal'si·fi·ca'tion

fal'si·fi'er

fal'si·fy

fal'si·ty

fal'ter

fal'tered

fal'ter·ing·ly

fame

famed

fa·mil'ial

fa·mil'iar

fa·mil'i·ar'i·ty

fa·mil'iar·ize

fa·mil'iar·ly

fam'i·lies

fam'i·ly

fam'ine

fam'ish

fa'mous

fa'mous·ly

fan

fa·nat'ic

fa·nat'i·cal

fa·nat'i·cism

fan'cied

fan'ci·er

fan'ci·est

fan'ci·ful

fan'cy

fan'fare

fang

fanged

fan'light'

fanned

fan'tail'

fan·ta'sia

fan·tas'tic

fan'ta·sy

far

far'ad

farce

far'cial

far'ci·cal

far'cy

fare

fared

fare'well'

far'fetched'

fa·ri'na

far'i·na'ceous

farm

farmed

farm'er

farm'house'

farm'yard'

far'o

far'ri·er

far'see'ing

far'sight'ed

far'ther

far'thest

far'thing

fas'ci·nate

fas'ci·nat'ed

fas'ci·na'tion

fas'ci·nat'ing·ly

fas'ci·na'tor

fas'cism

fas'cist

fash'ion

fash'ion·a·ble

fash'ioned

fast

fas'ten

fas'tened

fas'ten·ings

fast'er

fast'est

fas·tid'i·ous

fast'ness

fat

fa'tal

fa'tal·ism

fa'tal·ist

fa'tal·is'tic

fa'tal'i·ty

fa'tal·ly

fate

fat'ed

fate'ful

fa'ther

fa'thered

fa'ther·hood

fa'ther-in-law'

fa'ther·land'

fa'ther·less

fa'ther·li·ness

fa'ther·ly

fath'om

fath'omed

fath'om·less

fa·tigue'

fat'ness

fat'ten

fat'tened

fat'ter

fat'test

fat'ty

fa·tu'i·ty

fat'u·ous

fau'cet

fault

fault'i·ly

fault'less

fault'less·ly

fault'y

fau'na

fa'vor

fa'vor·a·ble

fa'vored

fa'vor·ite

fa'vor·it·ism

fawn

fawned

fe'al·ty

fear

feared

fear'ful

fear'less

fear'less·ly

fear'some

fea'si·bil'i·ty

fea'si·ble

feast

feat

feath'er

feath'ered

feath'er·edge'

feath'er·weight'

feath'er·y

fea'ture

fea'tured

fe'brile

Feb'ru·ar'y

fe'cund

fe'cun·date

fe·cun'di·ty

fed'er·al

fed'er·al·ism

fed'er·al·ist

fed'er·al·i·za'tion

fed'er·al·ize

fed'er·al·ized

fed'er·ate

fed'er·at'ed

fed'er·a'tion

fed'er·a'tive

fe·do'ra

fee

fee'ble

fee'ble·ness

fee'blest

fee'bly

feed

feed'-back'

feed'ings

feel

feel'er

feel'ing·ly

feel'ings

feer

feered

feet

feign

feigned

feint

feld'spar'

fe·lic'i·tate

fe·lic'i·tat'ed

fe·lic'i·ta'tion

fe·lic'i·tous

fe·lic'i·tous·ly

fe·lic'i·ty

fe'line

fel'low

fel'low·ship

fel'on

fe·lo'ni·ous

fel'o·ny

felt

fe·luc'ca

fe'male

fem'i·nine

fem'i·nin'i·ty

fem'i·nism

fem'i·nist

fem'o·ral

fe'mur

fen

fence

fenc'er

fend

fend'ed

fend'er

fe·nes'trat·ed

fen'es·tra'tion

Fe'ni·an

fen'nel

fe'ral

fer·ment'

fer'men·ta'tion

fer·ment'ed

fern

fe·ro'cious

fe·ro'cious·ly

fe·roc'i·ty

fer'ret

fer'ret·ed

fer'ric

fer'ro·chrome

fer'ro·type

fer'rous

fer'rule

fer'ry

fer'ry·boat'

fer'tile

fer·til'i·ty

fer'ti·li·za'tion

fer'ti·lize

fer'ti·lized

fer'ti·liz'er

fer'ule

fer'vent

fer'vent·ly

fer'vid

fer'vid·ly

fer'vor

fes'cue

fes'tal

fes'ter

fes'tered

fes'ti·val

fes'tive

fes·tiv'i·ty

fes·toon'

fes·tooned'

fetch

fet'id

fe'tish

fe'tish·ism

fet'lock

fet'ter

fet'tered

fet'tle

feud

feu'dal

feu'dal·ism

feu'da·to'ry

fe'ver

fe'ver·ish

fe'ver·ish·ly

few

few'er

few'est

fez

fi·as'co

fi'at

fib

fi'ber

fi'broid

fib'u·la

fick'le

fic'tion

fic'tion·al

fic·ti'tious

fid'dle

fid'dled

fid'dler

fi·del'i·ty

fidg'et		filed		find	
fi·du'ci·ar'y		fil'i·al		find'er	
fief		fil'i·bus'ter		find'ings	
field		fil'i·gree		fine	
field'ed		fil'ings		fined	
field'piece'		fill		fine'ly	
fiend		filled		fine'ness	
fiend'ish		fill'er		fin'er	
fiend'ish·ly		fil'let		fin'er·y	
fierce		fill'ings		fine'spun'	
fierce'ness		film		fi·nesse'	
fierc'er		filmed		fin'est	
fierc'est		film'y		fin'ger	
fi'er·y		fil'ter		fin'gered	
fife		fil'tered		fin'ger·print'	
fig		filth		fin'i·al	
fight		filth'i·er		fi'nis	
fig'ment		filth'i·est		fin'ish	
fig'u·ra'tion		filth'i·ness		fin'ished	
fig'ur·a·tive		filth'y		fin'ish·er	
fig'ur·a·tive·ly		fil'trate		fi'nite	
fig'ure		fil·tra'tion		fiord	
fig'ured		fin		fir	
fig'ure·head'		fi'nal		fire	
fig'u·rine'		fi'nal·ist		fire'arm'	
fil'a·ment		fi·nal'i·ty		fire'boat'	
fil'a·ri'a·sis		fi'nal·ly		fire'box'	
fil'a·ture		fi·nance'		fire'brand'	
fil'bert		fi·nan'cial		fire'break'	
filch		fi·nan'cial·ly		fire'brick'	
filched		fin'an·cier'		fired	
file		finch		fire'fly'	

fire′man	fit′ful	fla′grant
fire′place′	fit′ful·ly	fla′grant·ly
fire′proof′	fit′ness	flag′ship′
fire′side′	fit′ted	flag′staff′
fire′weed′	fit′ter	flag′stone′
fire′wood′	fit′ting·ly	flail
fire′works′	fit′tings	flailed
fir′kin	fix	flair
firm	fix·a′tion	flake
fir′ma·ment	fix′a·tive	flak′i·ness
firm′er	fixed	flak′y
firm′est	fix′er	flam′beau
firm′ly	fix′ings	flam·boy′ant
firm′ness	fix′i·ty	flame
first	fix′ture	flamed
first′ly	fiz′zle	fla·men′co
firth	fiz′zled	flame′proof′
fis′cal	flab′bi·er	flam′ing·ly
fish	flab′bi·est	fla·min′go
fish′er·man	flab′bi·ness	flan
fish′er·y	flab′by	flange
fish′hook′	flac′cid	flanged
fish′wife′	flag	flank
fish′y	flag′el·lant	flanked
fis′sile	flag′el·late	flan′nel
fis′sion	flag′el·la′tion	flan′nel·ette′
fis′sure	flag′eo·let′	flap
fist	flag′eo·lets′	flap′jack′
fist′ic	fla·gi′tious	flare
fist′i·cuffs	flag′on	flare′back′
fis′tu·la	flag′pole′	flared
fit	fla′grance	flash

flash'board'

flash'er

flash'i·ly

flash'i·ness

flash'ing·ly

flash'light'

flash'y

flask

flat

flat'-bed'

flat'boat'

flat'fish'

flat'-foot'ed

flat'head'

flat'i'ron

flat'ly

flat'ness

flat'ten

flat'tened

flat'ter

flat'tered

flat'ter·er

flat'ter·ing·ly

flat'ter·y

flat'test

flat'u·lence

flat'u·lent

flat'ware'

flat'wise'

flat'work'

flat'worm'

flaunt

flaunt'ed

flaunt'ing·ly

flau'tist

fla'vor

fla'vored

fla'vor·ings

fla'vors

flaw

flawed

flax

flax'en

flax'seed'

flay

flea

flea'bite'

fleck

fledge

fledg'ling

flee

fleece

fleeced

fleec'i·ness

fleec'y

fleet

fleet'ing·ly

Flem'ish

flesh

flesh'i·ness

flesh'ings

flesh'pot'

flesh'y

Fletch'er·ism

fleur'-de-lis'

flew

flex

flexed

flex'i·bil'i·ty

flex'i·ble

flex'ure

flick

flicked

flick'er

flick'er·ing·ly

fli'er

flight

flight'i·ness

flight'y

flim'si·er

flim'si·est

flim'si·ly

flim'si·ness

flim'sy

flinch

flinched

flinch'ing·ly

fling

flint

flint'i·ness

flint'lock'

flint'y

flip'pan·cy

flip'pant

flip'pant·ly

flip'per

flirt

flir·ta'tion

flir·ta'tious

flirt'ed

flit

flitch

fliv'ver

float

float'ed

float'er

floc'cu·lence

floc'cu·lent

flock

floe

flog

flogged

flog'gings

flood

flood'ed

flood'gate'

flood'light'

flood'wa'ter

floor

floor'walk'er

flop'pi·ness

flop'py

flo'ral

Flor'en·tine

flo'ret

flo'ri·cul'ture

flor'id

flo·rid'i·ty

flor'id·ly

flor'in

flo'rist

floss

floss'i·er

floss'i·est

floss'y

flo·ta'tion

flo·til'la

flot'sam

flounce

floun'der

floun'dered

floun'der·ing·ly

flour

flour'ish

flour'ish·ing·ly

flour'y

flout

flout'ed

flow

flowed

flow'er

flow'ered

flow'er·i·ness

flow'er·pot'

flow'er·y

flow'ing·ly

flown

fluc'tu·ate

fluc'tu·at'ed

fluc'tu·a'tion

flue

flu'en·cy

flu'ent

flu'ent·ly

fluff

fluff'i·ness

fluff'y

flu'id

flu'id·ly

flu'id·ex'tract

flu·id'i·ty

fluke

flume

flung

flunk

flunked

flunk'y

flu'o·res'cence

flu'o·res'cent

flu·or'ic

flu'o·ri·date

flu'o·ri·da'tion

flu'o·ride

flu'o·ri·nate

flu'o·rine

flu'o·ro·scope

flu'or·os'co·py

flur'ry

flush

flushed

flus'ter

flus'tered

flute	foe	fond'er
flut'ed	foe'man	fond'est
flut'ings	fog	fon'dle
flut'ist	fog'gi·er	fon'dled
flut'ter	fog'gi·est	fond'ly
flut'tered	fog'gy	fond'ness
flut'ter·ing·ly	fog'horn'	fon·due'
flut'ter·y	foi'ble	font
flux	foil	food
flux'ion	foiled	fool
fly	foist	fooled
fly'er	foist'ed	fool'har'di·ness
fly'leaf'	fold	fool'har'dy
fly'trap'	fold'ed	fool'ish
fly'wheel'	fold'er	fool'ish·ly
foal	fo'li·age	fool'ish·ness
foaled	fo'li·ate	fool'proof'
foam	fo'li·a'tion	fools'cap'
foamed	fo'li·o	foot
foam'i·er	folk	foot'age
foam'i·est	folk'way'	foot'ball'
foam'i·ness	fol'li·cle	foot'board'
foam'y	fol·lic'u·lar	foot'bridge'
fob	fol'low	foot'ed
fobbed	fol'lowed	foot'fall'
fo'cal	fol'low·er	foot'gear'
fo'cal·i·za'tion	fol'ly	foot'hill'
fo'cal·ize	fo·ment'	foot'hold'
fo'cal·ized	fo'men·ta'tion	foot'ings
fo'cus	fo·ment'ed	foot'less
fo'cused	fond	foot'lights'
fod'der	fon'dant	foot'-loose'

foot'man	for'ci·ble	fore'mast'
foot'mark'	ford	fore'most
foot'note'	ford'ed	fore'name'
foot'pace'	fore'arm'	fore'noon'
foot'pad'	fore'bear	fo·ren'sic
foot'path'	fore·bode'	fore'or·dain'
foot'print'	fore·bod'ing·ly	fore'or·dained'
foot'rest'	fore·bod'ings	fore'quar'ter
foot'sore'	fore·bore'	fore·run'ner
foot'step'	fore-cast'	fore·saw'
foot'stool'	fore'cas·tle	fore·see'
foot'wear'	fore·close'	fore·see'ing·ly
foot'work'	fore·closed'	fore·shad'ow
foot'worn'	fore·clo'sure	fore'shore'
foo'zle	fore'deck'	fore·short'en
foo'zled	fore·doom'	fore'sight'
fop'per·y	fore·doomed'	fore'sight'ed·ness
fop'pish	fore'fa'ther	for'est
for	fore'fin'ger	fore·stall'
for'age	fore'foot'	fore·stalled'
fo·ra'men	fore'front'	for'est·a'tion
for'as·much'	fore·gone'	for'est·ed
for'ay	fore'ground'	for'est·er
for·bear'	fore'hand'ed	for'est·ry
for·bear'ance	fore'head	fore·taste'
for·bid'	for'eign	fore·tell'
for·bid'den	for'eign·er	fore'thought'
for·bid'ding·ly	for'eign·ism	fore·told'
force	fore·knowl'edge	for·ev'er
force'ful	fore'leg'	fore·warn'
force'meat'	fore'lock'	fore·warned'
for'ceps	fore'man	fore'wom'an

fore'word'

for'feit

for'feit·ed

for'fei·ture

for·gath'er

for·gave'

forge

forged

for'ger

for'ger·y

for·get'

for·get'ful

for·get'ful·ly

for·get'ful·ness

for·give'

for·giv'en

for·give'ness

for·giv'ing·ly

for·go'

for·got'

for·got'ten

fork

forked

for·lorn'

form

for'mal

form·al'de·hyde

for'mal·ism

for·mal'i·ty

for'mal·i·za'tion

for'mal·ize

for'mal·ly

for'mat

for·ma'tion

form'a·tive

formed

form'er

for'mer·ly

for'mic

for'mi·da·ble

form'less

for'mu·la

for'mu·lar'y

for'mu·late

for'mu·lat'ed

for'mu·la'tion

for·sake'

for·sak'en

for·sook'

for·sooth'

for·swear'

for·syth'i·a

fort

for'ta·lice

forte

for'te

forth

forth'com'ing

forth'right'

forth'right'ness

forth'with'

for'ti·fi·ca'tion

for'ti·fy

for·tis'si·mo

for'ti·tude

fort'night

fort'night·ly

for'tress

for·tu'i·tous

for·tu'i·ty

for'tu·nate

for'tune

for'tune·tell'er

fo'rum

for'ward

for'ward·ed

for'ward·er

for'ward·ness

fos'sil

fos'sil·if'er·ous

fos'sil·i·za'tion

fos'sil·ize

fos'sil·ized

fos'ter

fos'tered

fought

foul

fou·lard'

foul'er

foul'est

foul'ly

foul'ness

found

foun·da'tion

found'ed

found'er

found'ling

found'lings

found'ry

fount

foun'tain

foun'tain·head'

four'some

four'square'

fourth

fowl

fox

foxes

fox'glove'

fox'i·er

fox'i·est

fox'y

fra'cas

frac'tion

frac'tion·al

frac'tion·al·ly

frac'tion·ate

frac'tion·a'tion

frac'tious

frac'ture

frac'tured

frag'ile

frag'ile·ly

fra·gil'i·ty

frag'ment

frag'men·tar'i·ly

frag'men·tar'y

frag'men·ta'tion

frag'ment·ed

fra'grance

fra'grant

fra'grant·ly

frail

frail'er

frail'est

frail'ty

frame

framed

frame'work'

franc

fran'chise

Fran·cis'can

frank

frank'er

frank'est

frank'furt·er

frank'ly

frank'ness

fran'tic

frap'pé'

fra·ter'nal

fra·ter'nal·ly

fra·ter'ni·ty

frat'er·ni·za'tion

frat'er·nize

frat'er·nized

frat'ri·cid'al

frat'ri·cide

fraud

fraud'u·lent

fraught

fray

fraz'zle

fraz'zled

freak

freak'ish

freck'le

freck'led

free

free'board'

free'born'

free'dom

free'hand'

free'hold'

free'ly

free'man

free'ma'son

free'ma'son·ry

fre'er

fre'est

free'stone'

free'think'er

free'wheel'ing

freeze

freez'er

freight

freight'er

French

fren'zied

fren'zy

fre'quen·cy

fre'quent

fre'quent·ly		fright'en		frond	
fres'co		fright'ened		frond'ed	
fresh		fright'en·ing·ly		front	
fresh'en		fright'ful		front'age	
fresh'en·er		fright'ful·ly		fron'tal	
fresh'er		fright'ful·ness		front'ed	
fresh'est		frig'id		fron·tier'	
fresh'ly		Frig'id·aire'		fron'tis·piece	
fresh'man		fri·gid'i·ty		frost	
fresh'ness		frig'id·ly		frost'bite'	
fret		frill		frost'ed	
fret'ful		frilled		frost'fish'	
fret'ted		frill'i·ness		frost'i·er	
fret'work'		frill'y		frost'i·est	
fri'a·bil'i·ty		fringe		frost'i·ly	
fri'a·ble		fringed		frost'i·ness	
fri'ar		frip'per·y		frost'work'	
fric'as·see'		frisk		frost'y	
fric'tion		frit'ter		froth	
fric'tion·al		frit'tered		frothed	
Fri'day		fri·vol'i·ty		froth'y	
fried		friv'o·lous		fro'ward	
friend		friv'o·lous·ly		frown	
friend'less		friz'zi·ness		frowned	
friend'li·er		friz'zle		frown'ing·ly	
friend'li·est		friz'zled		frowz'i·ly	
friend'li·ness		frock		frowz'y	
friend'ly		frog		froze	
friend'ship		frog'fish'		fro'zen	
frieze		frol'ic		fruc·tif'er·ous	
frig'ate		frol'icked		fruc'ti·fy	
fright		from		fru'gal	

fru·gal′i·ty	full′er	fun′gus
fru′gal·ly	full′est	fu·nic′u·lar
fruit	full′ness	fun′nel
fruit′er·er	ful′ly	fun′ni·er
fruit′ful	ful′mi·nate	fun′ni·est
fruit′ful·ly	ful′mi·nat′ed	fun′ny
fruit′i·ness	ful′mi·na′tion	fur
fru·i′tion	ful′some	fur′be·low
fruit′less	fum′ble	fur′bish
fruit′less·ly	fum′bling	fu′ri·ous
fruit′less·ness	fume	fu′ri·ous·ly
fruit′worm′	fumed	furl
fruit′y	fu′mi·gate	furled
frump	fu′mi·gat′ed	fur′long
frus′trate	fu′mi·ga′tion	fur′lough
frus·tra′tion	fu′mi·ga′tor	fur′loughed
fry	fun	fur′nace
fry′er	func′tion	fur′nish
fuch′sia	func′tion·al	fur′nished
fud′dle	func′tion·al·ly	fur′nish·ings
fud′dled	func′tion·ar′y	fur′ni·ture
fudge	fund	fu′ror
fu′el	fun′da·men′tal	fur′ri·er
fu′eled	fun′da·men′tal·ly	fur′ri·est
fu·ga′cious	fund′ed	fur′row
fu′gi·tive	fu′ner·al	fur′rowed
fugue	fu·ne′re·al	fur′ry
ful′crum	fu·ne′re·al·ly	fur′ther
ful·fill′	fun′gi	fur′ther·ance
ful·filled′	fun′gi·ble	fur′ther·more′
ful·fill′ment	fun′gi·cide	fur′thest
full	fun′goid	fur′tive

fur'tive·ly	fu'si·bil'i·ty	fu'tile
fu'run·cle	fu'si·ble	fu'tile·ly
fu'ry	fu'sil·lade'	fu·til'i·ty
furze	fu'sion	fu'ture
fuse	fuss	fu'tur·is'tic
fused	fussed	fu·tu'ri·ty
fu'sel	fuss'i·er	fuzz
fu'se·lage	fuss'y	fuzz'i·ly
fus'es	fus'tian	fuzz'i·ness

G

gab'ar·dine'

ga'ble

gad'fly'

gad'o·lin'i·um

ga·droon'

gaff

gag

gage

gagged

gag'gle

gai'e·ty

gai'ly

gain

gained

gain'er

gain'ful

gain'ful·ly

gain'say'

gait'ed

gai'ter

ga'la

gal'an·tine

gal'ax·y

gale

ga·le'na

gall

gal'lant

gal'lant·ry

galled

gal'ler·y

gal'ley

Gal'lic

gall'ing·ly

gal'li·um

gal'lon

gal'lop

gal'lows

gall'stone'

ga·lore'

gal'va·nism

gal'va·ni·za'tion

gal'va·nize

gal'va·nized

gal'va·nom'e·ter

gam'bit

gam'ble

gam'bled

gam'bler

gam·boge'

gam'bol

gam'brel

game

game'ness

gam'mon

gam'ut

gan'der

gang

ganged

gan'gli·a

gan'gli·on

gang'plank'

gan'grene

gan'gre·nous

gang'ster

gang'way'

gan'try

gap	gashed	gay'ly
gaped	gas'house'	gay'ness
ga·rage'	gas'ket	gaze
garb	gas'o·line	ga·ze'bo
gar'bage	gasp	ga·zelle'
gar'ble	gas'tight'	ga·zette'
gar'den	gas·tral'gi·a	ga·zet'ted
gar'den·er	gas'tric	gaz'et·teer'
gar·de'ni·a	gas·tri'tis	gear
gar'gle	gas'tro·nom'ic	geared
gar'goyle	gas·tron'o·my	gear'shift'
gar'ish	gate	gei'sha
gar'land	gate'house'	gel'a·tin
gar'lic	gate'post'	ge·lat'i·nize
gar'ment	gate'way'	ge·lat'i·noid
gar'ner	gath'er	ge·lat'i·nous
gar'nered	gath'ered	gem
gar'net	gath'er·er	gen'der
gar'nish	gau'che·rie'	gen'e·a·log'i·cal
gar'nished	gaud'i·er	gen'e·al'o·gist
gar'nish·ee'	gaud'i·est	gen'e·al'o·gy
gar'nish·er	gaud'y	gen'er·al
gar'nish·ment	gauge	gen'er·al·is'si·mo
gar'ni·ture	gauged	gen'er·al·ist
gar'ret	gaunt'let	gen'er·al'i·ty
gar'ri·son	gauze	gen'er·al·i·za'tion
gar'ri·soned	gave	gen'er·al·ize
gar'ru·lous	gav'el	gen'er·al·ized
gar'ter	ga·votte'	gen'er·al·ly
gas	gawk'y	gen'er·al·ship'
gas'e·ous	gay	gen'er·ate
gash	gay'e·ty	gen'er·at'ed

gen'er·a'tion	ge'nus	ges'ture
gen'er·a'tive	ge·od'e·sy	ges'tured
gen'er·a'tor	ge'o·det'ic	get
ge·ner'ic	ge·og'ra·pher	gew'gaw
gen'er·os'i·ty	ge·og'ra·phy	gey'ser
gen'er·ous	ge'o·log'i·cal	ghast'li·ness
gen'er·ous·ly	ge·ol'o·gist	ghast'ly
gen'e·sis	ge·ol'o·gy	gher'kin
ge·net'ics	ge'o·met'ric	ghet'to
ge·ni'al	ge'o·met'ri·cal	ghost
ge·ni·al'i·ty	ge·om'e·try	ghost'li·ness
gen'ial·ly	ge·ra'ni·um	ghost'ly
gen'i·tive	ge'rent	ghoul
gen'ius	ger'i·a·tri'cian	gi'ant
gen·teel'	ger'i·at'rics	gi'ant·ism
gen·teel'ly	germ	gib'ber
gen'tian	Ger'man	gib'ber·ish
gen'tile	ger·mane'	gib'bet
gen·til'i·ty	ger'mi·cide	gib'bon
gen'tle	ger'mi·nal	gibe
gen'tle·man	ger'mi·nant	gib'let
gen'tle·men	ger'mi·nate	gid'di·ly
gen'tle·ness	ger'mi·nat'ed	gid'di·ness
gen'tler	ger'mi·na'tion	gid'dy
gen'tlest	ger'mi·na'tive	gift
gen'tly	ger'und	gift'ed
gen'try	ge·run'di·al	gig
gen'u·flect	ge·run'dive	gi·gan'tic
gen'u·flec'tion	ges'so	gi·gan'ti·cal·ly
gen'u·ine	Ge·stalt'	gi·gan'tism
gen'u·ine·ly	ges·tic'u·late	gig'gle
gen'u·ine·ness	ges·tic'u·la'tion	gig'gled

gild

gild'ed

gild'er

gill

gill

gilt

gim'bals

gim'crack'

gim'let

gin

gin'ger

gin'ger·ly

ging'ham

gin'gi·vi'tis

gi·raffe'

gir'an·dole

gird

gird'er

gir'dle

gir'dled

gir'dler

girl

girl'hood

girl'ish

girt

girth

gist

give

giv'en

giv'er

giz'zard

gla'cial

gla'cier

glad

glad'den

glad'dened

glade

glad'i·a'tor

glad'i·a·to'ri·al

glad'i·o'lus

glad'ly

glad'ness

Glad'stone

glam'or·ous

glam'our

glance

gland

glan'dered

glan'ders

glan'du·lar

glare

glared

glar'ing·ly

glass

glass'ful

glass'house'

glass'i·ly

glass'i·ness

glass'ware'

glass'y

glau·co'ma

glaze

glazed

gla'zier

gleam

gleamed

glean

glean'er

glean'ings

glee'ful

glib

glib'ly

glide

glid'ed

glid'er

glim'mer

glim'mered

glim'mer·ings

glimpse

glimpsed

glint

glint'ed

gli·o'ma

glis·san'do

glis'ten

glis'tened

glis'ter

glit'ter

glit'tered

gloat

gloat'ed

glob'al

glob'al·ly

globe

glob'u·lar

glob'ule

glock'en·spiel'	glut'ton	god
gloom	glut'ton·ize	god'child'
gloom'i·ly	glut'ton·ous	god'dess
gloom'i·ness	glut'ton·y	god'fa'ther
glo'ri·fi·ca'tion	glyc'er·in	god'head
glo'ri·fy	gnarl	god'hood
glo'ri·ous	gnarled	god'less
glo'ry	gnash	god'like'
gloss	gnashed	god'li·ness
glos'sal	gnat	god'ly
glos'sa·ry	gnath'ic	god'moth'er
gloss'i·ly	gnaw	god'par'ent
gloss'i·ness	gnawed	god'send'
glos·si'tis	gnaw'ings	god'son'
gloss'y	gneiss	gog'gle
glot'tis	gnome	go'ings
glove	gno'mic	goi'ter
glov'er	gno'mon	gold
glow	gnu	gold'en
glowed	go	gold'en·rod'
glow'er	goad	gold'finch'
glow'ered	goal	gold'smith'
glow'ing·ly	goat	gold'weed'
glow'worm'	goat'fish'	golf
glu·ci'num	goat'herd'	golf'er
glu'cose	goat'skin'	gon'do·la
glue	goat'weed'	gon'do·lier'
glued	gob'ble	gone
glue'y	gob'bled	gong
glum	gob'let	goo'ber
glut	gob'lin	good
glut'ted	go'cart'	good'-by'

good'ly

good'-na'tured

good'ness

goose

goose'ber'ry

goose'neck'

go'pher

Gor'di·an

gore

gored

gorge

gorged

gor'geous

gor'get

gor'gon

go·ril'la

gos'hawk'

gos'ling

gos'pel

gos'sa·mer

gos'sip

got

Goth'ic

got'ten

gouache

gouge

gouged

gou'lash

gourd

gour'mand

gour'met

gout

gov'ern

gov'ern·ance

gov'erned

gov'ern·ess

gov'ern·ment

gov'ern·men'tal

gov'er·nor

gown

grab

grabbed

grace

grace'ful

grace'less

gra'cious

gra'cious·ly

grack'le

gra·da'tion

grade

grad'ed

gra'di·ent

grad'u·al

grad'u·al·ly

grad'u·ate

grad'u·at'ed

grad'u·a'tion

graft

graft'ed

graft'er

grail

grain

grained

grain'field'

gram'mar

gram·mar'i·an

gram·mat'i·cal

gram·mat'i·cal·ly

gram'pus

gran'a·ry

grand

grand'child'

gran·dee'

gran'deur

grand'fa'ther

gran·dil'o·quence

gran·dil'o·quent

gran'di·ose

grand'ly

grand'moth'er

grand'ness

grand'par'ent

grand'sire'

grand'son'

grand'stand'

grange

gran'ite

gran'it·oid

gra·niv'o·rous

grant

grant'ed

gran'u·lar

gran'u·late

gran'u·lat'ed

gran'u·la'tion

gran'ule

grape	grav'en	greed
grape'shot'	grav'er	greed'i·er
graph	grav'est	greed'i·est
graph'ic	grave'stone'	greed'i·ly
graph'ics	grave'yard'	greed'i·ness
graph'ite	grav'i·tate	greed'y
grap'nel	grav'i·tat'ed	Greek
grap'ple	grav'i·ta'tion	green
grap'pled	grav'i·ta'tion·al	green'back'
grasp	grav'i·ty	green'er
grasp'ing·ly	gra·vure'	green'er·y
grass	gra'vy	green'est
grass'hop'per	gray	green'horn'
grass'plot'	gray'beard'	green'house'
grate	gray'ish	green'ish
grat'ed	gray'ness	green'ness
grate'ful	graze	green'room'
grat'er	grazed	green'stick'
grat'i·fi·ca'tion	gra'zier	green'sward'
grat'i·fy	grease	green'wood'
grat'i·fy'ing·ly	greased	greet
grat'i·nate	grease'wood'	greet'ed
grat'ings	greas'i·er	greet'ings
gra'tis	greas'i·est	gre·gar'i·ous
grat'i·tude	greas'i·ly	Gre·go'ri·an
gra·tu'i·tous	greas'i·ness	gre·nade'
gra·tu'i·ty	greas'y	gren'a·dier'
gra·va'men	great	gren'a·dine'
grave	great'er	grew
grave'dig'ger	great'est	grey'hound'
grav'el	great'ly	grid
grav'el·ly	great'ness	grid'dle

grid'i'ron

grief

griev'ance

grieve

grieved

griev'ous

griev'ous·ly

grif'fin

grill

grilled

grim

gri·mace'

grime

grim'i·er

grim'i·est

grim'i·ly

grim'i·ness

grim'y

grin

grind

grind'er

grind'ing·ly

grind'stone'

grinned

grip

gripe

grip'per

gris'ly

grist

gris'tle

grist'mill'

grit

grit'ti·ness

grit'ty

griz'zle

griz'zled

griz'zly

groan

groaned

groan'ing·ly

gro'cer

gro'cer·y

grog

grog'gy

groin

grom'met

groom

groomed

groove

grooved

grope

grop'ing·ly

gros'beak'

gros'grain'

gross

gross'er

gross'est

gross'ly

gross'ness

gro·tesque'

gro·tesque'ly

grot'to

grouch

grouch'i·ly

grouch'y

ground

ground'ed

ground'less

ground'lings

ground'work'

group

group'ings

grouse

grout

grout'ed

grove

grov'el

grov'eled

grow

grow'er

growl

growled

grown

growth

grub

grubbed

grub'bi·ness

grub'by

grudge

grudg'ing·ly

gru'el

grue'some

gruff

gruff'er

gruff'est

gruff'ly

grum′ble	guile′ful	gun
grum′bled	guile′less	gun′boat′
grump′i·ly	guil′lo·tine	gun′cot′ton
grump′i·ness	guilt	gun′fire′
grump′y	guilt′i·er	gun′lock′
grunt	guilt′i·est	gun′man
grunt′ed	guilt′i·ly	gun′ner
guar′an·tee′	guilt′i·ness	gun′ner·y
guar′an·tor	guilt′y	gun′ny
guar′an·ty	guin′ea	gun′pa′per
guard	guise	gun′pow′der
guard′ed	guis′es	gun′run′ning
guard′i·an	gui·tar′	gun′shot′
guard′i·an·ship′	gulch	gun′smith′
guard′room′	gul′den	gun′stock′
guards′man	gulf	gun′wale
gua′va	gull	gur′gle
gu′ber·na·to′ri·al	gul′let	gu′ru
gudg′eon	gul′li·bil′i·ty	gush
guer′don	gul′li·ble	gush′er
guer·ril′la	gul′ly	gush′y
guess	gulp	gus′set
guess′work′	gum	gust
guest	gum′bo	gus′ta·to′ry
guid′ance	gum′boil′	gust′i·ly
guide	gummed	gus′to
guide′book′	gum·mo′sis	gust′y
guid′ed	gum′my	gut′ter
guide′line′	gump′tion	gut′ter·snipe′
gui′don	gum′shoe′	gut′tur·al
guild	gum′weed′	gut′tur·al·ly
guile	gum′wood′	guy

guz′zle

guz′zled

guz′zler

gym·kha′na

gym·na′si·um

gym′nast

gym·nas′tic

gyn′e·col′o·gist

gyn′e·col′o·gy

gyp′sum

gyp′sy

gy′rate

gy′rat·ed

gy·ra′tion

gy′ra·to′ry

gyr′fal′con

gy′ro

gy′ro·com′pass

gy′ro·scope

gy′ro·stat

gyves

H

hab′er·dash′er	hag′gard	half′heart′ed
hab′er·dash′er·y	hag′gle	half′tone′
ha·bil′i·ment	hag′gled	half′way′
hab′it	hail	half′-wit′ted
hab′it·a·ble	hailed	hal′i·but
hab′i·tat	hail′stone′	hal′ide
hab′i·ta′tion	hail′storm′	hal′ite
hab′it·ed	hair	hal′i·to′sis
ha·bit′u·al	hair′breadth′	hall
ha·bit′u·al·ly	hair′brush′	hall′mark′
ha·bit′u·ate	hair′cut′	hal′low
ha·bit′u·at′ed	hair′line′	hal′lowed
hab′i·tude	hair′pin′	Hal′low·een′
hack′le	hair′split′ter	hal·lu′ci·na′tion
hack′man	hair′spring′	hal·lu′ci·na·to′ry
hack′ney	hair′y	hal·lu′ci·no′sis
hack′neyed	hake	ha′lo
hack saw	ha·la′tion	hal′o·gen
had	hal′berd	halt
had′dock	hal′cy·on	halt′ed
haft	hale	hal′ter
hag	half	halt′ing·ly

128

halves	hand'some	hard
hal'yard	hand'spring'	hard'en
ham	hand'work'	hard'ened
ham'let	hand'writ'ing	hard'en·er
ham'mer	hand'y	hard'er
ham'mered	hang	hard'est
ham'mer·less	hang'ar	hard'fist'ed
ham'mock	hanged	hard'head'ed
ham'per	hang'er	har'di·hood
ham'pered	hang'ings	har'di·ness
ham'ster	hang'man	hard'ly
ham'string'	han'ker	hard'ness
ham'strung'	han'kered	hard'pan'
hand	han'som	hard'ship
hand'bag'	hap'haz'ard	hard'ware'
hand'ball'	hap'less	har'dy
hand'bill'	hap'loid	hare
hand'book'	hap'pen	hare'brained'
hand'cuff'	hap'pened	hare'lip'
hand'ed	hap'pen·ings	ha'rem
hand'ful	hap'pi·er	hark
hand'i·cap	hap'pi·est	har'le·quin
hand'i·capped	hap'pi·ly	har'le·quin·ade'
hand'i·craft	hap'pi·ness	harm
hand'i·er	hap'py	harmed
hand'i·est	ha·rangue'	harm'ful
hand'i·ly	ha·rangued'	harm'ful·ly
hand'i·ness	har'ass	harm'ful·ness
hand'ker·chief	har'ass·ment	harm'less
han'dle	har'bin·ger	harm'less·ly
han'dled	har'bor	harm'less·ness
hand'rail	har'bored	har·mon'ic

har·mon'i·ca

har·mo'ni·ous

har·mo'ni·ous·ly

har·mo'ni·ous·ness

har·mo'ni·um

har'mo·ni·za'tion

har'mo·nize

har'mo·nized

har'mo·ny

har'ness

har'nessed

harp

harp'er

harp'ist

har·poon'

har·pooned'

harp'si·chord

har'ri·er

har'row

harsh

harsh'er

harsh'est

harsh'ly

harsh'ness

har'te·beest'

har'vest

har'vest·ed

har'vest·er

has

hash

hashed

hash'ish

hasp

has'sock

haste

has'ten

has'tened

hast'i·er

hast'i·est

hast'i·ly

hast'i·ness

hast'y

hat

hat'band'

hatch

hatched

hatch'er·y

hatch'et

hatch'ment

hatch'way'

hate

hat'ed

hate'ful

hate'ful·ly

hate'ful·ness

hat'pin'

ha'tred

hat'ter

haugh'ti·er

haugh'ti·est

haugh'ti·ly

haugh'ty

haul

haul'age

hauled

haunch

haunt

haunt'ed

haunt'ing·ly

haut'boy

hau·teur'

have

ha'ven

hav'er·sack

hav'oc

Ha·wai'ian

hawk

hawk'er

hawk'weed'

hawse

haw'ser

haw'thorn

hay

hay'cock'

hay'fork'

hay'loft'

hay'mow'

hay'rack'

hay'seed'

hay'stack'

haz'ard

haz'ard·ed

haz'ard·ous

haz'ard·ous·ly

haze

ha'zel

ha'zel·nut'

ha'zi·er

ha'zi·est

ha'zi·ly

ha'zi·ness

ha'zy

he

head

head'ache'

head'band'

head'board'

head'cheese'

head'dress'

head'ed

head'er

head'first'

head'fore'most

head'gear'

head'i·ly

head'ings

head'land'

head'less

head'light'

head'line'

head'lock'

head'long

head'mas'ter

head'phone'

head'piece'

head'quar'ters

heads'man

head'spring'

head'stone'

head'strong

head'wa'ter

head'way'

head'work'

head'y

heal

healed

heal'er

health

health'ful

health'ful·ness

health'i·er

health'i·est

health'i·ly

health'y

heap

heaped

hear

heard

hear'er

hear'ings

heark'en

heark'ened

hear'say'

hearse

heart

heart'ache'

heart'beat'

heart'break'

heart'bro'ken

heart'burn'

heart'en

heart'ened

heart'felt'

hearth

hearth'stone'

heart'i·er

heart'i·est

heart'i·ly

heart'less

heart'sick'

heart'sore'

heart'string'

heart'wood'

heart'y

heat

heat'ed

heat'er

heath

hea'then

hea'then·ish

hea'then·ish·ly

heath'er

heat'stroke'

heave

heav'en

heav'en·ly

heav'en·ward

heav'i·er

heav'i·est

heav'i·ly

heav'i·ness

heav'y

He·bra'ic

He'brew

hec'a·tomb

heck'le

heck'led

heck'ler

hec'tic

hec'to·graph

hedge

hedged

hedge'hog'

hedge'row'

he'don·ism

heed

heed'ed

heed'ful·ly

heed'ful·ness

heed'less

heed'less·ness

heel

heft

he·gem'o·ny

he·gi'ra

heif'er

height

height'en

height'ened

hei'nous

heir

heir'ess

heir'loom'

hel'i·cal

hel'i·coid

hel'i·cop'ter

he'li·o·trope

he'li·um

he'lix

helm

hel'met

hel'met·ed

helms'man

help

help'er

help'ful

help'ful·ly

help'ful·ness

help'ing

help'less

help'less·ly

help'less·ness

help'mate'

hem

hem'a·tite

hem'i·cy'cle

hem'i·ple'gi·a

hem'i·sphere

hem'i·spher'i·cal

hem'lock

hemmed

hem'or·rhage

hemp

hemp'en

hem'stitch'

hem'stitched'

hence

hence'forth'

hence'for'ward

hench'man

hen'e·quen

hen'na

he·pat'ic

he·pat'i·ca

hep'a·ti'tis

hep'ta·gon

hep·tam'e·ter

her

her'ald

her'ald·ed

he·ral'dic

her'ald·ry

herb

her·ba'ceous

herb'age

herb'al

her·bar'i·um

her'bi·cide

her·biv'o·rous

Her·cu'le·an

herd

herd'ed

here

here'a·bouts'

here·aft'er

here·by'

he·red'i·ta·bil'i·ty

he·red'i·ta·ble

he·red'i·ta·bly	her'ring	hid
her'e·dit'a·ment	her'ring·bone'	hid'den
he·red'i·tar'y	hers	hide
he·red'i·ty	her·self'	hide'bound'
here'in·aft'er	hes'i·tance	hid'e·ous
here·in'be·fore'	hes'i·tan·cy	hid'e·ous·ly
here·on'	hes'i·tant	hid'e·ous·ness
her'e·sy	hes'i·tate	hi'er·arch'y
her'e·tic	hes'i·tat'ed	hi'er·at'ic
he·ret'i·cal	hes'i·tat'ing·ly	hi'er·o·glyph'ic
here·to'	hes'i·ta'tion	high
here'to·fore'	hes'i·ta'tive·ly	high'born'
here'un·to'	het'er·o·dox	high'boy'
here'up·on'	het'er·o·ge·ne'i·ty	high'er
here·with'	het'er·o·ge'ne·ous	high'est
her'it·a·bil'i·ty	het'er·o·nym'	high'land
her'it·a·ble	heu·ris'tic	high'land·er
her'it·a·bly	hew	high'ly
her'it·age	hewed	high'ness
her·met'ic	hew'er	high'road'
her·met'i·cal·ly	hewn	high'way'
her'mit	hex'a·gon	high'way'man
her'mit·age	hex·ag'o·nal	hike
her'ni·a	hex·am'e·ter	hiked
he'ro	hex·an'gu·lar	hik'er
he·ro'ic	hex'a·pod	hi·lar'i·ous
he·ro'i·cal	hey'day'	hi·lar'i·ty
her'o·ine	hi·a'tus	hill
her'o·ism	hi'ber·nate	hill'i·er
her'on	hi'ber·na'tion	hill'i·est
her'pes	hi·bis'cus	hill'i·ness
her'pe·tol'o·gy	hick'o·ry	hill'ock

hill'side'	hith'er	hoist'way'
hilt	hith'er·to'	ho'kum
him	hive	hold
him·self'	hoar	hold'er
hind	hoard	hold'ings
hin'der	hoard'ed	hole
hin'dered	hoard'er	hol'i·day
hin'drance	hoar'frost'	ho'li·ly
hinge	hoarse	ho'li·ness
hinged	hoars'er	Hol'land
hint	hoars'est	hol'low
hint'ed	hoax	hol'lowed
hin'ter·land'	hob'ble	hol'ly
hip'po·drome	hob'bled	hol'ly·hock
hip'po·pot'a·mus	hob'by	hol'o·caust
hire	hob'gob'lin	hol'o·graph
hired	hob'nail'	hol'o·graph'ic
hire'ling	hob'nailed'	hol'ster
hir'sute	hob'nob'	ho'ly
his	ho'bo	ho'ly·stone'
hiss	hock	hom'age
his·tol'o·gist	hock'ey	home
his·tol'o·gy	hod	home'land'
his·to'ri·an	hoe	home'like'
his·tor'ic	hog	home'li·ness
his·tor'i·cal	hog'back'	home'ly
his'to·ry	hog'fish'	ho'me·o·path'ic
his'tri·on'ic	hog'gish	ho'me·op'a·thy
hit	hogs'head	home'sick'ness
hitch	hog'weed'	home'site'
hitched	hoist	home'spun'
hitch'hike'	hoist'ed	home'stead

home'ward

home'work'

hom'i·cid'al

hom'i·cide

hom'i·let'ics

hom'i·lies

hom'i·ly

hom'i·ny

ho'mo·ge·ne'i·ty

ho'mo·ge'ne·ous

ho'mo·ge'ne·ous·ly

ho·mog'e·nize

ho·mol'o·gous

hom'o·nym

ho·mun'cu·lus

hone

honed

hon'est

hon'est·ly

hon'es·ty

hon'ey

hon'ey·bee'

hon'ey·comb'

hon'ey·dew'

hon'eyed

hon'ey·moon'

hon'ey·suck'le

honk

hon'or

hon'or·a·ble

hon'or·a·bly

hon'o·rar'i·um

hon'or·ar'y

hon'ored

hood

hood'ed

hood'lum

hoo'doo

hood'wink

hoof

hook

hooked

hook'er

hook'worm'

hoop

Hoo'sier

hope

hope'ful

hope'ful·ly

hope'ful·ness

hope'less

hope'less·ly

hope'less·ness

hop'lite

hop'per

hop'scotch'

horde

hore'hound'

ho·ri'zon

hor'i·zon'tal

hor'mone

horn

horn'book'

horned

hor'net

horn'pipe'

ho·rol'o·gy

hor'o·scope

hor·ren'dous

hor'ri·ble

hor'rid

hor'ri·fi·ca'tion

hor'ri·fied

hor'ri·fy

hor'ror

horse

horse'back'

horse chest'nut

horse'hair'

horse'man

horse'man·ship

horse'pow'er

horse'shoe'

horse'weed'

horse'whip'

horse'wom'an

hor'ta·tive

hor'ta·to'ry

hor'ti·cul'ture

hose

ho'sier

ho'sier·y

hos'pice

hos'pi·ta·ble

hos'pi·tal

hos'pi·tal'i·ty

hos'pi·tal·i·za'tion

hos'pi·tal·ize

host

hos'tage

hos'tel

host'ess

hos'tile

hos'tile·ly

hos·til'i·ty

hot

hot'bed'

hot'box'

ho·tel'

hot'head'ed

hot'house'

hot'ly

hot'ness

hot'ter

hot'test

hound

hound'ed

hour

hour'ly

house

housed

house'fly'

house'fur'nish·ings

house'hold

house'hold'er

house'keep'er

house'maid'

house'man

house'moth'er

house'room'

house'wares'

house'warm'ing

house'wife'

house'work'

hov'el

hov'er

hov'ered

hov'er·ing·ly

how

how·ev'er

how'itz·er

howl

how'so·ev'er

hoy'den

hub

hub'bub

huck'le·ber'ry

huck'ster

hud'dle

hud'dled

hue

huff

hug

huge

hug'er

hug'est

Hu'gue·not

hulk

hull

hulled

hum

hu'man

hu·mane'

hu·mane'ly

hu·mane'ness

hu'man·ism

hu'man·ist

hu'man·is'tic

hu·man'i·tar'i·an

hu·man'i·tar'i·an·ism

hu·man'i·ty

hu'man·i·za'tion

hu'man·ize

hu'man·ized

hu'man·kind'

hu'man·ly

hum'ble

hum'bled

hum'ble·ness

hum'bler

hum'blest

hum'bly

hum'bug'

hum'drum'

hu'mer·us

hu'mid

hu·mid'i·fi·ca'tion

hu·mid'i·fied

hu·mid'i·fi'er

hu·mid'i·fy

hu·mid'i·ty

hu'mi·dor

hu·mil′i·ate	hurl	hy′drant
hu·mil′i·at′ed	hurled	hy′drate
hu·mil′i·a′tion	hur′ri·cane	hy·drau′lic
hu·mil′i·ty	hur′ry	hy′dro·car′bon
hummed	hurt	hy′dro·chlo′ric
hum′ming·bird′	hurt′ful	hy′dro·cy·an′ic
hum′mock	hurt′ful·ly	hy′dro·e·lec′tric
hu′mor	hurt′ful·ness	hy′dro·flu·or′ic
hu′mored	hur′tle	hy′dro·foil′
hu′mor·esque′	hur′tled	hy′dro·gen
hu′mor·ist	hus′band	hy·drom′e·ter
hu′mor·ous	hus′band·ry	hy′dro·pho′bi·a
hu′mor·ous·ness	hush	hy′dro·plane
hump	hushed	hy′dro·stat′ics
hu′mus	husk	hy·drox′ide
hunch	husk′i·ly	hy·e′na
hun′dred	husk′i·ness	hy′giene
hun′dred·fold′	hus′ky	hy′gi·en′ic
hun′dredth	hus′sy	hy′gi·en′i·cal·ly
Hun·gar′i·an	hus′tings	hy′gi·en·ist
hun′ger	hus′tle	hy·grom′e·ter
hun′gered	hus′tled	hy′gro·scop′ic
hun′gri·er	hus′tler	hymn
hun′gri·est	hut	hym′nal
hun′gry	hutch	hymn′book′
hunk	hy′a·cinth	hy·per′bo·la
hunt	hy′a·loid	hy·per′bo·le
hunt′ed	hy′brid	hy′per·bol′ic
hunt′er	hy′brid·ism	hy′per·crit′i·cal
hunts′man	hy′brid·i·za′tion	hy′per·e′mi·a
hur′dle	hy′brid·ize	hy′per·o′pi·a
hur′dled	hy·dran′ge·a	hy′per·sen′si·tive

hy'per·thy'roid	hyp'no·tized	hy·poth'e·ca'tion
hy·per'tro·phy	hy'po·chon'dri·a	hy·poth'e·ses
hy'phen	hy'po·chon'dri·ac	hy·poth'e·sis
hy'phen·ate	hy·poc'ri·sy	hy·poth'e·size
hy'phen·at'ed	hyp'o·crite	hy'po·thet'i·cal
hy'phen·a'tion	hyp'o·crit'i·cal	hy'po·thet'i·cal·ly
hyp·no'sis	hy'po·der'mic	hys·te'ri·a
hyp·not'ic	hy'po·der'mi·cal·ly	hys·ter'i·cal
hyp'no·tist	hy·pot'e·nuse	hys·ter'ics
hyp'no·tize	hy·poth'e·cate	hys'ter·oid

I

i·am'bic

I·be'ri·an

i'bex

i'bis

ice

ice'berg'

ice'boat'

ice'box'

ice'break'er

ice'house'

ice'man'

ich·neu'mon

i'chor

ich'thy·ol'o·gy

i'ci·cle

i'ci·er

i'ci·est

i'ci·ly

i'ci·ness

i'con

i'cy

i·de'a

i·de'al

i·de'al·ism

i·de'al·ist

i·de'al·is'tic

i·de'al·i·za'tion

i·de'al·ize

i·de'al·ly

i'de·a'tion

i'de·a'tion·al

i·den'ti·cal

i·den'ti·fi·ca'tion

i·den'ti·fy

i·den'ti·ty

id'e·o·log'i·cal

id'e·ol'o·gy

id'i·o·cy

id'i·om

id'i·o·mat'ic

id'i·o·mat'i·cal·ly

id'i·o·syn'cra·sy

id'i·o·syn·crat'ic

id'i·ot

id'i·ot'ic

id'i·ot'i·cal·ly

i'dle

i'dled

i'dle·ness

i'dler

i'dlest

i'dly

i'dol

i·dol'a·ter

i·dol'a·trize

i·dol'a·trous

i·dol'a·try

i'dol·ize

i'dyl

i·dyl'lic

if

ig'loo

ig'ne·ous

ig·nite'

ig·nit'ed

ig·ni'tion

ig·no′ble

ig′no·min′i·ous

ig′no·min·y

ig′no·ra′mus

ig′no·rance

ig′no·rant

ig′no·rant·ly

ig·nore′

ig·nored′

i·gua′na

i′lex

Il′i·ad

ilk

ill

il·le′gal

il′le·gal′i·ty

il·leg′i·ble

il·leg′i·bly

il′le·git′i·ma·cy

il′le·git′i·mate

il·lib′er·al

il·lic′it

il·lim′it·a·ble

il·lit′er·a·cy

il·lit′er·ate

ill′ness

il·log′i·cal

il·lu′mi·nant

il·lu′mi·nate

il·lu′mi·nat′ed

il·lu′mi·na′tion

il·lu′mi·na′tor

il·lu′mine

il·lu′mined

il·lu′sion

il·lu′sive

il·lu′so·ry

il′lus·trate

il′lus·trat′ed

il′lus·tra′tion

il·lus′tra·tive

il′lus·tra′tor

il·lus′tri·ous

im′age

im′age·ry

im·ag′i·na·ble

im·ag′i·nar′y

im·ag′i·na′tion

im·ag′i·na′tive

im·ag′ine

im·ag′ined

im·ag′in·ings

i·ma′go

i·mam′

im′be·cile

im′be·cil′i·ty

im·bibe′

im·bibed′

im·bro′glio

im·bue′

im·bued′

im′i·ta·ble

im′i·tate

im′i·tat′ed

im′i·ta′tion

im′i·ta′tive

im′i·ta′tor

im·mac′u·late

im·mac′u·late·ly

im′ma·nent

im·ma·te′ri·al

im·ma·ture′

im·ma·ture′ly

im·ma·tu′ri·ty

im·meas′ur·a·ble

im·me′di·a·cy

im·me′di·ate

im·me′di·ate·ly

im·me′di·ate·ness

im′me·mo′ri·al

im·mense′

im·mense′ly

im·men′si·ty

im·merse′

im·mersed′

im·mer′sion

im′mi·grant

im′mi·grate

im′mi·grat′ed

im′mi·gra′tion

im′mi·nence

im′mi·nent

im·mo′bile

im′mo·bil′i·ty

im′mo·bi·li·za′tion

im·mo′bi·lize

im·mod'er·ate

im·mod'est

im'mo·late

im'mo·la'tion

im·mor'al

im'mo·ral'i·ty

im·mor'al·ly

im·mor'tal

im'mor·tal'i·ty

im·mor'tal·ize

im·mor'tal·ly

im'mor·telle'

im·mov'a·bil'i·ty

im·mov'a·ble

im·mov'a·ble·ness

im·mov'a·bly

im·mune'

im·mu'ni·ty

im'mu·ni·za'tion

im'mu·nize

im'mu·nol'o·gy

im·mure'

im'mu·ta·bil'i·ty

im·mu'ta·ble

imp

im'pact

im·pac'tion

im·pair'

im·paired'

im·pair'ment

im·pa'la

im·pale'

im·paled'

im·pale'ment

im·pal'pa·bil'i·ty

im·pal'pa·ble

im·pan'el

im·pan'eled

im·part'

im·part'ed

im·par'tial

im'par·ti·al'i·ty

im·par'tial·ly

im·pass'a·bil'i·ty

im·pass'a·ble

im·passe'

im·pas'sion

im·pas'sioned

im·pas'sive

im·pas'sive·ly

im'pas·siv'i·ty

im·pa'tience

im·pa'tient

im·peach'

im·peach'ment

im·pec'ca·bil'i·ty

im·pec'ca·ble

im'pe·cu'ni·os'i·ty

im'pe·cu'ni·ous

im·ped'ance

im·pede'

im·ped'ed

im·ped'i·ment

im·ped'i·men'ta

im·pel'

im·pelled'

im·pend'

im·pend'ed

im·pen'e·tra·bil'i·ty

im·pen'e·tra·ble

im·pen'i·tent

im·per'a·tive

im'per·cep'ti·ble

im'per·cep'tive

im·per'fect

im'per·fec'tion

im·per'fo·rate

im·pe'ri·al

im·pe'ri·al·ism

im·pe'ri·al·ist

im·pe'ri·al·is'tic

im·pe'ri·ous

im·per'ish·a·ble

im·per'ma·nent

im·per'me·a·ble

im'per·scrip'ti·ble

im·per'son·al

im·per'son·ate

im·per'son·at'ed

im·per'son·a'tion

im·per'ti·nence

im·per'ti·nent

im'per·turb'a·ble

im·per'vi·ous

im'pe·ti'go

im·pet'u·os'i·ty

im·pet′u·ous

im·pet′u·ous·ly

im·pet′u·ous·ness

im′pe·tus

im·pi′e·ty

im·pinge′

im·pinged′

im·pinge′ment

im′pi·ous

im′pi·ous·ly

imp′ish

im·pla′ca·bil′i·ty

im·pla′ca·ble

im·plant′

im·plant′ed

im·plau′si·bil′i·ty

im·plau′si·ble

im′ple·ment

im′ple·ment′ed

im′pli·cate

im′pli·cat′ed

im′pli·ca′tion

im·plic′it

im·plic′it·ly

im·plied′

im′plo·ra′tion

im·plore′

im·plored′

im·plor′ing·ly

im·plo′sion

im·ply′

im′po·lite′

im′po·lite′ly

im′po·lite′ness

im·pol′i·tic

im·pon′der·a·ble

im·port′

im·por′tance

im·por′tant

im′por·ta′tion

im′port′er

im·por′tu·nate

im′por·tune′

im′por·tu′ni·ty

im·pose′

im·posed′

im·pos′ing·ly

im′po·si′tion

im·pos′si·bil′i·ty

im·pos′si·ble

im′post

im·pos′tor

im·pos′ture

im′po·tence

im′po·tent

im·pound′

im·pov′er·ish

im·pov′er·ish·ment

im·pow′er

im·prac′ti·ca·ble

im·prac′ti·cal′i·ty

im′pre·cate

im′pre·ca′tion

im′pre·ca·to′ry

im·preg′na·bil′i·ty

im·preg′na·ble

im·preg′nate

im′preg·na′tion

im′pre·sa′ri·o

im′pre·scrip′ti·ble

im·press′

im·pressed′

im·pres′sion

im·pres′sion·a·ble

im·pres′sion·ism

im·pres′sive

im′pri·ma′tur

im·print′

im·print′ed

im·pris′on

im·pris′oned

im·pris′on·ment

im′prob·a·bil′i·ty

im·prob′a·ble

im·prob′a·bly

im·promp′tu

im·prop′er

im′pro·pri′e·ty

im·prov′a·ble

im·prove′

im·prove′ment

im·prov′i·dence

im·prov′i·dent

im′pro·vi·sa′tion

im′pro·vise

im′pro·vised

im·pru'dence
im·pru'dent
im·pru'dent·ly
im'pu·dence
im'pu·dent
im·pugn'
im·pugn'a·ble
im·pugned'
im·pugn'ment
im'pulse
im·pul'sion
im·pul'sive
im·pu'ni·ty
im·pure'
im·pure'ly
im·pu'ri·ty
im·put'a·ble
im'pu·ta'tion
im·put'a·tive
im·pute'
im·put'ed
in·a·bil'i·ty
in'ac·ces'si·bil'i·ty
in'ac·ces'si·ble
in·ac'cu·ra·cy
in·ac'cu·rate
in·ac'tion
in·ac'ti·vate
in·ac'tive
in·ac'tiv'i·ty
in·ad'e·qua·cy
in·ad'e·quate

in'ad·mis'si·bil'i·ty
in'ad·mis'si·ble
in'ad·vert'ence
in'ad·vert'ent
in'ad·vis'a·bil'i·ty
in'ad·vis'a·ble
in·al'ien·a·ble
in·am'o·ra'ta
in·ane'
in·an'i·mate
in·a'ni'tion
in·an'i·ty
in·ap'pli·ca·ble
in·ap'po·site
in'ap·pro'pri·ate
in·apt'
in·apt'i·tude
in'ar·tic'u·late
in'ar·tis'tic
in'as·much'
in'at·ten'tion
in'at·ten'tive
in·au'di·bil'i·ty
in·au'di·ble
in·au'di·bly
in·au'gu·ral
in·au'gu·rate
in·au'gu·rat'ed
in·au'gu·ra'tion
in'aus·pi'cious
in'board'
in'born'

in'bred'
in·cal'cu·la·ble
in'can·desce'
in'can·des'cence
in'can·des'cent
in'can·ta'tion
in'ca·pa·bil'i·ty
in·ca'pa·ble
in'ca·pac'i·tate
in'ca·pac'i·tat'ed
in'ca·pac'i·ta'tion
in'ca·pac'i·ty
in·car'cer·ate
in·car'cer·at'ed
in·car'cer·a'tion
in·car'nate
in'car·na'tion
in·cen'di·a·rism
in·cen'di·ar'y
in·cense'
in·censed'
in·cen'tive
in·cep'tion
in·cer'ti·tude
in·ces'sant
in·ces'sant·ly
in'cest
in·ces'tu·ous
inch
in·cho'ate
inch'worm'
in'ci·dence

in'ci·dent

in'ci·den'tal

in'ci·den'tal·ly

in·cin'er·ate

in·cin'er·at'ed

in·cin'er·a'tion

in·cin'er·a'tor

in·cip'i·ent

in·cise'

in·cised'

in·ci'sion

in·ci'sive

in·ci'sive·ly

in·ci'sive·ness

in·ci'sor

in'ci·ta'tion

in·cite'

in·cite'ment

in'ci·vil'i·ty

in·clem'en·cy

in·clem'ent

in'cli·na'tion

in·cline'

in·clined'

in·close'

in·closed'

in·clo'sure

in·clude'

in·clud'ed

in·clu'sive

in·clu'sive·ly

in·clu'sive·ness

in·cog'ni·to

in'co·her'ence

in'co·her'ent

in'com·bus'ti·bil'i·ty

in'com·bus'ti·ble

in'come

in'com·men'su·ra·ble

in'com·men'su·rate

in'com·mode'

in'com·mu'ni·ca'do

in·com'pa·ra·ble

in·com'pa·ra·bly

in'com·pat'i·bil'i·ty

in'com·pat'i·ble

in·com'pe·tence

in·com'pe·tent

in·com'pe·tent·ly

in'com·plete'

in'com·pre·hen'si·bil'i·ty

in'com·pre·hen'si·ble

in'com·press'i·bil'i·ty

in'com·press'i·ble

in'con·ceiv'a·bil'i·ty

in'con·ceiv'a·ble

in'con·clu'sive

in'con·clu'sive·ness

in'con·gru'i·ty

in·con'gru·ous

in'con·se·quen'tial

in'con·sid'er·a·ble

in'con·sid'er·ate

in'con·sid'er·ate·ly

in'con·sist'en·cy

in'con·sist'ent

in'con·sol'a·ble

in'con·spic'u·ous

in'con·spic'u·ous·ly

in·con'stan·cy

in·con'stant

in'con·test'a·ble

in·con'ti·nence

in·con'ti·nent

in'con·tro·vert'i·ble

in'con·ven'ience

in'con·ven'ienced

in'con·ven'ient

in'con·ven'ient·ly

in'con·ver'si·bil'i·ty

in'con·vert'i·bil'i·ty

in'con·vert'i·ble

in·cor'po·rate

in·cor'po·rat'ed

in·cor'po·ra'tion

in·cor'po·ra'tor

in'cor·rect'

in·cor'ri·gi·bil'i·ty

in·cor'ri·gi·ble

in'cor·rupt'i·bil'i·ty

in'cor·rupt'i·ble

in·crease'

in·creased'

in·creas'ing·ly

in·cred'i·bil'i·ty

in·cred'i·ble

in·cre·du'li·ty

in·cred'u·lous

in'cre·ment

in'cre·men'tal

in·cre'tion

in·crim'i·nate

in·crim'i·nat'ed

in·crim'i·na'tion

in·crim'i·na·to'ry

in'crus·ta'tion

in'cu·bate

in'cu·bat'ed

in'cu·ba'tion

in'cu·ba'tor

in'cu·bus

in·cul'cate

in·cul'cat·ed

in·cul·ca'tion

in·cul'pate

in·cul'pat·ed

in'cul·pa'tion

in·cul'pa·to'ry

in·cum'ben·cy

in·cum'bent

in'cu·nab'u·la

in·cur'

in·cur'a·ble

in·cur'a·bly

in·curred'

in·cur'sion

in·debt'ed

in·debt'ed·ness

in·de'cen·cy

in·de'cent

in·de'cent·ly

in·de·ci'sion

in·de·ci'sive

in·de·ci'sive·ly

in·de·ci'sive·ness

in·dec'o·rous

in·de·co'rum

in·deed'

in'de·fat'i·ga·bil'i·ty

in'de·fat'i·ga·ble

in'de·fea'si·ble

in'de·fen'si·ble

in'de·fin'a·ble

in·def'i·nite

in·def'i·nite·ly

in·def'i·nite·ness

in·del'i·bil'i·ty

in·del'i·ble

in·del'i·bly

in·del'i·ca·cy

in·del'i·cate

in·del'i·cate·ly

in·dem'ni·fi·ca'tion

in·dem'ni·fied

in·dem'ni·fy

in·dem'ni·ty

in·dent'

in'den·ta'tion

in·dent'ed

in·den'tion

in·den'ture

in·den'tured

in'de·pend'ence

in'de·pend'ent

in'de·scrib'a·ble

in'de·struct'i·ble

in'de·ter'mi·na·ble

in'de·ter'mi·nate

in'dex

in'dexed

in'dex·er

in'dex·es

In'di·an

in'di·cate

in'di·cat'ed

in'di·ca'tion

in·dic'a·tive

in'di·ca'tor

in'di·ca·to'ry

in'di·ces

in·di'ci·a

in·dict'

in·dict'a·ble

in·dict'ed

in·dict'ment

in·dif'fer·ence

in·dif'fer·ent

in·dif'fer·ent·ly

in'di·gence

in·dig'e·nous

in'di·gent

in'di·gest'i·bil'i·ty

in′di·gest′i·ble

in′di·ges′tion

in·dig′nant

in·dig′nant·ly

in′dig·na′tion

in·dig′ni·ty

in′di·go

in′di·rect′

in′di·rec′tion

in′di·rect′ly

in′di·rect′ness

in′dis·creet′

in′dis·creet′ly

in′dis·cre′tion

in′dis·crim′i·nate

in′dis·crim′i·nate·ly

in′dis·pen′sa·bil′i·ty

in′dis·pen′sa·ble

in′dis·pose′

in′dis·posed′

in′dis·po·si′tion

in·dis′pu·ta·ble

in·dis′so·lu·ble

in·dis′so·lu·bly

in′dis·tinct′

in′dis·tinct′ly

in·dis·tin′guish·a·ble

in·dite′

in·dit′ed

in′di·um

in′di·vid′u·al

in′di·vid′u·al·ism

in′di·vid′u·al·ist

in′di·vid′u·al′i·ty

in′di·vid′u·al·ize

in′di·vid′u·al·ly

in′di·vis′i·bil′i·ty

in′di·vis′i·ble

in·doc′tri·nate

in·doc′tri·nat′ed

in·doc′tri·na′tion

in′do·lence

in′do·lent

in′do·lent·ly

in·dom′i·ta·ble

in′doors′

in·dorse′

in·dorsed′

in·dorse′ment

in·dors′er

in·du′bi·ta·ble

in·duce′

in·duced′

in·duce′ment

in·duct′

in·duct′ance

in·duct′ed

in·duc′tion

in·duc′tive

in·duc′tor

in·due′

in·dued′

in·dulge′

in·dul′gence

in·dul′gent

in·dul′gent·ly

in′du·rate

in′du·rat′ed

in·dus′tri·al

in·dus′tri·al·ly

in·dus′tri·al·ism

in·dus′tri·al·ist

in·dus′tri·al·i·za′tion

in·dus′tri·al·ize

in·dus′tri·al·ized

in·dus′tri·ous

in·dus′tri·ous·ly

in·dus′tri·ous·ness

in′dus·try

in·e′bri·ate

in·e′bri·at′ed

in·e′bri·a′tion

in·e·bri′e·ty

in·ed′i·ble

in·ef′fa·ble

in·ef′fa·bly

in′ef·fec′tive

in′ef·fec′tu·al

in′ef·fec′tu·al·ly

in′ef·fi·ca′cious

in′ef·fi′cien·cy

in′ef·fi′cient

in′ef·fi′cient·ly

in′e·las′tic

in′e·las·tic′i·ty

in·el′e·gance

in·el'e·gant

in·el'e·gant·ly

in·el'i·gi·bil'i·ty

in·el'i·gi·ble

in·e·luc'ta·ble

in·ept'

in·ept'i·tude

in·e·qual'i·ty

in·eq'ui·ta·ble

in·eq'ui·ty

in·e·rad'i·ca·ble

in·e·rad'i·ca·bly

in·er'ran·cy

in·er'rant

in·ert'

in·er'tia

in·ert'ly

in·ert'ness

in·es·sen'tial

in·es'ti·ma·ble

in·es'ti·ma·bly

in·ev'i·ta·bil'i·ty

in·ev'i·ta·ble

in·ev'i·ta·bly

in'ex·act'

in'ex·act'i·tude

in'ex·cus'a·ble

in'ex·cus'a·bly

in'ex·haust'i·ble

in'ex·haust'i·bly

in·ex'o·ra·ble

in'ex·pe'di·ence

in'ex·pe'di·en·cy

in'ex·pe'di·ent

in'ex·pen'sive

in'ex·pe'ri·ence

in'ex·pert'

in·ex'pli·ca·ble

in·ex'pli·ca·bly

in·ex'tri·ca·ble

in·fal'li·bil'i·ty

in·fal'li·ble

in'fa·mous

in'fa·my

in'fan·cy

in'fant

in·fan'ti·cide

in'fan·tile

in'fan·ti·lism

in'fan·try

in'fan·try·man

in·farct'

in·farc'tion

in·fat'u·ate

in·fat'u·at'ed

in·fat'u·a'tion

in·fea'si·ble

in·fect'

in·fect'ed

in·fec'tion

in·fec'tious

in·fec'tious·ly

in·fec'tious·ness

in'fe·lic'i·tous

in'fe·lic'i·ty

in·fer'

in'fer·ence

in'fer·en'tial

in·fe'ri·or

in·fe'ri·or'i·ty

in·fer'nal

in·fer'nal·ly

in·fer'no

in·ferred'

in·fer'tile

in'fer·til'i·ty

in·fest'

in'fes·ta'tion

in'fi·del

in'fi·del'i·ty

in'field'

in'field'er

in·fil'trate

in·fil'trat·ed

in'fil·tra'tion

in'fi·nite

in·fin'i·tes'i·mal

in·fin'i·tes'i·mal·ly

in·fin'i·tive

in·fin'i·tude

in·fin'i·ty

in·firm'

in·fir'ma·ry

in·fir'mi·ty

in·flame'

in·flamed'

in·flam′ma·bil′i·ty
in·flam′ma·ble
in·flam′ma·bly
in′flam·ma′tion
in·flam′ma·to′ry
in·flate′
in·flat′ed
in·fla′tion
in·fla′tion·ar′y
in·fla′tion·ist
in·flect′
in·flect′ed
in·flec′tion
in·flex′i·bil′i·ty
in·flex′i·ble
in·flict′
in·flict′ed
in·flic′tion
in′flu·ence
in′flu·enced
in′flu·en′tial
in′flu·en′tial·ly
in′flu·en′za
in′flux
in·form′
in·for′mal
in′for·mal′i·ty
in·for′mal·ly
in·form′ant
in′for·ma′tion
in·form′a·tive
in·formed′

in·form′er
in·form′ing·ly
in·frac′tion
in·fran′gi·ble
in′fra·red′
in·fre′quent
in·fre′quent·ly
in·fringe′
in·fringed′
in·fringe′ment
in·fu′ri·ate
in·fu′ri·at′ed
in·fuse′
in·fused′
in·fus′es
in·fu′sion
in·gen′ious
in·gen′ious·ly
in′ge·nu′i·ty
in·gen′u·ous
in·gest′
in·gest′ed
in·ges′tion
in·ges′tive
in·glo′ri·ous
in′got
in·grain′
in·grained′
in′grate
in·gra′ti·ate
in·gra′ti·a′tion
in·gra′ti·a·to′ry

in·grat′i·tude
in·gre′di·ent
in′gress
in′grown′
in·hab′it
in·hab′it·a·ble
in·hab′it·ance
in·hab′it·ant
in·hab′i·ta′tion
in·hab′it·ed
in′ha·la′tion
in·hale′
in·haled′
in·hal′er
in′har·mo′ni·ous
in·here′
in·hered′
in·her′ence
in·her′ent
in·her′ent·ly
in·her′it
in·her′it·a·ble
in·her′it·ance
in·her′it·ed
in·her′i·tor
in·hib′it
in·hib′it·ed
in′hi·bi′tion
in·hib′i·to′ry
in·hos′pi·ta·ble
in·hos′pi·ta·bly
in·hos′pi·tal′i·ty

in·hu·man

in·hu·mane'

in·hu·man'i·ty

in·hu·ma'tion

in·hume'

in·humed'

in·im'i·cal

in·im'i·ta·ble

in·im'i·ta·bly

in·iq'ui·tous

in·iq'ui·tous·ly

in·iq'ui·ty

in·i'tial

in·i'tialed

in·i'tial·ly

in·i'ti·ate

in·i'ti·at'ed

in·i'ti·a'tion

in·i'ti·a'tive

in·i'ti·a'tor

in·i'ti·a·to'ry

in·ject'

in·ject'ed

in·jec'tion

in·jec'tor

in'ju·di'cious

in'ju·di'cious·ly

in·junc'tion

in·junc'tive

in'jure

in'jured

in·ju'ri·ous

in'ju·ry

in·jus'tice

in·jus'tic·es

ink

inked

ink'horn'

ink'ling

ink'lings

ink'stand'

ink'well'

ink'y

in·laid'

in'land

in·lay'

in·let'

in'mate

in'most

inn

in'nate

in'nate·ly

in'ner

in'ner·most

in'ning

in'nings

inn'keep'er

in'no·cence

in'no·cent

in'no·cent·ly

in·noc'u·ous

in·noc'u·ous·ly

in'no·vate

in'no·va'tion

in'no·va'tive

in'no·va'tor

in'nu·en'do

in·nu'mer·a·ble

in'ob·serv'ant

in·oc'u·late

in·oc'u·lat'ed

in·oc'u·la'tion

in·of·fen'sive

in·op'er·a·ble

in·op'er·a'tive

in·op'por·tune'

in·or'di·nate

in·or·gan'ic

in'pa'tient

in'put'

in'quest

in·qui'e·tude

in·quire'

in·quired'

in·quir'er

in·quires'

in·quir'ies

in·quir'ing·ly

in·quir'y

in'qui·si'tion

in·quis'i·tive

in·quis'i·tor

in·quis'i·to'ri·al

in·road'

in·rush'

in·sane'

in·sane′ly
in·san′i·tar′y
in·san′i·ta′tion
in·san′i·ty
in·sa′ti·a·bil′i·ty
in·sa′ti·a·ble
in·scribe′
in·scribed′
in·scrib′er
in·scrip′tion
in·scru′ta·bil′i·ty
in·scru′ta·ble
in′sect
in·sec′ti·cide
in′sec·tiv′o·rous
in′se·cure′
in′se·cu′ri·ty
in·sen′sate
in·sen′si·bil′i·ty
in·sen′si·ble
in·sen′si·tive
in·sen′si·tive·ness
in·sen′ti·ence
in·sen′ti·ent
in·sep′a·ra·ble
in·sep′a·ra·bly
in·sert′
in·sert′ed
in·ser′tion
in′set′
in′shore′
in′side′

in′sid′er
in·sides′
in·sid′i·ous
in·sid′i·ous·ly
in′sight′
in·sig′ne
in·sig′ni·a
in′sig·nif′i·cance
in′sig·nif′i·cant
in′sig·nif′i·cant·ly
in′sin·cere′
in′sin·cere′ly
in′sin·cer′i·ty
in·sin′u·ate
in·sin′u·at′ed
in·sin′u·at′ing·ly
in·sin′u·a′tion
in·sin′u·a′tive
in·sip′id
in′si·pid′i·ty
in·sip′id·ly
in·sist′
in·sist′ed
in·sist′ence
in·sist′ent
in·sist′ent·ly
in′so·bri′e·ty
in′sole′
in′so·lence
in′so·lent
in′so·lent·ly
in·sol′u·bil′i·ty

in·sol′u·ble
in·solv′a·ble
in·sol′ven·cy
in·sol′vent
in·som′ni·a
in·som′ni·ac
in′so·much′
in·sou′ci·ance
in·sou′ci·ant
in·spect′
in·spect′ed
in·spec′tion
in·spec′tor
in·spec′tor·ate
in′spi·ra′tion
in′spi·ra′tion·al
in′spi·ra′tion·al·ly
in·spir′a·to′ry
in·spire′
in·spired′
in·spir′er
in·spir′ing·ly
in·spir′it·ing·ly
in′sta·bil′i·ty
in·stall′
in′stal·la′tion
in·stalled′
in·stall′ment
in′stance
in′stant
in′stan·ta′ne·ous
in·stan′ter

in'stant·ly	in'stru·men·ta'tion	in·tagl'io
in·state'	in'sub·or'di·nate	in'take'
in·stat'ed	in'sub·or'di·na'tion	in·tan'gi·bil'i·ty
in·stead'	in·suf'fer·a·ble	in·tan'gi·ble
in'step	in'suf·fi'cien·cy	in·tar'si·a
in'sti·gate	in'suf·fi'cient	in'te·ger
in'sti·gat'ed	in'su·lar	in'te·gral
in'sti·ga'tion	in'su·lar'i·ty	in'te·gral·ly
in'sti·ga'tor	in'su·late	in'te·grate
in·still'	in'su·lat'ed	in'te·grat'ed
in·stilled'	in'su·la'tion	in'te·gra'tion
in·stinct'	in'su·la'tor	in·teg'ri·ty
in·stinc'tive	in'su·lin	in·teg'u·ment
in·stinc'tive·ly	in·sult'	in'tel·lect
in·stinc'tu·al	in·sult'ed	in'tel·lec'tu·al
in'sti·tute	in·sult'ing·ly	in'tel·lec'tu·al·ism
in'sti·tut'ed	in·su'per·a·ble	in'tel·lec'tu·al·ize
in'sti·tu'tion	in'sup·port'a·ble	in'tel·lec'tu·al·ly
in'sti·tu'tion·al	in'sup·press'i·ble	in·tel'li·gence
in'sti·tu'tion·al·ize	in·sur'a·bil'i·ty	in·tel'li·gent
in'sti·tu'tion·al·ly	in·sur'a·ble	in·tel'li·gent'si·a
in·struct'	in·sur'ance	in·tel'li·gi·bil'i·ty
in·struct'ed	in·sure'	in·tel'li·gi·ble
in·struc'tion	in·sured'	in·tem'per·ance
in·struc'tion·al	in·sur'er	in·tem'per·ate
in·struc'tive	in·sur'gen·cy	in·tem'per·ate·ly
in·struc'tor	in·sur'gent	in·tend'
in'stru·ment	in'sur·mount'a·ble	in·tend'ant
in'stru·men'tal	in'sur·rec'tion	in·tend'ed
in'stru·men'tal·ist	in'sur·rec'tion·ar'y	in·tense'
in'stru·men'tal'i·ty	in'sur·rec'tion·ist	in·ten'si·fi·ca'tion
in'stru·men'tal·ly	in·tact'	in·ten'si·fi'er

in·ten'si·fy

in·ten'si·ty

in·ten'sive

in·tent'

in·ten'tion

in·ten'tion·al

in·ten'tion·al·ly

in·tent'ly

in·tent'ness

in'ter·act'

in'ter·ac'tion

in'ter·bor'ough

in'ter·breed'

in'ter·cede'

in'ter·ced'ed

in'ter·cept'

in'ter·cept'ed

in'ter·cep'tion

in'ter·cep'tor

in'ter·ces'sion

in'ter·ces'so·ry

in'ter·change'

in'ter·change'a·bil'i·ty

in'ter·change'a·ble

in'ter·col·le'gi·ate

in'ter·com·mu'ni·cate

in'ter·con·nect'

in'ter·cos'tal

in'ter·course

in'ter·de·nom'i·na'tion·al

in'ter·de·part·men'tal

in'ter·de·pend'ence

in'ter·de·pend'ent

in'ter·dict

in'ter·dic'tion

in'ter·est

in'ter·est·ed

in'ter·est·ed·ly

in'ter·est·ing·ly

in'ter·fere'

in'ter·fered'

in'ter·fer'ence

in'ter·fer'ing·ly

in'ter·im

in·te'ri·or

in'ter·ject'

in'ter·ject'ed

in'ter·jec'tion

in'ter·lace'

in'ter·laced'

in'ter·lard'

in'ter·leaf'

in'ter·leave'

in'ter·line'

in'ter·lin'e·al

in'ter·lin'e·ar

in'ter·lin'e·a'tion

in'ter·lined'

in'ter·lock'

in'ter·locked'

in'ter·loc'u·tor

in'ter·loc'u·to'ry

in'ter·lop'er

in'ter·lude

in'ter·mar'riage

in'ter·mar'ry

in'ter·me'di·ar'y

in'ter·me'di·ate

in·ter'ment

in'ter·mez'zo

in·ter'mi·na·ble

in·ter'mi·na·bly

in·ter'min'gle

in·ter'min'gled

in·ter'mis'sion

in·ter'mit'

in·ter'mit'tence

in·ter'mit'tent

in·ter'mit'tent·ly

in'ter·mix'ture

in·tern'

in·ter'nal

in·ter'nal·ly

in'ter·na'tion·al

in'ter·na'tion·al·ize

in'ter·na'tion·al·ly

in'terne

in'ter·ne'cine

in·terned'

in·tern'ment

in·ter'pel'late

in·ter'pel·la'tion

in'ter·plan'e·tar'y

in·ter'po·late

in·ter'po·lat'ed

in·ter'po·la'tion

in·ter·pose'

in·ter·posed'

in·ter·po·si'tion

in·ter'pret

in·ter'pre·ta'tion

in·ter'pre·ta'tive

in·ter'pret·ed

in·ter'pret·er

in·ter·reg'num

in·ter·re·la'tion

in·ter'ro·gate

in·ter'ro·ga'tion

in·ter·rog'a·tive

in·ter·rog'a·to'ry

in·ter·rupt'

in·ter·rupt'ed·ly

in·ter·rup'tion

in·ter·scap'u·lar

in·ter·scho·las'tic

in·ter·sect'

in·ter·sect'ed

in·ter·sperse'

in·ter·spersed'

in'ter·state'

in'ter·stel'lar

in·ter'stice

in·ter'stic·es

in·ter·sti'tial

in·ter·sti'tial·ly

in·ter·twine'

in·ter·twined'

In'ter·type

in'ter·ur'ban

in'ter·val

in'ter·vene'

in'ter·vened'

in'ter·ven'tion

in'ter·ven'tion·ist

in'ter·ver'te·bral

in'ter·view

in'ter·viewed

in'ter·view'er

in'ter·weave'

in'ter·wo'ven

in·tes'ta·cy

in·tes'tate

in·tes'ti·nal

in·tes'tine

in'ti·ma·cy

in'ti·mate

in'ti·mat'ed

in'ti·mate·ly

in'ti·ma'tion

in·tim'i·date

in·tim'i·dat'ed

in·tim'i·da'tion

in'to

in·tol'er·a·ble

in·tol'er·ance

in·tol'er·ant

in'to·na'tion

in·tone'

in·toned'

in·tox'i·cate

in·tox'i·cat'ed

in·tox'i·cat'ing·ly

in·tox'i·ca'tion

in·trac'ta·bil'i·ty

in·trac'ta·ble

in'tra·mu'ral

in·tran'si·gence

in·tran'si·gent

in·tran'si·tive

in'tra·state'

in·trench'ment

in·trep'id

in'tre·pid'i·ty

in·trep'id·ly

in'tri·ca·cies

in'tri·ca·cy

in'tri·cate

in'tri·cate·ly

in·trigue'

in·trigued'

in·trin'sic

in·trin'si·cal

in·trin'si·cal·ly

in'tro·duce'

in'tro·duced'

in'tro·duc'tion

in'tro·duc'to·ry

in·tro'it

in'tro·jec'tion

in'tro·spect'

in'tro·spec'tion

in'tro·spec'tive

in'tro·ver'sion

in'tro·vert'

in'tro·vert'ed

in·trude'

in·trud'ed

in·trud'er

in·tru'sion

in·tru'sive

in·tru'sive·ly

in·tu·i'tion

in·tu·i'tion·al

in·tu'i·tive

in·tu'i·tive·ly

in'tu·mesce'

in'tu·mes'cence

in'tu·mes'cent

in·unc'tion

in'un·date

in'un·dat'ed

in'un·da'tion

in·ure'

in·ured'

in·ur'ed·ness

in·urn'

in·vade'

in·vad'ed

in'va·lid

in·val'i·date

in·val'i·dat'ed

in·val'i·da'tion

in'va·lid'i·ty

in·val'u·a·ble

In·var'

in·var'i·a·bil'i·ty

in·var'i·a·ble

in·var'i·a·ble·ness

in·va'sion

in·va'sive

in·vec'tive

in·veigh'

in·vei'gle

in·vei'gled

in·vent'

in·vent'ed

in·ven'tion

in·ven'tive

in·ven'tive·ly

in·ven'tive·ness

in·ven'tor

in'ven·to'ry

in·verse'

in·ver'sion

in·vert'

in·vert'ed

in·vert'i·ble

in·vest'

in·vest'ed

in·ves'ti·gate

in·ves'ti·gat'ed

in·ves'ti·ga'tion

in·ves'ti·ga'tive

in·ves'ti·ga'tor

in·ves'ti·ture

in·vest'ment

in·ves'tor

in·vet'er·ate

in·vid'i·ous

in·vid'i·ous·ly

in·vig'i·late

in·vig'or·ate

in·vig'or·at'ed

in·vig'or·at'ing·ly

in·vig'or·a'tion

in·vig'or·a'tive

in·vin'ci·bil'i·ty

in·vin'ci·ble

in·vi'o·la·bil'i·ty

in·vi'o·la·ble

in·vi'o·late

in·vis'i·bil'i·ty

in·vis'i·ble

in·vis'i·bly

in'vi·ta'tion

in'vi·ta'tion·al

in·vite'

in·vit'ed

in·vit'ing·ly

in'vo·ca'tion

in'voice

in'voiced

in'voic·es

in·voke'

in·voked'

in·vol'un·tar'i·ly

in·vol'un·tar'y

in'vo·lute

in'vo·lu'tion	i·ri'tis	ir're·den'ta
in·volve'	irk	ir're·duc'i·ble
in·volved'	irked	ir·ref'ra·ga·ble
in·vul'ner·a·bil'i·ty	irk'some	ir're·fran'gi·ble
in·vul'ner·a·ble	i'ron	ir·ref'u·ta·ble
in'ward	i'ron·bound'	ir·reg'u·lar
in'ward·ly	i'ron·clad'	ir·reg'u·lar'i·ty
in'ward·ness	i'roned	ir·reg'u·lar·ly
i'o·date	i·ron'ic	ir·rel'e·vance
i·od'ic	i·ron'i·cal	ir·rel'e·vant
i'o·dide	i·ron'i·cal·ly	ir're·li'gious
i'o·dine	i'ron·ings	ir're·me'di·a·ble
i'o·dize	i'ron·side'	ir're·mis'si·ble
i·o'do·form	i'ron·ware'	ir're·mov'a·ble
i'on	i'ron·weed'	ir·rep'a·ra·ble
I·on'ic	i'ron·wood'	ir're·place'a·ble
i'on·i·za'tion	i'ron·work'	ir're·press'i·ble
i'on·ize	i'ron·work'er	ir're·proach'a·ble
i·o'ta	i'ro·ny	ir're·sist'i·ble
ip'e·cac	Ir'o·quois	ir·res'o·lute
I·ra'ni·an	ir·ra'di·ate	ir·res'o·lu'tion
i·ras'ci·bil'i·ty	ir·ra'di·at'ed	ir're·solv'a·ble
i·ras'ci·ble	ir·ra'di·a'tion	ir're·spec'tive
i'rate	ir·ra'tion·al	ir're·spon'si·bil'i·ty
i'rate·ly	ir·ra'tion·al'i·ty	ir're·spon'si·ble
ire	ir·ra'tion·al·ly	ir're·spon'si·bly
ir'i·des'cence	ir're·claim'a·ble	ir're·trace'a·ble
ir'i·des'cent	ir·rec'on·cil'a·ble	ir're·triev'a·ble
i·rid'i·um	ir·rec'on·cil'i·a·bil'i·ty	ir·rev'er·ence
i'ris	ir·rec'on·cil'i·a·ble	ir·rev'er·ent
I'rish	ir're·cov'er·a·ble	ir're·vers'i·ble
I'rish·man	ir're·deem'a·ble	ir·rev'o·ca·ble

ir'ri·ga·ble

ir'ri·gate

ir'ri·gat'ed

ir'ri·ga'tion

ir'ri·ta·bil'i·ty

ir'ri·ta·ble

ir'ri·tant

ir'ri·tate

ir'ri·tat'ed

ir'ri·ta'tion

ir'ri·ta'tive

ir·rup'tion

ir·rup'tive

is'chi·um

i'sin·glass'

Is'lam

is'land

is'land·er

isle

is'let

i'so·bar

i'so·late

i'so·lat'ed

i·so·la'tion

i'so·la'tion·ism

i'so·la'tion·ist

i'so·mer

i'so·mer'ic

i'so·mor'phic

i·sos'ce·les

i'so·therm

i'so·tope

is'su·ance

is'sue

is'sued

is'sues

isth'mi·an

isth'mus

it

I·tal'ian

I·tal'ian·ate

i·tal'ic

i·tal'i·cize

itch

itched

itch'i·er

itch'i·est

itch'y

i'tem

i'tem·ize

i'tem·ized

it'er·ate

it'er·a'tion

it'er·a'tive

i·tin'er·a·cy

i·tin'er·an·cy

i·tin'er·ant

i·tin'er·ar'y

i·tin'er·ate

its

it·self'

i'vo·ry

i'vy

J

jab'ber
jab'ber·ing·ly
ja'bot'
jack
jack'al
jack'a·napes'
jack'daw'
jack'et
jack'et·ed
jack'knife'
jack'stone'
jack'straw'
jack'weed'
Jac·o·be'an
jade
jad'ed
jade'ite
jagged
jag'uar
jail
jailed
jail'er

jal'ou·sie
jam
jam'bo·ree'
jammed
jan'gle
jan'i·tor
jan'i·tress
Jan'u·ar'y
Ja·pan'
Jap'a·nese'
ja·panned'
jar
jar'gon
jarred
jas'mine
jas'per
jaun'dice
jaunt
jaun'ti·er
jaun'ti·est
jaun'ti·ly
jaun'ti·ness

jaun'ty
jave'lin
jaw
jaw'bone'
jazz
jazz'y
jeal'ous
jeal'ous·y
jeer
jeered
jeer'ing·ly
Je·ho'vah
je·june'
je·ju'num
jel'lied
jel'ly
jel'ly·fish'
jen'net
jeop'ard·ize
jeop'ard·y
jer'e·mi'ad
jerk

jerked	jit'ney	jol'li·er
jerk'i·ly	jit'ters	jol'li·est
jer'kin	jit'ter·y	jol'li·fi·ca'tion
jerk'y	job	jol'li·ty
jer'sey	job'ber	jol'ly
jest	jock'ey	jolt
jest'er	jo·cose'	jolt'ed
jest'ing·ly	jo·cose'ly	jon'quil
Jes'u·it	jo·cos'i·ty	jos'tle
Je'sus	joc'u·lar	jos'tled
jet	joc'u·lar'i·ty	jot
jet'sam	joc'u·lar·ly	jot'ted
jet'ti·son	joc'und	jounce
jet'ty	jo·cun'di·ty	jour'nal
jew'el	jodh'purs	jour'nal·ism
jew'eled	jog	jour'nal·ist
jew'el·er	jogged	jour'nal·is'tic
jew'el·ry	jog'gle	jour'nal·ize
Jew'ish	jog'gled	jour'nal·ized
Jew'ry	join	jour'ney
jibe	join'der	jour'neyed
jig	joined	jour'ney·man
jig'ger	join'er	jo'vi·al
jig'gle	join'ings	jo'vi·al'i·ty
jig'gled	joint	jo'vi·al·ly
jig'saw'	joint'ed	jowl
jin'gle	joint'ly	joy
jin'gled	join'ture	joy'ful
jin'go	joist	joy'ful·ly
jin'go·ism	joke	joy'ful·ness
jin·rik'i·sha	jok'er	joy'less
jinx	jok'ing·ly	joy'ous

ju'bi·lance

ju'bi·lant

ju'bi·late

ju'bi·la'tion

ju'bi·lee

Ju'da·ism

judge

judged

judge'ship

judg'ment

ju'di·ca'tive

ju'di·ca·to·ry

ju'di·ca·ture

ju·di'cial

ju·di'cial·ly

ju·di'ci·ar'y

ju·di'cious

jug'gle

jug'gled

jug'gler

jug'u·lar

juice

juic'y

ju'lep

ju'li·enne'

Ju·ly'

jum'ble

jum'bled

jum'bo

jump

jumped

jump'er

junc'tion

junc'ture

June

jun'gle

jun'ior

ju'ni·per

junk

jun'ket

jun'ta

ju'rat

ju·rid'i·cal

ju'ris·con·sult'

ju'ris·dic'tion

ju'ris·pru'dence

ju'rist

ju'ror

ju'ry

ju'ry·man

just

jus'tice

jus·ti'ci·a·ble

jus'ti·fi'a·ble

jus'ti·fi·ca'tion

jus'ti·fi·ca'to·ry

jus'ti·fied

jus'ti·fy

just'ly

just'ness

jut

jute

jut'ted

ju've·nile

ju've·nil'i·ty

jux'ta·po·si'tion

K

kai′ser

kale

ka·lei′do·scope

ka·lei′do·scop′ic

kal′so·mine

kan′ga·roo′

ka′o·lin

ka′pok

kar′ma

kay′ak

keel

keen

keen′er

keen′est

keen′ly

keen′ness

keep

keep′er

keep′sake′

keg

kelp

ken′nel

kept

ker′a·tin

ker′chief

ker′nel

ker′o·sene′

ker′sey

ketch

ke·to′sis

ket′tle

key

key′board′

keyed

key′hole′

key′note′

key′stone′

khak′i

khe·dive′

kib′itz·er

ki′bosh

kick

kick′back′

kick′er

kick′off′

kick′shaw′

kid

kid′nap

kid′naped

kid′ney

kid′skin′

kill

killed

kill′er

kill′ings

kiln

kil′o·cy′cle

kil′o·gram

kil′o·me′ter

kilt

kilt′ed

kin

kind

kind′er

kind′est

kin′der·gar′ten

kin'dle

kin'dled

kind'li·ness

kind'ly

kind'ness

kin'dred

kine

kin'es·thet'ic

ki·net'ic

king

king'bird'

king'bolt'

king'craft

king'dom

king'fish'

king'fish'er

king'let

king'li·ness

king'ly

king'pin'

king'ship

kink

kinked

kink'y

kin'ship

kins'man

ki·osk'

kip'per

kiss

kissed

kitch'en

kitch'en·ette'

kite

kith

kit'ten

klep'to·ma'ni·a

klep'to·ma'ni·ac

knap'sack'

knave

knav'er·y

knav'ish

knead

knead'ed

knee'cap'

kneel

kneeled

knelt

knew

knick'ers

knick'knack'

knife

knifed

knight

knight'ed

knight'hood

knight'li·ness

knight'ly

knit

knit'ter

knives

knob

knock

knock'down'

knock'er

knock'out'

knoll

knot

knot'hole'

knot'ted

knot'ty

knot'work'

knout

know

know'a·ble

know'ing·ly

know'ing·ness

knowl'edge

known

knuck'le

knuck'led

knurl

knurled

knurl'y

ko'bold

ko'dak

kohl'ra'bi

ko'peck

Ko·ran'

Ko·re'an

ko'sher

kraft

krem'lin

kryp'ton

ku·lak'

ky'mo·graph

ky·pho'sis

la'bel	lach'ry·mose	la'dy
la'beled	lac'ings	la'dy·like'
la'bi·al	lack	la'dy·ship
la'bor	lack'a·dai'si·cal	lag
lab'o·ra·to'ry	lack'ey	la'ger
la'bored	lack'lus'ter	lag'gard
la'bor·er	la·con'ic	lagged
la·bo'ri·ous	lac'quer	la·goon'
la·bur'num	lac'quered	lair
lab'y·rinth	la·crosse'	laird
lab'y·rin'thine	lac'tase	la'i·ty
lace	lac'tate	lake
laced	lac·ta'tion	lamb'doid
lac'er·ate	lac'te·al	lam'bent
lac'er·at'ed	lac'tic	lamb'kin
lac'er·a'tion	lac'tose	lamb'like'
lac'er·a'tive	la·cu'na	lam'bre·quin
lace'wing'	la·cu'nae	la·mé'
lace'wood'	lad'der	lame
lace'work'	lad'en	lamed
lach'es	la'dle	lame'ly
lach'ry·mal	la'dled	lame'ness

162

la·ment'	land'slip'	large
lam'en·ta·ble	lands'man	large'ly
lam'en·ta'tion	land'ward	large'ness
la·ment'ed	lan'guage	larg'er
lam'i·na	lan'guid	lar'gess
lam'i·nae	lan'guish	larg'est
lam'i·nate	lan'guor	lar'i·at
lam'i·nat'ed	lan'guor·ous	lark
lam'i·na'tion	lank	lark'spur
lamp	lank'er	lar'va
lamp'black'	lank'est	lar'vae
lam·poon'	lank'y	lar'val
lam·pooned'	lan'o·lin	la·ryn'ge·al
lam'prey	lans'downe	lar'yn·gi'tis
lance	lan'tern	lar'ynx
lanc'er	lan'tha·num	las'car
lan'cet	lan'yard	las·civ'i·ous
lan'ci·nate	lap	lash
lan'ci·nat'ed	la·pel'	lashed
lan'ci·na'tion	lap'ful	lash'ings
land	lap'i·dar'y	lass
lan'dau	lap'i·da'tion	las'si·tude
land'ed	lapse	las'so
land'fall'	lapsed	last
land'hold'er	lap'wing'	last'ed
land'la'dy	lar'board	last'ing·ly
land'locked'	lar'ce·nous	last'ly
land'lord'	lar'ce·ny	lasts
land'mark'	larch	Lat'a·ki'a
land'own'er	lard	latch
land'scape	lard'ed	latched
land'slide'	lard'er	latch'key'

latch'string'

late

la·teen'

late'ly

la'ten·cy

late'ness

la'tent

lat'er

lat'er·al

lat'er·al·ly

lat'est

la'tex

lath

lath'er

laths

Lat'in

Lat'in·ism

La·tin'i·ty

Lat'in·i·za'tion

Lat'in·ize

lat'i·tude

lat'i·tu'di·nal

lat'i·tu'di·nar'i·an

lat'ter

lat'ter·most

lat'tice

lat'tice·work'

laud

laud'a·bil'i·ty

laud'a·ble

lau'da·num

lau·da'tion

laud'a·to'ry

laud'ed

laugh

laugh'a·ble

laugh'ing·ly

laugh'ing·stock'

laugh'ter

launch

launch'ings

laun'der

laun'dered

laun'der·ings

laun'dress

laun'dry

laun'dry·man

lau're·ate

lau'rel

la'va

lav'a·liere'

lav'a·to'ry

lav'en·der

lay'ish

lav'ished

lav'ish·ness

law

law'break'er

law'ful

law'ful·ly

law'giv'er

law'less

law'less·ness

law'mak'er

lawn

law'suit'

law'yer

lax

lax'a·tive

lax'i·ty

lax'ly

lax'ness

lay'er

lay'man

laz'a·ret'to

la'zi·er

la'zi·est

la'zi·ly

la'zi·ness

la'zy

leach

leached

lead

lead'en

lead'er

lead'er·ship

leads'man

leaf

leaf'let

league

leagued

leak

leak'age

leak'i·ness

leak'y

lean

leaned	leered	le·git′i·ma·cy
lean′ings	leer′ing·ly	le·git′i·mate
leap	lee′ward	le·git′i·mate·ly
leaped	lee′way′	le·git′i·mate·ness
learn	left	le·git′i·ma′tion
learned	left′-hand′ed	le·git′i·mist
learnt	leg	le·git′i·mize
lease	leg′a·cy	leg′ume
leased	le′gal	le·gu′mi·nous
lease′hold′	le′gal·ism	lei′sure
lease′hold′er	le′gal·is′tic	lei′sure·li·ness
leash	le·gal′i·ty	lei′sure·ly
leashed	le′gal·i·za′tion	lem′mings
least	le′gal·ize	lem′on
leath′er	le′gal·ly	lem′on·ade′
leath′ern	leg′ate	lem′on·weed′
leath′er·oid	leg′a·tee′	le′mur
leath′er·y	le·ga′tion	lend
leave	le·ga′to	length
leav′en	leg′end	length′en
leav′ened	leg′end·ar′y	length′ened
leav′ing	leg′er·de·main′	length′i·er
lec′i·thin	leg′gings	length′i·est
lec′tern	leg′i·bil′i·ty	length′i·ly
lec′ture	leg′i·ble	length′i·ness
lec′tured	le′gion	length′ways
lec′tur·er	le′gion·ar′y	length′wise
ledge	leg′is·late	length′y
ledg′er	leg′is·la′tion	le′ni·ence
leech	leg′is·la′tive	le′ni·en·cy
leek	leg′is·la′tor	le′ni·ent
leer	leg′is·la′ture	le′ni·ent·ly

Len'in·ism	let'tered	li'beled
len'i·tive	let'ter·head'	li'bel·ous
len'i·ty	let'ter·press'	lib'er·al
lens	let'ter·space'	lib'er·al·ism
lent	let'tuce	lib'er·al'i·ty
Lent'en	leu'co·cyte	lib'er·al·i·za'tion
len·tic'u·lar	leu'co·cy·to'sis	lib'er·al·ize
len'til	leu'co·der'ma	lib'er·al·ized
len'toid	leu·ke'mi·a	lib'er·al·ly
le'o·nine	lev'ant	lib'er·ate
leop'ard	lev'ee	lib'er·at'ed
le'o·tard	lev'el	lib'er·a'tion
lep'er	lev'eled	lib'er·a'tor
lep're·chaun'	lev'el·head'ed	lib'er·tar'i·an
lep'ro·sy	le'ver	lib'er·tine
lep'rous	le'ver·age	lib'er·ty
le'sion	lev'i·tate	li·bi'do
less	lev'i·tat'ed	li·brar'i·an
les·see'	lev'i·ta'tion	li'brar'y
less'en	lev'i·ty	li·bret'to
less'ened	lev'u·lose	lice
less'er	lev'y	li'cense
les'son	lex'i·cog'ra·pher	li'cen·see'
les'sor	lex'i·cog'ra·phy	li·cen'ti·ate
lest	lex'i·con	li·cen'tious
let	li'a·bil'i·ty	li·cen'tious·ness
le'thal	li'a·ble	li'chen
le·thar'gic	li·a'na	li'chen·oid
le·thar'gi·cal	li'ar	lic'it
leth'ar·gy	li·ba'tion	lick
let's	li'bel	lic'o·rice
let'ter	li'bel·ant	lic'tor

lie	light'ness	lime'wa'ter
liege	light'ning	lim'i·nal
li'en	light'ship'	lim'it
lieu	light'weight'	lim'it·a·ble
lieu·ten'an·cy	lig'ne·ous	lim'i·ta'tion
lieu·ten'ant	lig'ni·fy	lim'it·ed
life	lig'nite	lim'it·less
life'guard'	lik'a·ble	limn
life'less	like	limned
life'like'	liked	lim·nol'o·gy
life'long'	like'li·er	lim'ou·sine'
life'time'	like'li·est	limp
life'work'	like'li·hood	limped
lift	like'ly	limp'er
lift'ed	lik'en	limp'est
lig'a·ment	like'ness	lim'pet
li'gate	like'wise'	lim'pid
li·ga'tion	lik'ings	lim·pid'i·ty
lig'a·ture	li'lac	lim'pid·ly
lig'a·tured	lil'i·a'ceous	limp'ly
light	lilt	limp'ness
light'ed	lilt'ing·ly	lin'age
light'en	lil'y	lin'den
light'ened	limb	line
light'er	lim'ber	lin'e·age
light'er·age	lim'bo	lin'e·al
light'est	lime	lin'e·al'i·ty
light'face'	lime'kiln'	lin'e·a·ment
light'head'ed	lime'light'	lin'e·ar
light'heart'ed	li'men	lined
light'house'	Lim'er·ick	line'man
light'ly	lime'stone'	lin'en

lin'er

lines'man

lin'ger

lin'gered

lin'ge·rie'

lin'ger·ing·ly

lin'go

lin'gual

lin'guist

lin·guis'tic

lin·guis'ti·cal·ly

lin·guis'tics

lin'i·ment

lin'ings

link

link'age

linked

Lin·nae'an

lin'net

li·no'le·um

Lin'o·type

lin'seed'

lint

lin'tel

li'on

li'on·ess

li'on·ize

lip'oid

li·po'ma

liq'ue·fa'cient

liq'ue·fac'tion

liq'ue·fac'tive

liq'ue·fi'a·ble

liq'ue·fied

liq'ue·fy

li'ques'cence

li·queur'

liq'uid

liq'ui·date

liq'ui·dat'ed

liq'ui·da'tion

liq'ui·da'tor

liq'uor

li'ra

lisp

lisped

lisp'ing·ly

lis'some

list

list'ed

lis'ten

lis'tened

lis'ten·er

list'ings

list'less

lit'a·ny

li'ter

lit'er·a·cy

lit'er·al

lit'er·al·ism

lit'er·al'i·ty

lit'er·al·ize

lit'er·al·ly

lit'er·ar'y

lit'er·ate

lit'er·a·ture

lith'arge

lithe

lithe'some

lith'i·a

lith'i·um

lith'o·graph

li·thog'ra·pher

lith'o·graph'ic

li·thog'ra·phy

li·tho'sis

li·thot'o·my

lit'i·ga·ble

lit'i·gant

lit'i·gate

lit'i·gat'ed

lit'i·ga'tion

li·ti'gious

lit'mus

lit'ter

lit'tered

lit'tle

lit'tlest

lit'to·ral

li·tur'gi·cal

lit'ur·gist

lit'ur·gy

liv'a·ble

live

live

lived

live′li·er

live′li·est

live′li·hood

live′li·ness

live′long′

live′ly

liv′er

liv′er·y

liv′er·y·man

liv′id

li·vid′i·ty

liv′ings

liz′ard

lla′ma

lla′no

load

load′ed

load′ings

loaf

loaf′er

loam

loan

loaned

loathe

loathed

loath′er

loath′ful

loath′ly

loath′some

lo′bar

lob′bied

lob′by

lob′by·ist

lob′ster

lo′cal

lo·cal·ism

lo·cal′i·ty

lo′cal·i·za′tion

lo′cal·ize

lo′cal·ized

lo′cal·ly

lo′cate

lo′cat·ed

lo·ca′tion

lo′ci

lock

lock′age

lock′er

lock′et

lock′jaw′

lock′out′

lock′smith′

lock′up′

lo′co·mo′tion

lo′co·mo′tive

lo′cus

lo′cust

lo·cu′tion

lode

lode′star′

lodge

lodged

lodg′er

lodg′ings

lodg′ment

loft

loft′i·ly

loft′i·ness

loft′y

log

lo′gan·ber′ry

log′a·rithm

log′book′

loge

log′ger·heads′

log′gia

log′ic

log′i·cal

log′i·cal·ly

lo·gi′cian

lo·gis′tics

log′or·rhe′a

log′o·type

log′wood′

loin

loi′ter

loi′tered

loi′ter·er

loll

lolled

lol′li·pop

lone

lone′li·ness

lone′ly

lone′some

lone′some·ly

lone'some·ness

long

long'boat'

longed

lon'ger

long'est

lon·gev'i·ty

long'hand'

long'horn'

long'ing·ly

long'ings

lon'gi·tude

lon'gi·tu'di·nal

long'shore'man

look

look'out'

loom

loomed

loon

loon'y

loop

loop'hole'

loose

loose'ly

loos'en

loos'ened

loose'ness

loos'er

loos'est

loot

loot'ed

lop

lop'sid'ed

lo·qua'cious

lo·qua'cious·ly

lo·quac'i·ty

lord

lord'li·ness

lord'ly

lor·do'sis

lord'ship

lore

lor'gnette'

lor'ry

los'a·ble

lose

los'er

los'es

los'ings

loss

lost

lo'tion

lot'ter·y

lo'tus

loud

loud'er

loud'est

loud'ly

loud'ness

lounge

louse

lout

lout'ish

lou'ver

lov'a·ble

love

love'less

love'li·ness

love'lorn'

love'ly

lov'er

love'sick'

lov'ing·ly

low

low'born'

low'boy'

low'bred'

low'er

low'est

low'land

low'li·er

low'li·est

low'li·ness

low'ly

low'most

loy'al

loy'al·ism

loy'al·ist

loy'al·ly

loy'al·ty

loz'enge

lu'bri·cant

lu'bri·cate

lu'bri·ca'tion

lu'bri·ca'tor

lu·bric'i·ty

lu'cent	lu'mi·nif'er·ous	lus'ter
lu'cid	lu'mi·nos'i·ty	lust'ful
lu·cid'i·ty	lu'mi·nous	lust'i·ly
lu'cid·ly	lump	lust'i·ness
lu'cid·ness	lump'i·er	lus'trous
luck	lump'i·est	lus'trous·ly
luck'i·ly	lump'y	lus'trum
luck'i·ness	lu'na·cy	lust'y
luck'less	lu'nar	lute
luck'y	lu'na·tic	Lu'ther·an
lu'cra·tive	lunch	lux·u'ri·ance
lu'cre	lunch'eon	lux·u'ri·ant
lu'cu·bra'tion	lunch'eon·ette'	lux·u'ri·ate
lu'di·crous	lunch'room'	lux·u'ri·at'ed
lug	lu·nette'	lux·u'ri·ous
lug'gage	lung	lux'u·ry
lugged	lunge	ly·ce'um
lug'ger	lunged	lydd'ite
lu·gu'bri·ous	lurch	lymph
luke'warm'	lurched	lym·phat'ic
lull	lurch'ing	lymph'oid
lull'a·by'	lure	lynx
lulled	lured	ly'on·naise'
lum·ba'go	lu'rid	lyre
lum'ber	lurk	lyre'bird'
lum'ber·yard'	lurked	lyr'ic
lu'mi·nar'y	lus'cious	lyr'i·cal
lu'mi·nes'cence	lush	lyr'i·cism
lu'mi·nes'cent	lust	

M

ma·ca′bre
mac·ad′am
mac·ad′am·ize
mac′a·ro′ni
mac′a·roon′
ma·caw′
mac′er·ate
mac′er·at′ed
mac′er·a′tion
Mach
ma·che′te
ma·chic′o·la′tion
mach′i·nate
mach′i·na′tion
ma·chine′
ma·chined′
ma·chin′er·y
ma·chin′ist
mack′er·el
mac′ro·cosm
mac′ro·cyte
ma′cron

mac′u·late
mad
mad′am
mad′den·ing·ly
mad′der
mad′dest
mad′house′
mad′ly
mad′man
mad′ness
ma·don′na
mad′ri·gal
mael′strom
maf′fi·a
mag′a·zine′
ma·gen′ta
mag′got
Ma′gi
mag′ic
mag′i·cal
mag′i·cal·ly
ma·gi′cian

mag′is·te′ri·al
mag′is·tra·cy
mag′is·tral
mag′is·trate
mag′is·tra·ture
mag′na·nim′i·ty
mag·nan′i·mous
mag′nate
mag·ne′sia
mag·ne′si·um
mag′net
mag·net′ic
mag·net′i·cal·ly
mag′net·ism
mag′net·i·za′tion
mag′net·ize
mag′net·ized
mag·ne′to
mag′ni·fi·ca′tion
mag·nif′i·cence
mag·nif′i·cent
mag·nif′i·co

mag'ni·fi'er

mag'ni·fy

mag·nil'o·quent

mag'ni·tude

mag·no'li·a

mag'num

mag'pie

mag'uey

ma·ha·ra'ja

ma·ha·ra'ni

ma·hat'ma

ma·hog'a·ny

maid

maid'en

maid'en·hair'

maid'en·hood

maid'en·ly

maid'serv'ant

mail

mail'a·ble

mail'bag'

mail'box'

mailed

mail'er

mail'ings

maim

maimed

main

main'land'

main'ly

main'mast'

main'sail'

main'sheet'

main'spring'

main'stay'

main·tain'

main·tain'a·ble

main'te·nance

ma·jes'tic

maj'es·ty

ma·jol'i·ca

ma'jor

ma·jor'i·ty

ma·jus'cule

make

make'-be·lieve'

mak'er

make'shift'

mak'ings

mal'a·chite

mal'ad·just'ed

mal'ad·just'ment

mal'a·droit'

mal'a·dy

mal'a·pert

mal'a·prop·ism

mal'ap·ro·pos'

ma·lar'i·a

ma·lar'i·al

mal'as·sim'i·la'tion

Ma·lay'

mal'con·tent'

male

mal'e·dic'tion

mal'e·dic'to·ry

mal'e·fac'tor

ma·lef'i·cence

ma·lef'i·cent

ma·lev'o·lence

ma·lev'o·lent

mal·fea'sance

mal·fea'sor

mal'for·ma'tion

mal·formed'

mal'ice

ma·li'cious

ma·li'cious·ly

ma·li'cious·ness

ma·lign'

ma·lig'nan·cy

ma·lig'nant

ma·lig'nant·ly

ma·ligned'

ma·lig'ni·ty

ma·lign'ly

ma·lin'ger

ma·lin'ger·er

mall

mal'lard

mal'le·a·bil'i·ty

mal'le·a·ble

mal·le'o·lar

mal·le'o·lus

mal'let

mal'low

malm'sey

mal'nu·tri'tion	man'da·to'ry	man'i·fold'er
mal·o'dor·ous	man'di·ble	man'i·kin
mal·po·si'tion	man·dib'u·lar	ma·nip'u·late
mal'prac'tice	man'do·lin	ma·nip'u·lat'ed
malt	man'drake	ma·nip'u·lates
malt'ase	man'drel	ma·nip'u·la'tion
Mal'tese'	ma·neu'ver	ma·nip'u·la'tive
malt'ose	ma·neu'vered	ma·nip'u·la'tor
mal·treat'	man'ga·nate	ma·nip'u·la·to'ry
mal·ver·sa'tion	man'ga·nese	man'kind'
mam'ba	mange	man'like'
mam'mal	man'ger	man'li·ness
mam·ma'li·an	man'gi·ly	man'ly
mam'ma·ry	man'gi·ness	man'na
mam'mon	man'gle	man'ner
mam'moth	man'gled	man'nered
man	man'go	man'ner·ism
man'a·cle	man'grove	man'ner·ly
man'a·cled	man'gy	man'nish
man'age	man'hole'	ma·nom'e·ter
man'age·a·ble	man'hood	man'o·met'ric
man'aged	ma'ni·a	man'or
man'age·ment	ma'ni·ac	ma·no'ri·al
man'ag·er	ma·ni'a·cal	man'sard
man'a·ge'ri·al	man'i·cure	man'serv'ant
man'a·ge'ri·al·ly	man'i·cur'ist	man'sion
man'ag·er·ship'	man'i·fest	man'slaugh'ter
man'a·tee'	man'i·fes·ta'tion	man'teau
man·da'mus	man'i·fest·ed	man'tel
man·da·rin	man'i·fes'to	man·til'la
man'date	man'i·fold	man'tis
man'dat·ed	man'i·fold'ed	man·tis'sa

man'tle	mar'gi·na'li·a	mar'mo·set
man'u·al	mar'gin·al·ly	mar'mot
man'u·al·ly	mar'grave	ma·roon'
man'u·fac'to·ry	mar'i·gold	ma·rooned'
man'u·fac'ture	mar'i·jua'na	mar'plot'
man'u·fac'tured	ma·rim'ba	mar·quee'
man'u·fac'tur·er	ma·ri'na	mar'qui·sette'
man'u·mis'sion	mar'i·nade'	marred
ma·nure'	mar'i·nate	mar'riage
man'u·script	mar'i·nat'ed	mar'riage·a·ble
Manx	ma·rine'	mar'ried
man'y	mar'i·ner	mar'row
Ma'o·ri	mar'i·o·nette'	mar'row·bone'
map	Mar'ist	mar'row·fat'
ma'ple	mar'i·tal	mar'row·y
mapped	mar'i·tal·ly	mar'ry
mar	mar'i·time	Mars
mar'a·bou	mar'jo·ram	mar'shal
mar'a·schi'no	mark	mar'shaled
ma·raud'	marked	marsh'i·ness
ma·raud'er	mark'ed·ly	marsh'mal'low
mar'ble	mark'er	marsh'y
mar'bled	mar'ket	mar·su'pi·al
mar'ca·site	mar'ket·a·bil'i·ty	mart
march	mar'ket·a·ble	mar'ten
march'er	mark'ings	mar'tial
mar'chion·ess	marks'man	mar'tial·ly
mar·co'ni·gram	marks'man·ship	Mar'ti·an
mare	mark'weed'	mar'ti·net'
mar'ga·rine	marl	mar'tin·gale
mar'gin	mar'lin	mar'tyr
mar'gin·al	mar'ma·lade	mar'tyr·dom

mar'tyred

mar'vel

mar'veled

mar'vel·ous

mar'zi·pan

mas·car'a

mas'cot

mas'cu·line

mas'cu·lin'i·ty

mash

mashed

mash'er

mash'ie

mask

masked

mask'er

ma'son

ma·son'ic

ma'son·ry

mas'quer·ade'

mas'quer·ad'ed

mass

mas'sa·cre

mas·sage'

mas·seur'

mas'sive

mast

mas'ter

mas'tered

mas'ter·ful

mas'ter·ful·ly

mas'ter·ful·ness

mas'ter·ly

mas'ter·piece'

mas'ter·ship

mas'ter·work'

mas'ter·y

mast'head'

mas'tic

mas'ti·cate

mas'ti·cat'ed

mas'ti·ca'tion

mas'ti·ca'tor

mas'ti·ca·to'ry

mas'tiff

mas'to·don

mas'toid

mas'toid·i'tis

mat

mat'a·dor

match

matched

match'less

match'less·ly

match'mak'er

match'wood'

ma·té'

ma·te'ri·al

ma·te'ri·al·ism

ma·te'ri·al·ist

ma·te'ri·al·is'tic

ma·te'ri·al'i·ty

ma·te'ri·al·i·za'tion

ma·te'ri·al·ize

ma·te'ri·al·ized

ma·te'ri·al·ly

ma·ter'nal

ma·ter'nal·ly

ma·ter'ni·ty

math'e·mat'i·cal

math'e·ma·ti'cian

math'e·mat'ics

mat'in

mat'i·nee'

ma'tri·arch

ma'tri·arch'y

ma'tri·ces

ma'tri·cide

ma·tric'u·lant

ma·tric'u·late

ma·tric'u·lat'ed

ma·tric'u·lates

ma·tric'u·la'tion

mat'ri·mo'ni·al

mat'ri·mo'ni·al·ly

mat'ri·mo'ny

ma'trix

ma'tron

ma'tron·li·ness

ma'tron·ly

matte

mat'ted

mat'ter

mat'tered

mat'tings

mat'tock

mat'tress	maze	me·a'tus
mat'u·rate	ma·zur'ka	me·chan'ic
mat'u·rat'ed	me	me·chan'i·cal
mat'u·ra'tion	mead'ow	me·chan'i·cal·ly
ma·tur'a·tive	mead'ow·land'	mech'a·ni'cian
ma·ture'	mea'ger	me·chan'ics
ma·tured'	meal	mech'a·nism
ma·ture'ly	meal'i·er	mech'a·ni·za'tion
ma·ture'ness	meal'i·est	mech'a·nize
ma·tu'ri·ty	meal'time'	med'al
ma·tu'ti·nal	meal'y	med'al·ist
maud'lin	meal'y·mouthed'	me·dal'lion
maul	mean	med'dle
mauled	me·an'der	med'dled
maun'der	mean'ing·ful	med'dle·some
mau·so·le'um	mean'ing·less	me'di·a
mauve	mean'ing·ly	me'di·al
mav'er·ick	mean'ings	me'di·an
ma'vis	mean'ly	me'di·ate
maw	mean'ness	me'di·at'ed
mawk'ish	mean'time'	me'di·a'tion
max'il·lar'y	mean'while'	me'di·a'tive
max'im	mea'sles	me'di·a'tor
max'i·mal	meas'ur·a·ble	med'i·cal
max'i·mize	meas'ur·a·bly	med'i·cal·ly
max'i·mum	meas'ure	me·dic'a·ment
may	meas'ured	med'i·cate
may'be	meas'ure·less	med'i·cat'ed
may'hem	meas'ure·ment	med'i·ca'tion
may'on·naise'	meas'ur·er	med'i·ca'tive
may'or	meat	me·dic'i·nal
may'or·al·ty	meat'cut'ter	me·dic'i·nal·ly

med'i·cine	mel'io·rate	mem'o·ran'da
me'di·e'val	mel'io·rat'ed	mem'o·ran'dum
me'di·e'val·ist	mel'io·ra'tion	mem'o·ran'dums
me'di·e'val·ly	mel'io·ra'tive	me·mo'ri·al
me'di·o'cre	me·lis'ma	me·mo'ri·al·i·za'tion
me'di·oc'ri·ty	mel'is·mat'ic	me·mo'ri·al·ize
med'i·tate	mel·lif'lu·ous	mem'o·ri·za'tion
med'i·tat'ed	mel'low	mem'o·rize
med'i·ta'tion	mel'lowed	mem'o·rized
med'i·ta'tive	mel'low·er	mem'o·ry
me'di·um	mel'low·est	men'ace
med'lar	me·lo'de·on	men'aced
me·dul'la	me·lod'ic	me·nage'
meek	me·lo'di·on	me·nag'er·ie
meek'er	me·lo'di·ous	mend
meek'est	me·lo'di·ous·ly	men·da'cious
meek'ly	mel'o·dra'ma	men·dac'i·ty
meek'ness	mel'o·dra·mat'ic	mend'ed
meer'schaum	mel'o·dy	Men·de'li·an
meet	mel'on	men'di·can·cy
meet'ings	me'los	men'di·cant
meet'ing·house'	melt	men'folk'
meg'a·cy'cle	melt'ed	men·ha'den
meg'a·phone	melt'ing·ly	me'ni·al
mei·o'sis	mem'ber	me'ni·al·ly
mei·ot'ic	mem'ber·ship	me·nin'ges
mel'an·cho'li·a	mem'brane	men'in·gi'tis
mel'an·chol'ic	mem'bra·nous	me·nis'cus
mel'an·chol'y	me·men'to	Men'non·ite
mel'a·nism	mem'oir	men'su·ra'tion
mel'a·no'sis	mem'o·ra·bil'i·a	men'su·ra'tive
meld	mem'o·ra·ble	men'tal

men·tal'i·ty

men'tal·ly

men'thol

men'tion

men'tioned

men'tor

men'u

me·phit'ic

mer'can·tile

mer'ce·nar'y

mer'cer·ize

mer'cer·ized

mer'chan·dise

mer'chan·dis'er

mer'chant

mer'chant·man

mer'ci·ful

mer'ci·less

mer'ci·less·ly

mer·cu'ri·al

mer'cu·ry

mer'cy

mere'ly

mer'est

mer'e·tri'cious

merge

merged

merg'er

me·rid'i·an

me·ringue'

me·ri'no

mer'it

mer'it·ed

mer'i·to'ri·ous

mer'i·to'ri·ous·ly

mer'lin

mer'maid'

mer'ri·er

mer'ri·est

mer'ri·ly

mer'ri·ment

mer'ri·ness

mer'ry

mer'ry·mak'ing

me'sa

mes·cal'

mes·cal'ine

mesh

mesh'work'

mes'mer·ism

mes'on

mess

mes'sage

mes'sen·ger

Mes·si'ah

mess'man

mess'mate'

mes·ti'zo

met'a·bol'ic

me·tab'o·lism

met'a·car'pal

met'a·car'pus

met'al

me·tal'lic

me·tal'li·cal·ly

met'al·loid

met'al·lur'gic

met'al·lur'gi·cal

met'al·lur'gy

met'al·ware'

met'al·work'

met'al·work'er

met'a·mor'phose

met'a·mor'phoses

met'a·mor'pho·sis

met'a·phor

met'a·phor'ic

met'a·phor'i·cal

met'a·phor'i·cal·ly

met'a·phys'i·cal

met'a·phys'i·cal·ly

met'a·phy·si'cian

met'a·phys'ics

me·tas'ta·sis

me·tas'ta·size

met'a·tar'sal

met'a·tar'sus

mete

met'ed

me'te·or

me'te·or'ic

me'te·or·ite

me'te·or·oid'

me'te·or·ol'o·gy

me'ter

me'tered

meth'ane	mi·crom'e·ter	mid'year'
me·thinks'	mi'cron	mien
meth'od	mi'cro·phone	might
me·thod'i·cal	mi'cro·scope	might'i·ly
me·thod'i·cal·ly	mi'cro·scop'ic	might'i·ness
meth'od·ist	mi·cros'co·py	might'y
meth'od·ize	mi'cro·spore	mi'graine
meth'od·ol'o·gy	mi'cro·struc'ture	mi'grant
meth'yl	mi'cro·tome	mi'grate
me·tic'u·lous	mi·crot'o·my	mi'grat·ed
mé·tier'	Mi'das	mi·gra'tion
me·ton'y·my	mid'brain'	mi'gra·to'ry
met'ric	mid'day'	mi·ka'do
met'ri·cal	mid'dle	milch
me·trol'o·gy	mid'dle·man'	mild
met'ro·nome	mid'dle·weight'	mild'er
me·trop'o·lis	midge	mild'est
met'ro·pol'i·tan	midg'et	mil'dew
met'tle	mid'i'ron	mild'ly
met'tled	mid'land	mild'ness
met'tle·some	mid'most	mile
Mex'i·can	mid'night'	mile'age
mez'za·nine	mid'riff	mile'post'
mi·as'ma	mid'ship'man	mil'er
mi·as'mal	mid'ships'	mile'stone'
mi'as·mat'ic	midst	mil'i·tant
mi'ca	mid'stream'	mil'i·ta·rism
mi·ca'ce·ous	mid'sum'mer	mil'i·ta·rist
mi'crobe	mid'way'	mil'i·ta·ris'tic
mi'cro·cosm	mid'week'	mil'i·ta·rize
mi'cro·de·ter'mi·na'tion	mid'wife'	mil'i·tar'y
mi'cro·dis·sec'tion	mid'win'ter	mil'i·tate

mil'i·tat'ed	mim'ic	min'is·try
mi·li'tia	mim'ic·ry	min'i·ver
milk	mi·mo'sa	mink
milk'maid'	min'a·ret'	min'now
milk'man'	min'a·to'ry	mi'nor
milk'weed'	mince	mi·nor'i·ty
milk'y	minced	min'ster
mill	mince'meat'	min'strel
mill'board'	minc'ing·ly	min'strel·sy
milled	mind	mint
mil'le·nar'y	mind'ed	mint'ed
mil·len'ni·al	mind'ful	min'u·end
mil·len'ni·um	mind'less	min'u·et'
mil'le·pede	mine	mi'nus
mill'er	min'er	mi·nus'cule
mil'let	min'er·al	min'ute
mil'line'	min'er·al'o·gy	mi·nute'
mil'li·ner	min'gle	mi·nute'ness
mil'li·ner'y	min'gled	mi·nu'ti·a
mil'lion	min'i·a·ture	mi·nu'ti·ae
mil'lion·aire'	min'i·a·tur·ist	minx
mil'lion·fold'	min'im	mir'a·cle
mil'lionth	min'i·mal	mi·rac'u·lous
mill'pond'	min'i·mi·za'tion	mi·rage'
mill'race'	min'i·mize	mire
mill'stone'	min'i·mum	mired
mill'work'	min'ion	mir'ror
mill'wright'	min'is·ter	mir'rored
Mil·ton'ic	min'is·tered	mirth
mime	min'is·te'ri·al	mirth'ful
mim'e·o·graph'	min'is·te'ri·al·ly	mirth'ful·ly
mi·met'ic	min'is·tra'tion	mirth'less

mis'ad·ven'ture
mis'al·li'ance
mis'an·thrope
mis'an·throp'ic
mis'an·throp'i·cal
mis·an'thro·pism
mis·an'thro·pist
mis·an'thro·py
mis'ap·pli·ca'tion
mis'ap·ply'
mis'ap·pre·hen'sion
mis'ap·pro'pri·ate
mis'ap·pro'pri·a'tion
mis'ar·range'
mis'be·got'ten
mis'be·have'
mis'be·haved'
mis'be·hav'ior
mis'be·liev'er
mis·brand'
mis·cal'cu·late
mis·cal'cu·lat'ed
mis·call'
mis·car'riage
mis·car'ried
mis·car'ry
mis·cast'
mis'ce·ge·na'tion
mis'cel·la'ne·a
mis'cel·la'ne·ous
mis'cel·la'nist
mis'cel·la'ny

mis·chance'
mis'chief
mis'chie·vous
mis'ci·ble
mis'con·ceive'
mis'con·cep'tion
mis'con·duct'
mis'con·struc'tion
mis'con·strue'
mis·count'
mis'cre·ant
mis·cue'
mis·date'
mis·deal'
mis·deed'
mis'de·mean'or
mis'di·rect'
mis'di·rect'ed
mis'di·rec'tion
mis·doubt'
mi'ser
mis'er·a·ble
mi'ser·li·ness
mi'ser·ly
mis'er·y
mis·fea'sance
mis·fire'
mis·fired'
mis·fit'
mis·formed'
mis·for'tune
mis·giv'ings

mis·gov'ern
mis·gov'erned
mis·guide'
mis·guid'ed
mis·hap'
mish'mash'
mis'in·form'
mis'in·formed'
mis'in·ter'pret
mis'in·ter'pre·ta'tion
mis'in·ter'pret·ed
mis·judge'
mis·judged'
mis·laid'
mis·lay'
mis·lead'
mis·lead'ing·ly
mis·like'
mis·liked'
mis·made'
mis·man'age
mis·man'age·ment
mis·mate'
mis·mat'ed
mis·name'
mis·named'
mis·no'mer
mi·sog'y·nist
mis·place'
mis·placed'
mis·print'
mis·pri'sion

mis'pro·nounce'

mis·pro·nun'ci·a'tion

mis'quo·ta'tion

mis·quote'

mis·read'

mis're·mem'ber

mis're·mem'brance

mis'rep·re·sent'

mis'rep·re·sen·ta'tion

mis·rule'

miss

mis'sal

missed

mis·shap'en

mis'sile

mis'sion

mis'sion·ar'y

mis'sion·er

mis'sive

mis·spell'

mis·spelled'

mis·spell'ings

mis·spend'

mis·spent'

mis·state'

mis·stat'ed

mis·state'ment

mis·step'

mist

mis·take'

mis·tak'en

mis·tak'en·ly

mis·taught'

mis·teach'

mist'i·er

mist'i·est

mist'i·ly

mist'i·ness

mis'tle·toe

mis·took'

mis·treat'

mis·treat'ment

mis'tress

mis·tri'al

mis·trust'

mis·trust'ful

mist'y

mis'un·der·stand'

mis'un·der·stand'ings

mis'un·der·stood'

mis·us'age

mis·use'

mis·used'

mite

mi'ter

mi'tered

mit'i·ga·ble

mit'i·gate

mit'i·gat'ed

mit'i·ga'tion

mit'i·ga'tive

mit'i·ga·to'ry

mi·to'sis

mi·tot'ic

mi'tral

mit'ten

mit'tened

mix

mixed

mix'er

mix'ture

miz'zen·mast'

mne·mon'ic

mo'a

moan

moaned

moat

mob

mob'cap'

mo'bile

mo·bil'i·ty

mo'bi·li·za'tion

mo'bi·lize

mo'bi·lized

mob·oc'ra·cy

moc'ca·sin

Mo'cha

mock

mock'er·y

mock'ing·ly

mod'al

mo·dal'i·ty

mode

mod'el

mod'eled

mod'er·ate

mod'er·at'ed

mod'er·ate·ly

mod'er·ate·ness

mod'er·a'tion

mod'er·a'tion·ist

mod'er·a'tor

mod'ern

mod'ern·ism

mod'ern·ist

mod'ern·is'tic

mo·der'ni·ty

mod'ern·i·za'tion

mod'ern·ize

mod'ern·ized

mod'est

mod'est·ly

mod'es·ty

mod'i·cum

mod'i·fi·ca'tion

mod'i·fi·ca'tion·ist

mod'i·fied

mod'i·fi'er

mod'i·fy

mod'ish

mod'ish·ly

mod'ish·ness

mod'u·lar

mod'u·late

mod'u·lat'ed

mod'u·la'tion

mod'u·la'tive

mod'u·la'tor

mod'u·la·to'ry

mod'ule

mod'u·lus

mog'a·dore'

Mo·gul'

mo'hair'

Mo·ham'med·an

Mo'hawk

mo'ho

moi'e·ty

moil

moiled

moi·re'

moist

mois'ten

mois'tened

mois'ten·er

mois'ture

mo'lal

mo'lar

mo·lar'i·ty

mo·las'ses

mold

mold'board'

mold'ed

mold'er

mold'ings

mold'y

mole

mo·lec'u·lar

mol'e·cule

mole'hill'

mole'skin'

mo·lest'

mo·les·ta'tion

mo·lest'ed

mol'li·fi·ca'tion

mol'li·fied

mol'li·fy

mol'lusk

mol'ly·cod'dle

molt

molt'ed

mol'ten

mo'ly

mo·lyb'de·num

mo'ment

mo'men·tar'i·ly

mo'men·tar'y

mo'ment·ly

mo·men'tous

mo·men'tum

mon'ad

mo·nad'nock

mon'arch

mo·nar'chi·al

mo·nar'chi·an·ism

mo·nar'chic

mon'arch·ism

mon'arch·ist

mon'arch·is'tic

mon'arch·y

mon'as·te'ri·al

mon'as·te'ri·al·ly

mon'as·ter'y	mon'o·lith'ic	month
mo·nas'tic	mon'o·logue	month'ly
mo·nas'ti·cism	mon'o·ma'ni·a	mon'u·ment
mon'a·tom'ic	mon'o·ma'ni·ac	mon'u·men'tal
Mon'day	mon'o·ma·ni'a·cal	mon'u·men'tal·ly
mo·nel'	mon'o·mor'phic	mood
mon'e·tar'y	mon'o·plane	mood'i·ly
mon'e·ti·za'tion	mon'o·ple'gi·a	mood'i·ness
mon'e·tize	mo·nop'o·lism	mood'y
mon'ey	mo·nop'o·list	moon
mon'eyed	mo·nop'o·lis'tic	moon'beam'
mon'goose	mo·nop'o·lis'ti·cal·ly	moon'faced'
mon'grel	mo·nop'o·li·za'tion	moon'fish'
mon'ism	mo·nop'o·lize	moon'flow'er
mon'i·tor	mo·nop'o·lized	moon'light'
mon'i·tored	mo·nop'o·ly	moon'light'ed
mon'i·to'ri·al	mon'o·rail'	moon'light'er
mon'i·to'ry	mon'o·syl·lab'ic	moon'light'ing
monk	mon'o·syl'la·ble	moon'rise'
mon'key	mon'o·the·ism	moon'shine'
monk'hood	mon'o·the·is'tic	moon'stone'
monk'ish	mon'o·tone	moon'-struck
mon'o·bas'ic	mo·not'o·nous	moor
mon'o·cle	mo·not'o·ny	moor'age
mon'o·cled	mon'o·type	moored
mo·noc'u·lar	mon·ox'ide	moor'ings
mon'o·dy	mon·si'gnor	Moor'ish
mo·nog'a·mous	mon·soon'	moor'land'
mo·nog'a·my	mon'ster	moose
mon'o·gram	mon'strance	moot
mon'o·graph	mon·stros'i·ty	mop
mon'o·lith	mon'strous	mopped

mop'pet

mo·raine'

mor'al

mo·rale'

mor'al·ist

mor'al·is'tic

mo·ral'i·ty

mor'al·i·za'tion

mor'al·ize

mor'al·ized

mor'al·ly

mo·rass'

mor'a·to'ri·um

mo·ray'

mor'bid

mor·bid'i·ty

mor'bid·ly

mor'dant

more

more·o'ver

mo'res

mor·ga·nat'ic

morgue

mor'i·bund

Mor'mon

morn

morn'ing

morn'ings

mo·roc'co

mo'ron

mo·rose'

mo·rose'ly

mor'phine

mor'phin·ism

mor'phin·ize

mor·phol'o·gy

mor'ris

mor'row

mor'sel

mor'tal

mor·tal'i·ty

mor'tal·ly

mor'tar

mor'tar·board'

mort'gage

mort'gaged

mort'ga·gee'

mort'ga·gor'

mor·ti'cian

mor'ti·fi·ca'tion

mor'ti·fied

mor'ti·fy

mor'tise

mort'main

mor'tu·ar'y

mo·sa'ic

Mos'lem

mosque

mos·qui'to

moss

moss'back'

moss'i·ness

moss'y

most

most'ly

mote

mo·tet'

moth

moth'er

moth'er·hood

moth'er-in-law'

moth'er·land'

moth'er·less

moth'er·li·ness

moth'er·ly

moth'er-of-pearl'

mo·tif'

mo'tile

mo'tion

mo'tioned

mo'tion·less

mo'ti·vate

mo'ti·vat'ed

mo'ti·va'tion

mo'ti·va'tion·al

mo'tive

mot'ley

mo'tor

mo'tor·boat'

mo'tor·cy'cle

mo'tored

mo'tor·ist

mo'tor·ize

mo'tor·man

mot'tle

mot'tled

mot'to	mow	mug
mound	mow	mug'gi·ness
mount	mow'er	mug'gy
moun'tain	much	mug'wump'
moun'tain·eer'	mu'ci·lage	mu·lat'to
moun'tain·ous	mu'ci·lag'i·nous	mul'ber'ry
moun'tain·ous·ly	muck	mulch
moun'te·bank	muck'er	mulched
mount'ed	muck'rak'er	mulct
mount'ings	muck'weed'	mulct'ed
mourn	muck'worm'	mule
mourned	mu'coid	mu'le·teer'
mourn'er	mu·co'sa	mu'li·eb'ri·ty
mourn'ful	mu'cous	mul'ish
mouse	mu'cus	mull
mous'er	mud	mulled
mouse'trap'	mud'di·er	mul'let
mousse	mud'di·est	mul'li·ga·taw'ny
mouth	mud'di·ly	mul'lion
mouthed	mud'di·ness	mul'ti·far'i·ous
mouth'ful	mud'dle	mul'ti·fold
mouth'fuls	mud'dled	mul'ti·form
mouth'piece'	mud'dle-head'ed	mul'ti·for'mi·ty
mov'a·bil'i·ty	mud'dy	Mul'ti·graph
mov'a·ble	mud'fish'	Mul'ti·lith'
mov'a·bly	mud'weed'	mul'ti·mil'lion·aire'
move	muff	mul'ti·ped
moved	muf'fin	mul'ti·ple
move'ment	muf'fle	mul'ti·plex
mov'er	muf'fled	mul'ti·pli·cand'
mov'ie	muf'fler	mul'ti·pli·cate
mov'ing·ly	muf'ti	mul'ti·pli·ca'tion

mul'ti·pli·ca'tive

mul'ti·plic'i·ty

mul'ti·plied

mul'ti·pli'er

mul'ti·ply

mul'ti·tude

mul'ti·tu'di·nous

mul'ti·va'lent

mum'ble

mum'bled

mum'mer

mum'mer·y

mum'mi·fi·ca'tion

mum'mi·fied

mum'mi·fy

mum'my

mumps

munch

munched

mun'dane

mu·nic'i·pal

mu·nic'i·pal'i·ty

mu·nic'i·pal·ly

mu·nif'i·cence

mu·nif'i·cent

mu'ni·ment

mu·ni'tion

mu'ral

mur'der

mur'dered

mur'der·er

mur'der·ous

mu'rex

mu'ri·at'ic

murk

murk'i·ly

murk'i·ness

murk'y

mur'mur

mur'mured

mur'mur·er

mur'mur·ous

mus'ca·dine

mus'cat

mus'ca·tel'

mus'cle

mus'cu·lar

mus'cu·lar'i·ty

mus'cu·lar·ly

mus'cu·la·ture

muse

mused

mu·sette'

mu·se'um

mush

mush'room

mush'roomed

mush'y

mu'sic

mu'si·cal

mu'si·cale'

mu'si·cal·ly

mu·si'cian

mu·si'cian·ly

musk

mus'keg

mus'kel·lunge

mus'ket

mus'ket·eer'

mus'ket·ry

musk'mel'on

musk'rat'

mus'lin

muss

mussed

mus'sel

muss'i·er

muss'i·est

muss'y

must

mus·tache'

mus·ta'chio

mus'tang

mus'tard

mus'ter

mus'tered

mus'ti·ness

mus'ty

mu'ta·bil'i·ty

mu'ta·ble

mu'tate

mu·ta'tion

mu'ta·tive

mute

mut'ed

mute'ness

mu'ti·late

mu'ti·lat'ed

mu'ti·la'tion

mu'ti·la'tor

mu'ti·neer'

mu'ti·nied

mu'ti·nous

mu'ti·ny

mut'ism

mut'ter

mut'tered

mut'ter·ings

mut'ton

mu'tu·al

mu'tu·al'i·ty

mu'tu·al·ly

muz'zle

muz'zled

my

my·col'o·gy

my·co'sis

my·dri'a·sis

myd'ri·at'ic

my'e·loid

my·o'ma

my·o'pi·a

my·op'ic

myr'i·ad

myrrh

myr'tle

my·self'

mys·te'ri·ous

mys·te'ri·ous·ly

mys'ter·y

mys'tic

mys'ti·cal

mys'ti·cal·ly

mys'ti·cism

mys'ti·fi·ca'tion

mys'ti·fied

mys'ti·fy

myth

myth'i·cal

myth'o·log'i·cal

my·thol'o·gist

my·thol'o·gy

N

na·celle'

na'cre

na'cre·ous

na'dir

nai'ad

nail

nailed

nail'head'

nain'sook

na·ïve'

na·ïve·té'

na'ked

na'ked·ly

na'ked·ness

nam'a·ble

name

named

name'less

name'less·ly

name'ly

name'sake'

nan·keen'

nap

na'per·y

naph'tha

naph'tha·lene

nap'kin

na·po'le·on

Na·po'le·on·a'na

Na·po'le·on'ic

napped

nar·cis'sism

nar·cis'sus

nar·co'sis

nar·cot'ic

nar·cot'i·cism

nar'co·tize

nar'co·tized

nar·rate'

nar·rat'ed

nar·ra'tion

nar'ra·tive

nar·ra'tor

nar'row

nar'rowed

nar'row·er

nar'row·est

nar'row·ly

nar'row·ness

nar'whal

na'sal

na·sal'i·ty

na'sal·ize

na'sal·ly

nas'cent

nas'ti·er

nas'ti·est

nas'ti·ly

nas'ti·ness

nas·tur'tium

nas'ty

na'tal

na·ta'tion

na'ta·to'ri·um

na'ta·to'ry

na'tion

na'tion·al

na'tion·al·ism

na'tion·al·is'tic

na'tion·al'i·ty

na'tion·al·i·za'tion

na'tion·al·ize

na'tion·al·ized

na'tion·al·ly

na'tive

na·tiv'i·ty

nat'u·ral

nat'u·ral·ism

nat'u·ral·ist

nat'u·ral·is'tic

nat'u·ral·i·za'tion

nat'u·ral·ize

nat'u·ral·ized

nat'u·ral·ly

nat'u·ral·ness

na'ture

na'tur·is'tic

naught

naugh'ti·ly

naugh'ti·ness

naugh'ty

nau'se·a

nau'se·ate

nau'se·at'ed

nau'seous

nau'ti·cal

nau'ti·lus

na'val

nave

na'vel

nav'i·ga·ble

nav'i·gate

nav'i·gat'ed

nav'i·ga'tion

nav'i·ga'tion·al

nav'i·ga'tor

na'vy

Naz'a·rene'

neap

Ne'a·pol'i·tan

near

near'by'

neared

near'er

near'est

near'ly

near'ness

near'sight'ed

neat

neat'er

neat'est

neat'herd'

neat'ly

neat'ness

neb'u·la

neb'u·lar

neb'u·los'i·ty

neb'u·lous

neb'u·lous·ly

nec'es·sar'i·ly

nec'es·sar'y

ne·ces'si·tar'i·an

ne·ces'si·tate

ne·ces'si·tat'ed

ne·ces'si·tous

ne·ces'si·ty

neck

neck'band'

neck'cloth'

neck'er·chief

neck'lace

neck'tie'

neck'wear'

nec'ro·log'i·cal

ne·crol'o·gy

nec'ro·man'cy

nec'ro·man'tic

nec'ro·pho'bi·a

ne·crop'o·lis

nec'rop·sy

ne·cro'sis

ne·crot'ic

nec'tar

nec'tar·ine'

need

need'ed

need'ful

need'ful·ly

need'i·er

need'i·est

need'i·ness

nee'dle

nee′dled

nee′dle·ful

need′less

need′less·ly

need′less·ness

nee′dle·work′

need′y

ne·far′i·ous

ne·gate′

ne·gat′ed

ne·ga′tion

neg′a·tive

neg′a·tived

neg′a·tiv·ism

neg·lect′

neg·lect′ed

neg·lect′ful

neg′li·gee′

neg′li·gence

neg′li·gent

neg′li·gi·ble

ne·go′ti·a·bil′i·ty

ne·go′ti·a·ble

ne·go′ti·ate

ne·go′ti·at′ed

ne·go′ti·a′tion

ne·go′ti·a′tor

Ne′gro

Ne′gro·phile

neigh′bor

neigh′bor·hood

neigh′bor·li·ness

neigh′bor·ly

nei′ther

nem′a·tode

Nem′e·sis

ne′o·for·ma′tion

ne′o·lith′ic

ne·ol′o·gism

ne·ol′o·gy

ne′on

ne′o·phyte

ne′o·plasm

ne·pen′the

neph′ew

ne·phrec′to·my

ne·phri′tis

nep′o·tism

nerve

nerve′less

ner′vous

nerv′ous·ly

nerv′ous·ness

nes′ci·ence

nes′ci·ent

nest

nest′ed

nes′tle

nes′tled

nest′lings

net

neth′er

neth′er·most

net′su·ke

net′ted

net′tings

net′tle

net′tled

net′work′

neu′ral

neu·ral′gia

neu′ras·the′ni·a

neu′ras·then′ic

neu·ri′tis

neu·ro′ses

neu·ro′sis

neu·rot′ic

neu′ter

neu′tral

neu′tral·ism

neu′tral·ist

neu·tral′i·ty

neu′tral·i·za′tion

neu′tral·ize

neu′tral·ized

neu′tral·iz′er

neu′tral·ly

neu′tron

nev′er

nev′er·more′

nev′er·the·less′

new

new′com′er

new′el

new′er

new′est

new'fan'gled

new'ly

new'ness

news'i·er

news'i·est

news'let'ter

news'pa'per

news'reel'

news'stand'

news'y

newt

next

nex'us

nib'ble

nib'bled

nib'lick

nice

nice'ly

nice'ness

nic'er

nic'est

ni'ce·ty

niche

nick

nicked

nick'el

nick'el·if'er·ous

nick'el·o'de·on

nick'name'

nick'named'

nic'o·tine

nic'o·tin'ic

niece

ni·el'lo

nig'gard

nig'gard·li·ness

nig'gard·ly

nig'gle

nig'gling·ly

nigh

night

night'cap'

night'fall'

night'fish'

night'gown'

night'hawk'

night'in·gale

night'ly

night'mare'

night'mar'ish

night'shade'

night'shirt'

night'time'

night'wear'

night'work'

night'work'er

ni'hil·ism

ni'hil·ist

ni'hil·is'tic

nim'ble

nim'bus

nin'com·poop

nine'pins'

nip'per

nip'ple

nip'py

nir·va'na

ni'ter

ni'trate

ni'tric

ni'tride

ni'tri·fi·ca'tion

ni'tri·fy

ni'tro·gen

ni·trog'e·nous

ni'tro·glyc'er·in

ni'trous

nit'wit'

no

no·bil'i·ty

no'ble

no'ble·man

no'bler

no'blest

no'bly

no'bod·y

noc·tur'nal

noc·tur'nal·ly

noc'turne

nod

nod'ded

node

nod'ule

no·el'

noise

noise'less

nois'i·er

nois'i·est

nois'i·ly

nois'i·ness

noi'some

nois'y

no'mad

no·mad'ic

no'men·cla'ture

nom'i·nal

nom'i·nal·ism

nom'i·nal·ly

nom'i·nate

nom'i·nat'ed

nom'i·na'tion

nom'i·na·tive

nom'i·nee'

non'a·ge·nar'i·an

non'a·gon

non'ap·pear'ance

non·call'a·ble

nonce

non'cha·lance

non'cha·lant

non'cha·lant·ly

non·com'bat·ant

non'com·mis'sioned

non·com·mit'tal

non'com·mu'ni·cant

non'con·duc'tor

non'con·form'ism

non'con·form'ist

non'con·form'i·ty

non'-co-op'er·a'tion

non'de·script

non·en'ti·ty

non'es·sen'tial

none'such'

non'ex·ist'ence

non·fea'sance

non·fea'sor

non·for'feit·ure

non'in·ter·ven'tion

non'met'al

non'me·tal'lic

non'pa·reil'

non'par·tic'i·pat'ing

non·par'ti·san

non·per'ma·nent

non'plus

non'plused

non·res'i·dence

non·res'i·dent

non're·sist'ance

non're·sist'ant

non'sense

non·sen'si·cal

non'skid'

non'stop'

non'sub·scrib'er

non'suit'

non'sup·port'

non·un'ion

noo'dle

nook

noon

noon'day'

noon'time'

noose

nor

norm

nor'mal

nor·mal'i·ty

nor'mal·ize

nor'mal·ized

nor'mal·ly

Nor'man

nor'ma·tive

Norse

north

north'east'

north'east'er

north'east'er·ly

north'east'ern

north'east'ward

north'east'ward·ly

north'er·ly

north'ern

north'ern·er

north'land

north'ward

north'west'

north'west'er·ly

north'west'ern

Nor·we'gian

nose

nose'band'

nose'bleed'

nose'gay'

nose'piece'

nos'ings

no·sol'o·gy

nos·tal'gi·a

nos·tal'gic

nos'tril

nos'trum

not

no'ta·bil'i·ty

no'ta·ble

no·tar'i·al

no·tar'i·al·ly

no'ta·ry

no·ta'tion

notch

notched

notch'weed'

note

note'book'

not'ed

note'wor'thi·ly

note'wor'thy

noth'ing

noth'ing·ness

no'tice

no'tice·a·ble

no'ticed

no'ti·fi·ca'tion

no'ti·fied

no'ti·fy

no'tion

no'to·ri'e·ty

no·to'ri·ous

no·to'ri·ous·ly

not'with·stand'ing

nou'gat

nou'ga·tine

nought

nou'me·non

noun

nour'ish

nour'ished

nour'ish·ing·ly

nour'ish·ment

nov'el

nov'el·ette'

nov'el·ist

nov'el·ize

no·vel'la

nov'el·ty

No·vem'ber

no·ve'na

nov'ice

no·vi'ti·ate

No'vo·cain'

now

now'a·days'

no'where

nox'ious

nox'ious·ness

noz'zle

nu·ance'

nu'cle·ar

nu'cle·ate

nu'cle·at'ed

nu'cle·a'tion

nu'cle·i

nu·cle'o·lus

nu'cle·us

nude

nudge

nudged

nud'ism

nud'ist

nu'di·ty

nu'ga·to'ry

nug'get

nui'sance

null

nul'li·fi·ca'tion

nul'li·fi·ca'tion·ist

nul'li·fied

nul'li·fy

nul'li·ty

numb

numbed

num'ber

num'bered

num'ber·less

numb'ness

nu'mer·al

nu'mer·ate

nu'mer·a'tion	nursed	nu·tri'tion
nu'mer·a'tor	nurse'maid'	nu·tri'tion·al
nu·mer'ic	nurs'er·y	nu·tri'tion·al·ly
nu·mer'i·cal	nurs'er·y·maid'	nu·tri'tion·ist
nu'mer·ous	nurs'er·y·man	nu·tri'tious
nu'mis·mat'ics	nurs'lings	nu·tri'tious·ly
nu·mis'ma·tist	nur'ture	nu'tri·tive
num'skull'	nur'tured	nu'tri·tive·ly
nun	nut	nut'shell'
nun'ci·a·ture	nut'hatch'	nuz'zle
nun'ci·o	nut'meg	nuz'zled
nun'ner·y	nu'tri·a	nyc'ta·lo'pi·a
nup'tial	nu'tri·ent	nymph
nurse	nu'tri·ment	nys·tag'mus

oaf	o·bit′u·ar′y	ob·lique′ness
oak	ob·ject′	ob·liq′ui·ty
oak′en	ob·ject′ed	ob·lit′er·ate
oa′kum	ob·jec′tion	ob·lit′er·at′ed
oar	ob·jec′tion·a·ble	ob·lit′er·a′tion
oar′lock′	ob·jec′tive	ob·liv′i·on
oars′man	ob·jec′tive·ly	ob·liv′i·ous
o·a′sis	ob·jec′tive·ness	ob·liv′i·ous·ly
oat′en	ob′jec·tiv′i·ty	ob·liv′i·ous·ness
oath	ob·jec′tor	ob′long
oat′meal′	ob′jur·gate	ob′lo·quy
ob′bli·ga′to	ob′late	ob·nox′ious
ob′du·ra·cy	ob·la′tion	ob·nox′ious·ly
ob′du·rate	ob′li·gate	o′boe
o·be′di·ence	ob′li·gat′ed	ob·scene′
o·be′di·ent	ob′li·ga′tion	ob·scen′i·ty
o·bei′sance	ob·lig′a·to′ry	ob·scure′
ob′e·lisk	o·blige′	ob·scure′ness
o·bese′	o·bliged′	ob·scu′ri·ty
o·bes′i·ty	o·blig′ing·ly	ob·se′qui·ous
o·bey′	ob·lique′	ob·se′qui·ous·ly
o·beyed′	ob·lique′ly	ob·se′qui·ous·ness

ob·se·quy
ob·serv'a·ble
ob·serv'ance
ob·serv'ant
ob'ser·va'tion
ob·serv'a·to'ry
ob·serve'
ob·served'
ob·serv'er
ob·serv'ing·ly
ob·sess'
ob·sessed'
ob·ses'sion
ob·ses'sion·al
ob·ses'sive
ob·sid'i·an
ob'so·les'cence
ob'so·les'cent
ob'so·lete
ob'so·lete·ly
ob'so·lete·ness
ob'sta·cle
ob·stet'ri·cal
ob·ste·tri'cian
ob·stet'rics
ob'sti·na·cy
ob'sti·nate
ob'sti·nate·ly
ob·strep'er·ous
ob·struct'
ob·struct'ed
ob·struc'tion

ob·struc'tion·ism
ob·struc'tion·ist
ob·struc'tive
ob·struc'tor
ob·tain'
ob·tain'a·ble
ob·tained'
ob·trude'
ob·trud'ed
ob·trud'er
ob·tru'sion
ob·tru'sive
ob·tuse'
ob·tuse'ly
ob·tuse'ness
ob'verse
ob'vi·ate
ob'vi·at'ed
ob'vi·a'tion
ob'vi·ous
ob'vi·ous·ly
oc'a·ri'na
oc·ca'sion
oc·ca'sion·al
oc·ca'sion·al·ly
oc·ca'sioned
oc'ci·dent
oc'ci·den'tal
oc'ci·den'tal·ly
oc·cip'i·tal
oc'ci·put
oc·clude'

oc·clud'ed
oc·clu'sion
oc·cult'
oc'cul·ta'tion
oc·cult'ism
oc·cult'ist
oc'cu·pan·cy
oc'cu·pant
oc'cu·pa'tion
oc'cu·pa'tion·al
oc'cu·pa'tion·al·ly
oc'cu·pied
oc'cu·py
oc·cur'
oc·curred'
oc·cur'rence
o'cean
o'ce·an'ic
o'ce·a·nog'ra·phy
o'ce·lot
o'cher
och·loc'ra·cy
oc'ta·gon
oc·tag'o·nal
oc·tag'o·nal·ly
oc·tam'e·ter
oc·tan'gu·lar
oc'tave
oc·ta'vo
oc·tet'
Oc·to'ber
oc'to·ge·nar'i·an

oc'to·pus

oc'u·lar

oc'u·list

odd

odd'er

odd'est

odd'i·ty

odd'ly

odd'ment

odd'ness

ode

o·de'um

o'di·ous

o'di·ous·ly

o'di·ous·ness

o'di·um

o·dom'e·ter

o'dor

o'dor·if'er·ous

o'dor·less

o'dor·ous

oe·nol'o·gy

of

off

off'fal

off'cast'

of·fend'

of·fend'ed

of·fense'

of·fen'sive

of'fer

of'fered

of'fer·ings

of'fer·to'ry

off'hand'

of'fice

of'fi·cer

of·fi'cial

of·fi'cial·ly

of·fi'ci·ate

of·fi'ci·at'ed

of·fi'ci·a'tion

of·fi'cious

of·fi'cious·ly

of·fi'cious·ness

off'ish

off'set'

off'shoot'

off'shore'

of'ten

of'ten·er

of'ten·est

of'ten·times'

o·gee'

o'give

o'gle

o'gled

o'gre

ohm

ohm'age

ohm'me'ter

oil

oiled

oil'er

oil'hole'

oil'i·er

oil'i·est

oil'i·ly

oil'i·ness

oil'man

oil'pa'per

oil'proof'

oil'seed'

oil'skin'

oil'stone'

oil'tight'

oil'y

oint'ment

o·ka'pi

o'kra

old

old'en

old'er

old'est

old'-fash'ioned

old'ish

old'ness

old'ster

o'le·ag'i·nous

o'le·an'der

o'le·ate

o·lec'ra·non

o'le·o

o'le·o·mar'ga·rine

ol·fac'to·ry

ol'i·garch'y

ol'ive

o·me'ga

om'e·let

o'men

o·men'tum

om'i·nous

o·mis'sion

o·mit'

o·mit'ted

om'ni·bus

om'nip'o·tence

om·nip'o·tent

om'ni·pres'ent

om·nis'cience

om·nis'cient

om·niv'o·rous

on

on'a·ger

once

one

one'ness

on'er·ous

one·self'

one'time'

on'ion

on'look·er

on'ly

on'o·mat'o·poe'ia

on'set'

on'slaught'

on'to

on·tog'e·ny

on·tol'o·gy

o'nus

on'ward

on'yx

o·öl'o·gy

oo'long

ooze

oozed

o·pac'i·ty

o'pal

o'pal·esce'

o'pal·es'cence

o'pal·es'cent

o·paque'

o'pen

o'pened

o'pen·er

o'pen·ings

o'pen·ly

o'pen·ness

o'pen·work'

op'er·a

op'er·a·ble

op'er·a·logue'

op'er·ate

op'er·at·ed

op'er·at'ic

op'er·at'i·cal·ly

op'er·a'tion

op'er·a'tive

op'er·a'tor

op'er·et'ta

oph'thal·mol'o·gist

oph'thal·mol'o·gy

o'pi·ate

o·pin'ion

o·pin'ion·at'ed

o·pin'ion·a'tive

o'pi·um

o·pos'sum

op·po'nent

op'por·tune'

op'por·tun'ism

op'por·tu'ni·ty

op·pos'a·ble

op·pose'

op·posed'

op·pos'er

op·pos'ing

op'po·site

op'po·si'tion

op·press'

op·pressed'

op·pres'sion

op·pres'sive

op·pres'sive·ly

op·pres'sive·ness

op·pres'sor

op·pro'bri·ous

op·pro'bri·ous·ly

op·pro'bri·ous·ness

op·pro'bri·um

opt

opt'ed

op'ta·tive
op'tic
op'ti·cal
op·ti'cian
op'tics
op'ti·mism
op'ti·mist
op'ti·mis'tic
op'ti·mis'ti·cal·ly
op'ti·mum
op'tion
op'tion·al
op'tion·al·ly
op·tom'e·trist
op·tom'e·try
op'u·lence
op'u·lent
o'pus
or
or'a·cle
o·rac'u·lar
o·rac'u·lar·ly
o'ral
o'ral·ly
or'ange
o·rang'u·tan'
o·ra'tion
or'a·tor
or'a·tor'i·cal
or'a·to'ri·o
or'a·to'ry
orb

or'bit
or'bit·al
or'bit·ed
or'chard
or'ches·tra
or·ches'tral
or'ches·trate
or'ches·trat'ed
or·ches·tra'tion
or'chid
or'chi·da'ceous
or·dain'
or·dained'
or·deal'
or'der
or'dered
or'der·li·ness
or'der·ly
or'di·nal
or'di·nance
or'di·nar'i·ly
or'di·nar'y
or'di·na'tion
ord'nance
ore
or'gan
or·gan'ic
or·gan'i·cal·ly
or'gan·ism
or'gan·ist
or'gan·i·za'tion
or'gan·i·za'tion·al

or'gan·ize
or'gan·ized
or'gy
o'ri·el
o'ri·ent
o'ri·en'tal
o'ri·en'tal·ism
o'ri·en'tal·ist
o'ri·en'tal·ly
o'ri·en·tate'
o'ri·en·ta'tion
o'ri·ent'ed
or'i·fice
or'i·gin
o·rig'i·nal
o·rig'i·nal'i·ty
o·rig'i·nal·ly
o·rig'i·nate
o·rig'i·nat'ed
o·rig'i·na'tion
o·rig'i·na'tive
o·rig'i·na'tor
o'ri·ole
O·ri'on
or'i·son
or'lop
or'mo·lu
or'na·ment
or'na·men'tal
or'na·men'tal·ly
or'na·men·ta'tion
or·nate'

or·nate′ly	os′se·ous	out′crop′
or′ni·tho·log′i·cal	os′si·fi·ca′tion	out′cry′
or′ni·thol′o·gist	os′si·fied	out·curve′
or′ni·thol′o·gy	os′si·fy	out·dis′tance
o′ro·tund	os·ten′si·ble	out·do′
o′ro·tun′di·ty	os·ten′si·bly	out′doors′
or′phan	os′ten·ta′tion	out′er
or′phan·age	os′ten·ta′tious	out′er·most
or′phaned	os′ten·ta′tious·ly	out·face′
or′phan·hood	os′te·o·path	out′field′
or′phe·um	os′te·op′a·thy	out′fit
or′rer·y	os′tra·cism	out′fit′ter
or′tho·dox	os′tra·cize	out·flank′
or′tho·ëp′y	os′tra·cized	out′flow′
or·thog′ra·phy	os′trich	out·go′
or′tho·pe′dic	o·tal′gi·a	out′growth′
or·thop′tic	oth′er	out′ings
or′to·lan	oth′er·wise′	out·land′ish
os′cil·late	o′ti·ose	out·land′ish·ness
os′cil·lat′ed	ot′ter	out·last′
os′cil·la′tion	Ot′to·man	out′law′
os′cil·la′tor	ought	out′law′ry
os′cil·la·to′ry	ounce	out′lay′
os·cil′lo·scope	our	out′let
os′cu·late	ours	out′lets
os′cu·la′tion	our·selves′	out′line′
os′cu·la·to′ry	oust	out′lined′
o′sier	oust′er	out·live′
os′mi·um	out	out·lived′
os·mo′sis	out′cast′	out·look′
os·mot′ic	out·class′	out′ly′ing
os′prey	out·come′	out′march′

out·mod'ed

out·num'ber

out'put'

out'rage

out·ra'geous

out·ra'geous·ly

out·ra'geous·ness

out·rank'

out·ranked'

out·reach'

out'rid·er

out'rig'ger

out'right'

out·run'

out'set'

out'side'

out'sid'er

out'size'

out'skirt'

out·stand'ing·ly

out·stay'

out·strip'

out·vote'

out'ward

out'ward·ly

out·wear'

out·wit'

out·work'

o'val

o'vate

o·va'tion

ov'en

ov'en·bird'

ov'en·ware'

o'ver

o'ver·age

o'ver·age'

o'ver·alls'

o'ver·awe'

o'ver·awed'

o'ver·bal'ance

o'ver·bear'

o'ver·bear'ing·ly

o'ver·bid'

o'ver·board'

o'ver·build'

o'ver·built'

o'ver·bur'den

o'ver·cap'i·tal·ize

o'ver·cast'

o'ver·charge'

o'ver·charged'

o'ver·clothes'

o'ver·coat'

o'ver·come'

o'ver·com'pen·sa'tion

o'ver·cor·rect'

o'ver·count'

o'ver·de·vel'op

o'ver·do'

o'ver·done'

o'ver·dose'

o'ver·draft'

o'ver·draw'

o'ver·drawn'

o'ver·dress'

o'ver·drew'

o'ver·drive'

o'ver·driv'en

o'ver·due'

o'ver·eat'

o'ver·es'ti·mate

o'ver·ex·pose'

o'ver·ex·po'sure

o'ver·flow'

o'ver·flow'ing·ly

o'ver·grown'

o'ver·hand'

o'ver·hang'

o'ver·haul'

o'ver·head'

o'ver·heat'

o'ver·is'sue

o'ver·land'

o'ver·lap'

o'ver·look'

o'ver·lord'

o'ver·ly

o'ver·mas'ter·ing·ly

o'ver·mod'u·la'tion

o'ver·night'

o'ver·pass'

o'ver·pay'

o'ver·pop'u·la'tion

o'ver·pow'er

o'ver·pow'ered

o'ver·pow'er·ing·ly	o'ver·sub·scribe'	o'vule
o'ver·pro·duc'tion	o'ver·sup·ply'	o'vum
o'ver·rate'	o'vert	owe
o'ver·rat'ed	o'ver·take'	owed
o'ver·reach'	o'ver·tax'	owl
o'ver·ride'	o'ver·taxed'	owl'et
o'ver·ripe'	o'ver·threw'	owl'ish
o'ver·rule'	o'ver·throw'	own
o'ver·ruled'	o'ver·thrown'	owned
o'ver·run'	o'ver·time'	own'er
o'ver·seas'	o'ver·tone'	own'er·ship
o'ver·see'	o'ver·ture	ox
o'ver·se'er	o'ver·turn'	ox'a·late
o'ver·sell'	o'ver·turned'	ox·al'ic
o'ver·shad'ow	o'ver·val'ue	ox'i·da'tion
o'ver·shad'owed	o'ver·ween'ing·ly	ox'ide
o'ver·shoe'	o'ver·weight'	ox'i·diz'a·ble
o'ver·side'	o'ver·whelm'	ox'i·dize
o'ver·sight'	o'ver·whelmed'	ox'i·dized
o'ver·size'	o'ver·whelm'ing·ly	ox'tongue'
o'ver·spread'	o'ver·wind'	ox'y·gen
o'ver·state'	o'ver·work'	ox'y·gen·ate
o'ver·state'ment	o'ver·worked'	oys'ter
o'ver·stay'	o'ver·wrought'	oys'ter·shell'
o'ver·step'	o'vi·duct	o'zone
o'ver·stock'	o·vip'a·rous	o'zo·nize
o'ver·strain'	o'vi·pos'i·tor	o'zo·nized

P

pab'u·lum

pace

pace'mak'er

pac'er

pach'y·derm

pach'y·san'dra

pa·cif'ic

pa·cif'i·cal·ly

pa·cif'i·cate

pac'i·fi·ca'tion

pa·cif'i·ca·to'ry

pac'i·fied

pac'i·fi'er

pac'i·fism

pac'i·fist

pac'i·fy

pack

pack'age

pack'aged

pack'er

pack'et

pack'ings

pack'sack'

pack'sad'dle

pack'thread'

pact

pad

pad'ded

pad'dings

pad'dle

pad'dled

pad'dle·fish'

pad'dock

pad'lock'

pae'an

pa'gan

pa'gan·ism

pa'gan·ize

page

pag'eant

pag'eant·ry

paged

pag'i·na'tion

pa·go'da

paid

pail

pain

pained

pain'ful

pain'kill'er

pain'less

pains'tak'ing·ly

paint

paint'ed

paint'er

paint'ings

paint'pot'

pair

paired

pair'ings

pa·ja'ma

pal'ace

pal'a·din

pal'an·quin'

pal'at·a·bil'i·ty

pal'at·a·ble

pal′a·tal

pal′a·tal·ize

pal′ate

pa·la′tial

pa·la′tial·ly

pa·lat′i·nate

pal′a·tine

pa·lav′er

pale

paled

pa′le·og′ra·phy

pal′er

pal′est

pal′ette

pal′frey

pal′imp·sest

pal′in·drome

pal′ings

pal′i·node

pal′i·sade′

pall

pal·la′di·um

pall′bear·er

palled

pal′let

pal′li·ate

pal′li·at′ed

pal′li·a′tion

pal′li·a′tive

pal′lid

pal·lid′i·ty

pal′lid·ly

pal′li·um

pal′lor

palm

pal′mate

palmed

palm′er

pal·met′to

palm′ist

palm′is·try

pal′pa·bil′i·ty

pal′pa·ble

pal′pate

pal′pat·ed

pal·pa′tion

pal′pa·to′ry

pal′pi·tant

pal′pi·tate

pal′pi·tat′ed

pal′pi·tat′ing·ly

pal′pi·ta′tion

pal′sied

pal′sy

pal′ter

pal′tered

pal′try

pam′pas

pam′per

pam′pered

pam′phlet

pam′phlet·eer′

pam′phlet·ize

pan

pan′a·ce′a

pan′a·ma′

Pan′-A·mer′i·can

Pan′-A·mer′i-
can·ism

pan′cake′

pan′chro·mat′ic

pan′cre·as

pan′cre·at′ic

pan′da

pan·dem′ic

pan′de·mo′ni·um

pan′der

pan′dered

pane

pan′e·gyr′ic

pan′e·gyr′i·cal

pan′e·gy·rize

pan′e·gy·rized

pan′el

pan′eled

pang

Pan′hel·len′ic

pan′ic

pan′icked

pan′ick·y

pan·jan′drum

panned

pan′nier

pan′ni·kin

pan′o·ply

pan′o·ra·ma

pan′o·ram′ic

pan'sy	pa·rab'o·loid	par'a·phras'tic
pant	par'a·chute	par'a·ple'gi·a
pan'ta·loon'	pa·rade'	par'a·pleg'ic
pant'ed	pa·rad'ed	par'a·site
pan'the·ism	par'a·digm	par'a·sit'ic
pan'the·ist	par'a·dise	par'a·sit'i·cal
pan'the·is'tic	par'a·dox	par'a·sit'i·cide
pan'the·on	par'a·dox'i·cal	par'a·sit·ism
pan'ther	par'af·fin	par'a·sit·ize
pan'to·graph	par'a·gon	par'a·sol
pan'to·mime	par'a·graph	par'a·thy'roid
pan'try	par'a·graphed	par'a·ty'phoid
pan'try·man	par'a·keet	par'a·vane
pa'pa·cy	par'al·lax	par'boil'
pa'pal	par'al·lel	par'boiled'
pa·pay'a	par'al·leled	par'cel
pa'per	par'al·lel·ism	par'celed
pa'per·back'	par'al·lel'o·gram	parch
pa'per·board'	pa·ral'y·sis	parched
pa'pered	par'a·lyt'ic	parch'ment
pa'per·er	par'a·lyt'i·cal·ly	par'don
pap'e·terie	par'a·lyze	par'don·a·ble
pa·poose'	par'a·lyzed	par'doned
pa·pri'ka	pa·ram'e·ter	pare
Pap'u·an	par'a·mount	pared
pap'ule	par'a·noi'a	par'e·gor'ic
pa·py'rus	par'a·noi'ac	pa·ren'chy·ma
par	par'a·noid	par'ent
par'a·ble	par'a·pet	par'ent·age
pa·rab'o·la	par'a·pher·na'li·a	pa·ren'tal
par'a·bol'ic	par'a·phrase	pa·ren'tal·ly
par'a·bol'i·cal	par'a·phrased	pa·ren'the·ses

pa·ren'the·sis
pa·ren'the·size
par'en·thet'i·cal
par'en·thet'i·cal·ly
par'ent·hood
pa·re'sis
par·fait'
pa·ri'ah
pa·ri'e·tal
par'ings
par'ish
pa·rish'ion·er
par'i·ty
park
par'ka
parked
park'way'
par'lance
par·lan'do
par'lay
par'ley
par'leyed
par'lia·ment
par'lia·men·tar'i·an
par'lia·men'ta·ri·ly
par'lia·men'ta·ry
par'lor
par'lous
Par'me·san'
Par·nas'sus
pa·ro'chi·al
pa·ro'chi·al·ism

pa·ro'chi·al·ly
par'o·dy
pa·role'
par'o·no·ma'si·a
pa·rot'id
par'ox·ysm
par'ox·ys'mal
par'ox·ys'mal·ly
par·quet'
par'ri·cid'al
par'ri·cid'al·ly
par'ri·cide
par'ried
par'rot
par'rot·ed
par'ry
parse
parsed
par'si·mo'ni·ous
par'si·mo'ny
pars'ley
pars'nip
par'son
par'son·age
part
par·take'
par·tak'er
part'ed
par·terre'
par'the·no·gen'e·sis
Par'the·non
Par'thi·an

par'tial
par'ti·al'i·ty
par'tial·ly
par·tic'i·pant
par·tic'i·pate
par·tic'i·pat'ed
par·tic'i·pa'tion
par·tic'i·pa'tive
par·tic'i·pa'tor
par'ti·cip'i·al
par'ti·cip'i·al·ly
par'ti·ci·ple
par'ti·cle
par·tic'u·lar
par·tic'u·lar'i·ty
par·tic'u·lar·ize
par·tic'u·lar·ized
par·tic'u·lar·ly
part'ings
par'ti·san
par'ti·san·ship'
par·ti'tion
par·ti'tioned
par'ti·tive
part'ner
part'ner·ship
par'tridge
par'ty
par've·nu
pas'chal
pa·sha'
pass

pass′a·ble

pas′sage

pas′sage·way′

pass′book′

passed

pas′sen·ger

pas′sion

pas′sion·ate

pas′sion·ate·ly

Pas′sion·ist

pas′sion·less

pas′sive

pas′sive·ness

pas′siv·ism

pas′siv·ist

pas·siv′i·ty

pass′key′

pass′o′ver

pass′port

pass′word′

past

paste

paste′board′

past′ed

pas·tel′

pas′tern

pas′teur·i·za′tion

pas′teur·ize

pas′teur·ized

pas·tiche′

pas·tille′

pas′time′

past′i·ness

pas′tor

pas′to·ral

pas′to·ral·ly

pas′tor·ate

pas′try

pas′try·man

pas′tur·age

pas′ture

pas′tured

past′y

pat

Pat′a·go′ni·an

patch

patched

patch′ou·li

patch′work′

patch′y

pa·tel′la

pa·tel′lar

pat′ent

pat′ent·a·ble

pat′ent·ed

pat′ent·ee′

pa′ter·fa·mil′i·as

pa·ter′nal

pa·ter′nal·ism

pa·ter′nal·is′tic

pa·ter′nal·ly

pa·ter′ni·ty

path

pa·thet′ic

pa·thet′i·cal·ly

path′less

pa·thol′o·gist

pa·thol′o·gy

pa′thos

path′way′

pa′tience

pa′tient

pat′i·na

pa′ti·o

pat′ness

pat′ois

pa′tri·arch

pa′tri·ar′chal

pa′tri·arch′ate

pa′tri·arch′y

pa·tri′cian

pat′ri·cide

pat′ri·mo′ni·al

pat′ri·mo′ny

pa′tri·ot

pa′tri·ot′ic

pa′tri·ot′i·cal·ly

pa′tri·ot·ism

pa·tris′tic

pa·trol′

pa·trolled′

pa·trol′man

pa′tron

pa′tron·age

pa′tron·ess

pa′tron·ize

pa'tron·ized

pat'ro·nym'ic

pa·troon'

pat'ted

pat'ten

pat'ter

pat'tered

pat'tern

pat'terned

pau'ci·ty

Paul'ist

paunch

paunch'i·ness

pau'per

pau'per·ism

pau'per·i·za'tion

pau'per·ize

pau'per·ized

pause

paused

pave

paved

pave'ment

pav'er

pa·vil'lion

paw

pawed

pawl

pawn

pawn'bro'ker

pawned

pawn'shop'

pay

pay'a·ble

pay'day'

pay'ee'

pay'ees'

pay'er

pay'mas'ter

pay'ment

pay'roll'

pea

peace

peace'a·ble

peace'a·bly

peace'ful

peace'mak'er

peach

pea'cock'

peak

peaked

peal

pealed

pea'nut'

pear

pearl

pearl'ite

pearl'y

peas'ant

peas'ant·ry

pea'shoot'er

peat

pea'vey

peb'ble

peb'bled

peb'ble·ware'

peb'bly

pe·can'

pec'ca·dil'lo

pec'can·cy

pec'cant

pec'ca·ry

peck

pec'tase

pec'tin

pec'to·ral

pec'u·late

pec'u·lat'ed

pec'u·la'tion

pec'u·la'tor

pe·cul'iar

pe·cu'li·ar'i·ty

pe·cul'iar·ly

pe·cu'ni·ar'y

ped'a·gog'ic

ped'a·gog'i·cal

ped'a·gog'i·cal·ly

ped'a·gogue

ped'a·go'gy

ped'al

ped'aled

ped'ant

pe·dan'tic

pe·dan'ti·cal

pe·dan'ti·cism

ped'ant·ry

ped'dle

ped'dled

ped'dler

ped'es·tal

pe·des'tri·an

pe·des'tri·an·ism

pe'di·a·tri'cian

pe'di·at'rics

pe·dic'u·lar

pe·dic'u·lo'sis

ped'i·cure

ped'i·gree

ped'i·greed

ped'i·ment

pe·dom'e·ter

peek

peel

peeled

peel'ings

peen

peep

peer

peer'age

peered

peer'less

pee'vish

peg

Peg'a·sus

pegged

pe'jo·ra'tive

pe'koe

pe·lag'ic

pelf

pel'i·can

pe·lisse'

pel·la'gra

pel'let

pel·lu'cid

pe·lo'ta

pelt

pelt'ed

pel'try

pel'vic

pel'vis

pem'mi·can

pen

pe'nal

pe'nal·i·za'tion

pe'nal·ize

pe'nal·ized

pen'al·ty

pen'ance

pen'chant'

pen'cil

pen'ciled

pend'ant

pend'en·cy

pend'ing

pen'du·lous

pen'du·lum

pen'e·tra·bil'i·ty

pen'e·tra·ble

pen'e·trant

pen'e·trate

pen'e·trat'ed

pen'e·trat'ing·ly

pen'e·tra'tion

pen'e·tra'tive

pen'guin

pen'hold'er

pen'i·cil'lin

pen·in'su·la

pen·in'su·lar

pen'i·tence

pen'i·tent

pen'i·ten'tial

pen'i·ten'tial·ly

pen'i·ten'tia·ry

pen'i·tent·ly

pen'knife'

pen'man

pen'man·ship

pen'nant

pen'ni·less

pen'non

pen'ny

pen'ny·roy'al

pen'ny·weight'

pe·nol'o·gist

pe·nol'o·gy

pen'sion

pen'sion·ar'y

pen'sioned

pen'sion·er

pen'sive

pen'stock'

pent

pen'ta·gon

pen·tag'o·nal

pen·tam'e·ter

Pen'ta·teuch

pen·tath'lon

pen'ta·ton'ic

Pen'te·cost

pent'house'

pent·ox'ide

pe'nult

pe·nul'ti·mate

pe·num'bra

pe·nu'ri·ous

pen'u·ry

pe'on

pe'on·age

pe'o·ny

peo'ple

peo'pled

pep'lum

pep'per

pep'pered

pep'per·i·ness

pep'per·mint

pep'per·y

pep'sin

pep'tic

pep'tone

per'ad·ven'ture

per·am'bu·late

per·am'bu·la'tor

per·bo'rate

per·cale'

per·ceiv'a·ble

per·ceive'

per·ceived'

per cent

per·cent'age

per·cen'tile

per'cept

per·cep'ti·bil'i·ty

per·cep'ti·ble

per·cep'tion

per·cep'tive

per·cep'tu·al

per·cep'tu·al·ly

perch

per·chance'

per·cip'i·en·cy

per·cip'i·ent

per'co·late

per'co·la'tion

per'co·la'tor

per·cus'sion

per·cus'sive

per·di'tion

per·du'

per·dur'a·ble

per'e·gri·na'tion

per·emp'to·ri·ly

per·emp'to·ri·ness

per·emp'to·ry

per·en'ni·al

per·en'ni·al·ly

per'fect

per·fect'ed

per·fect'i·bil'i·ty

per·fect'i·ble

per·fec'tion

per·fec'tion·ism

per·fec'tion·ist

per'fect·ly

per·fec'to

per·fid'i·ous

per'fi·dy

per'fo·rate

per'fo·rat'ed

per'fo·ra'tion

per'fo·ra'tive

per'fo·ra'tor

per·force'

per·form'

per·form'a·ble

per·form'ance

per·formed'

per·form'er

per·fume'

per·fumed'

per·fum'er

per·fum'er·y

per·func'to·ri·ly

per·func'to·ri·ness

per·func'to·ry

per·fuse'

per·fused'

per'go·la

per·haps'

per'i·car'di·al

per'i·car·di'tis

per'i·car'di·um

per'il

per'il·ous

per'il·ous·ly

per·im'e·ter

pe'ri·od

per·i'o·date

pe'ri·od'ic

pe'ri·od'i·cal

pe'ri·od'i·cal·ly

pe'ri·o·dic'i·ty

per'i·os'te·um

per'i·pa·tet'ic

pe·riph'er·al

pe·riph'er·al·ly

pe·riph'er·y

per'i·phras'tic

per'i·scope

per'i·scop'ic

per'ish

per'ish·a·ble

per'ished

per'i·stal'sis

per'i·stal'tic

per'i·stal'ti·cal·ly

per'i·style

per'i·to·ne'um

per'i·to·ni'tis

per'i·win'kle

per'jure

per'jured

per'jur·er

per·ju'ri·ous·ly

per'ju·ry

perk'y

perm'al·loy'

per'ma·nence

per'ma·nent

per'ma·nent·ly

per·man'ga·nate

per'me·a·bil'i·ty

per'me·a·ble

per'me·ate

per'me·at'ed

per'me·a'tion

per·mis'si·bil'i·ty

per·mis'si·ble

per·mis'sion

per·mis'sive

per·mit'

per·mit'ted

per'mu·ta'tion

per·mute'

per·mut'ed

per·ni'cious

per·o·ra'tion

per·ox'ide

per'pen·dic'u·lar

per'pen·dic'u·lar'i·ty

per'pe·trate

per'pe·trat'ed

per'pe·tra'tion

per'pe·tra'tor

per·pet'u·al

per·pet'u·al·ly

per·pet'u·ate

per·pet'u·at'ed

per·pet'u·a'tion

per·pet'u·a'tor

per'pe·tu'i·ty

per·plex'

per·plexed'

per·plex'ed·ly

per·plex'ing·ly

per·plex'i·ty

per'qui·site

per'qui·si'tion

per'se·cute

per'se·cut'ed

per'se·cu'tion

per'se·cu'tor

per'se·ver'ance

per·sev'er·a'tion

per'se·vere'

per'se·vered'

per'si·flage

per·sim'mon

per·sist'

per·sist'ence

per·sist'en·cy

per·sist'ent

per·sist'ing·ly

per'son

per'son·a·ble

per'son·age

per'son·al

per'son·al'i·ty

per'son·al·ize

per'son·al·ly

per'son·al·ty

per·son'i·fi·ca'tion

per·son'i·fied

per·son'i·fy

per'son·nel'

per·spec'tive

per'spi·ca'cious

per'spi·cac'i·ty

per·spic'u·ous

per'spi·ra'tion

per·spir'a·to·ry

per·spire'

per·spired'

per·suade'

per·suad'ed

per·suad'er

per·sua'sion

per·sua'sive

per·sua'sive·ness

per·sul'phate

pert

per·tain'

per·tained'

per'ti·na'cious

per'ti·nac'i·ty

per'ti·nence

per'ti·nent

per·turb'

per·turb'a·ble

per'tur·ba'tion

per·turbed'

pe·rus'al

pe·ruse'

pe·rused'

Pe·ru'vi·an

per·vade'

per·vad'ed

per·vad'ing·ly

per·va'sion

per·va'sive

per·verse'

per·ver'sion

per·ver'si·ty

per·ver'sive

per·vert'

per·vert'ed

per'vi·ous

pes'si·mism

pes'si·mist

pes'si·mis'tic

pes'si·mis'ti·cal·ly

pest

pes'ter

pes'tered

pest'hole'

pest'house'

pes·tif'er·ous

pes'ti·lence

pes'ti·lent

pes'ti·len'tial

pes'ti·len'tial·ly

pes'tle

pet

pet'al

pe·tard'

pe·tite'

pe·ti'tion

pe·ti'tioned

pe·ti'tion·er

pet'rel

pet'ri·fac'tion

pet'ri·fac'tive

pet'ri·fy

pet'rol

pet'ro·la'tum

pe·tro'le·um

pe·trol'o·gy

pet'ted

pet'ti·coat

pet'ti·er

pet'ti·est

pet'ti·fog'ger

pet'ti·ly

pet'ti·ness

pet'tish

pet'ty

pet'u·lance

pet'u·lant

pe·tu'ni·a

pew	phil'an·throp'i·cal	phon'ic
pew'ter	phi·lan'thro·pist	pho'no·graph
pha'e·ton	phi·lan'thro·py	phos'phate
phag'o·cyte	phil'a·tel'ic	phos'phide
phal'ange	phi·lat'e·list	phos'phite
phal'an·ster'y	phi·lat'e·ly	phos'pho·resce'
pha'lanx	phil'har·mon'ic	phos'pho·res'cence
phan'tasm	phi·lip'pic	phos·phor'ic
phan·tas'ma·go'ri·a	Phil'ip·pine	phos'pho·rous
phan'tom	Phil·is'tine	phos'pho·rus
Phar'aoh	phi·lol'o·gist	pho'to·cop'i·er
phar'ma·ceu'tic	phi·lol'o·gy	pho'to·e·lec'tric
phar'ma·ceu'ti·cal	phi·los'o·pher	pho'to·en·grav'ing
phar'ma·ceu'tics	phil'o·soph'ic	pho'to·gen'ic
phar'ma·cist	phil'o·soph'i·cal	pho'to·graph
phar'ma·col'o·gy	phi·los'o·phize	pho'to·graphed
phar'ma·co·poe'ia	phi·los'o·phy	pho·tog'ra·pher
phar'ma·cy	phil'ter	pho'to·graph'ic
phar'yn·gi'tis	phle·bi'tis	pho·tog'ra·phy
phar'ynx	phle·bot'o·my	pho'to·gra·vure'
phase	phlegm	pho'to·lith'o·graph
phased	phleg·mat'ic	pho'to·mi'cro·graph
pheas'ant	phleg·mat'i·cal·ly	pho'ton
phe'nol	phlo'em	pho'to·play'
phe·nom'e·na	phlox	pho'to·sen'si·tize
phe·nom'e·nal	pho'bi·a	Pho'to·stat
phe·nom'e·nol'o·gy	phoe'nix	pho'to·syn'the·sis
phe·nom'e·non	phone	phrase
phi'al	pho·net'ic	phrased
phi·lan'der	pho·net'i·cal·ly	phra'se·ol'o·gy
phi·lan'der·er	pho·ne·ti'cian	phre·net'ic
phil'an·throp'ic	pho·net'ics	phren'ic

phre·nol′o·gist

phre·nol′o·gy

phthi′sis

phy·lac′ter·y

phys′ic

phys′i·cal

phys′i·cal·ly

phy·si′cian

phys′i·cist

phys′ics

phys′i·og′no·my

phys′i·o·log′i·cal

phys′i·o·log′i·cal·ly

phys′i·ol′o·gy

phy·sique′

pi′a·nis′si·mo

pi·an′ist

pi·a′no

pi·an′o·for′te

pi·az′za

pi′ca

pic′a·resque′

pic′co·lo

pick

pick′ax

picked

pick′er

pick′er·el

pick′et

pick′et·ed

pick′ings

pick′le

pick′led

pick′lock′

pick′pock′et

pick′up′

pic′nic

pic′nick·er

pic′ric

pic′to·graph

pic·to′ri·al

pic·to′ri·al·ly

pic′ture

pic′tured

pic′tur·esque′

pie

pie′bald′

piece

piece′meal′

piece′work′

pie′crust′

pied

pie′plant′

pier

pierce

pierced

pi′e·ty

pig

pi′geon

pi′geon·hole′

pig′fish′

pig′ger·y

pig′gish

pig′head′ed

pig′let

pig′ment

pig′men·tar′y

pig′men·ta′tion

pig′ment·ed

pig′nut′

pig′pen′

pig′skin′

pig′stick′er

pig′sty′

pig′tail′

pig′weed′

pike

pik′er

pike′staff′

pi·las′ter

pil′chard

pile

piled

pile′work′

pile′worm′

pil′fer

pil′fer·age

pil′fered

pil′fer·ings

pil′grim

pil′grim·age

pill

pil′lage

pil′laged

pil′lar

pil′lion

pil'lo·ry

pil'low

pil'low·case'

pil'lowed

pi'lot

pi'lot·ed

pi·men'to

pim'per·nel

pim'ple

pin

pin'a·fore'

pin'cers

pinch

pinched

pin'cush'ion

pine

pine'ap'ple

pined

pin'feath'er

pin'fish'

ping'-pong'

pin'guid

pin'hole'

pin'ion

pink

pink'ish

pink'weed'

pink'wood'

pin'nace

pin'na·cle

pinned

pi'noch'le

pin'prick'

pint

pin'to

pin'weed'

pin'worm'

pi'o·neer'

pi'o·neered'

pi'ous

pi'ous·ly

pip

pip'age

pipe

piped

pipe'line'

pip'er

pipe'stem'

pipe'stone'

pi·pette'

pipe'wood'

pip'ing·ly

pip'ings

pip'it

pip'kin

pip·sis'se·wa

pi'quan·cy

pi'quant

pique

pi·qué'

piqued

pi'ra·cy

pi'rate

pi'rat·ed

pi·rat'ic

pi·rat'i·cal

pi·rogue'

pir'ou·ette'

pir·ou·et'ted

pis'ca·tol'o·gy

pis'ca·to'ri·al

pis'ca·to'ri·al·ly

pis·tach'i·o

pis'tol

pis·tole'

pis'ton

pit

pitch

pitched

pitch'er

pitch'fork'

pit'e·ous

pit'e·ous·ness

pit'fall'

pith

pith'i·ly

pith'i·ness

pith'y

pit'i·a·ble

pit'i·ful

pit'i·less

pit'i·less·ly

pit'i·less·ness

pit'tance

pit'ted

pi·tu'i·tar'y

pit'y	plain'ly	plas'ma
pit'y·ing·ly	plain'ness	plas'ter
piv'ot	plaint	plas'tered
piv'ot·al	plain'tiff	plas'ter·er
piv'ot·ed	plain'tive	plas'ter·work'
pla'ca·bil'i·ty	plait	plas'tic
pla'ca·ble	plait'ed	plas·tic'i·ty
plac'ard	plait'ings	plas'tron
pla'cate	plan	plate
pla'cat·ed	plan·chette'	pla·teau'
pla'ca·tive·ly	plane	plat'ed
pla'ca·to'ry	plan'et	plate'hold'er
place	plan'e·tar'i·an	plate'let
pla·ce'bo	plan'e·tar'i·um	plat'en
place'man	plan'e·tar'y	plat'er
place'ment	plan'et·oid	plat'form'
pla·cen'ta	plan'gent	plat'i·na
plac'er	plan'i·sphere	plat'i·nate
plac'id	plank	plat'ings
pla·cid'i·ty	planked	pla·tin'ic
plac'id·ly	plank'ton	plat'i·nize
plack'et	plan'less	plat'i·noid
pla'gi·a·rism	planned	plat'i·num
pla'gi·a·rist	pla'no·graph'ic	plat'i·tude
pla'gi·a·rize	plant	plat'i·tu'di·nize
pla'gi·a·ry	plan'tain	plat'i·tu'di- nous
plague	plan'tar	pla·toon'
plagued	plan·ta'tion	plat'ter
plaid	plant'ed	plat'y·pus
plain	plant'er	plau'dit
plain'er	plant'ings	plau'si·bil'i·ty
plain'est	plaque	plau'si·ble

play	pleat	plinth
play'back'	ple·be'ian	plod
play'bill'	pleb'i·scite	plod'ded
play'boy'	pledge	plod'der
played	pledged	plod'ding·ly
play'er	pledg'ee'	plot
play'ful	pledge'or'	plot'ted
play'ful·ness	pledg'er	plot'ter
play'ground'	pledg'et	plough
play'ings	ple'na·ri·ly	plov'er
play'mate'	ple'na·ry	plow
play'read'er	plen'i·po·ten'ti·ar'y	plow'boy
play'room'	plen'i·tude	plow'ings
play'script'	plen'te·ous	plow'man
play'thing'	plen'ti·ful	plow'share'
play'time'	plen'ty	pluck
play'wright'	ple'num	plucked
pla'za	ple'o·nasm	pluck'i·er
plea	ple'o·nas'tic	pluck'i·est
plead	pleth'o·ra	pluck'i·ly
plead'ed	ple·thor'ic	pluck'i·ness
plead'er	pleu'ra	pluck'y
plead'ing·ly	pleu'ral	plug
plead'ings	pleu'ri·sy	plugged
pleas'ant	plex'us	plum
pleas'ant·ly	pli'a·bil'i·ty	plum'age
pleas'ant·ness	pli'a·ble	plumb
pleas'ant·ry	pli'an·cy	plum·ba'go
please	pli'ant	plum'bate
pleased	pli'ers	plumbed
pleas'ur·a·ble	plight	plumb'er
pleas'ure	plight'ed	plum'bic

plum'bous

plume

plumed

plum'met

plum'met·ed

plump

plump'er

plump'est

plump'ly

plump'ness

plun'der

plun'dered

plun'der·er

plunge

plunged

plung'er

plunk

plunked

plu'ral

plu'ral·ism

plu'ral·ist

plu·ral·is'tic

plu·ral'i·ty

plu'ral·ize

plu'ral·ized

plus

plush

plu·toc'ra·cy

plu'to·crat

plu'to·crat'ic

plu'to·crat'i·cal·ly

plu·ton'ic

plu·to'ni·um

ply

pneu·mat'ic

pneu·mat'i·cal·ly

pneu·mat'ics

pneu·mo'ni·a

poach

poach'er

pock'et

pock'et·book'

pock'et·knife'

pock'mark'

pod

po·dag'ra

po·di'a·try

po'di·um

po'em

po'e·sy

po'et

po'et·as'ter

po·et'ic

po·et'i·cal

po'et·ry

po'i

poign'an·cy

poign'ant

poin'ci·an'a

poin·set'ti·a

point

point'ed

point'ed·ly

point'er

point'less

point'less·ly

poise

poised

poi'son

poi'soned

poi'son·er

poi'son·ous

poke

poked

pok'er

poke'weed'

po'lar

po·lar'i·ty

po'lar·i·za'tion

po'lar·ize

po'lar·ized

po'lar·iz'er

pole

pole'cat'

po·lem'ic

po·lem'i·cal

po·lem'i·cist

po·lem'ics

pole'star'

po·lice'

po·liced'

po·lice'man

pol'i·cy

pol'ish

pol'ished

pol'ish·er

po·lite′

po·lite′ly

po·lite′ness

pol′i·tic

po·lit′i·cal

po·lit′i·cal·ly

pol′i·ti′cian

pol′i·tics

pol′ka

poll

pol′lard

pol′lard·ed

polled

pol′len

pol′li·nate

pol′li·na′tion

pol′li·nif′er·ous

pol·lute′

pol·lut′ed

pol·lu′tion

po′lo

pol′o·naise′

po·lo′ni·um

pol·troon′

pol′y·an′drous

pol′y·an′dry

pol′y·chrome

pol′y·clin′ic

po·lyg′a·mist

po·lyg′a·mous

po·lyg′a·my

pol′y·glot

pol′y·gon

po·lyg′o·nal

pol′y·mer′ic

po·lym′er·ism

pol′y·mer·i·za′tion

pol′y·mer·ize

pol′y·no′mi·al

pol′yp

po·lyph′o·ny

pol′y·syl·lab′ic

pol′y·tech′nic

po·made′

po′man·der

po·ma′tum

pome′gran′ate

Pom′er·a′ni·an

pom′mel

pom′meled

po·mol′o·gy

pomp

pom′pa·dour

pom′pa·no

Pom·pe′ian

pom′pon

pom·pos′i·ty

pomp′ous

pon′cho

pond

pon′der

pon′der·a·ble

pon′dered

pon′der·o′sa

pon′der·os′i·ty

pon′der·ous

pond′fish′

pond′weed′

pon·gee′

pon′iard

pon′tiff

pon·tif′i·cal

pon·tif′i·cal·ly

pon·tif′i·cate

pon·toon′

po′ny

poo′dle

pool

pooled

pool′room′

poor

poor′er

poor′est

poor′house′

poor′ly

poor′ness

pop

pop′corn′

pop′gun′

pop′in·jay

pop′lar

pop′lin

pop′o′ver

popped

pop′pet

pop′py

pop′u·lace	por·ten′tous	pos′si·bil′i·ty
pop′u·lar	por′ter	pos′si·ble
pop′u·lar′i·ty	por′ter·house′	pos′si·bly
pop′u·lar·i·za′tion	port·fo′li·o	pos′sum
pop′u·lar·ize	port′hole′	post
pop′u·lar·ized	por′ti·co	post′age
pop′u·late	por·tiere′	post′al
pop′u·lat′ed	por′tion	post′box′
pop·u·la′tion	por′tioned	post′date′
pop′u·lous	port·man′teau	post′dat′ed
por′ce·lain	por′trait	post′ed
porch	por′trait·ist	post′er
por′cu·pine	por′trai·ture	pos·te′ri·or
pore	por·tray′	pos·ter′i·ty
pored	por·tray′al	pos′tern
por′gy	por·trayed′	post·grad′u·ate
pork	Por′tu·guese	post′haste′
por·nog′ra·phy	por′tu·la′ca	post′hole′
po·ros′i·ty	pose	post′hu·mous
po′rous	posed	pos·til′ion
por′phy·ry	po·si′tion	post′im·pres′sion·ism
por′poise	pos′i·tive	post′ings
por′ridge	pos′i·tiv·ism	post′lude
por′rin·ger	pos′i·tiv·is′tic	post′man
port	pos′i·tron	post·mar′i·tal
port′a·ble	pos′se	post′mark′
por′tage	pos·sess′	post′mas′ter
por′tal	pos·sessed′	post′me·rid′i·an
port·cul′lis	pos·ses′sion	post′mis′tress
por·tend′	pos·ses′sive	post′-mor′tem
por·tend′ed	pos·ses′sor	post·nup′tial
por′tent	pos·ses′sor·ship	post′op′er·a·tive

post'paid'	pot'house'	pow'ered
post·pone'	po'tion	pow'er·ful
post·poned'	pot'latch'	pow'er·ful·ly
post·pone'ment	pot'luck'	pow'er·less
post·pran'di·al	pot'pie'	pow'er·less·ly
post'script	pot'pour'ri'	pow'er·less·ness
pos'tu·lant	pot'sherd'	pow'wow'
pos'tu·late	pot'tage	prac'ti·ca·bil'i·ty
pos'tu·lat'ed	pot'ter	prac'ti·ca·ble
pos'tu·la'tion	pot'ter·y	prac'ti·ca·bly
pos'ture	pouch	prac'ti·cal
pos'tured	poult	prac'ti·cal'i·ty
pos'tur·ings	poul'ter·er	prac'ti·cal·ly
po'sy	poul'tice	prac'tice
pot	poul'ticed	prac'ticed
po'ta·bil'i·ty	poul'try	prac'ti·cum
po'ta·ble	pounce	prac·ti'tion·er
pot'ash'	pounced	prag·mat'ic
po·tas'si·um	pound	prag·mat'i·cal
po·ta'tion	pound'age	prag·mat'i-cal·ly
po·ta'to	pound'cake'	prag'ma·tism
pot'boil'er	pound'ed	prag'ma·tist
po'ten·cy	pound'ings	prai'rie
po'tent	pour	praise
po'ten·tate	poured	praised
po·ten'tial	pout	praise'wor·thy
po·ten'ti·al'i·ty	pout'ed	pra'line
po·ten'tial·ly	pov'er·ty	prance
po·ten'ti·om'e·ter	pow'der	pranced
pot'herb'	pow'dered	pranc'ing·ly
pot'hole'	pow'der·y	prank
pot'hook'	pow'er	prank'ster

prate	pre·cep'tress	pre·cool'
prat'ed	pre·ces'sion	pre·cur'sor
prat'ings	pre·chill'	pre·cur'so·ry
pra·tique'	pre'cinct	pre·da'ceous
prat'tle	pre'ci·os'i·ty	pre·dac'i·ty
prat'tling·ly	pre'cious	pre·date'
prawn	pre'cious·ly	pre·da'tion
pray	prec'i·pice	pred'a·tive
prayed	pre·cip'i·tan·cy	pred'a·tor
prayer	pre·cip'i·tant	pred'a·to'ry
prayer'ful	pre·cip'i·tate	pre·de·cease'
prayer'ful·ly	pre·cip'i·tat'ed	pred'e·ces'sor
preach	pre·cip'i·tate·ly	pre·de·cide'
preached	pre·cip'i·ta'tion	pre·des'ig·nat'ed
preach'er	pre·cip'i·tous	pre'des·ig·na'tion
preach'ment	pré·cis'	pre·des'ti·nar'i·an
preach'y	pre·cise'	pre·des'ti·nar·i·an·ism
pre'ad·o·les'cent	pré·cised'	pre·des'ti·na'tion
pre'am'ble	pre·cise'ly	pre·des'tine
pre'ar·range'	pre·cise'ness	pre·des'tined
pre'ar·range'ment	pre·ci'sion	pre'de·ter'mi·nant
preb'en·dar'y	pre·ci'sion·ist	pre'de·ter'mi·nate
pre·can'celed	pre·clin'i·cal	pre'de·ter'mi·na·tion
pre·car'i·ous	pre·clude'	pre'de·ter'mine
pre·cau'tion	pre·clud'ed	pre'de·ter'mined
pre·cau'tion·ar'y	pre·clu'sion	pre'di·as·tol'ic
pre·cede'	pre·co'cious	pre·dic'a·ment
pre·ced'ed	pre·co'cious·ly	pred'i·cate
pre·ced'ence	pre·coc'i·ty	pred'i·cat'ed
prec'e·dent	pre·con·ceived'	pred'i·ca'tion
pre'cept	pre'con·cep'tion	pred'i·ca'tive
pre·cep'tor	pre·cook'	pre·dict'

pre·dict'a·ble
pre·dict'ed
pre·dic'tion
pre·dic'tion·al
pre·dic'tive
pre'di·gest'
pre'di·gest'ed
pre'di·ges'tion
pre'di·lec'tion
pre'dis·clo'sure
pre'dis·pose'
pre'dis·posed'
pre'dis·po·si'tion
pre·dom'i·nance
pre·dom'i·nant
pre·dom'i·nate
pre·dom'i·nat'ed
pre·dom'i·nate·ly
pre·dom'i·nat'ing·ly
pre·draft'
pre·dry'
pre-em'i·nence
pre-em'i·nent
pre-empt'
pre-empt'ed
pre-emp'tion
pre-emp'tive
preen
preened
pre-es'ti·mate
pre'-ex·ist'
pre'-ex·ist'ent

pref'ace
pref'aced
pre·fash'ion
pref'a·to'ry
pre'fect
pre'fec·ture
pre·fer'
pref'er·a·ble
pref'er·a·bly
pref'er·ence
pref'er·en'tial
pref'er·en'tial·ly
pre·fer'ment
pre·ferred'
pre·fig'ure
pre·fig'ured
pre'fix
pre'fix·al
pre·fixed'
pre·form'
pre·formed'
pre·gath'er
preg'nan·cy
preg'nant
pre·har'vest
pre·hen'sile
pre'hen·sil'i·ty
pre'his·tor'ic
pre'im·ag'ine
pre'in·au'gu·ral
pre'in·cline'
pre'in·clined'

pre·in'ven·to'ry
pre·judge'
pre·judged'
prej'u·diced
prej'u·di'cial
prej'u·di'cial·ly
prel'a·cy
prel'ate
pre·lim'i·nar'y
pre·lit'er·ate
prel'ude
pre·ma·ter'ni·ty
pre·ma·ture'
pre·med'i·cal
pre·med'i·tate
pre·med'i-tat'ed
pre'med·i·ta'tion
pre'mi·er
prem'ise
prem'is·es
pre'mi·um
pre'mo·ni'tion
pre·mon'i·to'ry
pre·na'tal
pre·na'tal·ly
pre·oc'cu·pa'tion
pre·oc'cu·pied
pre·oc'cu·py
pre·op'er·a·tive
pre·or·dain'
pre·or·dained'
pre·paid'

prep'a·ra'tion

pre·par'a·tive

pre·par'a·to'ry

pre·pare'

pre·pared'

pre·par'ed·ness

pre·pay'

pre·pay'ment

pre·pense'

pre·pon'der·ance

pre·pon'der·ant

pre·pon'der·ate

pre·pon'der·at'ing·ly

prep'o·si'tion

prep'o·si'tion·al

pre·pos·sess'

pre·pos·ses'sion

pre·pos'ter·ous

pre·print'

pre're·lease'

pre·req'ui·site

pre·rog'a·tive

pre·sage'

pre·saged'

pres'by·ter

Pres'by·te'ri·an

pres'by·ter'y

pre'sci·ence

pre'sci·ent

pre·scribe'

pre·scribed'

pre·scrip'tion

pre·scrip'tive

pres'ence

pres'ent

pre·sent'a·bil'i·ty

pre·sent'a·ble

pres'en·ta'tion

pre·sent'ed

pre·sen'ti·ment

pres'ent·ly

pre·sent'ment

pres'er·va'tion

pre·serv'a·tive

pre·serve'

pre·serv'er

pre·side'

pre·sid'ed

pres'i·den·cy

pres'i·dent

pres'i·den'tial

press

press'board'

pressed

pres'sings

press'man

press'room'

pres'sure

press'work'

pres'ti·dig'i·ta'tor

pres·tige'

pres·tig'i·ous

pres'to

pre·sum'a·ble

pre·sume'

pre·sumed'

pre·sum'ed·ly

pre·sump'tion

pre·sump'tive

pre·sump'tu·ous

pre'sup·pose'

pre'sys·tol'ic

pre·tend'

pre·tend'ed

pre·tend'er

pre·tense'

pre·ten'sion

pre·ten'tious

pre·ten'tious·ly

pre·ten'tious·ness

pret'er·it

pre'ter·mit'

pre'ter·mit'ted

pre'ter·nat'u·ral

pre'text

pret'ti·er

pret'ti·est

pret'ti·ly

pret'ti·ness

pret'ty

pret'zel

pre·vail'

pre·vailed'

pre·vail'ing·ly

prev'a·lence

prev'a·lent

prev'a·lent·ly

pre·var'i·cate

pre·var'i·cat·ed

pre·var'i·ca'tion

pre·var'i·ca'tor

pre·vent'

pre·vent'a·bil'i·ty

pre·vent'a·ble

pre·vent'ed

pre·ven'tion

pre·ven'tive

pre'view'

pre'vi·ous

pre·vi'sion

pre'vo·ca'tion·al

prey

price

priced

price'less

prick

pricked

prick'le

prick'led

prick'li·ness

prick'ly

pride

pride'ful

priest

priest'ess

priest'hood

priest'ly

prig'gish

prim

pri'ma·cy

pri'mal

pri'ma·ri·ly

pri'ma·ry

pri'mate

pri'mate·ship

prime

primed

prim'er

pri·me'val

prim'i·tive

prim'i·tiv·ism

prim'ly

prim'ness

pri'mo·gen'i·ture

pri·mor'di·al

prim'rose'

prince

prince'li·ness

prince'ling

prince'ly

prin'ces

prin'cess

prin'ci·pal

prin'ci·pal'i·ty

prin'ci·pal·ly

prin'ci·ple

prin'ci·pled

print

print'a·ble

print'ed

print'er

print'er·y

print'ings

pri'or

pri·or'i·ty

pri'o·ry

prism

pris·mat'ic

pris'on

pris'on·er

pris'tine

pri'va·cy

pri'vate

pri'va·teer'

pri'vate·ly

pri'vate·ness

pri·va'tion

priv'et

priv'i·lege

priv'i·ly

priv'i·ty

priv'y

prize

prized

prob'a·bil'i·ty

prob'a·ble

prob'a·bly

pro'bate

pro·ba'tion

pro·ba'tion·ar'y

probe

prob'i·ty

prob'lem	prod'ded	prof'fered
prob'lem·at'ic	prod'i·gal	pro·fi'cien·cy
pro·bos'cis	prod'i·gal'i·ty	pro·fi'cient
pro·ce'dur·al	prod'i·gal·ly	pro·fi'cient·ly
pro·ce'dure	pro·di'gious	pro'file
pro·ceed'	pro·di'gious·ly	prof'it
pro·ceed'ed	prod'i·gy	prof'it·a·ble
pro·ceed'ings	pro·duce'	prof'it·a·bly
proc'ess	pro·duced'	prof'it·ed
proc'essed	pro·duc'er	prof'it·eer'
proc'ess·es	prod'uct	prof'it·less
pro·ces'sion	pro·duc'tion	prof'li·ga·cy
pro·ces'sion·al	pro·duc'tive	prof'li·gate
pro·claim'	pro'duc·tiv'i·ty	pro·found'
pro·claimed'	pro'em	pro·found'ness
proc'la·ma'tion	prof'a·na'tion	pro·fun'di·ty
pro·cliv'i·ty	pro·fan'a·to'ry	pro·fuse'
pro·con'sul	pro·fane'	pro·fuse'ly
pro·cras'ti·nate	pro·faned'	pro·fuse'ness
pro·cras'ti·nat'ed	pro·fan'i·ty	pro·fu'sion
pro·cras'ti·na'tion	pro·fess'	pro·gen'i·tor
pro·cras'ti·na'tor	pro·fessed'	prog'e·ny
pro'cre·a'tion	pro·fess'ed·ly	prog·no'sis
pro'cre·a'tive	pro·fes'sion	prog·nos'tic
proc'tor	pro·fes'sion·al	prog·nos'ti·cate
pro·cur'a·ble	pro·fes'sion·al·ism	prog·nos'ti-cat'ed
proc'u·ra'tion	pro·fes'sion·al·ize	prog·nos'ti-ca'tion
proc'u·ra'tor	pro·fes'sion·al·ly	pro'gram
pro·cure'	pro·fes'sor	pro'gramed
pro·cured'	pro'fes·so'ri·al	pro·gress'
pro·cure'ment	pro·fes'sor·ship	pro·gressed'
prod	prof'fer	pro·gres'sion

pro·gres'sive

pro·hib'it

pro·hib'it·ed

pro'hi·bi'tion

pro'hi·bi'tion·ist

pro·hib'i·tive

pro·hib'i·to'ry

pro·ject'

pro·ject'ed

pro·jec'tile

pro·jec'tion

pro·jec'tive

pro·jec'tor

pro'le·tar'i·an

pro'le·tar'i·at

pro·lif'er·ate

pro·lif'er·a'tion

pro·lif'ic

pro·lif'i·ca'tion

pro·lix'

pro·lix'i·ty

pro'logue

pro·long'

pro·lon'gate

pro'lon·ga'tion

pro·longed'

prom'e·nade'

prom'e·nad'ed

prom'i·nence

prom'i·nent

prom'is·cu'i·ty

pro·mis'cu·ous

pro·mis'cu·ous·ly

pro·mis'cu·ous·ness

prom'ise

prom'ised

prom'is·ing·ly

prom'is·so'ry

prom'on·to'ry

pro·mote'

pro·mot'ed

pro·mot'er

pro·mo'tion

pro·mo'tion·al

prompt

prompt'ed

prompt'er

prompt'est

promp'ti·tude

prompt'ly

prompt'ness

pro·mul'gate

pro·mul'gat·ed

pro'mul·ga'tion

pro'nate

pro·na'tion

prone

prong

prong'horn'

pro·nom'i·nal

pro'noun

pro·nounce'

pro·nounce'a·ble

pro·nounced'

pro·nounce'ment

pro·nun'ci·a'tion

proof

proofed

prop

prop'a·gan'da

prop'a·gan'dist

prop'a·gate

prop'a·gat'ed

prop'a·ga'tion

pro·pel'

pro·pel'lant

pro·pelled'

pro·pel'ler

pro·pen'si·ty

prop'er

prop'er·ly

prop'er·ty

proph'e·cy

proph'e·sied

proph'e·sy

proph'et

pro·phet'ic

pro·phet'i·cal·ly

pro'phy·lac'tic

pro'phy·lax'is

pro·pin'qui·ty

pro·pi'ti·ate

pro·pi'ti·at'ed

pro·pi'ti·a'tion

pro·pi'ti·a·to'ry

pro·pi'tious

pro·po'nent

pro·por'tion

pro·por'tion·a·ble

pro·por'tion·al

pro·por'tion·al·ly

pro·por'tion·ate

pro·por'tion·ate·ly

pro·por'tioned

pro·pos'al

pro·pose'

pro·posed'

prop'o·si'tion

pro·pound'

pro·pound'ed

pro·pri'e·tar'y

pro·pri'e·tor

pro·pri'e·to'ri·al

pro·pri'e·to'ri·al·ly

pro·pri'e·tor·ship'

pro·pri'e·to'ry

pro·pri'e·ty

pro·pul'sion

pro·pul'sive

pro'rate'

pro'rat'ed

pro·ra'tion

pro'ro·ga'tion

pro·rogue'

pro·rogued'

pro·sa'ic

pro·sa'i·cal·ly

pro·sce'ni·um

pro·scribe'

pro·scribed'

pro·scrip'tion

prose

pros'e·cute

pros'e·cut·ed

pros'e·cu'tion

pros'e·cu'tor

pros'e·lyte

pros'e·lyt'ed

pros'e·lyt·ize

pros'e·lyt·iz'er

pros'i·er

pros'i·est

pros'i·fy

pros'i·ly

pros'i·ness

pros'o·dy

pros'pect

pros'pect·ed

pro·spec'tive

pros'pec·tor

pro·spec'tus

pros'per

pros'pered

pros·per'i·ty

pros'per·ous

pros'per·ous·ly

pros'the·sis

pros·thet'ic

pros'trate

pros'trat·ed

pros·tra'tion

pros'y

pro·tag'o·nist

pro'te·an

pro·tect'

pro·tect'ed

pro·tect'ing·ly

pro·tec'tion

pro·tec'tion·ism

pro·tec'tion·ist

pro·tec'tive

pro·tec'tive·ly

pro·tec'tive·ness

pro·tec'tor

pro·tec'tor·ate

pro'té·gé

pro'te·in

pro·test'

prot'es·tant

prot'es·ta'tion

pro·test'ed

pro·test'ing·ly

pro·thon'o·tar'y

pro'to·col

pro'ton

pro'to·plasm

pro'to·type

pro·tox'ide

Pro'to·zo'a

pro·tract'

pro·tract'ed

pro·trac'tile

pro·trac'tion

pro·trac'tive

pro·trac'tor

pro·trude'

pro·trud·ed

pro·tru'sion

pro·tru'sive

pro·tu'ber·ance

pro·tu'ber·ant

proud

proud'er

proud'est

proud'ly

prov'a·ble

prove

proved

prov'en

prov'e·nance

Prov·en·çal'

prov'en·der

prov'erb

pro·ver'bi·al

pro·ver'bi·al·ly

pro·vide'

pro·vid'ed

prov'i·dence

prov'i·dent

prov'i·den'tial

prov'i·den'tial·ly

pro·vid'er

prov'ince

pro·vin'cial

pro·vin'cial·ism

pro·vin'ci·al'i·ty

pro·vin'cial·ly

pro·vi'sion

pro·vi'sion·al

pro·vi'sion·al·ly

pro·vi'so

pro·vi'so·ry

prov'o·ca'tion

pro·voc'a·tive

pro·voke'

pro·voked'

pro·vok'ing·ly

prov'ost

prow

prow'ess

prowl

prowled

prowl'er

prox'i·mal

prox'i·mal·ly

prox'i·mate

prox·im'i·ty

prox'i·mo

prox'y

prude

pru'dence

pru'dent

pru·den'tial

pru·den'tial·ly

pru'dent·ly

prud'er·y

prud'ish

prune

pruned

pru'ri·ence

pru'ri·ent

pru·ri'tus

Prus'sian

pry

pry'ing·ly

psalm

psalm'book'

psalm'ist

psal'mo·dist

psal'mo·dy

psal'ter

pseu'do·nym

pso·ri'a·sis

psy'chi·at'ric

psy'chi·at'ri·cal·ly

psy·chi'a·trist

psy·chi'a·try

psy'chic

psy'chi·cal

psy'chi·cal·ly

psy'cho·a·nal'y·sis

psy'cho·bi·ol'o·gy

psy'cho·dy·nam'ics

psy'cho·gen'e·sis

psy'cho·ge·net'ic

psy'cho·log'i·cal

psy·chol'o·gist

psy·chol'o·gy

psy'cho·path'ic

psy'cho·pa·thol'o·gy

psy'chop'a·thy

psy·cho'sis

psy·chot'ic

Ptol'e·ma'ic

pto'maine

pub'lic

pub'li·ca'tion

pub'li·cist

pub·lic'i·ty

pub'lic·ly

pub'lish

pub'lished

pub'lish·er

puce

puck

puck'er

puck'ered

pud'dings

pud'dle

pud'dled

pud'dler

pu'den·cy

pudg'i·ness

pudg'y

pueb'lo

pu'er·ile

pu'er·il'i·ty

puff

puf'fin

puff'i·ness

puff'y

pug

pu'gil·ism

pu'gil·ist

pu'gil·is'tic

pug·na'cious·ly

pug·nac'i·ty

pu'is·sance

pu'is·sant

pul'chri·tude

pul'chri·tu'di·nous

pul'ing

pul'ing·ly

pull

pulled

pul'let

pul'ley

Pull'man

pul'lu·late

pul'mo·nar'y

Pul'mo'tor

pulp

pulp'i·er

pulp'i·est

pulp'i·ness

pul'pit

pul'pit·eer'

pulp'y

pul'sate

pul'sat·ed

pul·sa'tion

pul·sa'tor

pul'sa·to'ry

pulse

pul'ver·i·za'tion

pul'ver·ize

pul'ver·iz'er

pum'ice

pump

pum'per·nick'el

pump'kin

pun

punch

punched

pun'cheon

punch'ings

punc·til'i·o

punc·til'i·ous

punc·til'i·ous·ly

punc·til'i·ous·ness

punc'tu·al

punc'tu·al'i·ty

punc'tu·al·ly

punc'tu·ate

punc'tu·at'ed

punc'tu·a'tion

punc'ture

punc'tured

pun'dit

pung

pun'gen·cy

pun'gent

pu'ni·ness

pun'ish

pun'ish·a·ble
pun'ished
pun'ish·ment
pu'ni·tive
punk
punt
pu'ny
pup
pu'pa
pu'pae
pu'pil
pup'pet
pup'pet·eer'
pup'pet·ry
pup'py
pur'blind'
pur'chase
pur'chased
pur'chas·er
pure
pure'ly
pur'er
pur'est
pur'ga·tive
pur'ga·to'ry
purge
purged
pu'ri·fi·ca'tion
pu'ri·fied
pu'ri·fi'er
pu'ri·fy
pur'ism

pur'ist
Pu'ri·tan
pu'ri·tan'ic
pu'ri·tan'i·cal
Pu'ri·tan·ism
pu'ri·ty
purl
pur'lieu
pur·loin'
pur'ple
pur'plish
pur·port'
pur·port'ed
pur'pose
pur'pose·ful
pur'pose·ful·ly
pur'pose·ful·ness
pur'pose·less
pur'pose·ly
pur'pos·ive
purr
purred
purse
pursed
purs'er
purs'lane
pur·su'ance
pur·su'ant
pur·sue'
pur·sued'
pur·suit'
pur'sui·vant

pur'sy
pu'ru·lence
pu'ru·len·cy
pu'ru·lent
pur·vey'
pur·vey'ance
pur·vey'or
pur'view
pus
push
push'cart'
push'er
pu'sil·la·nim'i·ty
pu'sil·lan'i·mous
puss'y·foot'
pus'tu·lant
pus'tu·lar
pus'tu·late
pus'tu·la'tion
pus'tule
put
pu'ta·tive
pu'tre·fac'tion
pu'tre·fac'tive
pu'tre·fied
pu'tre·fy
pu·tres'cence
pu·tres'cent
pu'trid
putt
putt'tee
putt'er

put'ty

puz'zle

puz'zled

puz'zler

puz'zles

py·e'mi·a

pyg'my

py·ja'ma

py'lon

py·lo'rus

py'or·rhe'a

pyr'a·mid

py·ram'i·dal

pyre

py'rex

py·rex'i·a

py·ri'tes

py·rog'ra·phy

py'ro·ma'ni·a

py·rom'e·ter

py'ro·tech'nics

py·rox'y·lin

Pyr'rhic

py'thon

Q

quack	quag'mire'	quan'ti·ty
quack'er·y	qua'hog	quan'tum
quad	quail	quar'an·tine
quad'ran'gle	quailed	quar'an·tined
quad·ran'gu·lar	quaint	quar'rel
quad'rant	quaint'ly	quar'reled
quad'rat	quaint'ness	quar'rel·some
quad·rat'ic	quake	quar'ri·er
quad·rat'ics	quaked	quar'ry
quad'ra·ture	quak'er	quar'ry·man
quad·ren'ni·al	quak'ing·ly	quart
quad·ren'ni·al·ly	qual'i·fi·ca'tion	quar'tan
quad·ren'ni·um	qual'i·fied	quar'ter
quad'ri·lat'er·al	qual'i·fi'er	quar'ter·back'
qua·drille'	qual'i·fy	quar'tered
quad'ri·par'tite	qual'i·ta'tive	quar'ter·ings
quad'ru·ped	qual'i·ties	quar'ter·ly
quad'ru'ple	qual'i·ty	quar'ter·mas'ter
quad'ru·plet	qualm	quar'ter·saw'
quad'ru·plex	quan'da·ry	quar·tet'
quad·ru'pli·cate	quan'ti·ta'tive	quar'tile
quaff	quan'ti·ties	quar'to

quartz	queue	quin·tet'
quash	quib'ble	quin'tu·plet
qua'si	quick	quip
qua·ter'na·ry	quick'en	qui'pu
quat'rain	quick'ened	quire
quat're·foil'	quick'er	quirk
qua'ver	quick'est	quirt
qua'vered	quick'lime'	quit
qua'ver·ing·ly	quick'ly	quit'claim'
quay	quick'ness	quite
quay'age	quick'sand'	quit'rent'
quea'sy	quick'sil'ver	quit'tance
queen	quick'step'	quit'ter
queen'ly	quid'di·ty	quiv'er
queer	qui·es'cence	quiv'ered
queer'er	qui'et	quiv'er·ing·ly
queer'est	qui'et·ed	quix·ot'ic
quell	qui'et·ly	quiz
quelled	qui'et·ness	quiz'zi·cal
quench	qui'e·tude	quoin
quenched	qui·e'tus	quoit
quench'less	quill	quon'dam
que'ried	quilled	quo'rum
quer'u·lous	quill'work'	quo'ta
que'ry	quilt	quot'a·ble
quest	quilt'ed	quo·ta'tion
quest'ing·ly	quince	quote
ques'tion	qui'nine	quot'ed
ques'tion·a·ble	quin·quen'ni·al	quoth
ques'tion·er	quin'tal	quo·tid'i·an
ques'tion·ing·ly	quint·es'sence	quo'tient
ques'tion·naire'	quin'tes·sen'tial	quot'ing

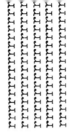

R

rab'bet	rac'y	ra'di·o·pho'to·graph
rab·bin'i·cal	ra'di·al	ra'di·o·scope'
rab'bit	ra'di·al·ly	ra'di·o·sen'si·tive
rab'bit·ry	ra'di·ance	ra'di·o·tel'e·gram
rab'ble	ra'di·ant	rad'ish
rab'id	ra'di·ant·ly	ra'di·um
rab'id·ly	ra'di·ate	ra'di·us
ra'bi·es	ra'di·at'ed	ra'di·us·es
rac·coon'	ra'di·a'tion	ra'dix
race	ra'di·a'tor	ra'don
raced	rad'i·cal	raf'fi·a
rac'er	rad'i·cal·ism	raf'fle
race'way'	rad'i·cal·ly	raf'fled
ra·chit'ic	ra·dic'u·lar	raft
ra·chi'tis	ra'di·i	raft'er
ra'cial	ra'di·o	rafts'man
ra'cial·ly	ra'di·o·ac'tive	rag
rac'i·ly	ra'di·o·ac·tiv'i·ty	rag'a·muf'fin
rac'i·ness	ra'di·o·gram'	rage
rack	ra'di·o·graph'	raged
rack'et	ra'di·om'e·ter	rag'ged
rac'on·teur'	ra'di·o·phone'	rag'lan

ra·gout'	ram	ranked
rag'pick'er	ram'ble	ran'kle
rag'time'	ram'bled	ran'kled
rag'weed'	ram'bler	rank'ling·ly
raid	ram·bunc'tious	ran'sack
rail	ram'e·kin	ran'som
rail'bird'	ram'i·fi·ca'tion	ran'somed
railed	ram'i·fied	rant
rail'head'	ram'i·fy	rant'ed
rail'ing·ly	rammed	rant'ing·ly
rail'ings	ram'mer	ra·pa'cious
rail'ler·y	ramp	ra·pac'i·ty
rail'road'	ram'page	rap'id
rail'road'er	ramp'ant	ra·pid'i·ty
rail'way'	ram'part	rap'id·ly
rai'ment	ram'rod'	ra'pi·er
rain	ram'shack'le	rap'ine
rain'bow'	ranch	rap·port'
rain'coat'	ranch'er	rap·scal'lion
rained	ran·che'ro	rapt
rain'fall'	ranch'man	rap·to'ri·al
rain'spout'	ran'cho	rap'ture
rain'storm'	ran'cid	rap'tur·ous
rain'y	ran·cid'i·ty	rap'tur·ous·ly
raise	ran'cid·ly	rap'tur·ous·ness
raised	ran'cor	rare
rai'sin	ran'cor·ous	rar'e·fac'tion
ra'ja	ran'dom	rar'e·fy
rake	range	rare'ly
rak'ish	ranged	rare'ness
ral'lied	rang'er	rar'er
ral'ly	rank	rar'est

rar'i·ty

ras'cal

ras·cal'i·ty

ras'cal·ly

rash

rash'er

rash'est

rash'ly

rash'ness

rasp

rasp'ber'ry

rasped

rasp'ing·ly

rat

rat'a·ble

ratch'et

rate

rat'ed

rath'er

raths'kel'ler

rat'i·fi·ca'tion

rat'i·fied

rat'i·fy

rat'ings

ra'tio

ra'ti·oc'i·na'tion

ra'ti·oc'i·na'tive

ra'tion

ra'tion·al

ra'tion·al·ism

ra'tion·al·ist

ra'tion·al·is'tic

ra'tion·al·i·za'tion

ra'tion·al·ize

ra'tion·al·ized

ra'tion·al·ly

ra'tioned

rat'line

rat·tan'

rat'ter

rat'tle

rat'tle·brain'

rat'tle·brained'

rat'tled

rat'tle·head'ed

rat'tler

rat'tle·snake'

rat'tlings

rat'tly

rau'cous

rav'age

rav'aged

rave

raved

rav'el

rav'eled

ra'ven

rav'en·ous

rav'en·ous·ly

rav'en·ous·ness

ra'vi'gote'

ra·vine'

rav'ings

ra·vi·o'li

rav'ish

rav'ished

rav'ish·er

rav'ish·ing·ly

rav'ish·ment

raw

raw'boned'

raw'er

raw'est

raw'hide'

raw'ness

ray

ray'less

ray'on

raze

razed

ra'zor

ra'zor·back'

ra'zor·edge'

reach

reached

reach'ings

re·act'

re·act'ance

re·ac'tion

re·ac'tion·ar'y

re·ac'ti·vate

re'ac·ti·va'tion

read

read'a·bil'i·ty

read'a·ble

read'er

read′i·ly

read′i·ness

read′ings

re′ad·just′

re′ad·just′a·ble

re′ad·just′ment

re′ad·mis′sion

re′ad·mit′

read′y

re′af·firm′

re′af·fir·ma′tion

re·a′gent

re′al

re′a·lign′

re′al·ism

re′al·ist

re′al·is′tic

re′al·is′ti·cal·ly

re·al′i·ty

re′al·iz′a·ble

re′al·i·za′tion

re′al·ize

re′al·ized

re′al·ly

realm

re′al·tor

re′al·ty

ream

reamed

ream′er

re·an′i·mate

reap

reap′er

re′ap·pear′

re′ap·pear′ance

re′ap·point′

re′ap·point′ment

rear

reared

re·ar′gue

re·arm′

re·ar′ma·ment

re·armed′

rear′most

re′ar·range′

re′ar·range′ment

rear′ward

rea′son

rea′son·a·ble

rea′son·a·ble·ness

rea′son·a·bly

rea′soned

re′as·sem′ble

re′as·sert′

re′as·sert′ed

re′as·sign′

re′as·sume′

re′as·sur′ance

re′as·sure′

re′as·sured′

re′bate

re′bat·ed

re·bel′

re·belled′

re·bel′lion

re·bel′lious

re·bind′

re·birth′

re·born′

re·bound′

re·buff′

re·buffed′

re·build′

re·built′

re·buke′

re·buked′

re·buk′ing·ly

re′bus

re·but′

re·but′tal

re·but′ted

re·but′ter

re·cal′ci·trance

re·cal′ci·trant

re·call′

re·called′

re·cant′

re′can·ta′tion

re·cant′ed

re·cap′i·tal·ize

re′ca·pit′u·late

re′ca·pit′u·lat′ed

re′ca·pit′u·la′tion

re′ca·pit′u·la·to′ry

re·cap′ture

re·cast′

re·cede'

re·ced'ed

re·ceipt'

re·ceipt'ed

re·ceiv'a·ble

re·ceiv'a·bles

re·ceive'

re·ceived'

re·ceiv'er

re·ceiv'er·ship

re'cent

re'cent·ly

re·cep'ta·cle

re·cep'tion

re·cep'tion·ist

re·cep'tive

re·cep'tive·ly

re·cep'tive·ness

re'cep·tiv'i·ty

re·cep'tor

re·cess'

re·cessed'

re·cess'es

re·ces'sion

re·ces'sion·al

re·ces'sive

re·charge'

re·charged'

re·cher'ché'

re·cid'i·vism

re·cid'i·vist

rec'i·pe

re·cip'i·ent

re·cip'ro·cal

re·cip'ro·cal·ly

re·cip'ro·cate

re·cip'ro·cat'ed

re·cip'ro·ca'tion

re·cip'ro·ca'tive

re·cip'ro·ca'tor

rec'i·proc'i·ty

re·cit'al

re·cit'al·ist

rec'i·ta'tion

rec'i·ta·tive'

re·cite'

re·cit'ed

reck

reck'less

reck'less·ly

reck'less·ness

reck'on

reck'oned

reck'on·er

reck'on·ings

re·claim'

re·claim'a·ble

re·claimed'

rec'la·ma'tion

re·cline'

re·clined'

re·cluse'

rec'og·ni'tion

rec'og·niz'a·ble

re·cog'ni·zance

rec'og·nize

rec'og·nized

re·coil'

re·coiled'

rec'ol·lect'

rec'ol·lect'ed

rec'ol·lec'tion

re'com·mence'

rec'om·mend'

rec'om·men·da'tion

rec'om·mend'a·to'ry

rec'om·mend'ed

re'com·mit'

rec'om·pen'sa·ble

rec'om·pense

rec'om·pensed

rec'on·cil'a·ble

rec'on·cile

rec'on·ciled

rec'on·cile'ment

rec'on·cil'i·a'tion

rec'on·cil'i·a·to'ry

rec'on·dite

re·con'nais·sance

rec'on·noi'ter

rec'on·noi'tered

re·con'quer

re·con·sid'er

re·con'sti·tute

re'con·struct'

re'con·struct'ed

re·con·struc'tion

re·con·struc'tive

re·con'vert

re·con·vey'

re·cord'

re·cord'ed

re·cord'er

re·cord'ings

re·count'

re·count'ed

re·coup'

re·couped'

re·coup'ment

re·course'

re·cov'er

re·cov'er·a·ble

re·cov'er·y

rec're·ant

re'-cre·ate'

rec're·a'tion

rec're·a'tion·al

re·crim'i·nate

re·crim'i·na'tion

re·crim'i·na'tive

re·crim'i·na·to'ry

re'cru·des'cence

re'cru·des'cent

re·cruit'

re·cruit'ed

re·cruit'ment

re'crys·tal·li·za'tion

re·crys'tal·lize

rec'tan'gle

rec·tan'gu·lar

rec·tan'gu·lar'i·ty

rec'ti·fi'a·ble

rec'ti·fi·ca'tion

rec'ti·fied

rec'ti·fi'er

rec'ti·fy

rec'ti·lin'e·ar

rec'ti·tude

rec'tor

rec'tor·ate

rec·to'ri·al

rec'to·ry

re·cum'ben·cy

re·cum'bent

re·cu'per·ate

re·cu'per·at'ed

re·cu'per·a'tion

re·cu'per·a'tive

re·cu'per·a·to'ry

re·cur'

re·curred'

re·cur'rence

re·cur'rent

re·cur'rent·ly

rec'u·sant

red

red'bird'

red'breast'

red'bud'

red'den

red'dened

red'der

red'dest

red'dish

re·deal'

re·deem'

re·deem'a·bil'i·ty

re·deem'a·ble

re·deemed'

re·deem'er

re·demp'tion

Re·demp'tor·ist

re·demp'to·ry

re'de·ter'mine

re'de·vel'op

re'di·rect'

re'di·rect'ed

re·dis'count

re'dis·cov'er

re'dis·trib'ute

re'dis·tri·bu'tion

re·dis'trict

red'ness

red'o·lence

red'o·lent

re·dou'ble

re·doubt'

re·doubt'a·ble

re·dound'

re·draft'

re·dress'

re·dressed'

re·duce'

re·duced'

re·duc'er

re·duc'i·ble

re·duc'tion

re·dun'dance

re·dun'dan·cy

re·dun'dant

re·dun'dant·ly

re·du'pli·cate

re·du'pli·cat'ed

re·du·pli·ca'tion

red'wood'

re-ech'o

re-ech'oed

reed

reed'bird'

reed'i·ness

re-ed'it

re-ed'u·cate

re'-ed·u·ca'tion

reed'y

reef

reef'er

reek

reek'ing·ly

reel

re'-e·lect'

re'-em·bark'

re'-em·bar·ka'tion

re'-em·ploy'

re'-en·act'

re'-en·force'

re'-en·force'ment

re'-en·gage'

re'-en·grave'

re'-en·list'

re-en'ter

re-en'trance

re-en'try

re'-es·tab'lish

re'-ex·am'i·na'tion

re'-ex·am'ine

re'-ex·port'

re'-ex·por·ta'tion

re·fec'to·ry

re·fer'

ref'er·a·ble

ref'er·ee'

ref'er·ence

ref'er·en'dum

re·ferred'

re·fig'ure

re'fill

re'fi·nance'

re·fine'

re·fined'

re·fine'ment

re·fin'er

re·fin'er·y

re·fit'

re·flect'

re·flect'ed

re·flect'ing·ly

re·flec'tion

re·flec'tive

re·flec'tor

re'flex

re·flex'ive

re'flux

re'for·est·a'tion

re·form'

ref'or·ma'tion

re·form'a·tive

re·form'a·to'ry

re·formed'

re·form'er

re·fract'

re·fract'ed

re·frac'tion

re·frac'tion·ist

re·frac'tive

re'frac·tiv'i·ty

re·frac'tor

re·frac'to·ry

re·frain'

re·frained'

re·fresh'

re·freshed'

re·fresh'er

re·fresh'ing·ly

re·fresh'ment

re·frig'er·ant

re·frig'er·ate

re·frig'er·at'ed

re·frig'er·a'tion

re·frig′er·a′tive
re·frig′er·a′tor
ref′uge
ref′u·gee′
re·ful′gence
re·ful′gent
re·fund′
re·fund′ed
re·fur′nish
re·fus′al
re·fuse′
re·fused′
ref′u·ta′tion
re·fute′
re·fut′ed
re·gain′
re·gained′
re′gal
re·gale′
re·galed′
re·gale′ment
re·ga′li·a
re·gal′i·ty
re′gal·ly
re·gard′
re·gard′ed
re·gard′ful
re·gard′less
re·gat′ta
re′ge·la′tion
re′gen·cy
re·gen′er·a·cy

re·gen′er·ate
re·gen′er·at′ed
re·gen′er·a′tion
re·gen′er·a′tive
re·gen′er·a′tor
re′gent
reg′i·cid′al
reg′i·cide
re·gime′
reg′i·men
reg′i·ment
reg′i·men′tal
reg′i·men′tals
reg′i·men·ta′tion
reg′i·ment′ed
re′gion
re′gion·al
re′gion·al·ism
re′gion·al·ize
re′gion·al·ly
reg′is·ter
reg′is·tered
reg′is·trar
reg′is·tra′tion
reg′is·try
re′gress
re·gres′sion
re·gres′sive
re·gret′
re·gret′ful
re·gret′ful·ly
re·gret′ful·ness

re·gret′ta·ble
re·gret′ted
reg′u·lar
reg′u·lar′i·ty
reg′u·lar·i·za′tion
reg′u·lar·ize
reg′u·late
reg′u·lat′ed
reg′u·lates
reg′u·la′tion
reg′u·la′tor
re·gur′gi·tate
re·gur′gi·tat′ed
re·gur′gi·ta′tion
re′ha·bil′i·tate
re′ha·bil′i·tat′ed
re′ha·bil′i·ta′tion
re·hash′
re·hears′al
re·hearse′
re·hearsed′
re·heat′
reign
reigned
re′im·burse′
re′im·bursed′
re′im·port′
re′im·por·ta′tion
rein
re′in·car′nate
re′in·car·na′tion
rein′deer′

reined	re·ju've·nes'cence	rel'e·vant
re'in·force'	re·ju've·nes'cent	re·li'a·bil'i·ty
re'in·forced'	re·kin'dle	re·li'a·ble
re'in·sert'	re·lapse'	re·li'ant
re'in·stall'	re·lapsed'	rel'ic
re'in·state'	re·late'	re·lief'
re'in·stat'ed	re·lat'ed	re·lieve'
re'in·state'ment	re·la'tion	re·lieved'
re'in·sur'ance	re·la'tion·al	re·li'gion
re'in·sure'	re·la'tion·ship	re·li'gious
re·in'te·grate	rel'a·tive	re·li'gious·ly
re'in·tro·duce'	rel'a·tive·ly	re·lin'quish
re'in·vest'	rel'a·tiv·ism	re·lin'quished
re'in·vig'o·rate	rel'a·tiv'i·ty	re·lin'quish·ment
re·is'sue	re·la'tor	rel'i·quar'y
re·it'er·ate	re·lax'	rel'ish
re·it'er·at'ed	re'lax·a'tion	rel'ished
re·it'er·a'tion	re·laxed'	re·live'
re·it'er·a'tive	re·lax'es	re·load'
re·ject'	re·lay'	re·lo'cate
re·ject'ed	re·layed'	re·lo'cat·ed
re·jec'tion	re·lease'	re'lo·ca'tion
re·joice'	re·leased'	re·lo'ca·tor
re·joiced'	rel'e·gate	re·lu'cent
re·joic'es	rel'e·gat'ed	re·luc'tance
re·joic'ing·ly	rel'e·ga'tion	re·luc'tant
re·join'	re·lent'	re·luc'tant·ly
re·join'der	re·lent'ed	re·ly'
re·ju've·nate	re·lent'ing·ly	re·main'
re·ju've·nat'ed	re·lent'less	re·main'der
re·ju've·na'tion	rel'e·vance	re·mained'
re·ju've·na'tive	rel'e·van·cy	re·make'

re·mand'

re·mand'ed

re·mark'

re·mark'a·ble

re·mar'ried

re·mar'ry

re·me'di·a·ble

re·me'di·al

rem'e·died

rem'e·dy

re·mem'ber

re·mem'bered

re·mem'brance

re·mind'

re·mind'ed

re·mind'er

re·mind'ful

re·mind'ing·ly

rem'i·nis'cence

rem'i·nis'cent

re·miss'

re·mis'sion

re·mit'

re·mit'tal

re·mit'tance

re·mit'ted

re·mit'tent

re·mit'ter

rem'nant

re·mod'el

re·mon'e·ti·za'tion

re·mon'e·tize

re·mon'strance

re·mon'strant

re·mon'strate

re·mon'strat·ed

re·mon'strat·ing·ly

re'mon·stra'tion

re'mon'stra·tive

re·morse'

re·morse'ful

re·morse'ful·ly

re·morse'less

re·mote'

re·mote'ness

re·mot'er

re·mot'est

re·mount'

re·mov'a·bil'i·ty

re·mov'a·ble

re·mov'al

re·move'

re·moved'

re·moves'

re·mu'ner·ate

re·mu'ner·at'ed

re·mu'ner·a'tion

re·mu'ner·a'tive

ren'ais·sance'

re'nal

re·nas'cent

rend

ren'der

ren'dered

ren'der·ings

ren'dez·vous

ren·di'tion

ren'e·gade

re·nege'

re·ne·go'ti·ate

re·new'

re·new'a·ble

re·new'al

re·newed'

ren'net

re·nom'i·nate

re·nom'i·na'tion

re·nounce'

re·nounced'

ren'o·vate

ren'o·vat'ed

ren'o·va'tion

re·nown'

re·nowned'

rent

rent'al

rent'ed

re·num'ber

re·nun'ci·a'tion

re·nun'ci·a'tive

re·nun'ci·a·to'ry

re·o'pen

re·or'der

re·or'gan·i·za'tion

re·or'gan·ize

re·o'ri·ent

re·paid'

re·paint'

re·pair'

re·paired'

re·pair'er

rep'a·ra·ble

rep'a·ra'tion

re·par'a·tive

rep'ar·tee'

re·past'

re·pa'tri·ate

re·pay'

re·pay'ment

re·peal'

re·pealed'

re·peal'er

re·peat'

re·peat'ed·ly

re·peat'er

re·pel'

re·pelled'

re·pel'lence

re·pel'len·cy

re·pel'lent

re·pel'ling·ly

re·pent'

re·pent'ance

re·pent'ed

re'per·cus'sion

re'per·cus'sive

rep'er·toire'

rep'er·to'ry

rep'e·tend

rep'e·ti'tion

rep'e·ti'tious

re·pet'i·tive

re·phrase'

re·pine'

re·pined'

re·place'

re·placed'

re·place'ment

re·plant'

re·plen'ish

re·plen'ished

re·plen'ish·ment

re·plete'

re·ple'tion

re·plev'in

rep'li·ca

rep'li·ca'tion

re·plied'

re·ply'

re·port'

re·port'ed

re·port'er

re·pose'

re·posed'

re·pose'ful

re·pos'i·to'ry

re'pos·sess'

re'pos·sessed'

rep're·hend'

rep're·hen'si·ble

rep're·hen'sion

rep're·hen'sive

rep're·sent'

rep're·sen·ta'tion

rep're·sent'a·tive

rep're·sent'ed

re·press'

re·pres'sion

re·pres'sive

re·prieve'

re·prieved'

rep'ri·mand

rep'ri·mand'ed

rep'ri·mand'ing·ly

re'print'

re·print'ed

re·pris'al

re·prise'

re·proach'

re·proached'

re·proach'ful

re·proach'ful·ly

re·proach'ful·ness

rep'ro·bate

rep'ro·ba'tion

re'pro·duce'

re'pro·duc'er

re'pro·duc'tion

re'pro·duc'tive

re·proof'

re·prove'

re·proved'

re·prov′ing·ly

rep′tile

rep·til′i·an

re·pub′lic

re·pub′li·can

re·pub′li·can·ism

re·pub′li·can·ize

re·pub′lish

re·pu′di·ate

re·pu′di·a′tion

re·pug′nance

re·pug′nant

re·pulse′

re·pulsed′

re·pul′sion

re·pul′sive

re·pul′sive·ness

re·pur′chase

rep′u·ta·ble

rep′u·ta′tion

re·pute′

re·put′ed

re·put′ed·ly

re·quest′

re′qui·em

re·quire′

re·quired′

re·quire′ment

req′ui·site

req′ui·si′tion

re·quit′al

re·quite′

re·quit′ed

rere′dos

re·run′

re·sale′

re·scind′

re·scind′ed

re·scis′sion

re·score′

res′cue

res′cued

re·search′

re·search′er

re·sec′tion

re·sem′blance

re·sem′ble

re·sem′bled

re·sent′

re·sent′ed

re·sent′ful

re·sent′ful·ness

re·sent′ment

res′er·va′tion

res′er·va′tion·ist

re·serve′

re·served′

re·serv′ist

res′er·voir

re·set′

re·set′tle

re·set′tle·ment

re·ship′

re·ship′ment

re·side′

re·sid′ed

res′i·dence

res′i·den·cy

res′i·dent

res′i·den′tial

re·sid′u·al

re·sid′u·ar′y

res′i·due

re·sid′u·um

re·sign′

res′ig·na′tion

re·signed′

re·sign′ed·ly

re·sil′i·en·cy

re·sil′i·ent

res′in

res′in·ous

re·sist′

re·sist′ance

re·sist′ant

re·sist′i·ble

re·sis′tive

re′sis·tiv′i·ty

re·sist′less

re·sol′u·ble

res′o·lute

res′o·lute·ness

res′o·lu′tion

re·solv′a·ble

re·solve′

re·solved′

re·sol'vent

res'o·nance

res'o·nant

res'o·nate

res'o·na'tor

re·sort'

re·sort'ed

re·sound'

re·sound'ed

re·sound'ing·ly

re·source'

re·source'ful

re·source'ful·ness

re·spect'

re·spect'a·bil'i·ty

re·spect'a·ble

re·spect'ed

re·spect'er

re·spect'ful

re·spec'tive

re·spec'tive·ly

re·spell'

re·spir'a·ble

res'pi·ra'tion

res'pi·ra·tor

re·spir'a·to'ry

re·spire'

re·spired'

res'pite

re·splend'ence

re·splend'en·cy

re·splend'ent

re·spond'

re·spond'ed

re·spond'ent

re·sponse'

re·spon'si·bil'i·ties

re·spon'si·bil'i·ty

re·spon'si·ble

re·spon'sive

re·spon'sive·ness

rest

re·state'

re·state'ment

res'tau·rant

res'tau·ra·teur'

rest'ed

rest'ful

rest'ful·ly

rest'ful·ness

res'ti·tu'tion

res'tive

res'tive·ly

res'tive·ness

rest'less

rest'less·ness

re·stock'

res'to·ra'tion

re·stor'a·tive

re·store'

re·stored'

re·strain'

re·strained'

re·strain'ed·ly

re·strain'ing·ly

re·straint'

re·strict'

re·strict'ed

re·stric'tion

re·stric'tive

re·sult'

re·sult'ant

re·sum'a·ble

re·sume'

re·sumed'

re·sump'tion

re·sur'gence

re·sur'gent

res'ur·rect'

res'ur·rect'ed

res'ur·rec'tion

re·sus'ci·tate

re·sus'ci·tat'ed

re·sus'ci·ta'tion

re·sus'ci·ta'tive

re·sus'ci·ta'tor

re'tail

re'tailed

re'tail·er

re·tain'

re·tained'

re·tain'er

re·take'

re·tal'i·ate

re·tal'i·at'ed

re·tal'i·a'tion

re·tal'i·a'tion·ist

re·tal'i·a'tive

re·tal'i·a·to'ry

re·tard'

re'tar·da'tion

re·tard'ed

re·tard'er

retch

retched

re·tell'

re·tell'ings

re·ten'tion

re·ten'tive

re'ten·tiv'i·ty

ret'i·cence

ret'i·cent

ret'i·cent·ly

ret'i·cle

re·tic'u·lar

re·tic'u·late

re·tic'u·lat'ed

re·tic'u·la'tion

ret'i·cule

ret'i·na

ret'i·nal

ret'i·ni'tis

ret'i·nue

re·tire'

re·tired'

re·tire'ment

re·tir'ing·ly

re·told'

re·tort'

re·tort'ed

re·touch'

re·touch'er

re·trace'

re·trace'a·ble

re·tract'

re·tract'ed

re·trac'tile

re·trac'tion

re·trac'tive

re·trac'tor

re-tread'

re·treat'

re·treat'ed

re·trench'

re·trenched'

re·trench'ment

re·tri'al

ret'ri·bu'tion

re·trib'u·tive

re·triev'al

re·trieve'

re·trieved'

re·triev'er

ret'ro·ac'tive

ret'ro·ac·tiv'i·ty

ret'ro·cede'

ret'ro·ces'sion

ret'ro·ces'sive

ret'ro·flex

ret'ro·flex'ion

ret'ro·grade

ret'ro·grad'ed

ret'ro·gress

ret'ro·gres'sion

ret'ro·gres'sive

ret'ro·spect

ret'ro·spec'tion

ret'ro·spec'tive

ret'ro·ver'sion

re·turn'

re·turn'a·ble

re·turned'

re·un'ion

re·u·nite'

re-use'

re-used'

re·vac'ci·nate

re·val'i·date

re·val'or·ize

re·val·u·a'tion

re·val'ue

re·vamp'

re·veal'

re·vealed'

re·veal'ing·ly

re·veal'ment

rev'eil·le

rev'el

rev'e·la'tion

rev'e·la·to'ry

rev'eled

rev'el·er

rev'el·ry

re·venge'

re·venged'

re·venge'ful

rev'e·nue

re·ver'ber·ant

re·ver'ber·ate

re·ver'ber·at'ed

re·ver'ber·a'tion

re·ver'ber·a'tive

re·ver'ber·a'tor

re·ver'ber·a·to'ry

re·vere'

re·vered'

rev'er·ence

rev'er·end

rev'er·ent

rev'er·en'tial

rev'er·ie

re·ver'sal

re·verse'

re·versed'

re·vers'i·bil'i·ty

re·vers'i·ble

re·ver'sion

re·ver'sion·ar'y

re·vert'

re·vert'ed

re·vert'i·ble

re·vest'

re·vet'

re·vet'ment

re·vict'ual

re·view'

re·viewed'

re·view'er

re·vile'

re·viled'

re·vile'ment

re·vil'ing·ly

re·vin'di·cate

re·vise'

re·vised'

re·vis'er

re·vi'sion

re·vi'sion·ism

re·vi'sion·ist

re·vis'it

re·viv'al

re·viv'al·ism

re·viv'al·ist

re·vive'

re·vived'

re·viv'i·fi·ca'tion

re·viv'i·fi'er

re·viv'i·fy

rev'o·ca'tion

re·vok'a·ble

re·voke'

re·voked'

re·volt'

re·volt'ed

re·volt'ing·ly

rev'o·lu'tion

rev'o·lu'tion·ar'y

rev'o·lu'tion·ist

rev'o·lu'tion·ize

rev'o·lu'tion·ized

re·volve'

re·volved'

re·volv'er

re·vue'

re·vul'sion

re·vul'sive

re·ward'

re·ward'ed

re·ward'ing·ly

re·wind'

re·wire'

re·word'

re·worked'

re·write'

re·writ'ten

rhap·sod'ic

rhap'so·dist

rhap'so·dize

rhap'so·dized

rhap'so·dy

rhe'ni·um

rhe'o·stat

rhe'sus

rhet'o·ric

rhe·tor'i·cal

rhet'o·ri'cian

rheum

rheu·mat'ic

rheu′ma·tism	rich′ness	right′eous
rheu′ma·toid	rich′weed′	right′eous·ly
rheum′y	rick′ets	right′eous·ness
rhine′stone′	ric′o·chet′	right′ful
rhi·ni′tis	rid′dance	right′ful·ly
rhi·noc′er·os	rid′den	right′ly
rhi·nol′o·gy	rid′dle	right′ness
rhi′no·scope	ride	rig′id
rhi·nos′co·py	rid′er	ri·gid′i·ty
rhi′zome	rid′er·less	rig′id·ly
rho′di·um	ridge	rig′id·ness
rhom′boid	ridged	rig′or
rhom′bus	rid′i·cule	rig′or·ous
rhu′barb	rid′i·culed	rig′or·ous·ly
rhyme	ri·dic′u·lous	rile
rhymed	ri·dic′u·lous·ly	riled
rhythm	ri·dot′to	rill
rhyth′mic	rife	rim
rhyth′mi·cal	rif′fle	rime
Ri·al′to	rif′fled	rind
ri′ant	riff′raff′	ring
rib	ri′fle	ring′bolt′
rib′ald	ri′fled	ring′bone′
rib′ald·ry	ri′fle·man	ringed
ribbed	ri′flings	ring′er
rib′bon	rift	ring′ing·ly
rice	rig	ring′lead′er
rich	rig′a·doon′	ring′let
rich′er	rigged	ring′let·ed
rich′es	rig′ger	ring′mas′ter
rich′est	right	ring′side′
rich′ly	right′ed	ring′worm′

rink		rite		roared	
rinse		rit'u·al		roar'ings	
rinsed		rit'u·al·ism		roast	
ri'ot		rit'u·al·ist		roast'ed	
ri'ot·ed		rit'u·al·is'tic		roast'er	
ri'ot·er		rit'u·al·ly		rob	
ri'ot·ous		ri'val		robbed	
ri'ot·ous·ly		ri'valed		rob'ber	
ri'ot·ous·ness		ri'val·ry		rob'ber·y	
rip		rive		robe	
ri·par'i·an		riv'er		robed	
ripe		riv'er·side'		rob'in	
ripe'ly		riv'et		ro'bot	
rip'en		riv'et·ed		ro·bust'	
rip'ened		riv'et·er		ro·bust'ly	
rip'er		riv'u·let		ro·bust'ness	
rip'est		roach		rock	
ri·poste'		road		rock'er	
rip'ple		road'a·bil'i·ty		rock'et	
rip'pled		road'bed'		rock'fish'	
rip'pling·ly		road'house'		rock'weed'	
rip'ply		road'man		rock'work'	
rip'rap'		road'side'		rock'y	
rise		road'stead		ro·co'co	
ris'en		road'ster		rod	
ris'er		road'way'		ro'dent	
ris'i·bil'i·ty		road'weed'		ro'de·o	
ris'i·ble		roam		rod'man	
ris'ings		roamed		roe	
risk		roam'er		roent'gen	
risked		roam'ings		rogue	
risk'y		roar		ro'guer·y	

ro'guish

ro'guish·ly

ro'guish·ness

roil

roiled

roist'er

roll

rolled

roll'er

roll'mop'

ro·maine'

Ro'man

ro·mance'

Ro'man·esque'

ro·man'tic

ro·man'ti·cal·ly

ro·man'ti·cism

ro·man'ti·cist

ro·man'ti·cize

romp

romp'ers

ron'deau

ron'do

roof

roof'er

roof'less

roof'tree'

rook'er·y

room

roomed

room'er

room'ful

room'i·ness

room'mate'

room'y

roost

roost'er

root

root'ed

root'er

root'let

root'worm'

rope

rope'danc'er

rope'mak'er

rope'work'

ro·quet'

ro·sa'ceous

ro'sa·ry

rose

ro'se·ate

rose'mar'y

ro·sette'

rose'wood'

ros'i·ly

ros'in

ros'i·ness

ros'ter

ros'trum

ros'y

rot

Ro·tar'i·an

ro'ta·ry

ro'tate

ro'tat·ed

ro·ta'tion

ro·ta'tion·al

ro'ta·tive

ro'ta·tor

ro'ta·to'ry

rote

ro'te·none

ro'to·gra·vure'

ro'tor

rot'ten

rot'ten·ness

rot'ter

ro·tund'

ro·tun'da

ro·tun'di·ty

rouge

rouged

rough

rough'age

rough'cast'

rough'dry'

rough'en

rough'ened

rough'er

rough'est

rough'hew'

rough'hewn'

rough'house'

rough'ish

rough'ly

rough'neck'

rough'ness

rough'rid'er

rou·lade'

rou·leau'

rou·lette'

round

round'a·bout'

round'ed

roun'de·lay

round'er

round'est

round'fish'

round'house'

round'ish

round'ly

round'ness

rounds'man

round'worm'

rouse

roused

rous'ing·ly

roust'a·bout'

rout

route

rout'ed

rout'ed

rou·tine'

rou·tin'i·za'tion

rou·tin'ize

rov'er

rov'ing·ly

rov'ings

row

row

row'boat

row'dy

rowed

row'el

row'eled

row'en

row'er

row'lock

roy'al

roy'al·ism

roy'al·ist

roy'al·ly

roy'al·ty

rub

rubbed

rub'ber

rub'ber·ize

rub'ber·ized

rub'ber·y

rub'bings

rub'bish

rub'ble

rub'down'

ru'be·fa'cient

ru'be·fac'tion

ru·be'o·la

ru'bi·cund

ru·bid'i·um

ru'ble

ru'bric

ru'bri·ca'tor

ru'by

ruch'ing

ruck'sack'

ruck'us

rud'der

rud'der·post'

rud'di·er

rud'di·est

rud'di·ly

rud'di·ness

rud'dy

rude

rude'ly

rude'ness

rud'er

rud'est

ru'di·ment

ru'di·men'tal

ru'di·men'ta·ry

rue

rued

rue'ful

ruff

ruf'fi·an

ruf'fi·an·ism

ruf'fle

ruf'fled

Rug'by

rug'ged

rug'ged·ness

ru'gose

ru·gos'i·ty	rum'ple	rus'set
ru'in	rum'pled	Rus'sian
ru'in·a'tion	rum'pus	rust
ru'ined	run	rust'ed
ru'in·ous	run'a·bout'	rus'tic
rule	run'a·gate	rus'ti·cate
ruled	rune	rus'ti·cat'ed
rul'er	rung	rus'ti·ca'tion
rul'ings	ru'nic	rus'ti·cism
rum	run'ner	rus·tic'i·ty
rum'ble	run'off'	rus'tic·ly
rum'bled	runt	rust'i·er
rum'bling·ly	run'way'	rust'i·est
rum'blings	ru·pee'	rus'tle
ru'mi·nant	rup'ture	rus'tled
ru'mi·nate	rup'tured	rus'tler
ru'mi·nat'ed	ru'ral	rus'tling·ly
ru'mi·nat'ing·ly	ru'ral·ism	rus'tlings
ru'mi·na'tion	ru'ral·i·za'tion	rust'proof'
ru'mi·na'tive	ru'ral·ize	rust'y
rum'mage	ru'ral·ly	rut
rum'maged	ruse	ru'ta·ba'ga
rum'my	rush	ruth
ru'mor	rush'ing·ly	ru·the'ni·um
ru'mored	rush'light'	ruth'less
rump	rusk	rye

Sab'ba·tar'i·an	sa'cred	sad'ly
Sab'bath	sa'cred·ly	sad'ness
sab·bat'i·cal	sa'cred·ness	sa·fa'ri
sab'ba·tine	sac'ri·fice	safe
sa'ber	sac'ri·ficed	safe'guard'
sa'ble	sac'ri·fi'cial	safe'keep'ing
sab'o·tage'	sac'ri·lege	safe'ly
sac'cha·rine	sac'ri·le'gious	safe'ness
sac'er·do'tal	sac'ris·tan	saf'er
sa'chem	sac'ris·ty	saf'est
sa·chet'	sac'ro·sanct	safe'ty
sack'but	sa'crum	saf'fron
sack'cloth'	sad	sag
sacked	sad'der	sa'ga
sack'ful	sad'dest	sa·ga'cious
sa'cral	sad'dle	sa·ga'cious·ly
sac'ra·ment	sad'dle·back'	sa·gac'i·ty
sac'ra·men'tal	sad'dle·bag'	sag'a·more
sac'ra·men'tal·ism	sad'dled	sage
sac'ra·men'tal·ist	sad'dler	sagged
sac'ra·men'tal·ly	sad'dler·y	sag'it·tal
sac'ra·men·tar'i·an	sad'i'ron	sa'go

sa'hib

said

sail

sail'boat'

sailed

sail'fish'

sail'ings

sail'or

saint

saint'ed

saint'hood

saint'li·ness

saint'ly

sake

sa'ker

sa·laam'

sal'a·bil'i·ty

sal'a·ble

sa·la'cious

sa·la'cious·ly

sa·la'cious·ness

sal'ad

sal'a·man'der

sal'a·ried

sal'a·ry

sale

sal'e·ra'tus

sales'man

sales'man·ship

sales'peo'ple

sales'per'son

sales'room'

sales'wom'an

sal'i·cyl'ic

sa'li·ence

sa'li·ent

sa·lif'er·ous

sa'line

sa·li'va

sal'i·vant

sal'i·vate

sal'i·va'tion

sal'low

sal'low·er

sal'low·est

sal'ly

salm'on

sa·loon'

sal'si·fy

salt

sal'ta·to'ry

salt'cel'lar

salt'ed

salt'i·er

salt'i·est

salt'pe'ter

salt'y

sa·lu'bri·ous

sa·lu'bri·ty

sal'u·tar'y

sal'u·ta'tion

sa·lu'ta·to'ri·an

sa·lu'ta·to'ry

sa·lute'

sa·lut'ed

sal'vage

sal'vaged

sal·va'tion

salve

salved

sal'ver

sal'vo

Sa·mar'i·tan

sa·ma'ri·um

same

same'ness

sam'ite

Sa·mo'an

sam'o·var

sam'pan

sam'ple

sam'pled

sam'pler

sam'plings

sam'u·rai

san'a·tive

san'a·to'ri·um

san'a·to'ry

sanc'ti·fi·ca'tion

sanc'ti·fied

sanc'ti·fy

sanc'ti·mo'ni·ous

sanc'ti·mo'ni·ous·ly

sanc'ti·mo'ni·ous·ness

sanc'tion

sanc'tioned

sanc'ti·tude	san'guine	sar'do·nyx
sanc'ti·ty	san'i·tar'i·um	sar·gas'so
sanc'tu·ar'y	san'i·tar'y	sa'ri
sanc'tum	san'i·ta'tion	sa·rong'
sand	san'i·ty	sar'sa·pa·ril'la
san'dal	sank	sar·to'ri·al
san'dal·wood'	San'skrit	sash
sand'bag'	sap	sas'sa·fras
sand'bank'	sa'pi·ence	sat
sand'blast'	sa'pi·ent	Sa'tan
sand'box'	sap'lings	sa·tan'ic
sand'bur'	sa·pon'i·fi·ca'tion	satch'el
sand'ed	sa·pon'i·fy	sate
sand'er	sap'per	sat'ed
sand'fish'	sap'phire	sa·teen'
sand'flow'er	sap'pi·er	sat'el·lite
sand'i·ness	sap'pi·est	sa'ti·ate
sand'man'	sap'py	sa'ti·at'ed
sand'pa'per	sap'wood'	sa'ti·a'tion
sand'pip'er	sar'a·band	sa·ti'e·ty
sand'stone'	Sar'a·cen	sat'in
sand'storm'	sar'casm	sat'i·nette'
sand'wich	sar·cas'tic	sat'ire
sand'wiched	sar·cas'ti·cal·ly	sa·tir'ic
sand'worm'	sar·co'ma	sa·tir'i·cal
sand'y	sar·co'ma·ta	sa·tir'i·cal·ly
sane	sar'co·phag'ic	sat'i·rist
sane'ly	sar·coph'a·gus	sat'i·rize
san'er	sar·dine'	sat'i·rized
san'est	Sar·din'i·an	sat'is·fac'tion
sang	sar·don'ic	sat'is·fac'to·ri·ly
san'gui·nar'y	sar·don'i·cal·ly	sat'is·fac'to·ry

sat'is·fied	sav'a·ble	sca'lar
sat'is·fy	sav'age	scald
sat'is·fy'ing·ly	sav'age·ly	scald'ed
sa'trap	sav'age·ry	scale
sat'u·rate	sa·van'na	scaled
sat'u·rat'ed	sa·vant'	sca·lene'
sat'u·ra'tion	save	scal'er
Sat'ur·day	saved	scal'lion
Sat'urn	sav'ings	scal'lop
sat'ur·nine	sav'ior	scalp
sat'yr	sa'vor	scalped
sat'yr·esque'	sa'vor·less	scal'pel
sauce	sa'vor·y	scalp'er
sauce'boat'	saw	scal'y
sauce'dish'	saw'dust'	scamp
sauce'pan'	sawed	scamped
sau'cer	saw'fish'	scam'per
sau'cer·like'	saw'fly'	scam'pered
sau'ci·er	saw'horse'	scan
sau'ci·est	saw'mill'	scan'dal
sau'ci·ly	saw'yer	scan'dal·i·za'tion
sau'cy	Sax'on	scan'dal·ize
saun'ter	say	scan'dal·ized
saun'tered	say'ings	scan'dal·ous
saun'ter·er	says	scan'dal·ous·ly
saun'ter·ing·ly	scab	Scan'di·na'vi·a
saun'ter·ings	scab'bard	scan'di·um
sau'ri·an	scab'by	scanned
sau'sage	sca'bi·es	scan'ner
sau·té'	sca'bi·ous	scan'sion
sau·téed'	sca'brous	scan·so'ri·al
sau·terne'	scaf'fold	scant

scant'ed

scant'i·ly

scant'i·ness

scant'lings

scant'y

scape'goat'

scape'grace'

scap'u·la

scap'u·lar

scar

scar'ab

scarce

scarce'ly

scarc'er

scarc'est

scar'ci·ty

scare

scared

scarf

scar'i·fi·ca'tion

scar'i·fied

scar'i·fi'er

scar'i·fy

scar'la·ti'na

scar'let

scarred

scathed

scathe'less

scath'ing

scath'ing·ly

scat'ter

scat'ter·brain'

scat'tered

scat'ter·ing·ly

scat'ter·ings

scav'en·ger

sce·na'ri·o

scen'er·y

scene'shift'er

sce'nic

sce'ni·cal

scent

scent'ed

scent'less

scent'wood'

scep'ter

scep'tered

sched'ule

sched'uled

sche·mat'ic

sche·mat'i·cal·ly

sche'ma·tize

sche'ma·tized

scheme

schemed

schem'er

schem'ing·ly

scher·zan'do

scher'zo

schism

schis·mat'ic

schis·mat'i·cal

schist

schiz'oid

schiz'o·phre'ni·a

schiz'o·phren'ic

schnapps

schnau'zer

schnit'zel

schol'ar

schol'ar·ly

schol'ar·ship

scho·las'tic

scho·las'ti·cal

scho·las'ti·cal·ly

scho·las'ti·cism

scho'li·ast

scho'li·um

school

school'book'

schooled

school'house'

school'man

school'mas'ter

schoon'er

schot'tische

sci·at'ic

sci·at'i·ca

sci'ence

sci'en·tif'ic

sci'en·tif'i·cal·ly

sci'en·tist

scim'i·tar

scin·til'la

scin'til·lant

scin'til·late

scin'til·lat'ed

scin'til·lat'ing·ly

scin'til·la'tion

sci'on

scis'sors

scle·ri'tis

scle·ro'sis

scle·rot'ic

scle'ro·ti'tis

scle·rot'o·my

scoff

scoffed

scoff'er

scoff'ing·ly

scoff'law'

scold

scold'ed

scold'ing·ly

scold'ings

sco'li·o'sis

sconce

scone

scoop

scooped

scoop'ing·ly

scoot

scoot'er

scope

scorch

scorched

scorch'er

scorch'ing·ly

score

scored

scor'er

scor'ings

scorn

scorned

scorn'er

scorn'ful

scorn'ful·ly

scor'pi·on

Scot

Scotch

Scotch'man

Scots'man

Scot'tish

scoun'drel

scoun'drel·ly

scour

scoured

scour'er

scourge

scourged

scourg'ing·ly

scour'ings

scout

scout'ed

scow

scowl

scowled

scowl'ing·ly

scrab'ble

scrab'bled

scrab'blings

scrag'gy

scram'ble

scram'bled

scram'blings

scrap

scrap'book'

scrape

scraped

scrap'er

scrap'ing·ly

scrap'ings

scrap'man

scrap'pi·er

scrap'pi·est

scrap'ple

scrap'py

scratch

scratched

scratch'i·ness

scratch'ings

scratch'y

scrawl

scrawled

scrawl'ings

scraw'ni·ly

scraw'ni·ness

scraw'ny

scream

screamed

scream'ing·ly

screech

screeched

screech'i·er

screech'i·est

screech'y

screed

screen

screened

screen'ings

screen'play'

screw

screw'driv'er

screwed

scrib'ble

scrib'bled

scrib'bler

scrib'bling·ly

scrib'blings

scribe

scrib'er

scrim

scrim'mage

scrimp

scrimped

scrimp'i·ly

scrimp'i·ness

scrimp'ing·ly

scrim'shaw'

scrip

script

scrip'tur·al

scrip'tur·al·ism

scrip'tur·al·ist

scrip'ture

scrive'ner

scrod

scrof'u·la

scrof'u·lous

scroll

scrolled

scroll'work'

scroug'er

scrounge

scrub

scrub'bed

scrub'bi·er

scrub'bi·est

scrub'bings

scrub'by

scrub'land'

scruff

scrum'mage

scrump'tious

scrunch

scrunched

scru'ple

scru'pled

scru'pu·los'i·ty

scru'pu·lous

scru'pu·lous·ly

scru'pu·lous·ness

scru'ti·ni·za'tion

scru'ti·nize

scru'ti·nized

scru'ti·niz'ing·ly

scru'ti·ny

scud

scud'ded

scuff

scuffed

scuf'fle

scuf'fled

scuf'fling·ly

scuf'flings

scull

sculled

scull'er

scul'ler·y

scul'lion

scul'pin

sculp'tor

sculp'tur·al

sculp'ture

sculp'tur·esque'

scum

scum'my

scup'per

scup'per·nong

scurf

scur·ril'i·ty

scur'ril·ous

scur'ril·ous·ly

scur'ril·ous·ness

scur'ry

scur'vy

scut'tle

scut'tled

scut'tle·ful

scu'tum

scythe

sea

sea'board'

sea'coast'

sea'far'er

sea'fowl'

sea'go'ing

seal

sealed

seal'er

seal'skin'

seam

sea'man

sea'man·like'

sea'man·ship

seamed

seam'stress

seam'y

sea'plane'

sea'port'

sear

search

searched

search'er

search'ing·ly

search'light'

seared

sea'scape

sea'shore'

sea'sick'

sea'sick'ness

sea'side'

sea'son

sea'son·a·ble

sea'son·al

sea'son·al·ly

sea'soned

sea'son·ings

seat

seat'ed

sea'ward

sea'wor'thi·ness

sea'wor'thy

se·ba'ceous

se'cant

se·cede'

se·ced'ed

se·ces'sion

se·ces'sion·ism

se·ces'sion·ist

se·clude'

se·clud'ed

se·clu'sion

sec'ond

sec'ond·ar'i·ly

sec'ond·ar'y

sec'ond·ed

sec'ond·er

sec'ond·hand'

sec'ond·ly

se'cre·cy

se'cret

sec're·tar'i·al

sec're·tar'i·at

sec're·tar'y

se·crete'

se·cret'ed

se·cre'tion

se·cre'tive

se·cre'tive·ly

se·cre'tive·ness

se'cret·ly

se·cre'to·ry

sect

sec·tar'i·an

sec·tar'i·an·ism

sec'ta·ry

sec'tion

sec'tion·al

sec'tion·al·ism

sec'tion·al·ize

sec'tion·al·ized

sec'tion·al·ly

sec'tor

sec'u·lar

sec'u·lar·ism

sec'u·lar·ist

sec'u·lar'i·ty

sec'u·lar·i·za'tion

sec'u·lar·ize

sec'u·lar·ized

sec'u·lar·iz'er

se·cure'

se·cured'

se·cure'ly

se·cu'ri·ty

se·dan'

se·date'

se·date'ly

se·date'ness

se·da'tion

sed'a·tive

sed'en·tar'y

sedge

sed'i·ment

sed'i·men'tal

sed'i·men'ta·ry

sed'i·men·ta'tion

se·di'tion

se·di'tious

se·di'tious·ly

se·di'tious·ness

se·duce'

se·duced'

se·duc'er

se·duc'i·ble

se·duc'tion

se·duc'tive

se·duc'tive·ly

se·duc'tive·ness

sed'u·lous

sed'u·lous·ly

sed'u·lous·ness

se'dum

see

seed

seed'ed

seed'i·er

seed'i·est

seed'i·ness

seed'less

seed'less·ness

seed'lings

seed'y

seek

seek'er

seem

seemed

seem'ing·ly

seem'ly

seen

seep

seep'age

seep'weed'

se'er

seer'ess

seer'suck'er

see'saw'

seethe

seethed

seg'ment

seg·men'tal

seg'men·tar'y

seg'men·ta'tion

seg're·gate

seg're·gat'ed

seg're·ga'tion

seg're·ga'tion·ist

se'gui·dil'la

seine

seis'mic

seis'mo·graph

seis·mol'o·gy

seiz'a·ble

seize

seized

sei'zure

sel'dom

se·lect'

se·lect'ed

se·lec'tion

se·lec'tive

se·lec'tiv'i·ty

se·lect'man

se·lect'men

se·lec'tor

sel'e·nate

se·le'nic

sel'e·nide

sel'e·nite

se·le'ni·um

self

self'-as·ser'tion

self'-as·ser'tive

self'-as·sured'

self'-cen'tered

self'-col'ored

self'-com·mand'

self'-com·pla'cent

self'-com·posed'

self'-con·ceit'

self'-con·cern'

self'-con'fi·dence

self'-con'scious

self'-con'scious·ness

self'-con·tained'

self'-con'tra·dic'tion

self'-con·trol'

self'-cov'ered

self'-de·ceit'

self'-de·fense'

self'-de·ni·al

self'-de·struc'tion

self'-de·ter'mi·na'tion

self'-de·ter'mined

self'-dis'ci·pline

self'-dis·trust'

self'-ed'u·cat·ed

self'-ef·face'ment

self'-ef·fac'ing·ly

self'-es·teem'

self'-ev'i·dent

self'-ex·am'i·na'tion

self'-ex'e·cut'ing

self'-ex·plain'ing

self'-ex·plan'a·to'ry

self'-ex·pres'sion

self'-for·get'ful

self'-gov'erned

self'-gov'ern·ment

self'-help'

self'-im·por'tance

self'-im·prove'ment

self'-in·duced'

self'-in·duc'tance

self'-in·dul'gent

self'-in'ter·est

self'ish

self'ish·ly

self'ish·ness

self'-knowl'edge

self'less

self'-lim'it·ed

self'-liq'ui·dat'ing

self'-love'

self'-made'

self'-mas'ter·y

self'-o·pin'ion·at·ed

self'-pos·sessed'

self'-pos·ses'sion

self'-pres'er·va'tion

self'-pro·pel'ling

self'-rat'ing

self'-read'ing

self'-re'al·i·za'tion

self'-re·gard'

self'-reg'is·ter·ing

self'-re·li'ance

self'-re·li'ant

self'-re·nun'ci·a'tion

self'-re·proach'

self'-re·proach'ful

self'-re·proach'ing·ly

self'-re·spect'

self'-re·straint'

self'-right'eous

self'-right'eous·ness

self'-sac'ri·fice

self'-sac'ri·fic'ing·ly

self'same'

self'-sat'is·fied

self'-seek'er

self'-serv'ice

self'-start'er

self'-stud'y

self'-styled'

self'-suf·fi'cien·cy

self'-suf·fi'cient

self'-sup·port'

self'-sur·ren'der

self'-sus·tain'ing

self'-un'der·stand'ing

self'-will'

self'-willed'

self'-wind'ing

sell

sell'er

sell'out'

Selt'zer

sel'vage

se·man'tic

sem'a·phore

sem'blance

se·mes'ter

sem'i·cir'cle

sem'i·cir'cu·lar

sem'i·civ'i·lized

sem'i·co'lon

sem'i·con'scious

sem'i·de·tached'

sem'i·fi'nal

sem'i·fi'nal·ist

sem'i·fin'ished

sem'i·month'ly

sem'i·nar'

sem'i·nar'i·an

sem'i·nar'y

Sem'i·nole

sem'i·per'me·a·ble

sem'i·pre'cious

sem'i·se'ri·ous

sem'i·skilled'

Sem'ite

Se·mit'ic

Sem'i·tism

sem'i·tone'

sem'i·week'ly

sem'o·li'na

sem'pi·ter'nal

sen'ate

sen'a·tor

sen'a·to'ri·al

sen'a·to'ri·al·ly

sen'a·tor·ship'

send

send'er

Sen'e·ca

se·nes'cence

se·nes'cent

sen'es·chal

se'nile

se·nil'i·ty

sen'ior

sen·ior'i·ty

sen'na

sen'nit

sen'sate

sen·sa'tion

sen·sa'tion·al

sen·sa'tion·al·ism

sen·sa'tion·al·ly

sense

sense'less

sense'less·ly

sense'less·ness

sen'si·bil'i·ty

sen'si·ble

sen'si·tive

sen'si·tive·ly

sen'si·tive·ness

sen'si·tiv'i·ty

sen'si·ti·za'tion

sen'si·tize

sen'si·tized

sen'si·tiz'er

sen'si·tom'e·ter

sen·so'ri·um

sen'so·ry

sen'su·al

sen'su·al·ism

sen'su·al·ist

sen'su·al·is'tic

sen'su·al'i·ty

sen'su·al·i·za'tion

sen'su·al·ize

sen'su·al·ized

sen'su·al·ly

sen'su·ous

sen'su·ous·ly

sen'su·ous·ness

sen'tence

sen'tenced

sen·ten'tious

sen·ten'tious·ly

sen·ten'tious·ness

sen'ti·ence

sen'ti·en·cy

sen'ti·ment

sen'ti·men'tal

sen'ti·men'tal·ism

sen'ti·men'tal·ist

sen'ti·men'tal'i·ty

sen'ti·men'tal·ize

sen'ti·men'tal·ized

sen'ti·nel

sen'try

sep'a·ra·bil'i·ty

sep'a·ra·ble

sep'a·rate

sep'a·rat'ed

sep'a·rate·ly

sep'a·ra'tion

sep'a·ra'tion·ist

sep'a·ra·tism

sep'a·ra'tist

sep'a·ra'tive

sep'a·ra'tor

sep'a·ra·to'ry

se'pi·a

se'poy

sep'sis

Sep·tem'ber

sep·ten'ni·al

sep·tet'

sep'tic

sep'ti·ce'mi·a

Sep'tu·a·gint

sep'tum

sep'ul·cher

se·pul'chral

se·pul'tur·al

sep'ul·ture

se'quel

se·que'la

se·que'lae

se'quence

se·quen'tial

se·quen'tial·ly

se·ques'ter

se·ques'tered

se·ques'trate

se·ques'trat·ed

se'ques·tra'tion

se'quin

Se·quoi'a

se·ragl'io

se·ra'pe

ser'aph

se·raph'ic

se·raph'i·cal

ser'a·phim

Ser'bi·an

sere

ser'e·nade'

ser'e·nad'ed

ser'e·nad'er

ser'e·na'ta

ser'en·dip'i·ty

se·rene'

se·rene'ly

se·rene'ness

se·ren'i·ty

serf

serf'dom

serge

ser'geant

se'ri·al

se'ri·al·i·za'tion

se'ri·al·ize

se'ri·al·ly

se'ri·a'tim

ser'i·cul'ture

se'ries

ser'if

se'ri·ous

se'ri·ous·ly

se'ri·ous·ness

ser'mon

ser'mon·ize

ser'mon·ized

se'rous

ser'pent

ser'pen·tine

ser·pig'i·nous

ser'rate

ser·ra'tion

ser'ried

se'rum

serv'ant

serve

served

serv'er

serv'ice

serv'ice·a·bil'i·ty

serv'ice·a·ble

serv'ice·a·bly

serv'iced

Serv'i·dor

ser'vile

ser·vil'i·ty

serv'ings

ser'vi·tor

ser'vi·tude

ser'vo·mech'-
a·nism

ser'vo·mo'tor

ses'a·me

ses'qui·sul'phide

ses'sion

ses'terce	sex·tet'	shak'en
ses·tet'	sex'ton	shak'er
set	sex'tu·ple	Shake·spear'e·an
set'back'	sex·tu'pli·cate	shake'-up'
set'off'	shab'bi·ly	shak'i·er
set·tee'	shab'bi·ness	shak'i·est
set'ter	shab'by	shak'i·ly
set'tings	shack	shak'i·ness
set'tle	shack'le	shak'o
set'tled	shack'led	shak'y
set'tle·ment	shade	shale
set'tler	shad'ed	shall
sev'er	shad'i·er	shal'lop
sev'er·a·ble	shad'i·est	shal·lot'
sev'er·al	shad'i·ly	shal'low
sev'er·al·ly	shad'i·ness	shal'lowed
sev'er·al·ty	shad'ings	shal'low·er
sev'er·ance	shad'ow	shal'low·est
sev'er·a'tion	shad'owed	shal'low·ly
se·vere'	shad'ow·less	shal'low·ness
sev'ered	shad'ow·y	sham
se·vere'ly	shad'y	sha'man
se·ver'er	shaft	sham'ble
se·ver'est	shag	sham'bled
se·ver'i·ty	shag'bark'	sham'bling·ly
sew	shag'gi·er	shame
sew'age	shag'gi·est	shamed
sewed	shag'gi·ly	shame'faced'
sew'er	shag'gy	shame·fac'ed·ly
sew'er·age	sha·green'	shame'ful
sewn	shake	shame'ful·ly
sex'tant	shake'down'	shame'ful·ness

shame'less·ly	sharp'ness	sheep'skin'
shame'less·ness	sharp'shoot'er	sheer
shammed	sharp'-wit'ted	sheer'er
sham'mer	shas'tra	sheer'est
sham·poo'	shat'ter	sheer'ly
sham·pooed'	shat'tered	sheet
sham'rock	shat'ter·ing·ly	sheet'ed
shan'dy·gaff	shat'ter·proof'	sheet'ings
shang·hai'	shave	sheet'ways'
shang·haied'	shaved	sheet'wise'
shank	shav'er	sheet'work'
shan't	shave'tail'	shek'el
shan'ty	shav'ings	shel'drake'
shape	shaw	shelf
shaped	shawl	shell
shape'less	she	shel·lac'
shape'less·ly	sheaf	shell'back'
shape'less·ness	shear	shell'burst'
shape'li·ness	sheared	shelled
shape'ly	shear'ings	shell'fish'
shard	shears	shell'proof'
share	sheathe	shell'work'
shared	sheathed	shel'ter
share'hold'er	sheaves	shel'tered
shark	shed	shel'ter·ing·ly
sharp	sheen	shel'ter·less
sharp'en	sheep	shelve
sharp'ened	sheep'herd'er	shelved
sharp'en·er	sheep'ish	shelves
sharp'er	sheep'ish·ly	shep'herd
sharp'est	sheep'ish·ness	shep'herd·ed
sharp'ly	sheep'man	shep'herd·ess

Sher'a·ton	shin'gled	shirt'ings
sher'bet	shin'i·ly	shirt'less
sher'iff	shin'i·ness	shiv'er
Sher'pa	shin'ing·ly	shiv'ered
sher'ry	shin'ny	shiv'er·ing·ly
Shet'land	shin'plas'ter	shiv'er·ings
shew'bread'	Shin'to'	shoal
shib'bo·leth	Shin'to·ism	shoal'ness
shied	Shin'to·ist	shock
shield	Shin'to·is'tic	shocked
shield'ed	shin'y	shock'ing·ly
shift	ship	shod
shift'ed	ship'board'	shod'di·er
shift'i·er	ship'build'er	shod'di·est
shift'i·est	ship'load'	shod'dy
shift'i·ly	ship'mas'ter	shoe
shift'i·ness	ship'mate'	shoe'horn'
shift'less	ship'ment	shoe'lace'
shift'y	ship'own'er	shoe'less
shil·le'lagh	ship'per	shoe'mak'er
shil'lings	ship'shape'	shoe'man
shim	ship'worm'	shoes
shimmed	ship'wreck'	shoe'string'
shim'mer	ship'wright'	sho'gun'
shim'mered	ship'yard'	shook
shim'mer·ing·ly	shire	shoot
shim'mer·y	shirk	shoot'er
shin	shirked	shoot'ings
shin'bone'	shirk'er	shop
shine	shirr	shop'keep'er
shin'er	shirred	shop'lift'er
shin'gle	shirt	shop'man

shop'per

shop'work'

shop'worn'

shore

shored

shorn

short

short'age

short'bread'

short'cake'

short'change'

short'com'ings

short'en

short'ened

short'en·ing

short'er

short'est

short'fall'

short'hand'

short'hand'ed

short'horn'

short'ish

short'leaf'

short'-lived'

short'ly

short'ness

short'-range'

short'sight'ed

short'-time'

shot

shot'gun'

shot'ted

should

shoul'der

shoul'dered

shout

shout'ed

shove

shoved

shov'el

shov'eled

shov'el·head'

show

show'boat'

show'down'

showed

show'er

show'ered

show'i·er

show'i·est

show'i·ly

show'i·ness

show'ings

show'man

show'man·ship

shown

show'room'

show'y

shrank

shrap'nel

shred

shred'ded

shred'der

shrew

shrewd

shrewd'er

shrewd'est

shrewd'ly

shrewd'ness

shriek

shrieked

shrift

shrike

shrill

shrilled

shrill'er

shrill'est

shrill'ness

shrill'y

shrimp

shrimp'er

shrine

Shrin'er

shrink

shrink'age

shrink'er

shrink'ing·ly

shrive

shriv'el

shriv'eled

shriv'en

shroud

shroud'ed

shrub

shrub'ber·y

shrub'wood'

shrug

shrugged

shrunk

shrunk'en

shuck

shucked

shud'der

shud'dered

shud'der·ing·ly

shud'der·ings

shuf'fle

shuf'fled

shuf'fling·ly

shuf'flings

shun

shunt

shunt'ed

shut

shut'off'

shut'ter

shut'tered

shut'tle

shut'tled

shy

shy'ly

shy'ness

shy'ster

Si'a·mese'

sib'i·lance

sib'i·lant

sib'i·late

sib'ling

sib'yl

sib'yl·line

Si·cil'i·an

sick

sick'bed'

sick'en

sick'ened

sick'en·ing·ly

sick'er

sick'est

sick'le

sick'li·er

sick'li·est

sick'li·ness

sick'ly

sick'ness

sick'room'

side

side'board'

side'car'

sid'ed

side'long'

side'piece'

si·de're·al

sid'er·ite

side'split'ting

side'walk'

side'ways'

side'wise'

sid'ings

si'dle

si'dled

siege

si·en'na

si·er'ra

si·es'ta

sieve

sift

sift'age

sift'ed

sift'ings

sigh

sighed

sigh'ing·ly

sigh'ings

sight

sight'ed

sight'ings

sight'less

sight'li·ness

sight'ly

sig'ma

sign

sig'nal

sig'naled

sig'nal·ize

sig'nal·ized

sig'nal·ly

sig'na·to'ry

sig'na·ture

sign'board'

signed

sign'er

sig'net

sig·nif'i·cance

sig·nif'i·cant

sig·nif'i·cant·ly

sig'ni·fi·ca'tion

sig'ni·fied

sig'ni·fy

sign'post'

sign'writ·er

si'lage

si'lence

si'lenced

si'lenc·er

si'lent

si'lent·ly

si'lent·ness

si'lex

sil'hou·ette'

sil'i·ca

sil'i·cate

sil'i·con

sil'i·co'sis

silk

silk'en

silk'i·er

silk'i·est

silk'i·ly

silk'i·ness

silk'weed'

silk'worm'

silk'y

sil'la·bub

sil'li·er

sil'li·est

sil'li·ness

sil'ly

si'lo

silt

silt·ta'tion

silt'ed

sil'van

sil'ver

sil'vered

sil'ver·smith'

sil'ver·ware'

sil'ver·y

sim'i·an

sim'i·lar

sim'i·lar'i·ty

sim'i·lar·ly

sim'i·le

si·mil'i·tude

sim'mer

sim'mered

sim'mer·ing·ly

sim'o·ny

si·moon'

sim'per

sim'pered

sim'per·ing·ly

sim'ple

sim'pler

sim'plest

sim'ple·ton

sim'plex

sim·plic'i·ty

sim'pli·fi·ca'tion

sim'pli·fied

sim'pli·fy

sim'ply

sim'u·la'crum

sim'u·late

sim'u·la'tion

si'mul·ta'ne·ous

si·mul·ta'ne·ous·ly

sin

since

sin·cere'

sin·cere'ly

sin·cere'ness

sin·cer'er

sin·cer'est

sin·cer'i·ty

sine

si'ne·cure

sin'ew

sin'ew·y

sin'ful

sin'ful·ly

sin'ful·ness

sing

sing'a·ble

singe

singed

sing'er

sin'gle

sin'gled

sin'gle·ness		sip'per		siz'es	
sin'gle·ton		sir		siz'ings	
sin'gly		sir·dar'		siz'zle	
sin'gu·lar		sire		siz'zled	
sin'gu·lar'i·ty		sired		siz'zling·ly	
sin'gu·lar·ly		si'ren		skate	
sin'is·ter		sir'loin'		skat'ed	
sin'is·tral		si·roc'co		skat'er	
sink		sir'up		skein	
sink'age		sir'up·y		skel'e·tal	
sink'er		si'sal		skel'e·ton	
sink'hole'		sis'kin		skel'e·ton·ize	
sink'ings		sis'si·fied		skel'e·ton·ized	
sink'less		sis'sy		skep'tic	
sin'less		sis'ter		skep'ti·cal	
sin'less·ly		sis'ter·hood		skep'ti·cal·ly	
sin'less·ness		sis'ter-in-law'		skep'ti·cism	
sinned		sis'ter·ly		sketch	
sin'ner		Sis'tine		sketched	
Sin'o·log'i·cal		sis'trum		sketch'i·ly	
Si·nol'o·gist		sit		sketch'i·ness	
Sin'o·logue		site		sketch'y	
Sin'o·phile		sit'ter		skew	
sin'ter		sit'tings		skewed	
sin'u·os'i·ty		sit'u·ate		skew'er	
sin'u·ous		sit'u·at'ed		skew'ered	
si'nus·i'tis		sit'u·a'tion		skew'ings	
Sioux		sixth		ski	
sip		siz'a·ble		ski'a·gram	
si'phon		size		ski'a·graph	
si'phoned		sized		ski·am'e·try	
sipped		siz'er		skid	

skid'ded	skir'mished	sky'writ'ing
skied	skir'mish·er	slab
skiff	skir'mish·ing·ly	slack
ski·jor'ing	skirt	slacked
skill	skirt'ed	slack'en
skilled	skirt'ings	slack'ened
skil'let	skit	slack'er
skill'ful	skit'ter	slack'est
skill'ful·ly	skit'tish	slack'ness
skill'ful·ness	skit'tish·ly	slag
skim	skit'tish·ness	slain
skimmed	skit'tles	slake
skim'mer	skive	slaked
skim'ming·ly	skived	slam
skimp	skiv'er	slammed
skimped	skiv'ings	slan'der
skimp'i·ness	skoal	slan'dered
skimp'y	skulk	slan'der·er
skin	skulked	slan'der·ing·ly
skin'flint'	skull	slan'der·ous
skink'er	skunk	slan'der·ous·ly
skinned	skunk'weed'	slan'der·ous·ness
skin'ner	sky	slang
skin'ni·er	sky'lark'	slang'y
skin'ni·est	sky'larked'	slank
skin'ny	sky'light'	slant
skin'worm'	sky'rock'et	slant'ed
skip	sky'scape	slant'ing·ly
skipped	sky'scrap'er	slant'ways'
skip'per	sky'shine'	slant'wise'
skip'ping·ly	sky'ward	slap
skir'mish	sky'writ'er	slap'dash'

slap'stick'	sleek'er	slick'est
slash	sleek'est	slid
slashed	sleek'ly	slide
slash'er	sleek'ness	sli'er
slash'ing·ly	sleep	sli'est
slash'ings	sleep'er	slight
slate	sleep'i·er	slight'ed
slat'er	sleep'i·est	slight'er
slat'ted	sleep'i·ly	slight'est
slat'tern	sleep'i·ness	slight'ing·ly
slat'tern·ly	sleep'less	slight'ly
slaugh'ter	sleep'less·ness	slight'ness
slaugh'tered	sleep'y	slim
slaugh'ter·er	sleet	slime
slaugh'ter·house'	sleeve	slim'i·er
slave	sleigh	slim'i·est
slaved	sleight	slim'i·ly
slav'er	slen'der	slim'i·ness
slav'er·y	slen'der·er	slim'mer
slav'ish	slen'der·est	slim'mest
slav'ish·ly	slen'der·ness	slim'ness
slav'ish·ness	slept	slim'y
slaw	sleuth	sling
slay	sleuthed	slink
slay'er	sleuth'hound'	slink'i·er
slay'ings	slew	slink'i·est
sleave	slewed	slink'y
slea'zi·ness	slice	slip
slea'zy	sliced	slip'case'
sled	slic'er	slip'knot'
sledge	slick	slip'page
sleek	slick'er	slipped

slip'per

slip'per·i·ness

slip'per·y

slip'shod'

slit

slith'er

slith'ered

slit'ter

sliv'er

sliv'ered

sliv'er·y

slob

slob'ber

sloe

sloe'ber'ry

slog

slo'gan

slo'gan·eer'

slogged

sloop

slop

slope

sloped

slop'ing·ly

slopped

slop'py

slosh

sloshed

slot

sloth

sloth'ful

sloth'ful·ly

sloth'ful·ness

slot'ted

slouch

slouched

slouch'i·ly

slouch'i·ness

slouch'ing·ly

slough

slough

sloughed

slov'en

slov'en·li·ness

slov'en·ly

slow

slowed

slow'er

slow'est

slow'go'ing

slow'ly

slow'poke'

sloyd

slub

slubbed

sludge

slug

slug'gard

slug'gard·ly

slugged

slug'ger

slug'gish

slug'gish·ly

slug'gish·ness

sluice

sluiced

sluice'way'

sluic'ings

slum

slum'ber

slum'bered

slum'ber·er

slum'ber·ing·ly

slum'ber·land'

slum'ber·ous

slump

slumped

slung

slur

slurred

slur'ring·ly

slur'ry

slush

slush'i·ly

slush'i·ness

slush'y

slut'tish

sly

sly'boots'

sly'ly

sly'ness

smack

smacked

smack'ing·ly

small

small'er

small'est	smil'ing·ly	smooth'ing·ly
small'ness	smirch	smooth'ly
small'pox'	smirched	smooth'ness
smart	smirk	smote
smart'ed	smirked	smoth'er
smart'en	smirk'ing·ly	smoth'ered
smart'ened	smirk'ish	smoth'er·ing·ly
smart'er	smite	smudge
smart'est	smith	smudged
smart'ing·ly	Smith·so'ni·an	smudg'i·ly
smart'ly	smith'y	smudg'i·ness
smart'ness	smit'ten	smudg'y
smash	smock	smug
smash'up'	smoke	smug'gle
smat'ter	smoked	smug'gled
smat'ter·ings	smoke'house'	smug'gler
smear	smoke'less	smug'ly
smeared	smoke'proof'	smug'ness
smear'i·er	smok'er	smut
smear'i·est	smoke'stack'	smut'ted
smear'i·ness	smoke'wood'	smut'ti·er
smear'y	smok'i·er	smut'ti·est
smell	smok'i·est	smut'ti·ly
smelled	smok'i·ness	smut'ti·ness
smelt	smok'y	smut'ty
smelt'ed	smol'der	snack
smelt'er	smol'dered	snaf'fle
smelt'er·y	smooth	sna·fu'
smidg'en	smooth'bore'	snag
smi'lax	smoothed	snag'ged
smile	smooth'er	snag'gled
smiled	smooth'est	snail

snake	snatch'y	snip'pet
snake'bird'	snath	snip'pi·er
snaked	sneak	snip'pi·est
snake'like'	sneaked	snip'pi·ness
snake'stone'	sneak'er	snip'py
snake'weed'	sneak'i·er	sniv'el
snake'wood'	sneak'i·est	sniv'eled
snak'i·er	sneak'ing·ly	sniv'el·er
snak'i·est	sneak'y	sniv'el·ings
snak'i·ly	sneer	snob
snak'i·ness	sneered	snob'ber·y
snak'y	sneer'ing·ly	snob'bish
snap	sneeze	snob'bish·ly
snap'drag'on	sneezed	snob'bish·ness
snapped	sneeze'weed'	snood
snap'per	snick'er	snook'er
snap'pi·er	snick'ered	snoop
snap'pi·est	snick'er·ing·ly	snoop'er
snap'ping·ly	snick'er·ings	snoot
snap'pish	sniff	snooze
snap'py	sniffed	snore
snap'shot'	sniff'i·ly	snored
snap'weed'	sniff'i·ness	snor'ing·ly
snare	sniff'ing·ly	snor'ings
snared	sniff'ings	snor'kel
snarl	snif'fle	snort
snarled	snif'fled	snort'ing·ly
snarl'ing·ly	sniff'y	snort'ings
snarl'y	snig'ger·ing·ly	snout
snatch	snip	snow
snatched	snipe	snow'ball'
snatch'ing·ly	snipped	snow'bell'

snow'ber'ry

snow'bird'

snow'bound'

snow'bush'

snow'cap'

snow'drift'

snow'drop'

snowed

snow'fall'

snow'flake'

snow'flow'er

snow'i·er

snow'i·est

snow'plow'

snow'shed'

snow'shoe'

snow'slide

snow'slip

snow'storm

snow'worm'

snow'y

snub

snubbed

snub'ber

snub'bing·ly

snub'bings

snuff

snuffed

snuff'er

snuf'fle

snuf'fled

snuf'fling·ly

snuf'flings

snug

snug'ger

snug'ger·y

snug'gest

snug'gle

snug'gled

snug'ly

snug'ness

so

soak

soaked

soap

soap'box'

soaped

soap'i·ness

soap'root'

soap'stone'

soap'suds'

soap'y

soar

soared

soar'ing·ly

sob

sobbed

sob'bing·ly

so·be'it

so'ber

so'bered

so'ber·er

so'ber·est

so'ber·ing·ly

so'ber·ly

so'ber·sides'

so·bri'e·ty

so'bri·quet

soc'age

soc'cer

so'cia·bil'i·ty

so'cia·ble

so'cia·bly

so'cial

so'cial·ism

so'cial·ist

so'cial·is'tic

so'cial·i·za'tion

so'cial·ize

so'cial·ized

so'cial·iz'er

so·ci'e·tal

so·ci'e·tar'i·an

so·ci'e·tar'i·an·ism

so·ci'e·ty

so'ci·o·log'i·cal

so'ci·o·log'i·cal·ly

so'ci·ol'o·gist

so'ci·ol'o·gy

sock

sock'et

sock'et·ed

So·crat'ic

sod

so'da

so·dal'i·ty

sod'den	sol'e·cism	sol'i·tude
so'di·um	soled	so'lo
so'fa	sole'ly	so'loed
soft	sol'emn	so'lo·ist
sof'ten	so·lem'ni·ty	sol'stice
sof'tened	sol'em·ni·za'tion	sol'u·bil'i·ty
sof'ten·er	sol'em·nize	sol'u·ble
soft'er	sol'em·nized	sol'ute
soft'est	sol'emn·ly	so·lu'tion
soft'ly	so'le·noid	solv'a·ble
soft'ness	so'le·noi'dal	sol'vate
soft'wood'	sole'print'	sol·va'tion
sog'gi·ly	sol'fe·ri'no	solve
sog'gi·ness	so·lic'it	solved
sog'gy	so·lic'i·ta'tion	sol'ven·cy
soil	so·lic'it·ed	sol'vent
soiled	so·lic'i·tor	so·mat'ic
so·journ'	so·lic'it·ous	so'ma·tol'o·gy
so·journed'	so·lic'i·tude	som'ber
so·journ'er	sol'id	som·bre'ro
sol'ace	sol'i·dar'i·ty	some
sol'aced	so·lid'i·fi'a·ble·ness	some'bod'y
so'lar	so·lid'i·fi·ca'tion	some'how
so·lar'i·um	so·lid'i·fy	some'one'
sold	so·lid'i·ty	som'er·sault
sol'der	sol'id·ly	some'thing
sol'dered	so·lil'o·quize	some'time'
sol'dier	so·lil'o·quized	some'what'
sol'diered	so·lil'o·quy	some'where'
sol'dier·ly	sol'i·taire'	som·nam'bu·lism
sol'dier·y	sol'i·tar'i·ly	som·nam'bu·list
sole	sol'i·tar'y	som'no·lent

son	so·phis'tic	sort
so'nant	so·phis'ti·cal	sort'ed
so·na'ta	so·phis'ti·cate	sort'er
so'na·ti'na	so·phis'ti·cat'ed	sor'tie
song	so·phis'ti·ca'tion	sor'ti·lege
song'bird'	soph'ist·ry	sos'te·nu'to
song'book'	soph'o·more	sot
song'ful	soph'o·mor'ic	sot'tish
song'ful·ness	soph'o·mor'i·cal	sot'tish·ness
song'ster	so'po·rif'ic	sou·brette'
son'ic	so'pra·ni'no	souf'flé'
son'-in-law'	so·pra'no	sought
son'net	sor'cer·er	soul
son'net·eer'	sor'cer·ess	soul'ful
so·nor'i·ty	sor'cer·y	soul'ful·ly
so·no'rous	sor'did	soul'ful·ness
soon	sor'did·ness	soul'less
soon'er	sore	soul'less·ly
soon'est	sore'head'	soul'less·ness
soot	sore'ly	sound
soot'ed	sore'ness	sound'ed
soothe	sor'ghum	sound'er
soothed	so·ror'i·ty	sound'est
sooth'ing·ly	so·ro'sis	sound'ing·ly
sooth'say'er	sor'rel	sound'ings
soot'i·er	sor'ri·er	sound'less
soot'i·est	sor'ri·est	sound'less·ly
soot'i·ly	sor'row	sound'less·ness
soot'y	sor'rowed	sound'ly
sop	sor'row·ful	sound'ness
soph'ism	sor'row·ful·ly	sound'proof'
soph'ist	sor'ry	soup

soup'bone'	sowed	spare'rib'
sour	sow'er	spar'ing·ly
source	sow'ings	spark
soured	soy	spark'ed
sour'er	soy'bean'	spar'kle
sour'est	spa	spar'kled
souse	space	spar'kler
soused	spaced	spar'kling·ly
sou·tane'	spac'ings	sparred
south	spa'cious	spar'ring·ly
south'east'	spa'cious·ly	spar'row
south'east'er	spa'cious·ness	sparse
south'east'er·ly	spade	sparse'ly
south'east'ern	spad'ed	sparse'ness
south'er·ly	spade'fish'	spars'er
south'ern	spade'work'	spars'est
south'ern·er	spa·ghet'ti	spar'si·ty
south'ern·most	spal·peen'	Spar'tan
south'ward	span	spasm
south'west'	span'drel	spas·mod'ic
south'west'er	span'gle	spas·mod'i·cal
south'west'er·ly	span'gled	spas·mod'i·cal·ly
sou've·nir'	Span'iard	spas'tic
sov'er·eign	span'iel	spas'ti·cal·ly
sov'er·eign·ty	Span'ish	spas·tic'i·ty
so'vi·et'	spank	spat
so'vi·et'ism	spanked	spat'ter
so'vi·et'i·za'tion	spank'ing·ly	spat'tered
so'vi·et·ize	spank'ings	spat'ter·ing·ly
so'vi·et·ol'o·gist	span'ner	spat'ter·ings
sow	spare	spat'ter·proof'
sow	spared	spat'ter·work'

spat'u·la	specked	speed'i·ly
spat'u·late	speck'le	speed'i·ness
spav'ined	speck'led	speed'ing·ly
spawn	spec'ta·cle	speed·om'e·ter
spawned	spec'ta·cles	speed'way'
speak	spec·tac'u·lar	speed'y
speak'er	spec·tac'u·lar·ly	spe'le·ol'o·gist
spear	spec·ta'tor	spe'le·ol'o·gy
speared	spec'ter	spell
spear'fish'	spec'tral	spell'bind'er
spear'head'	spec·trom'e·ter	spell'bound'
spear'mint'	spec'tro·scope	spelled
spear'wood'	spec'trum	spell'er
spe'cial	spec'u·late	spell'ings
spe'cial·ist	spec'u·lat'ed	spel'ter
spe'cial·i·za'tion	spec'u·la'tion	Spen·ce'ri·an
spe'cial·ize	spec'u·la'tive	spend
spe'cial·ized	spec'u·la'tive·ly	spend'er
spe'cial·ly	spec'u·la'tive·ness	spend'ings
spe'cial·ty	spec'u·la'tor	spend'thrift'
spe'cie	spec'u·la·to'ry	spent
spe'cies	spec'u·lum	sper'ma·ce'ti
spe·cif'ic	speech	spew
spe·cif'i·cal·ly	speech'less	spewed
spec'i·fi·ca'tion	speech'less·ly	sphag'num
spec'i·fied	speech'less·ness	sphere
spec'i·fy	speed	spher'i·cal
spec'i·men	speed'boat'	spher'i·cal·ly
spe'cious	speed'ed	sphe·ric'i·ty
spe'cious·ly	speed'er	sphe'roid
spe'cious·ness	speed'i·er	sphinx
speck	speed'i·est	spice

spiced	spin'y	splash'ings
spic'i·ly	spi'ral	splash'y
spic'i·ness	spi'raled	splat'ter
spic'y	spi'ral·ly	splat'ter·work'
spi'der	spire	splayed
spi'der·y	spired	splay'foot'
spied	spir'it	spleen
spig'ot	spir'it·ed	splen'did
spike	spir'it·ed·ly	splen'did·ly
spiked	spir'it·u·al	splen'dor
spik'y	spir'it·u·al·ism	splen'dor·ous
spile	spir'it·u·al·ist	sple·net'ic
spiled	spir'it·u·al·is'tic	splen'i·tive
spill	spir'it·u·al'i·ty	splice
spilled	spir'it·u·al·ize	spliced
spill'way'	spir'it·u·al·ized	splic'er
spin	spir'it·u·al·ly	splic'ings
spin'ach	spir'it·u·ous	splint
spi'nal	spi'ro·chete	splint'ed
spin'dle	spit	splin'ter
spine	spit'ball'	splin'tered
spine'less	spite	splin'ter·proof'
spin'et	spite'ful	split
spin'i·er	spite'ful·ly	split'tings
spin'i·est	spite'ful·ness	split'worm'
spin'na·ker	spit'fire'	splotch
spin'ner	spit·toon'	splotched
spin'ner·et	splash	splotch'y
spin'ney	splashed	splurge
spin'ning·ly	splash'i·er	splurged
spin'ster	splash'i·est	splut'ter
spin'ster·hood	splash'ing·ly	splut'tered

spoil	spooled	spout'ings
spoil'age	spoon	sprain
spoiled	spoon'bill'	sprained
spoils'man	spooned	sprang
spoil'sport'	spoon'er·ism	sprat
spoke	spoon'ful	sprawl
spo'ken	spoon'fuls	sprawled
spoke'shave'	spoor	sprawl'ing·ly
spokes'man	spo·rad'ic	spray
spo'li·a'tion	spore	sprayed
spo'li·a'tive	sport	spray'er
spo'li·a·to'ry	sport'ed	spread
spon'dee	spor'tive	spread'er
sponge	spor'tive·ly	spread'ing·ly
sponge'cake'	spor'tive·ness	spree
sponged	sports'man	sprig
spong'er	sports'man·ship	spright'li·er
spon'gi·er	sports'wear'	spright'li·est
spon'gi·est	sport'y	spright'li·ness
spong'ings	spot	spright'ly
spon'gy	spot'less	spring
spon'sor	spot'less·ly	spring'board'
spon'sor·ship	spot'less·ness	spring'bok'
spon'ta·ne'i·ty	spot'light'	spring'fish'
spon·ta'ne·ous	spot'ted	spring'i·ly
spon·ta'ne·ous·ly	spot'ter	spring'i·ness
spon·ta'ne·ous·ness	spot'ti·er	spring'ing·ly
spoof	spot'ti·est	spring'time'
spook	spot'ty	spring'wood'
spook'i·ness	spouse	spring'y
spook'y	spout	sprin'kle
spool	spout'ed	sprin'kled

sprin'kler	spurt'ed	squashed
sprin'kling·ly	sput'nik	squat
sprin'klings	sput'ter	squat'ted
sprint	sput'tered	squat'ter
sprint'er	sput'ter·ing·ly	squaw
sprite	sput'ter·ings	squaw'fish'
sprit'sail'	spu'tum	squawk
sprock'et	spy	squeak
sprout	spy'glass'	squeal
sprout'ed	squab	squealed
sprout'ling	squab'ble	squeam'ish
spruce	squab'bled	squee'gee
spruc'er	squab'bling·ly	squeeze
spruc'est	squab'blings	squeezed
sprung	squad	squelch
spry	squad'ron	squelched
spud	squal'id	squelch'ing·ly
spume	squa·lid'i·ty	squib
spumed	squal'id·ly	squid
spu·mo'ne	squall	squig'gle
spun	squalled	squig'gly
spunk	squall'ings	squint
spunk'i·er	squall'y	squint'ed
spunk'i·est	squal'or	squint'ing·ly
spunk'y	squan'der	squire
spur	squan'dered	squirm
spu'ri·ous	square	squirmed
spu'ri·ous·ly	squared	squirm'ing·ly
spurn	square'head'	squirm'ings
spurned	square'ly	squir'rel
spurred	square'ness	squir'rel·fish'
spurt	squash	squir'rel·proof'

squirt	stag'nat·ed	stamped
stab	stag·na'tion	stam·pede'
stabbed	staid	stam·ped'ed
stab'bing·ly	stain	stamp'er
stab'bings	stained	stamp'ings
sta·bil'i·ty	stain'less	stance
sta·bi·li·za'tion	stair	stanch
sta'bi·lize	stair'case'	stan'chion
sta'bi·lized	stair'way'	stand
sta'bi·liz'er	stake	stand'ard
sta'ble	staked	stand'ard·i·za-tion
stac·ca'to	sta·lac'tite	stand'ard·ize
stack	sta·lag'mite	stand'ings
sta'di·a	stale	stand'off'
sta'di·um	stale'mate'	stand'pipe'
staff	stal'er	stand'point'
stag	stal'est	stand'still'
stage	stalk	stank
stage'coach'	stalked	stan'nate
stage'craft'	stalk'er	stan'nic
staged	stalk'ing·ly	stan'nous
stage'hand'	stall	stan'za
stag'er	stalled	sta'ple
stage'wor'thy	stal'lion	sta'pled
stag'ger	stal'wart	sta'pler
stag'gered	sta'men	star
stag'ger·ing·ly	stam'i·na	star'board
stag'horn'	stam'mer	starch
stag'hound'	stam'mered	starched
stag'hunt'	stam'mer·er	starch'y
stag'nant	stam'mer·ing·ly	stare
stag'nate	stamp	stared

star'fish'		states'man·like'		steak	
star'gaz'er		stat'ic		steal	
star'ing·ly		sta'tion		stealth	
stark		sta'tion·ar'y		stealth'i·er	
star'less		sta'tioned		stealth'i·est	
star'let		sta'tion·er		stealth'i·ly	
star'light'		sta'tion·er'y		steam	
star'like'		stat'ism		steam'boat'	
star'lings		stat'ist		steamed	
starred		sta·tis'ti·cal		steam'er	
star'ri·er		sta·tis'ti·cal·ly		steam'i·er	
star'ri·est		stat'is·ti'cian		steam'i·est	
star'ry		sta·tis'tics		steam'i·ness	
start		stat'u·ar'y		steam'ship'	
start'ed		stat'ue		steam'y	
start'er		stat'u·esque'		ste'a·tite	
star'tle		stat'u·ette'		steel	
star'tled		stat'ure		steel'head'	
star'tling·ly		sta'tus		steel'work'	
star·va'tion		stat'ute		steel'yard	
starve		stat'u·to'ry		steep	
starved		stave		steep'er	
starve'ling		stay		steep'est	
state		stayed		stee'ple	
stat'ed		stead		stee'ple·chase'	
state'hood		stead'fast		steer	
State'house'		stead'fast·ly		steer'age	
state'li·ness		stead'fast·ness		steered	
state'ly		stead'i·er		steer'ing	
state'ment		stead'i·est		steers'man	
state'room'		stead'i·ly		stein	
states'man		stead'y		stel'lar	

stem	stern'er	stiff'est
stemmed	stern'est	stiff'ness
stench	stern'ly	sti'fle
sten'cil	stern'ness	sti'fled
sten'ciled	stern'post'	sti'fling·ly
ste·nog'ra·pher	ster'num	stig'ma
sten'o·graph'ic	ster'nu·ta'tion	stig·mat'a
ste·nog'ra·phy	ster'to·rous	stig·mat'ic
ste·no'sis	stet	stig'ma·tism
sten·to'ri·an	steth'o·scope	stig'ma·ti·za'tion
step	ste've·dore'	stig'ma·tize
step'child'	stew	stig'ma·tized
step'daugh'ter	stew'ard	stile
step'lad'der	stew'ard·ess	sti·let'to
step'moth'er	stewed	still
steppe	stick	still'born'
stepped	stick'er	stilled
step'sis'ter	stick'ful	still'er
step'son'	stick'i·er	still'est
ster'e·o	stick'i·est	still'ness
ster'e·o·phon'ic	stick'i·ly	still'room'
ster'e·op'ti·con	stick'i·ness	still'y
ster'e·o·scope'	stick'le·back'	stilt
ster'e·o·scop'ic	stick'ler	stilt'ed
ster'ile	stick'pin'	stim'u·lant
ste·ril'i·ty	stick'weed'	stim'u·late
ster'i·li·za'tion	stick'y	stim'u·lat'ed
ster'i·lize	stiff	stim'u·lat'ing·ly
ster'i·lized	stiff'en	stim'u·la'tion
ster'i·liz'er	stiff'ened	stim'u·lus
ster'ling	stiff'en·er	sting
stern	stiff'er	sting'er

sting'fish'

stin'gi·er

stin'gi·est

sting'ing·ly

stin'gy

stink

stink'bug'

stink'er

stink'ing·ly

stink'pot'

stink'weed'

stink'wood'

stint

stint'ed

stint'ing·ly

stipe

sti'pend

sti·pen'di·ar'y

sti·pen'di·um

stip'ple

stip'pled

stip'plings

stip'u·late

stip'u·lat'ed

stip'u·lates

stip'u·la'tion

stip'u·la·to'ry

stir

stir'pes

stirps

stirred

stir'ring·ly

stir'rings

stir'rup

stitch

stitched

stitch'er

stitch'ings

stitch'work'

sti'ver

sto'a

stoat

stock

stock·ade'

stock·ad'ed

stock'breed'er

stock'bro'ker

stocked

stock'fish'

stock'hold'er

stock'house'

stock'i·ness

stock'i·net'

stock'ings

stock'job'ber

stock'keep'er

stock'mak'er

stock'man

stock'own'er

stock'pile'

stock'pot'

stock'tak'er

stock'y

stock'yard'

stodg'i·er

stodg'i·est

stodg'y

sto'gy

sto'ic

sto'i·cal

sto'i·cal·ly

sto'i·cism

stoke

stoked

stoke'hold'

stok'er

stole

sto'len

stol'id

sto·lid'i·ty

stol'id·ly

stom'ach

stom'ach·ful

sto·mach'ic

stone

stone'boat'

stoned

stone'fish'

stone'ma'son

stone'ware'

stone'weed'

stone'wood'

stone'work'

stone'yard'

ston'i·er

ston'i·est

ston'i·ly	sto'ry	strain
ston'y	sto'ry·tell'er	strained
stood	stoup	strain'er
stool	stout	strain'ing·ly
stoop	stout'er	strain'ings
stooped	stout'est	strait
stoop'ing·ly	stout'heart'ed	strait'en
stop	stout'ly	strait'ened
stop'cock'	stout'ness	strait'er
stope	stove	strait'est
stop'gap'	stow	strake
stop'o'ver	stow'age	strand
stop'page	stra·bis'mus	strand'ed
stopped	strad'dle	strange
stop'per	strad'dled	strange'lings
stop'pered	strad'dling·ly	strange'ly
stop'ple	strafe	strange'ness
stor'age	strag'gle	stran'ger
store	strag'gled	strang'est
stored	strag'gler	stran'gle
store'house'	strag'gling·ly	stran'gled
store'keep'er	straight	stran'gler
store'room'	straight'edge'	stran'gles
sto'ried	straight'en	stran'gling·ly
stork	straight'ened	stran'glings
storm	straight'er	stran'gu·late
storm'bound'	straight'est	stran'gu·lat'ed
stormed	straight'for'ward	stran'gu·la'tion
storm'i·er	straight'for'ward·ly	strap
storm'i·est	straight'for'ward·ness	strap'less
storm'ing·ly	straight'way'	strap·pa'do
storm'y	straight'ways'	strapped

strap'pings	strength'en·er	strik'er
stra'ta	stren'u·ous	strik'ing·ly
strat'a·gem	stren'u·ous·ly	string
stra·te'gic	stren'u·ous·ness	stringed
stra·te'gi·cal	stress	strin'gen·cy
strat'e·gist	stressed	strin'gent
strat'e·gy	stress'ful	strin'gent·ly
strat'i·fi·ca'tion	stretch	string'er
strat'i·fied	stretched	string'i·er
strat'i·fy	stretch'er	string'i·est
strat'o·sphere	stretch'er·man	string'piece'
stra'tum	stretch'-out'	string'y
straw	strew	strip
straw'ber'ry	strewed	stripe
straw'flow'er	strewn	striped
stray	stri'ate	strip'lings
strayed	stri'at·ed	strip'per
streak	stri·a'tion	strip'pings
streaked	strick'en	strive
streak'i·er	strict	striv'en
streak'i·est	strict'ly	strob'o·scope
streak'y	strict'ness	strode
stream	stric'ture	stroke
streamed	stride	stroked
stream'er	stri'dent	strok'ings
stream'ing·ly	stri'dent·ly	stroll
stream'line'	strid'ing·ly	strolled
stream'way'	strid'u·lous	stroll'er
street	strife	strong
strength	strig'il	strong'box'
strength'en	strike	strong'er
strength'ened	strike'break'er	strong'est

strong'hold'

strong'ly

stron'ti·um

strop

stro'phe

stroph'ic

strove

struck

struc'tur·al

struc'tur·al·ly

struc'ture

struc'tured

stru'del

strug'gle

strug'gled

strug'gler

strug'gling·ly

strug'glings

strum

strummed

strung

strut

strut'ted

strut'ter

strut'ting·ly

strut'tings

strych'nine

stub

stubbed

stub'bi·ness

stub'ble

stub'bly

stub'born

stub'by

stuc'co

stuck

stud

stud'book'

stud'ded

stu'dent

stud'fish'

stud'horse'

stud'ied

stu'di·o

stu'di·ous

stu'di·ous·ly

stu'di·ous·ness

stud'work'

stud'y

stuff

stuffed

stuff'er

stuff'ings

stuff'i·er

stuff'i·est

stuff'i·ly

stuff'i·ness

stuff'y

stul'ti·fi·ca'tion

stul'ti·fied

stul'ti·fy

stum'ble

stum'bled

stum'bling·ly

stump

stump'age

stumped

stump'i·er

stump'i·est

stump'y

stun

stung

stunk

stunned

stun'ner

stun'ning·ly

stunt

stunt'ed

stu'pe·fa'cient

stu'pe·fac'tion

stu'pe·fied

stu'pe·fy

stu·pen'dous

stu'pid

stu·pid'i·ty

stu'pid·ly

stu'por

stu'por·ous

stur'di·ly

stur'di·ness

stur'dy

stur'geon

stut'ter

stut'tered

stut'ter·er

stut'ter·ing·ly

sty

Styg'i·an

style

style'book'

styled

styl'ings

styl'ish

styl'ish·ness

styl'ist

sty·lis'tic

sty·lis'ti·cal·ly

styl'ize

styl'ized

sty'lo·graph

sty'lo·graph'ic

sty'lus

sty'mie

styp'tic

Styx

su'a·bil'i·ty

su'a·ble

sua'sion

suave

suave'ly

suave'ness

suav'i·ty

sub'a·cute'

sub'a·dult'

sub·a'gent

sub·al'tern

sub'a·quat'ic

sub·a'que·ous

sub·arc'tic

sub'a·tom'ic

sub·cal'i·ber

sub'cap'tion

sub'cel'lar

sub'class'

sub'com·mit'tee

sub·con'scious

sub·con'scious·ly

sub·con'scious·ness

sub'con·stel·la'tion

sub·con'ti·nent

sub'con'tract

sub'con·tract'ed

sub'con·trac'tor

sub'cu·ta'ne·ous

sub·dea'con

sub'di·vide'

sub'di·vid'ed

sub'di·vi'sion

sub·due'

sub·dued'

sub·du'ing·ly

sub·ed'i·tor

sub·fam'i·ly

sub'foun·da'tion

sub'grade'

sub'group'

sub'head'

sub·head'ings

sub·hu'man

sub'ject

sub·ject'ed

sub·jec'tion

sub·jec'tive

sub·jec'tive·ly

sub·jec'tive·ness

sub·jec'tiv·ism

sub'jec·tiv'i·ty

sub·join'

sub·join'der

sub·joined'

sub'ju·gate

sub'ju·gat'ed

sub'ju·ga'tion

sub·junc'tive

sub·king'dom

sub'lap·sar'i·an

sub'lease'

sub'les·see'

sub·les'sor

sub·let'

sub'li·mate

sub'li·mat'ed

sub'li·ma'tion

sub·lime'

sub·limed'

sub·lim'er

sub·lim'est

sub·lim'i·nal

sub·lim'i·ty

sub'lu·nar'y

sub'lux·a'tion

sub·mar'gin·al

sub'ma·rine'
sub'ma·rin'er
sub·merge'
sub·merged'
sub·mer'gence
sub·mers'i·ble
sub·mer'sion
sub·me'ter·ing
sub·mis'sion
sub·mis'sive
sub·mis'sive·ly
sub·mis'sive·ness
sub·mit'
sub·mit'tal
sub·mit'ted
sub·mit'ting·ly
sub·nor'mal
sub'nor·mal'i·ty
sub'o·ce·an'ic
sub·or'der
sub·or'di·nate
sub·or'di·nat·ed
sub·or'di·nat'ing·ly
sub·or'di·na'tion
sub·or'di·na'tive
sub·orn'
sub'or·na'tion
sub·orned'
sub·orn'er
sub·phy'lum
sub'plinth'
sub'plot'

sub·poe'na
sub·poe'naed
sub·ro·ga'tion
sub·scribe'
sub·scribed'
sub·scrib'er
sub'script
sub·scrip'tion
sub'se·quent
sub'se·quent·ly
sub·serve'
sub·served'
sub·ser'vi·ence
sub·ser'vi·en·cy
sub·ser'vi·ent
sub·side'
sub·sid'ed
sub·sid'ence
sub·sid'i·ar'y
sub'si·dize
sub'si·dized
sub'si·dy
sub·sist'
sub·sist'ed
sub·sist'ence
sub'soil'
sub'spe'cies
sub'stance
sub·stand'ard
sub·stan'tial
sub·stan'tial·ly
sub·stan'ti·ate

sub·stan'ti·at'ed
sub·stan'ti·a'tion
sub'stan·tive
sub'sta'tion
sub'sti·tute
sub'sti·tut'ed
sub'sti·tu'tion
sub·stra'tum
sub·struc'ture
sub·sur'face
sub·tan'gent
sub·ten'ant
sub·tend'
sub·tend'ed
sub'ter·fuge
sub'ter·ra'ne·an
sub'ter·ra'ne·ous
sub'ti'tle
sub'tle
sub'tler
sub'tlest
sub'tle·ty
sub'tly
sub·tract'
sub·tract'ed
sub·trac'tion
sub'tra·hend'
sub·treas'ur·y
sub·trop'i·cal
sub'urb
sub·ur'ban
sub·ur'ban·ite

sub·ven'tion

sub·ver'sion

sub·ver'sive

sub·vert'

sub·vert'ed

sub'way'

suc·ceed'

suc·ceed'ed

suc·ceed'ing·ly

suc·cess'

suc·cess'ful

suc·cess'ful·ly

suc·ces'sion

suc·ces'sive

suc·ces'sor

suc·cinct'

suc·cinct'ly

suc'cor

suc'cored

suc'co·tash

suc'cu·lence

suc'cu·lent

suc'cu·lent·ly

suc·cumb'

suc·cumbed'

such

suck

sucked

suck'er

suck'le

suck'led

suck'lings

suc'tion

sud'den

sud'den·ly

sud'den·ness

su'dor·if'er·ous

su'dor·if'ic

suds

sue

sued

suède

su'et

suf'fer

suf'fer·a·ble

suf'fer·ance

suf'fered

suf'fer·er

suf'fer·ing·ly

suf'fer·ings

suf·fice'

suf·ficed'

suf·fi'cien·cy

suf·fi'cient

suf'fix

suf'fo·cate

suf'fo·cat'ed

suf'fo·cat'ing·ly

suf'fo·ca'tion

suf'fo·ca'tive

suf'fra·gan

suf'frage

suf'fra·gist

suf·fuse'

suf·fused'

suf·fu'sion

sug'ar

sug'ared

sug'ar·plum'

sug'ar·y

sug·gest'

sug·gest'ed

sug·gest'i·bil'i·ty

sug·gest'i·ble

sug·ges'tion

sug·ges'tive

sug·ges'tive·ness

su'i·cid'al

su'i·cid'al·ly

su'i·cide

suit

suit'a·bil'i·ty

suit'a·ble

suit'case'

suite

suit'ed

suit'ing·ly

suit'ings

suit'or

sulk

sulked

sulk'i·er

sulk'i·est

sulk'i·ly

sulk'i·ness

sulk'y

sul'len	sump	sun'rise'
sul'len·ly	sump'ter	sun'room'
sul'len·ness	sump'tu·ar'y	sun'set'
sul'lied	sump'tu·ous	sun'shade'
sul'ly	sump'tu·ous·ly	sun'shine'
sul'phate	sump'tu·ous·ness	sun'shin'y
sul'phide	sun	sun'spot'
sul'phite	sun'beam'	sun'stone'
sul'phur	sun'bon'net	sun'stroke'
sul·phu'ric	sun'burn'	sun'ward
sul'phu·rous	sun'burned	sup
sul'tan	sun'burst'	su'per·a·ble
sul·tan'a	sun'dae	su'per·a·bun'dance
sul'tan·ate	Sun'day	su'per·a·bun'dant
sul'tri·er	sun'der	su'per·an'nu·ate
sul'tri·est	sun'der·ance	su'per·an'nu·at'ed
sul'try	sun'dered	su'per·an'nu·a'tion
sum	sun'di'al	su·perb'
su'mac	sun'dry	su'per·cal'en·der
sum'ma·ri·ly	sun'fish'	su'per·cal'en- dered,
sum'ma·ri·ness	sun'flow'er	su'per·car'go
sum'ma·rize	sun'glass'	su'per·charg'er
sum'ma·rized	sun'glow'	su'per·cil'i·ous
sum'ma·ry	sunk	su'per·cil'i·ous·ly
sum·ma'tion	sunk'en	su'per·cil'i·ous·ness
summed	sun'less	su'per·con·duc- tance
sum'mer	sun'light'	su'per·con'duc- tiv'i·ty
sum'mered	sun'lit'	su'per·con·duc- tor
sum'mer·y	sunned	su'per·cool'
sum'mit	sun'ni·ness	su'per·dread- nought'
sum'mon	sun'ny	su'per·em'i·nence
sum'moned	sun'proof'	su'per·em'i·nent

su'per·er'o·ga'tion

su'per·fam'i·ly

su'per·fi'cial

su'per·fi'ci·al'i·ty

su'per·fi'cial·ly

su'per·fine'

su'per·flu'i·ty

su·per'flu·ous

su·per'flu·ous·ly

su·per'flu·ous·ness

su'per·heat'

su'per·heat'ed

su'per·het'er·o·dyne'

su'per·hu'man

su'per·hu'man·ly

su'per·im·pose'

su'per·im·posed'

su'per·im'po·si'tion

su'per·im·po'sure

su'per·in·duce'

su'per·in·duced'

su'per·in·tend'

su'per·in·tend'ed

su'per·in·tend'ence

su'per·in·tend'en·cy

su'per·in·tend'ent

su·pe'ri·or

su·pe'ri·or'i·ty

su·per'la·tive

su·per'la·tive·ly

su'per·man'

su·per'nal

su·per'nal·ly

su'per·nat'u·ral

su'per·nat'u·ral·ly

su'per·nat'u·ral·ism

su'per·nat'u·ral·ist

su'per·nor'mal

su'per·nu'mer·ar'y

su'per·po·si'tion

su'per·sat'u·rate

su'per·sat'u·rat'ed

su'per·sat'u·ra'tion

su'per·scribe'

su'per·scribed'

su'per·scrip tion

su'per·sede'

su'per·sed'ed

su'per·ses'sion

su'per·son'ic

su'per·sti'tion

su'per·sti'tious

su'per·sti'tious·ly

su'per·stra'tum

su'per·struc'ture

su'per·tax'

su'per·vene'

su'per·vened'

su'per·vise'

su'per·vised'

su'per·vi'sion

su'per·vi'sor

su'per·vi'so·ry

su·pine'

su·pine'ness

sup'per

sup·plant'

sup·plant'ed

sup'ple

sup'ple·ment

sup'ple·men'tal

sup'ple·men'ta·ry

sup'ple·men·ta'tion

sup'ple·ment'ed

sup'pli·ant

sup'pli·cant

sup'pli·cate

sup'pli·cat'ed

sup'pli·cat'ing·ly

sup'pli·ca'tion

sup'pli·ca·to'ry

sup·plied'

sup·pli'er

sup·ply'

sup·port'

sup·port'ed

sup·port'er

sup·pose'

sup·posed'

sup·pos'ed·ly

sup'po·si'tion

sup·pos'i·ti'tious

sup·pos'i·ti'tious·ly

sup·press'

sup·pressed'

sup·pres'sion

sup·pres'sive

sup'pu·rate

sup'pu·rat'ed

sup'pu·ra'tion

sup'pu·ra'tive

su·prem'a·cy

su·preme'

su·preme'ly

sur'base'

sur·cease'

sur·charge'

sur·charged'

sur·cin'gle

surd

sure

sure'ly

sure'ness

sure'ty

sure'ty·ship

surf

sur'face

sur'faced

sur'fac·ings

sur'feit

sur'feit·ed

surge

surged

sur'geon

sur'ger·y

sur'gi·cal

sur'li·er

sur'li·est

sur'li·ness

sur'ly

sur·mise'

sur·mised'

sur·mount'

sur·mount'ed

sur'name'

sur'named'

sur·pass'

sur·passed'

sur·pass'ing·ly

sur'plice

sur'pliced

sur'plus

sur'plus·age

sur·prise'

sur·prised'

sur·pris'ed·ly

sur·pris'ing·ly

sur're·but'tal

sur're·but'ter

sur're·join'der

sur·ren'der

sur·ren'dered

sur'rep·ti'tious

sur'rep·ti'tious·ly

sur'rep·ti'tious·ness

sur'rey

sur'ro·gate

sur'ro·ga'tion

sur·round'

sur·round'ed

sur·round'ings

sur'tax'

sur·tout'

sur·veil'lance

sur·vey'

sur·veyed'

sur·vey'or

sur·viv'al

sur·viv'al·ism

sur·vive'

sur·vived'

sur·vi'vor

sur·vi'vor·ship

sus·cep'ti·bil'i·ty

sus·cep'ti·ble

sus·cep'ti·bly

sus·pect'

sus·pect'ed

sus·pend'

sus·pend'ed

sus·pend'ers

sus·pense'

sus·pense'ful

sus·pen'sion

sus·pen'sive

sus·pen'sive·ly

sus·pen'sive·ness

sus·pi'cion

sus·pi'cious

sus·pi'cious·ly

sus·pi'cious·ness

sus·pire'

sus·tain'	swal'low-tailed'	sweat'box'
sus·tained'	swa'mi	sweat'er
sus·tain'ed·ly	swamp	sweat'i·er
sus·tain'ing·ly	swamped	sweat'i·est
sus'te·nance	swan	sweat'i·ly
sus'ten·tac'u·lar	swan'herd'	sweat'i·ness
sus'ten·ta'tion	swank	sweat'shop
su'sur·ra'tion	swank'i·er	sweat'y
sut'ler	swank'i·est	Swed'ish
sut·tee'	swank'y	sweep
su'ture	swans'down'	sweep'er
su'tured	swap	sweep'ing·ly
su'ze·rain	swapped	sweep'ings
su'ze·rain·ty	sward	sweep'stake'
svelte	swarm	sweet
swab	swarmed	sweet'bread'
swabbed	swart	sweet'bri'er
swad'dle	swarth'y	sweet'en
swad'dled	swash	sweet'ened
swad'dling	swas'ti·ka	sweet'en·er
swad'dlings	swat	sweet'en·ings
swag	swatch	sweet'heart'
swage	swath	sweet'ish
swaged	swathe	sweet'ish·ly
swag'ger	swat'ter	sweet'ly
swag'gered	sway	sweet'meat'
swag'ger·ing·ly	swayed	sweet'ness
Swa·hi'li	sway'ing·ly	sweet'root'
swain	swear	sweet'shop'
swal'low	swear'ing·ly	sweet'wa'ter
swal'lowed	sweat	sweet'weed'
swal'low·er	sweat'band'	sweet'wood'

swell

swelled

swell'er

swell'fish'

swell'ings

swel'ter

swel'tered

swel'ter·ing·ly

swept

swerve

swerved

swift

swift'er

swift'est

swift'ly

swift'ness

swig

swigged

swill

swilled

swim

swim'mer

swim'ming·ly

swin'dle

swin'dled

swin'dler

swine

swine'herd'

swing

swing'ing·ly

swin'ish

swink

swipe

swiped

swirl

swirled

swirl'ing·ly

swish

swished

Swiss

switch

switch'board'

switched

switch'gear'

switch'keep'er

switch'man

switch'tail'

switch'yard'

swiv'el

swiv'eled

swol'len

swoon

swooned

swoon'ing·ly

swoop

swooped

sword

sword'bill'

sword'fish'

sword'play'

swords'man

sword'stick'

sword'tail'

swore

sworn

swung

swum

syb'a·rite

syc'a·more

syc'o·phan·cy

syc'o·phant

syc'o·phan'tic

syl'la·bi

syl·lab'ic

syl·lab'i·cate

syl·lab'i·cat'ed

syl·lab'i·ca'tion

syl·lab'i·fi·ca'tion

syl·lab'i·fy

syl'la·ble

syl'la·bus

syl'la·bus·es

syl'lo·gism

syl'lo·gis'tic

syl'lo·gize

sylph

syl'van

sym'bi·o'sis

sym'bi·ot'ic

sym'bol

sym·bol'ic

sym·bol'i·cal

sym·bol'i·cal·ly

sym'bol·ism

sym'bol·ist

sym'bol·i·za'tion

sym'bol·ize

sym'bol·ized

sym·met'ri·cal

sym'me·try

sym'pa·thec'to·my

sym'pa·thet'ic

sym'pa·thet'i·cal·ly

sym'pa·thize

sym'pa·thized

sym'pa·thiz'er

sym'pa·thiz'ing·ly

sym'pa·thy

sym·phon'ic

sym'pho·ny

sym'phy·sis

sym·po'si·um

symp'tom

symp'to·mat'ic

symp'tom·a·tol'o·gy

syn'a·gogue

syn·apse'

syn·ap'sis

syn'chro·nism

syn'chro·ni·za'tion

syn'chro·nize

syn'chro·nized

syn'chro·nous

syn'co·pate

syn'co·pat'ed

syn'co·pa'tion

syn'co·pe

syn'cre·tism

syn'dic

syn'di·cal

syn'di·cal·ism

syn'di·cal·ize

syn'di·cate

syn'di·cat'ed

syn'di·ca'tion

syn'dro·me

syn·ec'do·che

syn'od

syn'od·ist

syn'o·nym

syn·on'y·mous

syn·op'ses

syn·op'sis

syn·op'tic

syn·o'vi·al

syn·o·vi'tis

syn·tac'ti·cal

syn'tax

syn'the·ses

syn'the·sis

syn'the·size

syn'the·sized

syn·thet'ic

syn·thet'i·cal·ly

syr'inge

syr'up

sys'tem

sys'tem·at'ic

sys'tem·a·ti·za'tion

sys'tem·a·tize

sys'tem·a·tized

sys'tem·a·tiz'er

sys'tem·a·tol'o·gy

sys·tem'ic

sys·tem'i·cal·ly

sys'to·le

sys·tol'ic

syz'y·gy

T

tab	tab'u·late	tac'ti·cal
tab'ard	tab'u·lat'ed	tac·ti'cian
ta·bas'co	tab'u·la'tion	tac'tics
tab'er·nac'le	tab'u·la'tor	tac'tile
tab'er·nac'led	ta·chis'to·scope	tact'less
ta'bes	ta·chom'e·ter	tact'less·ly
tab'la·ture	ta·chyg'ra·pher	tact'less·ness
ta'ble	ta·chyg'ra·phy	tad'pole'
ta'bleau	tac'it	taf'fe·ta
ta'ble·cloth'	tac'it·ly	taff'rail
ta'bled	tac'i·turn	taf'fy
ta'ble·maid'	tac'i·tur'ni·ty	tag
ta'ble·man	tack	tag'board'
ta'ble·spoon'	tacked	tagged
tab'let	tack'le	Ta·hi'ti·an
ta'ble·ware'	tack'led	tail
tab'loid	tack'ler	tail'board'
ta·boo'	tack'y	tailed
ta'bor	tact	tail'first'
tab'o·ret	tact'ful	tail'ings
ta·bu'	tact'ful·ly	tail'less
tab'u·lar	tact'ful·ness	tai'lor

305

tai'lored
tail'piece'
tail'race'
tail'stock'
taint
taint'ed
take
take'down'
tak'en
tak'er
tak'ing·ly
tak'ing·ness
tak'ings
talc
tal'cum
tale
tale'bear'er
tal'ent
tal'ent·ed
tal'i·pes
tal'is·man
tal'is·man'ic
talk
talk'a·tive
talked
talk'er
tall
tall'er
tall'est
tall'ish
tall'ness
tal'low

tal'lowed
tal'low·i·ness
tal'low·root'
tal'low·wood'
tal'low·y
tal'ly
tal'ly·ho'
tal'ly·man
Tal'mud
Tal·mud'ic
tal'on
tal'oned
tam'a·rack
tam'a·rind
tam'bour
tam'bou·rine'
tame
tamed
tame'ness
tam'er
tam'est
Tam'il
Tam'ma·ny
tamp'er
tam'pered
tam'per·proof'
tam'pon
tan
tan'a·ger
tan'bark'
tan'dem
tang

tan'gent
tan·gen'tial
tan·gen'ti·al'i·ty
tan'ge·rine'
tan'gi·ble
tan'gi·bly
tan'gle
tan'gled
tan'gle·root'
tan'gling·ly
tan'go
tang'y
tank
tank'age
tank'ard
tanked
tank'er
tan'nage
tanned
tan'ner
tan'ner·y
tan'nic
tan'nin
tan'nings
tan'sy
tan'ta·li·za'tion
tan'ta·lize
tan'ta·lized
tan'ta·lum
tan'ta·lus
tan'ta·mount'
tan'trum

tan·vat

tan'wood'

tap

tape

taped

tape'line'

tape'man

ta'per

ta'pered

ta'per·ing·ly

tap'es·try

tape'worm'

tap'hole'

tap'house'

tap'i·o'ca

ta'pir

tap'per

tap'pet

tap'pings

tap'room'

tap'root'

tap'ster

tar

tar'an·tel'la

ta·ran'tu·la

tar'board'

tar·boosh'

tar'brush'

tar'bush'

tar'di·er

tar'di·est

tar'di·ly

tar'di·ness

tar'dy

tare

tar'flow'er

targe

tar'get

tar'iff

tar'la·tan

tar'nish

tar'nished

tar'ot

tar·pau'lin

tar'pon

tar'ra·gon

tarred

tar'ried

tar'ry

tar'ry·ing·ly

tart

tar'tan

tar'tar

tart'let

tart'ness

tar'trate

tar'weed'

task

task'mas'ter

task'mis'tress

task'work'

Tas·ma'ni·an

tas'sel

tas'seled

taste

tast'ed

taste'ful

taste'ful·ly

taste'ful·ness

taste'less

taste'less·ly

taste'less·ness

tast'er

tast'i·er

tast'i·est

tast'i·ly

tast'ing·ly

tast'ings

tast'y

Ta'tar

tat'ter

tat'tered

tat'ting

tat'tle

tat'tled

tat'tler

tat·too'

tat·tooed'

tat·too'er

taught

taunt

taunt'ed

taunt'ing·ly

taupe

tau'rine

taut

taut'en	teach'er·age	tech'ni·cal·ly
taut'ened	teach'ing·ly	tech·ni'cian
tau·to·log'i·cal	teach'ings	tech·nique'
tau·tol'o·gy	tea'cup'	tech·noc'ra·cy
tav'ern	teak	tech'no·crat
taw'dri·er	tea'ket'tle	tech'no·log'i·cal
taw'dri·est	teal	tech·nol'o·gy
taw'dri·ly	team	te'di·ous
taw'dri·ness	teamed	te'di·ous·ly
taw'dry	team'mate'	te'di·ous·ness
taw'ny	team'ster	te'di·um
tax	team'work'	tee
tax'a·ble	tea'pot'	teed
tax·a'tion	tear	teem
taxed	tear	teemed
tax'es	tear'ful	teem'ing·ly
tax'i	tear'ful·ly	tee'ter
tax'i·cab'	tear'ful·ness	tee'ter·board'
tax'i·der'mist	tear'less	tee'tered
tax'i·der'my	tear'less·ly	teeth
tax'i·me'ter	tea'room'	tee·to'tal
tax'ing·ly	tear'stain'	tee·to'tal·er
tax·on'o·my	tear'y	tee·to'tal·ly
tax'paid'	tease	tel·au'to·graph
tax'pay'er	teased	tel'e·cast
tea	teas'er	tel'e·com·mu'ni·ca'tion
tea'ber'ry	teas'ing·ly	tel'e·gram
tea'cart'	tea'spoon'	tel'e·graph
teach	tea'spoon·ful	te·leg'ra·pher
teach'a·bil'i·ty	tea'tast'er	tel'e·graph'ic
teach'a·ble	tech'ni·cal	te·leg'ra·phy
teach'er	tech'ni·cal'i·ty	tel'e·ol'o·gy

tel′e·path′ic

te·lep′a·thy

tel′e·phone

tel′e·phon′ic

te·leph′o·ny

tel′e·pho′to

tel′e·scope

tel′e·scop′ic

tel′e·type

tel′e·type′set′ter

tel′e·type′writ′er

tel′e·vise

tel′e·vised

tel′e·vi′sion

tel′ford

tell

tell′er

tell′ing·ly

tell′ings

tell′tale′

tel·lu′ri·um

tel′pher

tel′pher·age

te·mer′i·ty

tem′per

tem′per·a·ment

tem′per·a·men′tal

tem′per·a·men′tal·ly

tem′per·ance

tem′per·ate

tem′per·ate·ly

tem′per·a·ture

tem′pered

tem′pest

tem·pes′tu·ous

tem·pes′tu·ous·ly

tem·pes′tu·ous·ness

tem′plate

tem′ple

tem′pled

tem′po

tem′po·ral

tem′po·ral·ty

tem′po·rar′i·ly

tem′po·rar′y

tem′po·ri·za′tion

tem′po·rize

tem′po·rized

tem′po·riz′er

tem′po·riz′ing·ly

tempt

temp·ta′tion

tempt′ed

tempt′er

tempt′ing·ly

tempt′ing·ness

tempt′ress

ten′a·bil′i·ty

ten′a·ble

te·na′cious

te·na′cious·ly

te·na′cious·ness

te·nac′i·ty

ten′an·cy

ten′ant

ten′ant·a·ble

ten′ant·ed

ten′ant·less

ten′ant·ry

tend

tend′ed

tend′en·cy

tend′er

ten′dered

ten′der·er

ten′der·est

ten′der·foot′

ten′der·loin′

ten′der·ly

ten′der·ness

ten′don

ten′dril

Ten′e·brae

ten′e·brous

ten′e·ment

ten′et

ten′nis

ten′on

ten′or

ten′pins′

tense

tense′ly

tense′ness

tens′er

tens′est

ten′sile

ten'sion	ter'mite	ters'est
ten'sor	term'less	ter'tian
tent	tern	ter'ti·ar'y
ten'ta·cle	ter'na·ry	tes'sel·late
ten'ta·tive	ter'race	tes'sel·lat'ed
ten'ter·er	ter'raced	tes'sel·la'tion
ten'ter·hooks'	ter·rain'	test
ten·u'i·ty	ter'ra·pin	tes'ta·ment
ten'u·ous	ter·raz'zo	tes'ta·men'ta·ry
ten'u·ous·ly	ter·res'tri·al	tes·ta'tor
ten'ure	ter'ri·ble	test'ed
te'pee	ter'ri·bly	tes'ter
tep'id	ter'ri·er	tes'ti·fied
te·pid'i·ty	ter·rif'ic	tes'ti·fy
tep'id·ly	ter·rif'i·cal·ly	tes'ti·mo'ni·al
ter'a·tol'o·gy	ter'ri·fied	tes'ti·mo'ny
ter·cen'te·nar'y	ter'ri·fy	test'ing·ly
te·re'do	ter'ri·fy'ing·ly	test'ings
ter'gi·ver·sate'	ter·rine'	tes'ty
term	ter'ri·to'ri·al	tet'a·nus
ter'ma·gant	ter'ri·to'ri·al'i·ty	teth'er
termed	ter'ri·to'ry	teth'ered
ter'mi·na·ble	ter'ror	tet'ra·gon
ter'mi·nal	ter'ror·ism	te·trag'o·nal
ter'mi·nate	ter'ror·ist	te·tral'o·gy
ter'mi·nat'ed	ter'ror·is'tic	te·tram'e·ter
ter'mi·na'tion	ter'ror·i·za'tion	te'trarch
ter'mi·na'tive	ter'ror·ize	te·trig'id
ter'mi·no·log'i·cal	ter'ror·ized	Tex'an
ter'mi·no·log'i·cal·ly	terse	tex'as
ter'mi·nol'o·gy	terse'ness	text
ter'mi·nus	ters'er	text'book'

tex′tile	the·at′ri·cal·ly	the′o·ry
tex′tu·al	the·at′ri·cals	the′o·soph′ic
tex′tu·al·ism	thee	the′o·soph′i·cal
tex′tu·al·ist	theft	the′o·soph′i·cal·ly
tex′tu·al·ly	their	the·os′o·phism
tex′tur·al	theirs	the·os′o·phist
tex′tur·al·ly	the′ism	the·os′o·phy
tex′ture	the′ist	ther′a·peu′tic
tex′tured	the·is′tic	ther′a·peu′ti·cal
tha·las′sic	them	ther′a·peu′ti·cal·ly
thal′li·um	the·mat′ic	ther′a·py
than	the·mat′i·cal	there
than′a·top′sis	theme	there′a·bouts′
thane	them·selves′	there′a·bove′
thank	then	there·aft′er
thanked	thence	there·at′
thank′ful	thence′forth′	there·by′
thank′ful·ly	thence′for′ward	there′fore
thank′ful·ness	the·oc′ra·cy	there·from′
thank′less	the·od′o·lite	there·in′
thank′less·ly	the′o·lo′gi·an	there·in·aft′er
thanks·giv′ing	the′o·log′i·cal	there·in′be·fore′
that	the′o·log′i·cal·ly	there·of′
thatch	the·ol′o·gy	there·on′
thatched	the′o·rem	there·to′
thau′ma·tur′gist	the′o·ret′ic	there′to·fore′
thau′ma·tur′gy	the′o·ret′i·cal	there·un′der
thaw	the′o·ret′i·cal·ly	there·un·to′
the′a·ter	the′o·rist	there′up·on′
the·at′ri·cal	the′o·rize	there·with′
the·at′ri·cal·ism	the′o·rized	ther′mal
the·at′ri·cal′i·ty	the′o·riz′er	therm′i′on

therm'i·on'ic

ther'mite

ther'mo·e·lec'tric

ther·mom'e·ter

ther'mo·met'ric

ther'mo·met'ri·cal

ther'mo·met'ri·cal·ly

ther'mo·stat

the·sau'rus

these

the'ses

the'sis

thew

they

thick

thick'en

thick'ened

thick'en·er

thick'er

thick'est

thick'et

thick'et·ed

thick'head'ed

thick'ly

thick'ness

thick'set'

thick'-skinned'

thick'-wit'ted

thief

thiev'er·y

thiev'ing·ly

thiev'ish

thigh

thill

thim'ble

thim'ble·ful

thim'ble·rig'ger

thin

thing

things

think

think'a·ble

think'er

think'ing·ly

thinks

thin'ly

thin'ner

thin'ness

thin'nest

third

thirst

thirst'ed

thirst'i·ly

thirst'i·ness

thirst'ing·ly

thirst'y

this

this'tle

thith'er

thole

thong

tho·rac'ic

tho'rax

tho'ri·um

thorn

thorn'bush'

thorned

thorn'i·er

thorn'i·est

thorn'y

thor'ough

thor'ough·bred'

thor'ough·fare'

thor'ough·go'ing

thor'ough·ly

thor'ough·ness

those

thou

though

thought

thought'ful

thought'ful·ly

thought'ful·ness

thought'less

thought'less·ly

thought'less·ness

thou'sand

thou'sand·fold'

thou'sandth

thrall

thrall'dom

thrash

thrashed

thrash'er

thrash'ings

thra·son'i·cal

thread

thread'bare'

thread'ed

thread'weed'

thread'worm'

thread'y

threat

threat'en

threat'ened

threat'en·ing·ly

three

three'some

thren'o·dy

thre'nos

thresh

threshed

thresh'er

thresh'old

threw

thrice

thrift

thrift'i·er

thrift'i·est

thrift'i·ly

thrift'i·ness

thrift'less

thrift'less·ly

thrift'less·ness

thrift'y

thrill

thrilled

thrill'ing·ly

thrips

thrive

thriv'ing·ly

throat

throat'ed

throat'i·er

throat'i·est

throat'i·ly

throat'i·ness

throat'root'

throat'wort'

throat'y

throb

throbbed

throb'bing·ly

throes

throm·bo'sis

throm'bus

throne

throne'less

throne'like'

throng

thronged

throng'ing·ly

throt'tle

throt'tled

throt'tling·ly

through

through·out'

throw

throw'back'

throw'er

thrown

throw'off'

thrum

thrummed

thrush

thrust

thud

thud'ded

thud'ding·ly

thug

thug'ger·y

thu'li·um

thumb

thumbed

thumb'mark'

thumb'nail'

thumb'piece'

thumb'print'

thump

thumped

thump'ing·ly

thump'ings

thun'der

thun'der·bird'

thun'der·bolt'

thun'dered

thun'der·fish'

thun'der·head'

thun'der·ing

thun'der·ing·ly

thun'der·ings

thun'der·ous

thun'der·show'er	tick'lish·ness	tight'en·ing
thun'der·struck'	tid'al	tight'er
thun'der·y	tid'bit'	tight'est
thun'drous	tide	tight'fist'ed
thu'ri·ble	tid'ed	tight'ly
Thurs'day	tide'race'	tight'rope'
thus	tide'wa'ter	tight'wad'
thwack	tide'way'	til'bu·ry
thwacked	ti'died	til'de
thwack'ing·ly	ti'di·er	tile
thwart	ti'di·est	tiled
thwart'ed	ti'di·ly	tile'fish'
thwart'ing·ly	ti'di·ness	til'er
thy	ti'dings	tile'root'
thyme	ti'dy	till
thy'mus	tie	till'a·ble
thy'roid	tie'back'	till'age
thy·self'	tied	tilled
ti·ar'a	tier	till'er
tib'i·a	tiered	tilt
tick	tiff	tilt'ed
ticked	tif'fa·ny	tilth
tick'er	tiffed	tilt'yard'
tick'et	tif'fin	tim'bale
tick'et·ed	ti'ger	tim'ber
tick'ings	ti'ger·ish	tim'bered
tick'le	ti'ger·like'	tim'ber·land'
tick'led	ti'ger·wood'	tim'ber·wood'
tick'ler	tight	tim'ber·work'
tick'ling·ly	tight'en	time
tick'lish	tight'ened	timed
tick'lish·ly	tight'en·er	time'keep'er

time'less

time'less·ly

time'less·ness

time'li·ness

time'ly

time'piece'

tim'er

time'serv'ing

time'ta'ble

tim'id

ti·mid'i·ty

tim'id·ly

tim'ings

tim'or·ous

tim'or·ous·ly

tin

tinct

tinct'ed

tinc'ture

tinc'tured

tin'der

tin'der·box'

tine

tined

tine'weed'

tinge

tinged

tin'gle

tin'gled

tin'gling·ly

tin'glings

tin'horn'

tink'er

tink'ered

tin'kle

tin'kled

tin'kling·ly

tin'klings

tinned

tin'ni·er

tin'ni·est

tin'ni·ly

tin'ni·ness

tin·ni'tus

tin'ny

tin'sel

tin'seled

tin'smith'

tint

tint'ed

tin'tin·nab'u·la'tion

tin'type'

tin'ware'

tin'work'

ti'ny

tip

tipped

tip'pet

tip'ple

tip'pled

tip'pler

tip'si·er

tip'si·est

tip'ster

tip'sy

tip'toe'

tip'toed'

tip'toe'ing·ly

tip'top'

ti'rade

tire

tired

tire'less

tire'less·ly

tire'less·ness

tire'some

tire'some·ly

tire'some·ness

tir'ing·ly

tis'sue

tis'sued

tis'sues

Ti'tan

ti·tan'ic

ti'tan·if'er·ous

ti·ta'ni·um

tit'bit'

tith'a·ble

tithe

tithed

tith'ings

ti'tian

tit'il·late

tit'il·lat'ed

tit'il·lat'ing·ly

tit'il·la'tion

tit′il·la′tive	to·bog′ganed	tol′er·ance
tit′i·vate	toc·ca′ta	tol′er·ant
tit′i·vat′ed	toc′sin	tol′er·ate
tit′i·va′tion	to·day′	tol′er·at′ed
ti′tle	tod′dle	tol′er·a′tion
ti′tled	tod′dled	tol′er·a′tion·ism
ti′tle·hold′er	tod′dler	tol′er·a′tive
tit′mouse′	tod′dy	toll
ti′trate	toe	tolled
ti′trat·ed	toe′cap′	toll′gate′
ti·tra′tion	toed	toll′house′
tit′ter	toe′nail′	tom′a·hawk
tit′tered	toe′plate′	to·ma′to
tit′ter·ingly	tof′fee	tomb
tit′ter·ings	to′ga	tombed
tit′tle	to·geth′er	tom′bo·la
tit′tup	to·geth′er·ness	tom′boy′
tit′u·lar	tog′gle	tomb′stone′
tit′u·lar·ly	tog′gled	tom′cat′
tit′u·lar′y	toil	tom′cod′
to	toiled	tome
toad	toil′er	tom′fool′
toad′fish′	toi′let	tom′fool′er·y
toad′root′	toi′let·ry	tom′fool′ish·ness
toad′stone′	toi′let·ware′	to·mor′row
toad′stool′	toil′ing·ly	ton
toad′y	To·kay′	ton′al
toast	to′ken	ton′al·ist
toast′ed	to′kened	to·nal′i·ty
toast′er	told	tone
to·bac′co	tol′er·a·ble	toned
to·bog′gan	tol′er·a·bly	tone′less

tongs	tooth'less·ness	top'side'
tongue	tooth'pick'	top'stone'
tongued	tooth'some	toque
ton'ic	too'tle	torch
ton'i·cal·ly	too'tled	torch'light'
to·nic'i·ty	top	torch'weed'
to·night'	to'paz	torch'wood'
ton'ka	top'coat'	tore
ton'nage	top'er	tor'e·a·dor'
ton·neau'	to'pi·a·rist	tor·ment'
ton'sil	to'pi·ar'y	tor·ment'ed
ton'sil·li'tis	top'ic	tor·ment'ing·ly
ton·so'ri·al	top'i·cal	tor·men'tor
ton'sure	top'knot'	tor·na'do
ton'tine	top'less	tor·pe'do
too	top'loft'y	tor·pe'doed
took	top'man	tor'pid
tool	top'mast'	tor·pid'i·ty
tool'box'	top'most	tor'pid·ly
tooled	to·pog'ra·pher	tor'por
tool'ings	top'o·graph'ic	torque
tool'mak'er	top'o·graph'i·cal	tor'rent
tool'room'	top'o·graph'i·cal·ly	tor·ren'tial
tool'smith'	to·pog'ra·phy	tor·ren'tial·ly
toot	topped	tor'rid
toot'ed	top'per	tor·rid'i·ty
tooth	top'piece'	tor'rid·ly
tooth'ache'	top'ping·ly	tor'sion
tooth'brush'	top'pings	tor'sion·al
toothed	top'ple	tor'so
tooth'less	top'pled	tort
tooth'less·ly	top'sail'	tor'toise

tor'tu·os'i·ty	tot'tered	tou'sle
tor'tu·ous	tot'ter·ing·ly	tou'sled
tor'tu·ous·ly	tot'ter·ings	tout
tor'tu·ous·ness	tot'ter·y	tout'ed
tor'ture	tou·can'	to·va'rish
tor'tured	touch	tow
tor'tur·er	touch'a·ble	tow'age
tor'tur·ing·ly	touch'down'	to'ward
tor'tur·ous	touched	to'wards
tor'tur·ous·ly	touch'hole'	tow'boat'
To'ry	touch'i·er	towed
toss	touch'i·est	tow'el
tossed	touch'i·ly	tow'el·ings
toss'ing·ly	touch'i·ness	tow'er
toss'ings	touch'ing·ly	tow'ered
toss'up'	touch'stone'	tow'er·ing·ly
to'tal	touch'wood'	tow'er·man
to'taled	touch'y	tow'head'
to·tal'i·tar'i·an	tough	tow'line'
to·tal'i·tar'i·an·ism	tough'en	town
to·tal'i·ty	tough'ened	town'folk'
to'tal·i·za'tion	tough'er	town'ship
to'tal·i·za'tor	tough'est	towns'man
to'tal·ize	tou·pee'	town'wear'
to'tal·ized	tour	tow'path'
to'tal·iz'er	toured	tow'rope'
to'tal·ly	tour'ism	tox·e'mi·a
tote	tour'ist	tox'ic
tot'ed	tour'ma·line	tox·ic'i·ty
to'tem	tour'na·ment	tox'i·co·log'i·cal
toth'er	tour'ney	tox'i·col'o·gist
tot'ter	tour'ni·quet	tox'i·col'o·gy

tox'i·co'sis

tox'oid

toy

toyed

toy'ing·ly

toy'man

toy'shop'

trace

trace'a·ble

traced

trac'er

trac'er·y

tra'che·a

tra'che·al

tra·cho'ma

trac'ings

track

track'age

tracked

track'er

track'lay'er

track'less

track'man

track'mas'ter

tract

trac'ta·bil'i·ty

trac'ta·ble

trac'ta·bly

trac·tar'i·an

trac'tate

trac'tile

trac'tion

trac'tive

trac'tor

trac'tor·ize

trade

trad'ed

trad'er

trades'man

tra·di'tion

tra·di'tion·al

tra·di'tion·al·ism

tra·di'tion·al·ly

tra·duce'

tra·duced'

tra·duc'er

tra·duc'ing·ly

traf'fic

traf'ficked

trag'a·canth

tra·ge'di·an

tra·ge'di·enne'

trag'e·dy

trag'ic

trag'i·cal

trag'i·cal·ly

trag'i·com'e·dy

tra'gus

trail

trailed

trail'er

trail'ing·ly

train

train'band'

trained

train'er

train'ful

train'load'

train'man

trait

trai'tor

trai'tor·ous

trai'tor·ous·ly

tra·jec'to·ry

tram

tram'car'

tram'mel

tram'meled

tram'mel·ing·ly

tra·mon'tane

tramp

tramped

tram'ple

tram'pled

tram'po·lin

tram'road'

tram'way'

trance

trance'like'

tran'quil

tran'quil·i·za'tion

tran'quil·ize

tran'quil·ized

tran'quil·iz'er

tran'quil·iz'ing·ly

tran·quil'li·ty

tran'quil·ly	trans·fig'ured	trans·la'tion
trans·act'	trans·fig'ure·ment	trans·la'tor
trans·act'ed	trans·fix'	trans·la'to·ry
trans·ac'tion	trans·fixed'	trans·lit'er·ate
trans·al'pine	trans·form'	trans·lu'cence
trans'at·lan'tic	trans'for·ma'tion	trans·lu'cen·cy
tran·scend'	trans·formed'	trans·lu'cent
tran·scend'ed	trans·form'er	trans·lu'cent·ly
tran·scend'ence	trans·form'ing·ly	trans'ma·rine'
tran·scend'en·cy	trans·fuse'	trans·mi'grant
tran·scend'ent	trans·fused'	trans'mi·gra'tion
tran'scen·den'tal	trans·fu'sion	trans·mis'si·ble
tran'scen·den'tal·ism	trans·fu'sions	trans·mis'sion
tran'scen·den'tal·ist	trans·gress'	trans·mit'
trans'con·ti·nen'tal	trans·gressed'	trans·mit'tal
tran·scribe'	trans·gress'ing·ly	trans·mit'ted
tran·scribed'	trans·gres'sion	trans·mit'ter
tran·scrib'er	trans·gres'sor	trans·mog'ri·fi·ca'-tion
tran'script	tran'sient	trans·mog'ri·fied
tran·scrip'tion	tran·sis'tor	trans·mog'ri·fy
trans·duc'er	tran·sis'tor·ize	trans·mut'a·ble
trans·duc'tion	trans'it	trans'mu·ta'tion
tran'sept	tran·si'tion	trans·mute'
trans·fer'	tran·si'tion·al	trans·mut'ed
trans·fer'a·bil'i·ty	tran·si'tion·al·ly	tran'som
trans·fer'a·ble	tran'si·tive	trans'pa·cif'ic
trans·fer'al	tran'si·tive·ly	trans·par'en·cy
trans·fer'ence	tran'si·tive·ness	trans·par'ent
trans'ferred'	tran'si·to'ry	tran'spi·ra'tion
trans·fer'rer	trans·lat'a·ble	tran·spir'a·to'ry
trans·fig'u·ra'tion	trans·late'	tran·spire'
trans·fig'ure	trans·lat'ed	tran·spired'

trans·plant'	trau'ma·ta	treas'ur·y
trans'plan·ta'tion	trau·mat'ic	treat
trans·plant'ed	trau·mat'i·cal·ly	treat'ed
trans·port'	trau'ma·tism	trea'tise
trans'por·ta'tion	trau'ma·tize	treat'ment
trans·port'ed	trav'ail	trea'ty
trans·port'ing·ly	trav'el	tre'ble
trans·pos'al	trav'eled	tre'bled
trans·pose'	trav'el·er	tree
trans·posed'	trav'e·logue	treed
trans'po·si'tion	trav'ers·a·ble	tree'nail'
trans·ship'	trav'ers·al	trek
trans·ship'ment	trav'erse	trekked
tran'sub·stan'ti·a'tion	trav'ersed	trel'lis
trans·ver'sal	trav'er·tine	trel'lised
trans·verse'	trav'es·ty	trem'ble
trap	trawl	trem'bled
trap door	trawl'er	trem'bling·ly
tra·peze'	tray	trem'blings
tra·pe'zi·um	treach'er·ous	tre·men'dous
trap'e·zoid	treach'er·ous·ly	tre·men'dous·ly
trapped	treach'er·ous·ness	tre'mo·lan'do
trap'per	treach'er·y	trem'o·lo
trap'pings	trea'cle	trem'or
Trap'pist	tread	trem'u·lous
trap'rock'	trea'dle	trem'u·lous·ly
trap'shoot'ing	tread'mill'	trem'u·lous·ness
trash	trea'son	trench
trash'i·er	trea'son·a·ble	trench'an·cy
trash'i·est	treas'ure	trench'ant
trash'y	treas'ured	trench'ant·ly
trau'ma	treas'ur·er	trench'er

trench'er·man

trend

trend'ed

tre·pan'

tre·phine'

tre·phined'

trep'i·da'tion

tres'pass

tres'passed

tres'pass·er

tress

tres'tle

tres'tle·work'

tri'ad

tri·ad'ic

tri'al

tri·an'gle

tri·an'gu·lar

tri·an'gu·lar'i·ty

tri·an'gu·late

tri·an'gu·lat'ed

tri·an'gu·la'tion

trib'al

trib'al·ism

tri·bas'ic

tribe

tribes'man

trib'u·la'tion

tri·bu'nal

trib'une

trib'u·tar'y

trib'ute

trice

tri'ceps

tri·chi'na

trich'i·no'sis

tri·chot'o·my

trick

tricked

trick'er·y

trick'i·er

trick'i·est

trick'i·ly

trick'i·ness

trick'le

trick'led

trick'ling·ly

trick'lings

trick'ster

trick'sy

trick'y

tri'col'or

tri'corn

tri'cot

tri'cy·cle

tri'dent

tried

tri·en'ni·al

tri·en'ni·al·ly

tri'fle

tri'fled

tri'fler

tri'fling·ly

tri'flings

trig

trig'ger

trig'gered

trig'ger·fish'

trig'glyph

trig'o·no·met'ric

trig'o·no·met'ri·cal

trig'o·nom'e·try

tri·lem'ma

tri·lin'gual

trill

trilled

tril'lion

Tril'li·um

tri'lo·bite

tril'o·gy

trim

trimmed

trim'mer

trim'mings

trim'ness

tri·month'ly

trin'i·ty

trin'ket

tri·no'mi·al

tri'o

tri'ode

tri'o·let

trip

tri·par'tite

tripe

triph'thong

tri'ple

tri'pled

tri'plet

tri'plex

trip'li·cate

trip'li·cat'ed

trip'li·ca'tion

tri'ply

tri'pod

tripped

trip'per

trip'ping·ly

trip'tych

tri'reme

tri'sect'

tri'sect'ed

tri·sec'tion

tri·sec'tor

tris·kel'i·on

tris'yl·lab'ic

trite

trite'ly

trite'ness

Tri'ton

tri'tone'

trit'u·rate

trit'u·rat'ed

trit'u·ra'tion

tri'umph

tri·um'phal

tri·um'phant

tri'umphed

tri'umph·ing·ly

tri·um'vir

tri·um'vi·rate

tri'une

tri·va'lent

triv'et

triv'i·a

triv'i·al

triv'i·al'i·ty

triv'i·al·ly

tro·cha'ic

tro'che

troi'ka

troll

trolled

trol'ley

trom'bone

troop

trooped

troop'er

troop'ship'

trope

tro'phy

trop'ic

trop'i·cal

trop'i·cal·ly

tro'pism

trop'ist

tro·pol'o·gy

trop'o·pause

trop'o·sphere

trot

troth

trot'line'

trot'ted

trot'ter

trou'ba·dour

trou'ble

trou'bled

trou'ble·some

trou'ble·some·ly

trou'ble·some·ness

trou'bling·ly

trou'blous

trough

trough'like'

trounce

trounced

trounc'ings

troupe

troup'er

trou'sers

trous'seau'

trout

trout'let

trout'ling

trow'el

trow'eled

troy

tru'an·cy

tru'ant

tru'ant·ism

truce

tru'cial

truck	trun'cat·ed	tub
truck'age	trun·ca'tion	tu'ba
trucked	trun'cheon	tubbed
truck'er	trun'dle	tub'bi·er
truck'le	trun'dled	tub'bi·est
truck'led	trunk	tub'bings
truck'ling·ly	trun'nion	tub'by
truck'man	truss	tube
truc'u·lence	trussed	tu'ber
truc'u·lent	truss'ings	tu'ber·cle
trudge	trust	tu·ber'cu·lar
trudged	trus·tee'	tu·ber'cu·lin
trudg'en	trus·tee'ship	tu·ber'cu·lo'sis
true	trust'ful	tu·ber'cu·lous
trued	trust'ful·ly	tu'ber·os'i·ty
true'love'	trust'ful·ness	tu'ber·ous
true'ness	trust'i·er	tub'ings
truf'fle	trust'i·est	tu'bu·lar
truf'fled	trust'ing·ly	tu'bu·la'tion
tru'ism	trust'wor'thi·ness	tuck
tru'ly	trust'wor'thy	tucked
trump	trust'y	Tu'dor
trumped	truth	Tues'day
trump'er·y	truth'ful	tuft
trum'pet	truth'ful·ly	tuft'ed
trum'pet·ed	truth'ful·ness	tuft'ings
trum'pet·er	try	tug
trum'pet·ings	try'ing·ly	tug'boat'
trum'pet·like'	try'sail'	tugged
trum'pet·weed'	tryst	tug'ging·ly
trum'pet·wood'	tryst'ed	tug'gings
trun'cate	tset'se	tu·i'tion

tu'la·re'mi·a

tu'lip

tu'lip·wood'

tulle

tum'ble

tum'bled

tum'bler

tum'ble·weed'

tum'bling·ly

tum'brel

tu'me·fac'tion

tu'me·fied

tu'me·fy

tu'mid

tu·mid'i·ty

tu'mor

tu'mor·ous

tu'mult

tu·mul'tu·ous

tu·mul'tu·ous·ly

tu·mul'tu·ous·ness

tu'mu·lus

tun

tu'na

tun'dra

tune

tuned

tune'ful

tune'less

tune'less·ly

tune'less·ness

tun'er

tung'sten

tu'nic

tun'ings

Tu·ni'sian

tun'nel

tun'neled

tun'ny

tu'pe·lo

tur'ban

tur'bid

tur·bid'i·ty

tur'bid·ly

tur'bi·nate

tur'bine

tur'bot

tur'bu·lence

tur'bu·lent

tur'bu·lent·ly

tu·reen'

turf

turfed

turf'man

tur'gid

tur·gid'i·ty

tur'gid·ly

Turk

tur'key

Turk'ish

tur'mer·ic

tur'moil

turn

turn'buck'le

turn'coat'

turn'cock'

turned

turn'er

turn'ings

tur'nip

turn'key'

turn'off'

turn'out'

turn'o'ver

turn'pike'

turn'spit'

turn'stile'

tur'pen·tine

tur'pi·tude

tur'quoise

tur'ret

tur'ret·ed

tur'tle

Tus'can

tusk

tusked

tus'sle

tus'sled

tus'sock

tu'te·lage

tu'te·lar'y

tu'tor

tu'tored

tu·to'ri·al

tux·e'do

twad'dle

twad'dled

twain

twang

twanged

tweak

tweaked

tweed

tweez'ers

twice

twid'dle

twid'dled

twig

twi'light'

twill

twilled

twin

twin'born'

twine

twined

twinge

twinged

twin'kle

twin'kled

twin'kling·ly

twin'klings

twirl

twirled

twist

twist'ed

twist'er

twist'ings

twit

twitch

twitched

twit'ted

twit'ter

twit'tered

twit'ter·ing·ly

twit'ter·ings

two

two'fold'

two'some

ty·coon'

type

typed

type'set'ter

type'writ'er

type'writ·ten

ty'phoid

ty·phoi'dal

ty·phoon'

ty'phous

ty'phus

typ'i·cal

typ'i·cal·ly

typ'i·fi·ca'tion

typ'i·fy

typ'ings

typ'ist

ty·pog'ra·pher

ty'po·graph'ic

ty·pog'ra·phy

ty·poth'e·tae

ty·ran'ni·cal

ty·ran'ni·cide

tyr'an·nize

tyr'an·nized

tyr'an·niz'ing·ly

tyr'an·nous

tyr'an·ny

ty'rant

ty'ro

U

u·biq'ui·tous
u·biq'ui·tous·ly
u·biq'ui·ty
ud'der
ug'li·er
ug'li·est
ug'li·ness
ug'ly
uh'lan
u·kase'
u'ku·le'le
ul'cer
ul'cer·ate
ul'cer·at·ed
ul'cer·a'tion
ul'cer·a'tive
ul'cer·ous
ul'cer·ous·ly
ul'na
ul'nar
ul'ster
ul·te'ri·or

ul'ti·mate
ul'ti·mate·ly
ul'ti·ma'tum
ul'ti·mo
ul'tra·ism
ul'tra·le·gal'i·ty
ul'tra·ma·rine'
ul'tra·mi'cro·scope
ul'tra·mod'ern
ul'tra·mon'tane
ul'tra·na'tion·al·ism
ul'tra·na'tion·al·ist
ul'tra·red'
ul'tra·son'ic
ul'tra·vi'o·let
ul'u·late
ul'u·lat'ed
ul'u·la'tion
um'ber
um'bra
um'brage
um·bra'geous

um·brel'la
um'laut
um'pire
um'pired
un·a'ble
un'a·bridged'
un'ac·cent'ed
un'ac·cept'a·ble
un'ac·com'mo·dat'ing
un'ac·com'pa·nied
un'ac·count'a·ble
un'ac·cus'tomed
un'ac·quaint'ed
un'a·dorned'
un'a·dul'ter·at·ed
un'af·fect'ed
un'al·loyed'
un·al'ter·a·ble
un·al'tered
un'-A·mer'i·can
un·a'mi·a·ble
u·nan'i·mous

327

un·an'swer·a·ble
un'ap·peas'a·ble
un'ap·proach'a·ble
un'ap·pro'pri·at'ed
un'ap·prov'ing·ly
un·armed'
un·a·shamed'
un·asked'
un'as·sail'a·ble
un'as·signed'
un'as·sim'i·lat'ed
un'as·sist'ed
un'as·sum'ing·ly
un'at·tached'
un'at·tain'a·ble
un'at·tempt'ed
un'at·trac'tive·ly
un·au'thor·ized
un'a·vail'a·ble
un'a·vail'ing·ly
un'a·void'a·ble
un'a·ware'
un·bal'anced
un·bal'last·ed
un·bar'
un·barred'
un·bear'a·bly
un·beat'a·ble
un'be·com'ing·ly
un'be·fit'ting·ly
un'be·known'
un'be·knownst'

unbe·lief'
un'be·liev'a·ble
un'be·liev'er
un'be·liev'ing·ly
un'be·liev'ing·ness
un·bend'
un·bend'ing·ly
un·bi'ased
un·bid'den
un·bind'
un·blem'ished
un·blessed'
un·blocked'
un·blush'ing·ly
un·bolt'
un·bolt'ed
un·born'
un·bos'om
un·bos'omed
un·bound'
un·bound'ed
un·bowed'
un·break'a·ble
un·bri'dled
un·bro'ken
un·buck'le
un·bur'den
un·bur'dened
un·burned'
un·busi'ness·like'
un·but'ton
un·but'toned

un·cage'
un·can'ny
un·cap'ti·vat'ed
un·car'pet·ed
un·cat'a·logued
un·ceas'ing·ly
un'cer·e·mo'ni·ous
un·cer'tain
un·cer'tain·ly
un·cer'tain·ness
un·cer'tain·ty
un·chal'lenged
un·change'a·ble
un·change'a·bly
un·chang'ing·ly
un·char'i·ta·ble
un·chid'ing·ly
un·chris'tened
un·chris'tian
un'ci·al
un·civ'il
un·civ'i·lized
un·clad'
un·claimed'
un·clasp'
un'cle
un·clean'
un·clean'ly
un·closed'
un·clothe'
un·coil'
un'col·lect'ed

un·colt'

un·com'fort·a·ble

un·com'fort·a·ble·ness

un·com'mon

un·com·mu'ni·ca'tive

un·com'pa·nied

un·com'pro·mis'ing

un'con·cerned'

un'con·di'tion·al

un'con·di'tion·al'i·ty

un'con·fined'

un'con·firmed'

un'con·form'i·ty

un'con·gen'ial

un·con'quer·a·ble

un·con'quered

un·con'scion·a·ble

un·con'scious

un·con'scious·ly

un·con'scious·ness

un·con'se·crat'ed

un·con'se·quen'tial

un·con·se·quen'tial·ly

un'con·sid'er·ate·ly

un'con·sid'ered

un'con·sti·tu'tion·al

un'con·sti·tu'tion·al·ly

un'con·strained'

un'con·strain'ed·ly

un'con·tam'i·nat'ed

un'con·tra·dic'to·ry

un'con·trol'la·ble

un'con·trolled'

un'con·ven'tion·al

un'con·ven'tion·al·ly

un'con·vert'ed

un'con·vinced'

un'con·vinc'ing·ly

un'co·op'er·a'tive

un·cork'

un·corked'

un'cor·rect'ed

un'cor·rupt'ed

un'count'a·ble

un·count'ed

un·cou'ple

un·cou'pled

un·couth'

un·couth'ness

un·cov'er

un·cov'ered

un·cowed'

un·creased'

un·crit'i·cal

un·crit'i·ciz'ing·ly

un·crowd'ed

un·crowned'

unc'tion

unc'tu·ous

un·cul'ti·vat'ed

un·cul'tured

un·curbed'

un·curl'

un·cut'

un·dam'aged

un·damped'

un·dashed'

un·dat'ed

un·daunt'ed

un'de·ceive'

un'de·ceived'

un'de·cid'ed

un'de·ci'pher·a·ble

un'de·ci'phered

un·dec'o·rous

un'de·feat'ed

un'de·fend'ed

un'de·filed'

un'de·fin'a·ble

un'de·liv'er·a·ble

un'dem·o·crat'ic,

un'de·mon'stra·tive

un'de·ni'a·ble

un'de·pend'a·ble

un'de·pos'it·ed

un'der

un'der·age'

un'der·arm'

un'der·bid'

un'der·bod'y

un'der·brush'

un'der·buy'

un'der·cap'i·tal·i·za'tion

un'der·cap'i·tal·ize

un'der·car'riage

un'der·charge'

un'der·charged'

un'der·class'man

un'der·clothes'

un'der·coat'

un'der·con·sump'tion

un'der·cov'er

un'der·cur'rent

un'der·cut'

un'der·done'

un'der·dose'

un'der·es'ti·mate

un'der·ex·pose'

un'der·feed'

un'der·foot'

un'der·gar'ment

un'der·glaze'

un'der·go'

un'der·grad'u·ate

un'der·ground'

un'der·growth'

un'der·hand'ed

un'der·hand'ed·ly

un'der·hand'ed·ness

un'der·hung'

un'der·laid'

un'der·lay'

un'der·lie'

un'der·line'

un'der·lined'

un'der·lings

un'der·manned'

un'der·mine'

un'der·mined'

un'der·neath'

un'der·nour'ish

un'der·nour'ished

un'der·nour'ish·ment

un'der·pass'

un'der·pin'nings

un'der·priv'i·leged

un'der·pro·duc'tion

un'der·quote'

un'der·rate'

un'der·rat'ed

un'der·score'

un'der·scored'

un'der·sec're·tar'y

un'der·sell'

un'der·shirt'

un'der·shot'

un'der·signed'

un'der·sized'

un'der·skirt'

un'der·slung'

un'der·sparred'

un'der·stand'

un'der·stand'ing·ly

un'der·stand'ings

un'der·state'

un'der·state'ment

un'der·stood'

un'der·stud'y

un'der·take'

un'der·tak'en

un'der·tak'er

un'der·tak'ings

un'der·things'

un'der·tone'

un'der·took'

un'der·tow'

un'der·turn'

un'der·val'ue

un'der·wa'ter

un'der·wear'

un'der·weight'

un'der·world'

un'der·write'

un'der·writ'er

un'de·scrib'a·ble

un'de·served'

un'de·sir'a·ble

un'de'sired'

un'de·stroyed'

un'de·tect'ed

un'de·ter'mined

un'de·vel'oped

un'di·ag·nosed'

un'di'a·pered

un'di·gest'ed

un·dig'ni·fied

un'di·lut'ed

un'di·min'ished

un·dimmed'

un'di·rect'ed

un·dis'ci·plined

un'dis·closed'

un'dis·cov'ered

un'dis·crim'i·nat'ing·ly

un'dis·guised'

un'dis·tin'guished

un'dis·trib'ut·ed

un'di·vid'ed

un·do'

un'do·mes'ti·cat'ed

un·done'

un·doubt'ed

un·doubt'ed·ly

un'dra·mat'i·cal·ly

un·draped'

un·drawn'

un·dress'

un·dressed'

un·drink'a·ble

un·due'

un'du·lant

un'du·late

un'du·lat'ed

un'du·la'tion

un·du'ly

un·du'ti·ful

un·dy'ing·ly

un·earned'

un·earth'

un·earthed'

un·earth'ly

un·eas'i·er

un·eas'i·est

un·eas'i·ly

un·eas'i·ness

un·eas'y

un·eat'a·ble

un·ed'u·ca·ble

un·ed'u·cat'ed

un'em·bar'rassed

un'em·bit'tered

un'em·broi'dered

un'e·mo'tion·al

un'em·ploy'a·ble

un'em·ploy'a·ble·ness

un'em·ployed'

un'em·ploy'ment

un'en·cum'bered

un'en·dan'gered

un·end'ing

un'en·dorsed'

un'en·dur'a·ble

un'en·force'a·ble

un'en·gaged'

un'en·graved'

un'en·grossed'

un'en·larged'

un'en·light'ened

un'en·slaved'

un·en'tered

un'en·ter·pris'ing

un'en·ter·tain'ing

un'en·thu'si·as'tic

un'en·thu'si·as'ti·cal·ly

un·en'vi·a·ble

un·en'vi·a·bly

un·en'vied

un·e'qual

un·e'qual·a·ble

un·e'qualed

un·e'qual·ize

un·e'qual·ized

un·e'qual·ly

un·e'quipped'

un·e·quiv'o·cal

un·e·rad'i·cat'ed

un·e·ras'a·ble

un·e·rased'

un·err'ing

un·err'ing·ly

un·es·sen'tial

un·es'ti·mat'ed

un·eth'i·cal

un·eth'i·cal·ly

un·e'ven

un·e'ven·ly

un·e'vent'ful

un·e'vent'ful·ly

un'ex·am'pled

un'ex·celled'

un'ex·cep'tion·a·ble

un'ex·cep'tion·al

un'ex·cit'a·ble

un'ex·cit'ing

un'ex·cused'

un·ex'e·cut'ed

un'ex·haust'ed

un'ex·pect'ed

un·ex·pect'ed·ly
un'ex·pect'ed·ness
un'ex·plain'a·ble
un'ex·plained'
un'ex·ploit'ed
un'ex·posed'
un'ex·pressed'
un'ex·press'i·ble
un·ex'pur·gat'ed
un·ex·tin'guished
un·ex·tri·cat'ed
un·fad'ed
un·fad'ing·ly
un·fail'ing·ly
un·fair'
un·fair'ly
un·fair'ness
un·faith'ful
un·faith'ful·ly
un·faith'ful·ness
un·fal'ter·ing
un'fa·mil'iar
un·farmed'
un·fash'ion·a·ble
un·fash'ion·a·bly
un·fas'ten
un·fas'tened
un·fa'ther·ly
un·fath'om·a·ble
un·fath'omed
un'fa·tigue'a·ble
un'fa·tigued'

un·fa'vor·able
un·fa'vor·a·bly
un·fear'ing·ly
un·fea'si·ble
un·fea'si·bly
un·fed'
un·feel'ing·ly
un·feigned'
un·felt'
un·fem'i·nine
un·fenced'
un'fe·nes'trat·ed
un'fer·ment'ed
un··fer'ti·lized
un·fet'ter
un·fet'tered
un·filed'
un·fil'i·al
un·fil'i·al·ly
un·fill'a·ble
un·fil'tered
un·fin'ished
un·fit'
un·fit'ting·ly
un·flag'ging·ly
un·flat'ter·ing·ly
un·flick'er·ing·ly
un·flinch'ing·ly
un·flinch'ing·ness
un·flood'ed
un·flur'ried
un·flus'tered

un·fo'cused
un·fold'
un·fold'ed
un·forced'
un'fore·see'a·ble
un'fore·seen'
un'fore·tell'a·ble
un·for'feit·ed
un'for·get'ta·ble
un'for·get'ting·ly
un'for·giv'a·ble
un'for·giv'en
un'for·giv'ing·ly
un'for·giv'ing·ness
un'for·got'ten
un·for'mal·ized
un·formed'
un·for'ti·fied
un·for'tu·nate
un·for'tu·nate·ly
un·found'ed
un·frayed'
un'fre·quent'ed
un·friend'ed
un·friend'li·ness
un·friend'ly
un·frock'
un·frocked'
un·fru'gal
un·fruit'ful
un·fu'eled
un'ful·filled'

un·fund'ed
un·fun'ny
un·fur'bished
un·furl'
un·furled'
un·fur'nished
un·gain'li·ness
un·gain'ly
un·gal'lant
un·gar'land·ed
un·gar'nished
un·gen'er·ous
un·gen'tle
un·gen'tle·man·ly
un·ger'mi·nat'ed
un·gift'ed
un·girt'
un·glazed'
un·glo'ri·ous
un·gloved'
un·god'li·ness
un·god'ly
un·gov'ern·a·ble
un·gov'ern·a·bly
un·gra'cious
un·gra'cious·ly
un·grad'ed
un'gram·mat'i·cal
un·grate'ful
un·grate'ful·ly
un·grate'ful·ness
un·ground'ed

un·grudg'ing·ly
un·guard'ed
un·guard'ed·ly
un'guent
un·guid'ed
un·gummed'
un·hack'neyed
un·hal'lowed
un·ham'pered
un·hand'i·ness
un·hand'some
un·hand'y
un·hanged'
un·hap'pi·er
un·hap'pi·est
un·hap'pi·ly
un·hap'pi·ness
un·hap'py
un·hard'ened
un·harmed'
un·har'ness
un·har'nessed
un·har'vest·ed
un·hatched'
un·healed'
un·health'ful
un·health'ful·ness
un·health'y
un·heard'
un·heat'ed
un·heed'ed
un·heed'ful·ly

un·heed'ing·ly
un·help'ful
un·her'ald·ed
un'he·ro'ic
un·hes'i·tat'ing
un·hes'i·tat'ing·ly
un·hin'dered
un·hinge'
un·hinged'
un·hitch'
un·hitched'
un·ho'li·ness
un·ho'ly
un·home'like'
un·hon'ored
un·hook'
un·hooked'
un·hoped'
un·horse'
un·hum'bled
un·hu'mor·ous
un·hurt'
un'hy·gi·en'ic
un·hy'phen·at'ed
u'ni·corn
u'ni·cy'cle
un'i·den'ti·fi'a·ble
un'i·den'ti·fied
u'ni·fi·ca'tion
u'ni·fied
u'ni·form
u'ni·formed

u′ni·form′i·ty

u′ni·fy

u′ni·lat′er·al

u′ni·lat′er·al·ly

un′il·lu′mi·nat′ing

un′im·ag′i·na·ble

un′im·ag′i·na′tive

un′im·paired′

un′im·peach′a·ble

un′im·ped′ed

un′im·por′tant

un′im·por′tant·ly

un′im·pos′ing

un′im·pressed′

un′im·pres′sion·a·ble

un′im·pres′sive

un′im·proved′

un′in·cor′po·rat′ed

un·in′dexed

un′in·dict′ed

un′in·flu′enced

un′in·formed′

un′in·hab′it·a·ble

un′in·hab′it·ed

un′in·hib′it·ed

un·in′jured

un·inked′

un′in·scribed′

un′in·spired′

un′in·spir′ing·ly

un′in·struct′ed

un′in·struc′tive

un·in′su·lat′ed

un′in·sur′a·ble

un′in·sured′

un·in′te·grat′ed

un′in·tel′li·gent

un′in·tel′li·gi·ble

un′in·tend′ed

un′in·ten′tion·al

un′in·ten′tion·al·ly

un·in′ter·est·ed

un·in′ter·est·ed·ly

un·in′ter·est·ing·ly

un′in·ter·mit′ting·ly

un′in·ter·rupt′ed·ly

un·in′ti·mat′ed

un′in·tim′i·dat′ed

un′in·tox′i·cat′ed

un′in·vad′ed

un′in·ven′tive

un′in·vig′o·rat′ed

un′in·vit′ing·ly

un′ion

un′ion·ism

un′ion·ist

un′ion·i·za′tion

un′ion·ize

un′ion·ized

u·nique′

u·nique′ly

u·nique′ness

un′ir·ra′di·at′ed

u′ni·son

un·is′sued

u′nit

U′ni·tar′i·an

U′ni·tar′i·an·ism

u′ni·tar′y

u·nite′

u·nit′ed

u·nit′ed·ly

u′ni·ty

u′ni·ver′sal

U′ni·ver′sal·ist

u′ni·ver·sal′i·ty

u′ni·ver′sal·ly

u′ni·verse

u′ni·ver′si·ty

un·jok′ing·ly

un·just′

un·jus′ti·fi′a·ble

un·jus′ti·fi′a·bly

un·jus′ti·fied

un·just′ly

un·kempt′

un·killed′

un·kind′

un·kind′li·ness

un·kind′ly

un·know′a·ble

un·know′ing·ly

un·known′

un·la′beled

un·lace′

un·laced'

un·la'dy·like'

un'la·ment'ed

un·lashed'

un·latch'

un·law'ful

un·law'ful·ly

un·law'ful·ness

un·lead'ed

un·learn'

un·leash'

un·leashed'

un·leav'ened

un·less'

un·let'tered

un·lib'er·at'ed

un·li'censed

un·light'ed

un·lik'a·ble

un·like'

un·like'li·hood

un·like'ly

un·lim'ber

un·lim'bered

un·lim'it·ed

un·lined'

un·list'ed

un·load'

un·load'ed

un·lo'cal·ized

un·lock'

un·locked'

un·looked'

un·loos'en

un·loved'

un·lov'ing·ly

un·luck'i·ly

un·luck'y

un·made'

un·mag'ni·fied

un·maid'en·ly

un·mail'a·ble

un·make'

un·man'

un·man'age·a·ble

un·man'li·ness

un·man'ly

un·manned'

un·man'ner·li·ness

un·man'ner·ly

un·marked'

un·mar'riage·a·ble

un·mar'ried

un·mask'

un·masked'

un·matched'

un·meas'ur·a·ble

un·meas'ured

un·men'tion·a·ble

un·men'tioned

un·mer'ci·ful

un·mer'ci·ful·ly

un·mer'it·ed

un·me'tered

un·mind'ful

un'mis·tak'a·ble

un·mit'i·gat'ed

un·mixed'

un'mo·lest'ed

un·moored'

un·mort'gaged

un·mo'ti·vat'ed

un·mount'ed

un·moved'

un·mov'ing·ly

un·named'

un·nat'u·ral

un·nat'u·ral·ly

un·nav'i·ga·ble

un·nec'es·sar'i·ly

un·nec'es·sar'y

un·need'ed

un·neigh'bor·ly

un·nerve'

un·no'tice·a·ble

un·no'ticed

un·num'bered

un'ob·serv'ant

un'ob·served'

un'ob·tain'a·ble

un·oc'cu·pied

un'of·fi'cial

un·o'pened

un'o·pin'ion·at'ed

un'op·posed'

un·or'ches·trat'ed

un·or′gan·ized	un·pleas′ant·ness	un′pro·fes′sion·al
un·or′tho·dox	un·pleas′ing·ly	un·prof′it·a·ble
un·os·ten·ta′tious	un·pledged′	un′pro·gres′sive
un·pac′i·fied	un·plowed′	un·prom′is·ing
un·pack′	un·plugged′	un·prompt′ed
un·paged′	un·plumbed′	un′pro·nounce′a·ble
un·paid′	un′po·et′ic	un′pro·pi′tious
un·paint′ed	un′po·liced′	un′pro·tect′ed
un·pal′at·a·ble	un·pol′ished	un·prov′a·ble
un·par′al·leled	un′pol·lut′ed	un·proved′
un·par′don·a·ble	un′pop′u·lar	un′pro·vid′ed
un·par′doned	un·pop′u·lat′ed	un′pro·voked′
un′par·lia·men′ta·ry	un·pop′u·lous	un·pub′lished
un·pas′teur·ized	un·prac′ticed	un·punc′tu·al
un·pat′ent·a·ble	un·prec′e·dent′ed	un′punc·tu·al′i·ty
un·pat′ent·ed	un·prec′e·dent′ed·ly	un·punc′tu·al·ly
un·pa·tri·ot′ic	un′pre·dict′a·ble	un·pun′ished
un·pa·tri·ot′i·cal·ly	un·prej′u·diced	un·qual′i·fied
un·pa·trolled′	un′pre·med′i·tat′ed	un·quelled′
un·paved′	un′pre·pared′	un·quench′a·bly
un′per·ceived′	un′pre·par′ed·ness	un·ques′tion·a·ble
un′per′fo·rat′ed	un′pre·pos·sess′ing	un·ques′tion·a·bly
un′per·formed′	un′pre·sent′a·ble	un·ques′tioned
un′per·turbed′	un′pre·tend′ing·ly	un·ques′tion·ing·ly
un·pit′y·ing	un′pre·ten′tious	un·ran′somed
un·pit′y·ing·ly	un′pre·ten′tious·ly	un·rav′el
un·planned′	un′pre·ten′tious·ness	un·rav′eled
un·plas′tered	un·prin′ci·pled	un·reach′a·ble
un·play′a·ble	un·print′a·ble	un·read′
un·pleas′a·ble	un·print′ed	un·read′a·ble
un·pleas′ant	un′pro·duced′	un·re′al
un·pleas′ant·ly	un′pro·duc′tive	un′re·al·is′tic

un're·al'i·ty

un're·al·ized

un·rea'son·a·ble

un·rea'son·a·bly

un·rea'soned

un·rea'son·ing·ly

un're·buked'

un're·ceipt'ed

un're·cep'tive

un're·claim'a·ble

un·rec'og·niz'a·ble

un·rec'og·nized

un·rec'og·niz'ing·ly

un·rec'on·cil'a·ble

un're·cord'ed

un're·deem'a·ble

un're·deemed'

un're·fill'a·ble

un're·fined'

un're·frig'er·at·ed

un're·fut'ed

un're·gen'er·ate

un·reg'u·lat·ed

un're·hearsed'

un're·lat'ed

un're·lent'ing·ly

un're·li'a·bil'i·ty

un're·li'a·ble

un're·mit'ting

un're·mu'ner·a'tive

un're·mu'ner·a'tive·ly

un·rent'a·ble

un·rent'ed

un're·pent'ed

un're·port'a·ble

un're·port'ed

un'rep·re·sent'a·tive

un're·proach'ing·ly

un're·proved'

un're·quit'ed

un're·served'

un're·serv'ed·ly

un're·sist'ing·ly

un're·solved'

un're·source'ful

un're·spon'sive

un·rest'

un·rest'ed

un're·strained'

un're·strict'ed

un're·veal'ing·ly

un're·ward'ed

un·rhymed'

un·right'eous

un·right'eous·ly

un·right'ful·ly

un·ripe'

un·ri'pened

un·ri'valed

un·roll'

un·rolled'

un·ruf'fle

un·ruf'fled

un·ruled'

un·rul'y

un·sad'dened

un·sad'dle

un·sad'dled

un·safe'

un·said'

un·sal'a·ble

un·sal'a·ried

un·sanc'ti·fied

un·sa'ti·at·ed

un'sat·is·fac'to·ri·ly

un'sat·is·fac'to·ry

un·sat'is·fied

un·sat'is·fy'ing·ly

un·sat'u·rat·ed

un·sa'vor·i·ly

un·sa'vor·y

un·scathed'

un·scent'ed

un·schooled'

un'sci·en·tif'ic

un·scram'ble

un·screw'

un·screwed'

un·scru'pu·lous

un·scru'pu·lous·ly

un·seal'

un·sealed'

un·sea'son·a·ble

un·sea'soned

un·seat'ed

un·sea'wor'thy

un·sec′ond·ed

un′se·cured′

un·see′ing·ly

un·seem′ing·ly

un·seem′ly

un·seen′

un′se·lect′ed

un·self′ish

un·self′ish·ly

un·sen′si·tized

un′sen·ti·men′tal

un·sep′a·rat′ed

un·serv′ice·a·ble

un·set′tle

un·set′tled

un·shack′le

un·shack′led

un·shad′ed

un·shak′a·ble

un·shak′en

un·sharp′ened

un·shav′en

un·sheathe′

un·shed′

un·shel′tered

un·shield′ed

un·ship′

un·shipped′

un·shrink′a·ble

un·shuf′fled

un·sight′ed

un·sight′ly

un·signed′

un·sing′a·ble

un·sink′a·ble

un·sis′ter·ly

un·sized′

un·skilled′

un·skill′ful

un·skimmed′

un·smil′ing·ly

un·smirched′

un·smoked′

un·smudged′

un·snarl′

un·so′cia·ble

un·soft′ened

un·soil′

un·soiled′

un·sold′

un·sol′dier·ly

un′so·lic′it·ed

un′so·phis′ti·cat′ed

un·sought′

un·sound′

un·sound′ly

un·speak′a·ble

un·spe′cial·ized

un·spec′i·fied

un·spoiled′

un·spo′ken

un·sports′man·like′

un·spot′ted

un·sprin′kled

un·sta′ble

un·stained′

un·stamped′

un·stead′i·ly

un·stead′y

un·ster′i·lized

un·stint′ed

un·stint′ing·ly

un·strained′

un·stressed′

un·strung′

un′sub·stan′tial

un′sub·stan′ti·at′ed

un′suc·cess′ful

un·suf′fer·a·ble

un·suit′a·ble

un·sul′lied

un·sum′moned

un·sung′

un′su·per·vised′

un·sure′

un′sur·pass′a·ble

un′sur·passed′

un′sus·pect′ed

un′sus·pect′ing

un′sus·pect′ing·ly

un·swayed′

un·sweet′ened

un·swerv′ing·ly

un·sworn′

un′sym·pa·thet′ic

un·sym′pa·thiz′ing·ly

un·sys·tem·at'ic

un·sys'tem·a·tized

un·taint'ed

un·tal'ent·ed

un·tamed'

un·tan'gle

un·tanned'

un·tast'ed

un·taught'

un·tax'a·ble

un·taxed'

un·teach'a·ble

un·tech'ni·cal

un·tempt'ed

un·ten'ant·a·ble

un·ten'ant·ed

un·tend'ed

un·ter'ri·fied

un·thick'ened

un·think'a·ble

un·think'ing

un·think'ing·ly

un·ti'di·ly

un·ti'dy

un·tie'

un·tied'

un·til'

un·time'ly

un·tint'ed

un·tir'ing·ly

un·ti'tled

un'to

un·told'

un·touch'a·ble

un·touched'

un·to'ward

un·trace'a·ble

un·trad'ed

un·trained'

un·tram'meled

un'trans·lat'a·ble

un·trav'eled

un·tried'

un·trimmed'

un·trod'den

un·trou'bled

un·true'

un·trussed'

un·trust'wor'thy

un·truth'

un·truth'ful

un·tuned'

un·turned'

un·tu'tored

un·twine'

un·twist'

un'un·der·stand'a·ble

un'up·braid'ing·ly

un·us'a·ble

un·used'

un·u'su·al

un·u'su·al·ly

un·ut'ter·a·ble

un·ut'ter·a·bly

un·ut'tered

un·val'i·dat'ed

un·val'ued

un·van'quished

un·var'ied

un·var'nished

un·var'y·ing·ly

un·vaunt'ing·ly

un·veil'

un·veiled'

un·ver'bal·ized

un·ver'i·fied

un·versed'

un·vis'it·ed

un·voiced'

un·walled'

un·war'i·ly

un·warned'

un·war'rant·a·ble

un·war'rant·ed

un·war'y

un·washed'

un·wa'tered

un·wa'ver·ing·ly

un·wea'ried

un·wea'ry·ing·ly

un·wed'

un·wed'ded

un·wel'come

un·well'

un·wept'

un·whole'some

un·whole'some·ly	un·yoked'	up·raised'
un·wield'i·ness	up	up'right'
un·wield'y	u'pas	up'right'ly
un·will'ing	up'beat'	up'right'ness
un·will'ing·ly	up·braid'	up·ris'ings
un·will'ing·ness	up·braid'ed	up'roar'
un·winc'ing·ly	up·braid'ing·ly	up·roar'i·ous
un·wind'	up·bring'ing	up·roar'i·ous·ness
un·wind'ing·ly	up'coun'try	up·root'
un·wink'ing·ly	up'draft'	up·root'ed
un·wise'	up'grade'	up·set'
un·wit'nessed	up'growth'	up·set'ting·ly
un·wit'ting·ly	up·heav'al	up'shot'
un·wom'an·ly	up·held'	up'side'
un·wont'ed	up'hill'	up'stairs'
un·work'a·ble	up·hold'	up'start'
un·work'man·like'	up·hold'er	up'state'
un·world'li·ness	up·hol'ster	up'stream'
un·world'ly	up·hol'stered	up'stroke'
un·worn'	up·hol'ster·er	up'take'
un·wor'ried	up·hol'ster·y	up'-to-date'
un·wor'thi·ly	up'keep'	up'town'
un·wor'thi·ness	up'land'	up·turn'
un·wor'thy	up·lift'	up·turned'
un·wound'	up·lift'ed	up'ward
un·wound'ed	up·lift'ing·ly	up'wind'
un·wrap'	up'most	u·ra'ni·um
un·wrapped'	up·on'	ur'ban
un·wreathe'	up'per	ur·bane'
un·wrin'kled	up'per·most	ur·bane'ly
un·writ'ten	up'pers	ur'ban·ite
un·yield'ing·ly	up·raise'	ur·ban'i·ty

ur'ban·i·za'tion

ur'ban·ize

ur'ban·ized

ur'chin

urge

urged

ur'gen·cy

ur'gent

ur'gent·ly

urg'ings

urn

us

us'a·bil'i·ty

us'a·ble

us'age

use

used

use'ful

use'ful·ly

use'ful·ness

use'less

use'less·ly

use'less·ness

us'er

us'es

ush'er

ush'ered

u'su·al

u'su·al·ly

u'su·fruct

u'su·rer

u·su'ri·ous

u·surp'

u'sur·pa'tion

u·surp'er

u'su·ry

u·ten'sil

u·til'i·tar'i·an

u·til'i·tar'i·an·ism

u·til'i·ties

u·til'i·ty

u'ti·liz'a·ble

u'ti·li·za'tion

u'ti·lize

u'ti·lized

ut'most

u·to'pi·a

u·to'pi·an

u·to'pi·an·ism

ut'ter

ut'ter·ance

ut'tered

ut'ter·ly

ut'ter·most

u'vu·la

u'vu·lar

V

va'can·cy

va'cant

va'cate

va'cat·ed

va·ca'tion

va·ca'tioned

va·ca'tion·ist

vac'ci·nate

vac'ci·nat'ed

vac'ci·na'tion

vac'ci·na'tor

vac'cine

vac'il·late

vac'il·lat'ed

vac'il·la'tion

vac'il·lat'ing·ly

vac'il·la·to'ry

va·cu'i·ty

vac'u·ous

vac'u·um

vag'a·bond

vag'a·bond'age

vag'a·bon'di·a

vag'a·bond·ism

vag'a·bond·ize

va·gar'y

va'gran·cy

va'grant

vague

va'guer

va'guest

va'gus

vain

vain'glo'ri·ous

vain'glo'ry

vain'ly

vain'ness

val'ance

vale

val'e·dic'tion

val'e·dic·to'ri·an

val'e·dic'to·ry

va'lence

val'en·tine

va·le'ri·an

val'et

val'.e·tu'di·nar'i·an

Val·hal'la

val'iant

val'id

val'i·date

val'i·dat'ed

val'i·da'tion

va·lid'i·ty

val'id·ly

va·lise'

val'ley

val'or

val'or·i·za'tion

val'or·ize

val'or·ous

val'u·a·ble

val'u·a'tion

val'ue

val'ued

val'ue·less

342

valve	var'i·a'tion	vault
val'vu·lar	var'i·col'ored	vault'ed
vamp	var'i·cose	vaunt
vam'pire	var'i·cos'i·ty	vaunt'ed
va·na'di·um	var'ied	vaunt'ing·ly
van'dal	var'i·e·gate	veal
van'dal·ism	var'i·e·gat'ed	vec'tor
van'dal·ize	var'i·e·ga'tion	ve·dette'
vane	va·ri'e·tal	veer
van'guard'	va·ri'e·ty	veered
va·nil'la	va·ri'o·la	veg'e·ta·ble
van'il·lin	var'i·o'rum	veg'e·tar'i·an
van'ish	var'i·ous	veg'e·tar'i·an·ism
van'ished	var'i·ous·ly	veg'e·tate
van'ish·ing·ly	var'let	veg'e·tat'ed
van'i·ty	var'nish	veg'e·ta'tion
van'quish	var'nished	veg'e·ta'tive
van'quished	var'nish·ings	ve'he·mence
van'tage	var'y	ve'he·ment
vap'id	var'y·ing·ly	ve'he·ment·ly
vap'id·ly	vas'cu·lar	ve'hi·cle
va'por	vase	ve'hi·cles
va'por·ings	Vas'e·line	ve·hic'u·lar
va'por·i·za'tion	vas'sal	veil
va'por·ize	vas'sal·age	veiled
va'por·ized	vast	vein
va'por·iz'er	vast'er	veined
va'por·ous	vast'est	vein'ings
var'i·a·bil'i·ty	vast'ly	vein'let
var'i·a·ble	vat	vel'lum
var'i·ance	Vat'i·can	ve·loc'i·pede
var'i·ant	vaude'ville	ve·loc'i·ty

ve'lo·drome	ven'om·ous	ver·bose'
ve·lours'	ven'om·ous·ly	ver·bos'i·ty
vel'vet	vent	ver'dant
vel'vet·een'	vent'ed	ver'dict
vel'vet·y	vent'hole'	ver'di·gris
ve'nal	ven'ti·late	ver'dure
ve·nal'i·ty	ven'ti·lat'ed	verge
ve'nal·i·za'tion	ven'ti·la'tion	verged
ve'nal·ize	ven'ti·la'tor	ver'ger
ve·na'tion	ven'tral	ver'i·est
vend	ven'tri·cle	ver'i·fi·a·ble
vend'ed	ven·tric'u·lar	ver'i·fi·ca'tion
vend·ee'	ven·tril'o·quism	ver'i·fied
ven·det'ta	ven·tril'o·quist	ver'i·fy
vend'i·ble	ven'ture	ver'i·ly
ven'dor	ven'tured	ver'i·si·mil'i-
ve·neer'	ven'ture·some	·tude
ve·neered'	ven'ue	ver'ism
ven'er·a·ble	ve·ra'cious	ver'i·ta·ble
ven'er·ate	ve·ra'cious·ly	ver'i·ta·bly
ven'er·at'ed	ve·rac'i·ty	ver'i·ties
ven'er·a'tion	ve·ran'da	ver'i·ty
ven'er·a'tive	ver'bal	ver'meil
Ve·ne'tian	ver'bal·ism	ver'mi·cel'li
venge'ance	ver'bal·ist	ver'mi·cide
venge'ful	ver'bal·i·za'tion	ver·mic'u·late
venge'ful·ness	ver'bal·ize	ver·mic'u·la'tion
ve'ni·al	ver'bal·ized	ver·mic'u·lite
ve'ni·al'i·ty	ver'bal·ly	ver'mi·form
ve'ni·al·ly	ver·ba'tim	ver'mi·fuge
ven'i·son	ver·be'na	ver·mil'ion
ven'om	ver'bi·age	ver'min
		ver'min·ous

ver·nac'u·lar

ver'nal

ver'ni·er

ver'sa·tile

ver'sa·til'i·ty

verse

ver'si·cle

ver'si·fi·ca'tion

ver'si·fied

ver'si·fi'er

ver'si·fy

ver'sion

ver'so

ver'sus

ver'te·bra

ver'te·brae

ver'te·brate

ver'tex

ver'ti·cal

ver'ti·cal·ly

ver·tig'i·nous

ver'ti·go

ver'vain

verve

ver'y

ves'i·cle

ves'per

ves'sel

vest

ves'tal

vest'ed

ves·tib'u·lar

ves'ti·bule

ves'tige

ves·tig'i·al

vest'ment

ves'try

ves'ture

vetch

vet'er·an

vet'er·i·nar'i·an

vet'er·i·nar'y

ve'to

ve'toed

vex

vex·a'tion

vex·a'tious

vexed

vi'a

vi·a·bil'i·ty

vi'a·ble

vi'a·duct

vi'al

vi'and

vi·at'i·cum

vi'bran·cy

vi'brant

vi'brate

vi'brat·ed

vi'brat·ing·ly

vi·bra'tion

vi·bra'tion·less

vi·bra'to

vi'bra·tor

vi'bra·to'ry

vic'ar

vic'ar·age

vi·car'i·ate

vi·car'i·ous

vi·car'i·ous·ly

vice

vice'ge'ral

vice'ge'rent

vice'reine

vice'roy

vic'i·nage

vi·cin'i·ties

vi·cin'i·ty

vi'cious

vi'cious·ly

vi'cious·ness

vi·cis'si·tude

vic'tim

vic'tim·ize

vic'tim·ized

vic'tor

Vic·to'ri·an

vic·to'ri·ous

vic·to'ri·ous·ly

vic'to·ry

Vic·tro'la

vict'ual

vi·cu'ña

vid'e·o

vie

vied

view

viewed

vig'il

vig'i·lance

vig'i·lant

vig'i·lan'te

vig'i·lant·ly

vi·gnette'

vi·gnett'ed

vig'or

vig'or·ous

vig'or·ous·ly

vi'kings

vile

vil'er

vil'est

vil'i·fi·ca'tion

vil'i·fi'er

vil'i·fy

vil'la

vil'lage

vil'lag·er

vil'lain

vil'lain·ous

vil'lain·ous·ly

vil'lain·y

vil'la·nelle'

vin'ai·grette'

vin'cu·lum

vin'di·ca·ble

vin'di·cate

vin'di·cat'ed

vin'di·ca'tion

vin·dic'tive

vine

vin'e·gar

vine'yard

vin'i·fi·ca'tion

vi'nous

vin'tage

vint'ner

vi'ol

vi·o'la

vi'o·late

vi'o·lat'ed

vi'o·la'tion

vi'o·la'tive

vi'o·la'tor

vi'o·lence

vi'o·lent

vi'o·lent·ly

vi'o·let

vi'o·lin'

vi'o·lin'ist

vi·o·lon·cel'list

vi·o·lon·cel'lo

vi'per

vi'per·ous

vi·ra'go

vir'e·o

vir'gin

vir'gin·al

vir·gin'i·ty

vir'ile

vi·ril'i·ty

vir'tu·al

vir'tu·al·ly

vir'tue

vir'tu·os'i·ty

vir'tu·o'so

vir'tu·ous

vir'tu·ous·ly

vir'tu·ous·ness

vir'u·lence

vir'u·len·cy

vir'u·lent

vi'rus

vi'sa

vis'age

vis'-à-vis'

vis'cer·a

vis'cer·al

vis'cid

vis·cid'i·ty

vis'cid·ly

vis'cose

vis·cos'i·ty

vis'count'

vis'cous

vise

vis'i·bil'i·ty

vis'i·ble

vis'i·bly

vi'sion

vi'sion·ar'y

vis'it

vis′it·a′tion

vis′it·ed

vis′i·tor

vis′ta

vis′u·al

vis′u·al·i·za′tion

vis′u·al·ize

vis′u·al·ized

vis′u·al·ly

vi′tal

vi·tal′i·ty

vi′tal·ize

vi′tal·ized

vi′tal·ly

vi′ta·min

vi′ti·ate

vi′ti·at′ed

vi′ti·a′tion

vit′re·ous

vit′ri·fac′tion

vit′ri·fi·ca′tion

vit′ri·fied

vit′ri·fy

vit′ri·ol

vit′ri·ol′ic

vi·tu′per·ate

vi·tu′per·at′ed

vi·tu′per·a′tion

vi·tu′per·a′tive

vi·tu′per·a′tive·ly

vi·va′cious

vi·va′cious·ly

vi·vac′i·ty

vi·var′i·um

viv′id

viv′id·ly

viv′i·fy

vi·vip′a·rous

viv′i·sect

viv′i·sec′tion

viv′i·sec′tion·ist

vix′en

vix′en·ish

viz′ard

vi·zier′

vo′ca·ble

vo·cab′u·lar′y

vo′cal

vo′cal·ism

vo′cal·ist

vo′cal·i·za′tion

vo′cal·ize

vo′cal·ized

vo′cal·ly

vo·ca′tion

vo·ca′tion·al

vo·ca′tion·al·ly

voc′a·tive

vo·cif′er·ate

vo·cif′er·at′ed

vo·cif′er·a′tion

vo·cif′er·ous

vod′ka

vogue

voice

voiced

voice′less

voice′less·ly

voice′less·ness

void

void′a·ble

void′ed

vol′a·tile

vol′a·til′i·ty

vol′a·til·i·za′tion

vol′a·til·ize

vol′a·til·ized

vol·can′ic

vol·ca′no

vol′can·ol′o·gy

vo·li′tion

vo·li′tion·al

vo·li′tion·al·ly

vol′ley

vol′ley·ball′

vol′leyed

volt

volt′age

vol·ta′ic

vol·tam′e·ter

volt′am′me·ter

volt′me′ter

vol′u·bil′i·ty

vol′u·ble

vol′u·bly

vol′ume

vol'u·met'ric
vo·lu'mi·nous
vo·lu'mi·nous·ly
vo·lu'mi·nous·ness
vol'un·tar'i·ly
vol'un·tar'y
vol'un·teer'
vol'un·teered'
vo·lup'tu·ar'y
vo·lup'tu·ous
vo·lup'tu·ous·ly
vo·lup'tu·ous·ness
vo·lute'
vol'vu·lus
vom'it
vom'it·ed
vom'i·to'ry
voo'doo
voo'doo·ism
vo·ra'cious

vo·rac'i·ty
vor'tex
vor'ti·cal
vor'ti·cal·ly
vo'ta·ry
vote
vot'ed
vot'er
vo'tive
vouch
vouched
vouch'er
vouch·safe'
vouch·safed'
vow
vowed
vow'el
vow'el·i·za'tion
vow'el·ize
voy'age

voy'aged
voy'ag·er
vul'can·i·za'tion
vul'can·ize
vul'can·ized
vul'can·iz'er
vul'gar
vul·gar'i·an
vul'gar·ism
vul·gar'i·ty
vul'gar·i·za'tion
vul'gar·ize
vul'gar·ized
vul'gar·iz'er
vul'gar·ly
vul'gate
vul'ner·a·bil'i·ty
vul'ner·a·ble
vul'ner·a·bly
vul'ture

wad	wag'gling·ly	wake
wad'ded	Wag·ne'ri·an	waked
wad'dings	wag'on	wake'ful
wad'dle	wag'tail'	wake'ful·ly
wad'dling·ly	waif	wake'ful·ness
wade	wail	wak'en
wad'ed	wailed	wak'ened
wad'er	wail'ing·ly	wak'ing·ly
wa'fer	wail'ings	wale
waf'fle	wain	waled
waft	wain'scot	walk
wag	waist	walked
wage	waist'band'	walk'er
waged	waist'coat'	walk'o'ver
wa'ger	waist'line'	walk'-up'
wa'gered	wait	walk'way'
wa'ger·ings	wait'ed	wall
wag'es	wait'er	wall'board'
wagged	wait'ress	walled
wag'gish	waive	wal'let
wag'gle	waived	wall'eyed'
wag'gled	waiv'er	wall'flow'er

349

Wal·loon′	ward′ed	war′rant
wal′lop	ward′en	war′rant·a·ble
wal′low	ward′er	war′rant·ed
wal′lowed	ward′robe′	war′ran·tor
wall′pa′per	ward′room′	war′ran·ty
wal′nut	ware′house′	warred
wal′rus	ware′house′man	war′ren
waltz	ware′room′	war′ship′
waltzed	wares	wart
wam′pum	war′fare′	war′time′
wan	war′i·ly	wart′less
wand	war′i·ness	war′y
wan′der	war′like′	was
wan′dered	war′lock	wash
wan′der·er	warm	wash′a·ble
wan′der·ing·ly	warmed	wash′board′
wan′der·ings	warm′er	wash′bowl′
wane	warm′est	wash′cloth′
waned	warm′heart′ed	washed
wan′gle	warm′ly	wash′er
wan′gled	warm′ness	wash′house′
want	war′mon′ger	wash′ings
want′ed	warmth	wash′out′
want′ing·ly	warn	wash′room′
wan′ton	warned	wash′stand′
war	warn′ing·ly	wash′-up′
war′ble	warn′ings	wash′wom′an
war′bled	warp	wasp
war′bler	warp′age	wasp′ish
war′bling·ly	war′path′	was′sail
war′blings	warped	wast′age
ward	war′plane′	waste

waste'bas'ket
wast'ed
waste'ful
waste'ful·ly
waste'ful·ness
waste'land'
waste'pa'per
wast'er
wast'ing·ly
wast'rel
watch
watch'case'
watch'dog'
watched
watch'er
watch'ful
watch'ful·ly
watch'ful·ness
watch'house'
watch'keep'er
watch'mak'er
watch'man
watch'tow'er
watch'word'
wa'ter
wa'tered
wa'ter·fall'
wa'ter·find'er
wa'ter·fowl'
wa'ter·i·ness
wa'ter·ings
wa'ter·line'

wa'ter·log'
wa'ter·logged'
Wa'ter·loo'
wa'ter·man
wa'ter·mark'
wa'ter·mel'on
wa'ter·proof'
wa'ter·proofed'
wa'ter·shed'
wa'ter·side'
wa'ter·spout'
wa'ter·way'
wa'ter·weed'
wa'ter·works'
wa'ter·y
watt
watt'age
wat'tle
wat'tled
watt'me'ter
wave
waved
wave'me'ter
wa'ver
wa'vered
wa'ver·ing·ly
wa'ver·ings
wav'i·ness
wav'y
wax
waxed
wax'en

wax'i·ness
wax'ing·ly
wax'wing'
wax'work'
wax'y
way
way'bill'
way'far'er
way'fel'low
way'laid'
way'lay'
way'side'
way'ward
we
weak
weak'en
weak'ened
weak'er
weak'est
weak'ling
weak'ly
weak'ness
weal
wealth
wealth'i·er
wealth'i·est
wealth'y
wean
weaned
weap'on
weap'on·less
wear

wear'a·bil'i·ty	weed'ed	wel'fare'
wear'a·ble	weed'i·er	wel'kin
wear'er	weed'i·est	well
wea'ried	weed'y	well'born'
wea'ri·er	week	welled
wea'ri·est	week'day'	well'head'
wea'ri·ly	week'end'	well'hole'
wea'ri·ness	week'lies	well'spring'
wear'ings	week'ly	welt
wea'ri·some	weep	welt'ed
wea'ri·some·ness	weep'ing·ly	wel'ter
wea'ry	wee'vil	wel'tered
wea'sel	weft	wen
weath'er	weigh	wench
weath'er·board'	weighed	wend
weath'er·cock'	weigh'ings	wend'ed
weath'ered	weigh'mas'ter	went
weath'er·proof'	weight	wept
weath'er·proofed'	weight'ed	were
weave	weight'i·er	were'wolf'
weav'er	weight'i·est	west
web	weight'ings	west'er·ly
webbed	weight'y	west'ern
web'bings	weir	west'ern·er
wed	weird	west'ward
wed'ded	weird'ly	wet
wed'dings	weird'ness	wet'ness
wedge	wel'come	wet'ta·bil'i·ty
wedged	wel'comed	wet'ta·ble
wed'lock	wel'com·ing·ly	wet'ted
Wednes'day	weld	wet'ter
weed	weld'ed	wet'test

wet'tings	wheez'ing·ly	which
we've	wheez'y	which·ev'er
whack	whelk	which'so·ev'er
whacked	whelp	whiff
whale	whelped	whiffed
whale'back'	when	whif'fle
whale'bone'	whence	whif'fled
whale'man	whence'forth'	Whig
whal'er	when·ev'er	while
wharf	when'so·ev'er	whiled
wharf'age	where	whi'lom
wharf'in·ger	where'a·bouts'	whim
what	where·aft'er	whim'per
what·ev'er	where·as'	whim'pered
what'not'	where·at'	whim'per·ing·ly
what'so·ev'er	where·by'	whim'per·ings
wheat	where'fore	whim'sey
wheat'en	where·from'	whim'si·cal
wheat'worm'	where·in'	whine
whee'dle	where·of'	whined
whee'dled	where·on'	whin'ing·ly
whee'dling·ly	where'so·ev'er	whin'ings
wheel	where'up·on'	whin'nied
wheel'bar'row	wher·ev'er	whin'ny
wheeled	where·with'	whip
wheel'house'	where'with·al'	whip'cord'
wheel'wright'	wher'ry	whipped
wheeze	whet	whip'per·snap'per
wheezed	wheth'er	whip'pet
wheez'i·er	whet'ted	whip'ping·ly
wheez'i·est	whet'stone'	whip'pings
wheez'i·ly	whey	whip'poor·will'

whip′saw′		whit′en		why	
whip′stitch′		whit′ened		wick	
whip′stock′		white′ness		wick′ed	
whip′worm′		white′wash′		wick′ed·ly	
whir		white′washed′		wick′ed·ness	
whirl		white′wing′		wick′er	
whirled		white′wood′		wick′er·work′	
whirl′i·gig′		whith′er		wick′et	
whirl′ing·ly		whit′ings		wide	
whirl′pool′		whit′ish		wide′ly	
whirl′wind′		whit′low		wid′en	
whirred		whit′tle		wid′ened	
whisk		whit′tled		wide′ness	
whisked		whit′tlings		wid′er	
whisk′er		who		wide′spread′	
whisk′ered		who·ev′er		wid′est	
whis′ky		whole		wid′ow	
whis′per		whole′heart′ed		wid′owed	
whis′pered		whole′heart′ed·ly		wid′ow·er	
whis′per·er		whole′sale′		wid′ow·hood	
whis′per·ing·ly		whole′sal′er		width	
whis′per·ings		whole′some		wield	
whist		whole′some·ly		wield′ed	
whis′tle		whol′ly		wife	
whis′tled		whom		wife′hood	
whis′tling·ly		whom·ev′er		wife′less	
whis′tlings		whom′so·ev′er		wife′ly	
whit		whoop		wig	
white		whooped		wig′gle	
white′cap′		whoop′ing·ly		wig′gled	
whit′ed		whose		wig′gler	
white′fish′		who′so·ev′er		wig′glings	

wight	wind'break'	wing'spread'
wig'mak'er	wind'ed	wink
wig'wag'	wind'er	winked
wig'wam'	wind'fall'	wink'ing·ly
wild	wind'i·ly	win'kle
wild'er	wind'i·ness	win'ner
wil'der·ness	wind'ing·ly	win'ning·ly
wild'est	wind'ings	win'nings
wild'fire'	wind'jam'mer	win'now
wild'ness	wind'lass	win'nowed
wile	wind'mill'	win'some
wil'i·er	win'dow	win'ter
wil'i·est	win'dowed	win'tered
will	win'dow·pane'	win'ter·ize
willed	wind'pipe'	wipe
will'ful	wind'row'	wiped
will'ful·ly	wind'rowed'	wip'er
will'ful·ness	wind'shield'	wire
will'ing·ly	wind'storm'	wired
will'ing·ness	wind'ward	wire'less
wil'low	wind'ward ly	wire'pull'er
wilt	wind'way'	wire'pull'ing
wilt'ed	wind'y	wire'way'
wil'y	wine	wire'work'
win	wine'ber'ry	wire'work'er
wince	wined	wire'worm'
winced	wine'glass'	wir'y
winc'ing·ly	wine'skin'	wis'dom
wind	wing	wise
wind	winged	wise'a'cre
wind'age	wing'fish'	wise'crack'
wind'bag'	wing'less	wise'crack'er

wise'ly	with'ered	woe'be·gone'
wise'ness	with'er·ing·ly	woe'ful
wis'er	with·held'	woe'ful·ly
wis'est	with·hold'	woe'ful·ness
wish	with·hold'ings	wolf
wish'bone'	with·in'	wolfed
wished	with·out'	wolf'hound'
wish'ful	with·stand'	wolf'ish
wish'ful·ly	with·stood'	wol'ver·ine'
wish'ful·ness	wit'less	wolves
wish'ing·ly	wit'less·ly	wom'an
wisp	wit'less·ness	wom'an·hood
wisp'i·er	wit'ness	wom'an·ish
wisp'i·est	wit'nessed	wom'an·kind'
wisp'y	wit'ti·cism	wom'an·like'
wis·te'ri·a	wit'ti·er	wom'an·li·ness
wist'ful	wit'ti·est	wom'an·ly
wist'ful·ly	wit'ting·ly	wom'en
wist'ful·ness	wit'ty	won
wit	wived	won'der
witch	wives	won'dered
witch'craft'	wiz'ard	won'der·ful
witch'er·y	wiz'ard·ly	won'der·ful·ly
witch'ing·ly	wiz'ard·ry	won'der·ing·ly
witch'weed'	wiz'ened	won'der·land'
with	woad	won'der·ment
with·al'	wob'ble	won'der·work'
with·draw'	wob'bled	won'drous
with·draw'al	wob'bli·ness	won'drous·ly
with·drawn'	wob'bling·ly	won't
with·drew'	wob'bly	wont
with'er	woe	woo

wood	word'age	work'peo'ple
wood'bin'	word'build'ing	work'place'
wood'bine'	word'ed	work'room'
wood'chuck'	word'i·er	work'shop'
wood'craft'	word'i·est	work'ta'ble
wood'cut'	word'i·ly	work'wom'an
wood'ed	word'i·ness	work'wom'en
wood'en	word'less	world
wood'en·head'	word'play'	world'li·ness
wood'fish'	word'y	world'ly
wood'land	wore	worm
wood'man	work	wormed
wood'peck'er	work'a·bil'i·ty	worm'hole'
wood'pile'	work'a·ble	worm'i·er
wood'shop'	work'bag'	worm'i·est
woods'man	work'bas'ket	worm'like'
wood'work'	work'bench'	worm'proof'
wood'work'er	work'book'	worm'wood'
wood'worm'	work'box'	worm'y
wooed	work'day'	worn
woo'er	worked	wor'ried
woof	work'er	wor'ried·ly
wool	work'house'	wor'ri·er
wool'en	work'ing·man'	wor'ri·ment
wool'li·er	work'ings	wor'ri·some
wool'li·est	work'less	wor'ri·some·ness
wool'li·ness	work'man	wor'ry
wool'ly	work'man·like'	worse
wool'work'	work'man·ship	wors'en
wool'work'er	work'men	wors'ened
wooz'y	work'out'	wor'ship
word	work'pan'	wor'shiped

wor'ship·er		wrath'ful		wrin'kli·er	
wor'ship·ful		wrath'ful·ly		wrin'kli·est	
wor'ship·ful·ly		wrath'ful·ness		wrin'kly	
worst		wreak		wrist	
worst'ed		wreaked		wrist'band'	
wor'sted		wreath		wrist'bone'	
worth		wreathed		wrist'let	
wor'thi·er		wreck		wrist'lock'	
wor'thi·est		wreck'age		writ	
wor'thi·ly		wrecked		writ'a·ble	
wor'thi·ness		wreck'er		write	
worth'less		wren		writ'er	
wor'thy		wrench		writhe	
would		wrenched		writhed	
wound		wrest		writh'ing·ly	
wound		wrest'ed		writ'ings	
wound'ed		wres'tle		writ'ten	
wound'ing·ly		wres'tled		wrong	
wound'less		wres'tler		wrong'do'er	
wove		wretch		wronged	
wo'ven		wretch'ed		wrong'ful	
wrack		wretch'ed·ly		wrong'ful·ly	
wraith		wretch'ed·ness		wrong'head'ed	
wraith'like'		wrig'gle		wrong'ly	
wran'gle		wrig'gled		wrong'ness	
wran'gled		wrig'gling·ly		wrote	
wrap		wrig'gly		wroth	
wrapped		wring		wrought	
wrap'per		wring'er		wrung	
wrap'pings		wrin'kle		wry	
wrath		wrin'kled		wry'neck'	

X Y Z

xe'non	yard'mas'ter	yell
xen'o·phile	yard'stick'	yelled
xen'o·pho'bi·a	yarn	yel'low
xe'ro·der'ma	yar'row	yel'lowed
xe·rog'ra·phy	yat'a·ghan	yel'low·er
xe·ro'sis	yaw	yel'low·est
X ray	yawl	yel'low·ish
xy'lo·phone	yawn	yel'low·ish·ness
xy·loph'o·nist	yawned	yelp
	yawn'ing·ly	yelped
yacht	ye	yeo'man
yachts'man	yea	yeo'man·ry
yak	year	yes
Yale	year'book'	yes'ter·day
yam	year'ling	yet
yam'mer	year'ly	yew
yank	yearn	Yid'dish
Yan'kee	yearned	yield
yard	yearn'ing·ly	yield'ed
yard'age	yearn'ings	yield'ing·ly
yard'arm'	yeast	yield'ing·ness
yard'man	yeast'y	yo'del

word		word		word	
yo'deled		youth'ful		ze'ro	
yo'del·er		youth'ful·ly		zest	
yo'ga		youth'ful·ness		zest'ful	
yo'ghurt		youths		zig'zag'	
yoke		yt·ter'bi·um		zinc	
yoked		yt'tri·um		Zi'on	
yoke'fel'low		Yuc'ca		Zi'on·ism	
yo'kel		yule		Zi'on·ist	
yo'kel·ry		yule'tide'		zip'per	
yolk				zir'con	
yon		za'ny		zir·co'ni·um	
yon'der		zeal		zith'er	
yore		zeal'ot		zo'di·ac	
you		zeal'ot·ry		zone	
young		zeal'ous		zoned	
young'er		zeal'ous·ly		zoo	
young'est		zeal'ous·ness		zo'o·log'i·cal	
young'ish		ze'bra		zo·ol'o·gist	
young'ster		ze'broid		zo·ol'o·gy	
your		ze'bu		zoom	
yours		ze'nith		zoomed	
your·self'		ze'o·lite		Zu'lu	
your·selves'		zeph'yr		zy'mase	
youth		Zep'pe·lin		zy·mol'o·gy	

PART TWO

Part Two consists of 1,314 entries of personal and geographical names divided approximately as follows:

835 Geographical Names. The largest group of names consists of the names of American cities and towns that are likely to be encountered in business dictation. The names of the American states are given. A relatively small group of foreign geographical names is given—the foreign countries and cities that are most likely to occur in American business dictation. The lists are not intended to be complete or exhaustive. The attempt has been made, however, to include the geographical names that occur most frequently in ordinary business dictation.

243 Surnames. This small group of names represents the commonest American surnames that are likely to be used in business dictation. There are tens of thousands of surnames in this country, and no attempt can be made to present a complete list.

113 First Names of Women. This list contains the more frequently used feminine first names.

123 First Names of Men. This list contains the more frequently used masculine first names.

The four groups of names listed above are combined in one alphabetical list in Part Two.

With the exception of the states and of a few of the largest cities, the geographical names are written very fully. This is done with the understanding that the writer will use these full outlines for the names that occur only occasionally in the dictation. When some name occurs more frequently in the dictation, an abbreviated form would be used.

The shorthand writer in Oregon would ordinarily have little occasion to use the outline for *Corpus Christi*. The shorthand writer in Texas might use it so frequently that he would abbreviate it to *kk*.

In order to keep the list in Part Two as short and at the same time as useful as possible, the names of many cities and towns are omitted. This is possible because many American city and town names are composed of nouns and adjectives that appear in Part One—for example, such names as *White River Junction* or *Egg Harbor City*.

Many city and town names are formed by adding to the name of another town a word like *Beach, Grove, Hill, City, Park,* or *Spring*. In most cases such names have been omitted, for they would cause no shorthand writing difficulty.

The writing and transcribing of proper names can present many traps for the shorthand writer. When you write in shorthand the name *Pittsburgh,* you will not know whether to transcribe it *Pittsburg* or *Pittsburgh* until you know whether the dictator had in mind *Pittsburg,* Kansas, or *Pittsburgh,* Pennsylvania. You can be tricked similarly by such pairs as *Worcester,* Massachusetts, and *Wooster,* Ohio.

You may confidently write *b-r-ow-n* in your shorthand notes without realizing that the dictator may not be referring to his familiar correspondent, Mr. *Brown,* but to some strange *Browne* or *Braun.*

Martin J. Dupraw, world's champion shorthand writer, tells of an error he made, but caught in time, because of an unusual proper name. He understood the witness to have said: "We gave it the hour test." Mr. Dupraw transcribed it like that, only to find out, just in time, that the witness had really said: "We gave it the Auer test."

Unless the writer is absolutely sure of the identity of the proper names used by the dictator, he should always check them with the greatest possible care. Almost everyone is annoyed when his name or the name of his city or town is spelled incorrectly.

PERSONAL AND GEOGRAPHICAL NAMES

Aaron	Algernon	Anniston
Aberdeen	Allentown	Anthony
Abilene	Allison	Antioch
Abington	Alphonsine	Antoinette
Abraham	Alphonso	Antwerp
Adams	Alton	Appleton
Adelbert	Altoona	Arabia
Adolph	Alvin	Archibald
Agatha	Amanda	Argentina
Aiken	Amarillo	Arizona
Aileen	Amelia	Arkansas
Ainsworth	Amesbury	Arlington
Akron	Amherst	Arnold
Alabama	Amityville	Arthur
Alameda	Amsterdam	Asheboro
Alaska	Anderson	Asheville
Albany	Andover	Ashley
Albert	Angela	Astoria
Albuquerque	Angelica	Atchison
Alexander	Angora	Atkinson
Alfred	Annabel	Atlanta
Algeria	Annapolis	Atlantic

Augusta	Bedford	Blairsville
Augustin	Belfast	Blakely
Aurelia	Belgium	Blanchard
Aurora	Belinda	Bloomington
Austin	Bellefontaine	Bloomsburg
Australia	Belleville	Bluffton
Austria	Bellevue	Bogota
Avery	Bellingham	Boise
Baird	Belmont	Bolivia
Bakersfield	Beloit	Bonham
Baldwin	Belvedere	Boniface
Ballard	Bemidji	Boonville
Baltimore	Benedict	Bordeaux
Bangkok	Benjamin	Boston
Bangor	Bennett	Bosworth
Barberton	Bennington	Boulder
Barcelona	Bentley	Bowen
Barlow	Bergenfield	Bowman
Barnard	Berkeley	Boyd
Barnesville	Bernard	Boyle
Barrington	Bernstein	Braddock
Bartholomew	Bertha	Bradenton
Bartlett	Berwick	Bradford
Bartow	Bethlehem	Bradley
Basil	Beulah	Brattleboro
Batavia	Beverly	Brazil
Batesville	Biloxi	Bremen
Baton Rouge	Binghamton	Bremerton
Bauer	Birmingham	Brenham
Bayonne	Bismarck	Brentwood
Beatrice	Blackstone	Brian
Beckley	Blackwell	Bridgeport

Bridgeton	Camden	Centralia
Brigham	Camilla	Chalmers
Brisbane	Campbell	Chambersburg
Bristow	Canada	Chandler
Brockton	Canfield	Chanute
Bronxville	Cannon	Chapman
Brookfield	Canonsburg	Charleston
Brownsville	Canton	Charlottesville
Brunswick	Caracas	Chattanooga
Bryan	Carbondale	Cheboygan
Bryant	Carlisle	Chelsea
Bucharest	Carlotta	Cherbourg
Budapest	Carlsbad	Cherokee
Buenos Aires	Carlson	Cheyenne
Buffalo	Carlstadt	Chicago
Bulgaria	Carlton	Chicopee
Burbank	Carmel	Childress
Burke	Carnegie	Chillicothe
Burlington	Carol	Chippewa Falls
Burma	Carpenter	Chisholm
Burns	Carrollton	Christabel
Burroughs	Carson	Christchurch
Burton	Carter	Christina
Butte	Cartersville	Christine
Byron	Carthage	Christopher
Cadillac	Casper	Cicely
Caesar	Catharine	Cicero
Calcutta	Catskill	Cincinnati
Calhoun	Cecelia	Claremont
California	Cedarhurst	Clarinda
Callahan	Cedartown	Clarksburg
Calumet City	Celia	Clarksville

Claudia	Connor	Curtis
Clearfield	Conrad	Cuthbert
Clearwater	Constance	Cynthia
Cleburne	Conway	Dagmar
Clement	Cooley	Dalton
Cleveland	Coolidge	Daly
Clifford	Copenhagen	Daniel
Coaldale	Corbin	Danville
Coatesville	Cork	Daphne
Coeur d'Alene	Cornelia	Darby
Coffeyville	Corning	Davenport
Cohen	Corona	Davidson
Coldwater	Corpus Christi	Dawson
Coleman	Cortland	Dearborn
Collier	Corvallis	Deborah
Collingdale	Corwin	Dedham
Collingswood	Costa Rica	Deerfield
Collinsville	Covington	Defiance
Cologne	Crafton	Delaware
Colorado	Crandall	Delhi
Colton	Cranford	Delia
Columbia	Crawford	Denise
Columbus	Creston	Denison
Comstock	Cromwell	Denmark
Concord	Crowley	Denver
Concordia	Cuba	Des Moines
Condon	Cudahy	Detroit
Conklin	Culbertson	Dewey
Conley	Cullman	Dexter
Connecticut	Cumberland	Diana
Connersville	Cummings	Dickinson
Connolly	Cummins	Dillon

District of Columbia

Dolores

Dominic

Donald

Donora

Donovan

Dormont

Dorothy

Dougherty

Doyle

Dresden

Dublin

Dubuque

Dudley

Duluth

Dunbar

Duncan

Dunkirk

Dunmore

Dunn

Duquesne

Durham

Dwight

Easthampton

Eastman

Easton

Eau Claire

Ecuador

Edgar

Edinburgh

Edmonton

Edward

Edwardsville

Edwin

Effingham

Egan

Egbert

Egypt

Eileen

Elbert

Eleanor

Electra

Elgin

Elizabeth

Elizabethton

Elkhart

Elkins

Ellensburg

Elliott

Ellsworth

Elmhurst

Elmira

El Paso

Elvira

Elwood

Ely

Elyria

Emil

Emily

Emmanuel

Emporia

Endicott

England

Englewood

Enrico

Enright

Ernest

Ernestine

Erwin

Esther

Esthonia

Ethel

Ethiopia

Euclid

Europe

Evangeline

Evanston

Evansville

Evelina

Everard

Everett

Exeter

Fairbanks

Fairbury

Fairfield

Fairmont

Fargo

Farrell

Fayetteville

Feldman

Ferdinand

Ferguson

Ferndale

Findlay

Finley

Fisher

Fitchburg	Galion	Greeley
Fitzgerald	Gallagher	Greensboro
Flagstaff	Gallup	Greensburg
Fleming	Galveston	Greenville
Florence	Gardner	Greenwood
Florida	Garfield	Gregory
Floyd	Gasper	Gretchen
Fond du Lac	Gastonia	Griffiths
Ford	Geneva	Grinnell
Fort Atkinson	Genevieve	Guam
Fort Lauderdale	Genoa	Guatemala
Fort Madison	George	Gutenberg
Fort Myers	Georgia	Guthrie
Fort Wayne	Gerald	Hackensack
Fort Worth	Germany	Haggerty
Foster	Gertrude	Halifax
Fostoria	Gettysburg	Hamburg
Framingham	Gibson	Hamilton
Frances	Gifford	Hammond
Francis	Gilbert	Hampton
Frankfort	Girard	Hancock
Franklin	Glasgow	Hanford
Frederic	Gleason	Hannibal
Fredonia	Gloria	Hanover
Freehold	Gloversville	Hanson
Freeport	Goddard	Harding
Fullerton	Godfrey	Harold
Fulton	Goodwin	Harriet
Gabriel	Gordon	Harriman
Gaffney	Gould	Harrington
Gainesville	Grafton	Harrisburg
Galesburg	Great Britain	Harrison

Hartford	Honolulu	Isolde
Hartman	Hopewell	Israel
Hattiesburg	Hopkinsville	Istanbul
Haverford	Horatio	Ithaca
Haverstraw	Hornel	Ivan
Hawaii	Hortense	Jacksonville
Hawthorne	Houston	Jacobs
Hayward	Howard	Jacqueline
Healy	Howell	Jamaica
Hedwig	Hubert	Jamestown
Heloise	Hudson	Janesville
Hempstead	Humboldt	Janet
Henderson	Humphrey	Japan
Henrietta	Hungary	Jason
Herbert	Huntington	Jasper
Herkimer	Huron	Jeannette
Herman	Hutchinson	Jeffersonville
Higgins	Hyattsville	Jeffrey
Hilda	Iceland	Jemima
Hillsboro	Idaho	Jennifer
Hinsdale	Illinois	Jeremiah
Hinton	India	Jersey City
Hobart	Indiana	Jerusalem
Hoboken	Indianapolis	Jessamine
Hoffman	Inglewood	Jessica
Holdenville	Iowa	Jocelin
Hollywood	Ironton	Johnson
Holt	Ironwood	Johnston
Holyoke	Irvington	Johnstown
Homewood	Irwin	Jonathan
Honduras	Isaac	Jonesboro
Hong Kong	Isidore	Joplin

Joseph	La Crosse	Leipsig
Judith	Lafayette	Leningrad
Julian	Lakeland	Lenoir
Juliet	Lakewood	Leominster
Julius	Lambert	Leon
Justin	Lancaster	Leonard
Kalamazoo	Lancelot	Leonia
Kalispell	Lansdale	Leopold
Kankakee	Lansford	Leroy
Kansas	Lansing	Leslie
Kansas City	La Paz	Lettice
Karl	La Porte	Lewiston
Katharine	Larchmont	Lexington
Kathleen	Laredo	Lillian
Kearny	Larksville	Lima
Keith	Larson	Lincoln
Kennedy	La Salle	Lindstrom
Kenneth	Las Vegas	Lionel
Kenosha	Latrobe	Lisbon
Kenton	Laughlin	Litchfield
Kentucky	Laura	Lithuania
Kerrville	Laurel	Liverpool
Keyser	Laurens	Livingston
Kilgore	Lavinia	Llewellyn
Kingsford	Lawrence	Lloyd
Kingston	Lawrenceville	Lockhart
Kirkwood	Lazarus	Lockport
Knoxville	Leah	Lodi
Kokomo	Leavenworth	Logansport
Korea	Lebanon	Lois
Lackawanna	Lehighton	Lombard
Laconia	Lehman	London

Longview	Manila	McCarthy
Lorain	Manistique	McCook
Lorenzo	Manitoba	McCormack
Los Angeles	Mannheim	McDonald
Louis	Manuel	McGregor
Louise	Maplewood	McKenzie
Louisiana	Marblehead	McKinney
Louisville	Marcella	McMillan
Lowell	Marcia	Meadville
Lubbock	Marcus	Medford
Lucretia	Margaret	Melbourne
Ludington	Marian	Melissa
Luella	Marianna	Menasha
Lufkin	Marion	Mercedes
Lumberton	Marlboro	Meriden
Luther	Marquette	Merrill
Luxembourg	Marseilles	Methuen
Lydia	Marshall	Mexico
Lynbrook	Martin	Meyer
Lynchburg	Martinsburg	Miami
Lyndhurst	Martinsville	Michigan
Lynwood	Mason	Middleboro
Lyons	Massachusetts	Midland
Madisonville	Massillon	Mildred
Magdalene	Mathilda	Milford
Maguire	Matthew	Millburn
Mahanoy City	Maxwell	Millbury
Mahoney	Maynard	Milledgeville
Malden	Maysville	Milton
Malvern	Mayville	Milwaukee
Manchester	Maywood	Minersville
Manhattan	McAdoo	Minneapolis

Minnesota	Naomi	New Zealand
Mississippi	Naperville	Niagara Falls
Missouri	Napoleon	Nicaragua
Mitchell	Nashua	Norfolk
Mobile	Nashville	Norma
Monica	Natalie	Norman
Monmouth	Natchez	Northampton
Monroe	Natchitoches	North Carolina
Montana	Nathaniel	North Dakota
Montebello	Natick	Norwalk
Montevideo	Naugatuck	Norway
Montpelier	Nazareth	Norwich
Montreal	Nebraska	Norwood
Mooresville	Needham	Nova Scotia
Moorhead	Nelson	Nyack
Morocco	Neptune	Oakwood
Morris	Netherlands	O'Brien
Morse	Nevada	Ocala
Mortimer	Newark	O'Connor
Moscow	Newberry	Odessa
Moultrie	New Britain	O'Donnell
Moundsville	New Brunswick	Oelwein
Muncie	Newburgh	Ogdensburg
Munhall	New Hampshire	Ohio
Munich	New Haven	Oklahoma
Murdock	New Jersey	Olean
Muriel	New London	Olney
Murray	New Mexico	Olson
Muscatine	New Orleans	Olympia
Muskegon	New Rochelle	Omaha
Myers	Newton	Oneida
Myrtle	New York	O'Neil

Ontario		Pelham		Portsmouth	
Ophelia		Pendleton		Portugal	
Oregon		Pennsylvania		Potter	
Orlando		Pensacola		Pottsville	
Oscar		Peoria		Poughkeepsie	
Oshkosh		Percival		Powell	
Oslo		Perth Amboy		Presque Isle	
Ossining		Petaluma		Prichard	
Oswald		Petersburg		Princeton	
Oswego		Petersen		Priscilla	
Ottawa		Peterson		Providence	
Owego		Philadelphia		Provo	
Owensboro		Philander		Pueblo	
Packard		Philippine Islands		Puerto Rico	
Paducah		Phillipsburg		Putnam	
Painesville		Phoenixville		Quebec	
Palestine		Piedmont		Quinn	
Pamela		Pittsburgh		Rachel	
Panama		Pittsfield		Racine	
Paraguay		Pius		Radford	
Parkersburg		Plainfield		Rahway	
Parsons		Plattsburg		Randall	
Pasadena		Pleasantville		Randolph	
Passaic		Plymouth		Rankin	
Patchogue		Ponca City		Raton	
Paterson		Pontiac		Ravenna	
Patrick		Portage		Raymond	
Pawtucket		Port Arthur		Rebecca	
Peabody		Port Chester		Redwood City	
Pearson		Porterville		Regina	
Peekskill		Port Huron		Reginald	
Pekin		Portland		Reinhardt	

Rensselaer

Reuben

Revere

Reynolds

Rhea

Rhinelander

Rhode Island

Richard

Richfield

Richmond

Richwood

Ridgeway

Rio de Janeiro

Roanoke

Robbinsdale

Robert

Robinson

Rochester

Rockford

Rockland

Rockville

Roderick

Romania

Roosevelt

Rosalind

Rosemary

Roseville

Rossville

Roswell

Rotterdam

Rowena

Ruby

Rudolph

Rupert

Rushville

Russia

Rutherford

Ryan

Ryerson

Sacramento

Saginaw

St. Albans

St. Augustine

St. Joseph

St. Louis

St. Petersburg

Salisbury

Salt Lake City

Sampson

Samuel

San Angelo

San Antonio

San Diego

Sandusky

San Fernando

Sanford

San Francisco

San Jose

San Luis Obispo

San Mateo

San Rafael

Santa Barbara

Santiago

Sarasota

Sault Ste. Marie

Savannah

Sawyer

Sayreville

Schenectady

Schneider

Schroeder

Schultz

Schuyler

Schwartz

Scotland

Seattle

Sedalia

Seminole

Serena

Seville

Seward

Sewickley

Sexton

Seymour

Shanghai

Sharon

Sharpsburg

Sheboygan

Sheffield

Shelbyville

Sheldon

Shenandoah

Sheridan

Sherman

Sherwood

Shippensburg

Shirley

Shorewood

Shreveport

Siam

Sicily

Silvester

Silvia

Simmons

Simpson

Sinclair

Singapore

Sioux Falls

Solomon

Somerset

Somerville

Sorensen

South America

Southampton

South Carolina

South Dakota

Southington

Sparks

Spartanburg

Spokane

Springfield

Stafford

Stamford

Stanford

Stanley

Statesboro

Staunton

Sterling

Steubenville

Stewart

Stillwater

Stockholm

Stoneham

Stoughton

Stratford

Straus

Stroudsburg

Struthers

Stuart

Sturgis

Stuttgart

Suffolk

Sullivan

Sumner

Sumter

Sunbury

Susan

Sweetwater

Switzerland

Sybil

Sydney

Sylvester

Syracuse

Tacoma

Tallahassee

Tampa

Tampico

Tarrytown

Taunton

Taylorville

Teaneck

Tenafly

Tennessee

Terre Haute

Texas

Thaddeus

The Hague

Theodore

Thomasville

Tifton

Timothy

Tipton

Titusville

Tokyo

Toledo

Topeka

Toronto

Torrington

Trenton

Trinidad

Truman

Tucson

Tulsa

Turkey

Tuscaloosa

Tyrone

Ukraine

Underhill

Union

United Kingdom

United States

Upton

Uruguay	Warsaw	Willmar
Utah	Washington	Wilmette
Utica	Waterbury	Wilmington
Valentine	Waterville	Wilson
Valeria	Watsonville	Winfield
Vanderlip	Waverly	Winifred
Van Horn	Waynesboro	Winnipeg
Venezuela	Weatherford	Winona
Vera Cruz	Webster	Winslow
Vermont	Welch	Winston-Salem
Vernon	Wellesley	Winthrop
Vicksburg	Wellington	Wisconsin
Victoria	Wellsburg	Woburn
Vienna	Westbrook	Woodbury
Vincennes	West Chester	Woodward
Vincent	Westfield	Woonsocket
Viola	Weston	Wooster
Virgil	West Virginia	Worcester
Virginia	Westwood	Worthington
Vivian	Weymouth	Wyoming
Wabash	Wheaton	Xenia
Waddington	Wheeling	Yakima
Wadsworth	Whitman	Yates
Wakefield	Whittier	Yokohama
Walker	Wichita	Yonkers
Wallace	Wilbur	York
Wallington	Wilfred	Youngstown
Walpole	Wilkes-Barre	Ypsilanti
Walsh	Wilkinsburg	Yugoslavia
Walter	Willard	Yuma
Waltham	Williamsport	Zanesville
Warrensburg	Williston	Zion